Lecture Notes in Computer Science 748

Edited by G. Goos and J. Hartmanis

Advisory Board: W. Brauer   D. Gries   J. Stoer

Robert H. Halstead, Jr. Takayasu Ito (Eds.)

Parallel Symbolic Computing: Languages, Systems, and Applications

US/Japan Workshop
Cambridge, MA, USA, October 14-17, 1992
Proceedings

Springer-Verlag

Berlin Heidelberg New York
London Paris Tokyo
Hong Kong Barcelona
Budapest

Series Editors

Gerhard Goos
Universität Karlsruhe
Postfach 69 80
Vincenz-Priessnitz-Straße 1
D-76131 Karlsruhe, Germany

Juris Hartmanis
Cornell University
Department of Computer Science
4130 Upson Hall
Ithaca, NY 14853, USA

Volume Editors

Robert H. Halstead, Jr.
Cambridge Research Lab, Digital Equipment Corporation
One Kendall Square, Bldg. 700, Cambridge, MA 02139, USA

Takayasu Ito
Department of Computer and Mathematical Sciences
Graduate School of Information Sciences, Tohoku University
Sendai 980, Japan

CR Subject Classification (1991):D.1.3, D.3.3-4, D.2.2, C.1.2

ISBN 3-540-57396-8 Springer-Verlag Berlin Heidelberg New York
ISBN 0-387-57396-8 Springer-Verlag New York Berlin Heidelberg

© Springer-Verlag Berlin Heidelberg 1993
Printed in Germany

Typesetting: Camera-ready by author
Printing and binding: Druckhaus Beltz, Hemsbach/Bergstr.
45/3140-543210 - Printed on acid-free paper

Preface

Parallel and distributed computing are becoming increasingly important as cost-effective ways to achieve high computational performance. Symbolic computing is widespread in applications and hence parallel symbolic computing is important, but symbolic computations are notable for their use of irregular data structures (such as trees, lists, and graphs) and irregular, data-driven operations on them. As a result, parallel symbolic computing has its own distinctive set of technical challenges.

To explore these issues, a workshop was held at MIT in Cambridge, Massachusetts, on October 14–17, 1992. This workshop brought together researchers interested in parallel symbolic computing to identify:

- Important common theoretical and implementation problems.
- The important application areas for parallel symbolic computing.
- How to move parallelism into wider use for symbolic computing.
- Opportunities for research collaboration.

The past ten years have seen the development of several small-scale (mostly shared-memory) systems for parallel symbolic computing based on Lisp and Prolog. Many symbolic programs written for serial computers have been successfully transformed into parallel programs using these systems. More recently, we have seen massively parallel processing and distributed computing take on greater importance, but these systems are more challenging to use and both their hardware and software are still immature.

The overriding technical objective driving this workshop and this book is to identify the common and fundamental technical issues in massively parallel symbolic computing and hasten the widespread availability and use of high-performance parallel symbolic computing systems. Accordingly, the papers included in this book cover a wide range of areas:

- Speculative computation.
- Scheduling techniques.
- Program development tools and environments.
- Programming languages and systems.
- Models of concurrency and distribution.
- Parallel computer architecture.
- Symbolic applications.

The workshop began on Wednesday afternoon, October 14, and concluded early in the afternoon on Saturday, October 17. The program included 24 presentations grouped roughly into the topic areas listed above. In addition there were two panel discussions, "Massively Parallel Architectures and Symbolic Computation," and "Applications for Parallel Symbolic Computation," focusing special attention on two areas of key importance to the future of parallel symbolic computing.

Workshop participants submitted papers which were distributed at the workshop. Based on the presentations and discussions at the workshop, all but one of the speakers revised their manuscripts and contributed them to this book. Contributions in this book are of two kinds: full papers and extended abstracts. Many participants contributed full papers based on their talks at the workshop; some participants contributed extended abstracts, because the work had already been published elsewhere or for other reasons. In addition, this book includes the questions for the panel discussions and position statements contributed by the panelists.

The papers and extended abstracts in this book are organized into groups by subject:

Part I: Speculative computation.
Part II: Implementation techniques.
Part III: Program development tools.
Part IV: Languages and conceptual models.
Part V: Systems.

Before the first group we include an overview of the papers. After the papers, we include the panel questions, position statements, and a list of the workshop participants.

The idea of having this workshop originated at an earlier workshop on parallel Lisp that was held in Sendai, Japan, in June, 1989. (The proceedings of that workshop were published in 1990 as *Lecture Notes in Computer Science* vol. 441 by Springer-Verlag.) Participants in that workshop felt it was a valuable experience that should be repeated in the future, so proposals were submitted to the U.S. National Science Foundation and the Japan Society for the Promotion of Science to have a follow-up workshop in 1992.

Although the 1989 workshop was exclusively a U.S./Japan meeting, the 1992 workshop also included participants from other countries (such as the U.K., France, and Canada). We hope the "new blood" thus brought into this workshop will expand our understanding of the opportunities and challenges of parallel symbolic computing and advance the ability of this computing discipline to contribute to solving real-world problems.

The workshop was held at the MIT Laboratory for Computer Science in Cambridge, Massachusetts, U.S.A., in a building where many ideas in symbolic computing originated—including Lisp, Macsyma, Actors, Scheme, Multilisp, and many artificial intelligence applications—and which has also seen many advances in parallel computing research. In addition to the formal workshop sessions, the workshop participants were hosted for lunch by the Mitsubishi Electric Research Lab in Cambridge, and enjoyed an evening reception *cum* panel discussion at the Cambridge Marriott Hotel. Following the formal portion of the workshop, a group of the participants traveled to Concord, Massachusetts, to explore a non-technical subject: the early history of the United States.

We are grateful for the support we received for this workshop from the Japan Society for the Promotion of Science, the National Science Foundation, the MIT Laboratory for Computer Science, Tohoku University, and the Mitsubishi Electric Research Lab. In addition, we are grateful to Anant Agarwal of MIT, who co-organized the workshop with us, and to Michelle Gillespie and Anne Mc-Carthy, who handled many of the logistical details.

The papers in this proceedings represent active projects in parallel symbolic computing by a distinguished and active group of researchers. We are happy that we have been able to bring this group together and collect their work in the form of this proceedings. We are sincerely grateful to Alfred Hofmann and Hans Wössner of Springer-Verlag for their assistance in this book's publication, and we also thank all who helped organize the workshop, and participated in it, for their invaluable contributions.

Cambridge, Massachusetts
July 1993

Robert H. Halstead, Jr.
Takayasu Ito

Table of Contents

Part V: Systems

Part VI: Panel Discussions

Overview of Papers
from the U.S./Japan Workshop
on Parallel Symbolic Computing

Robert H. Halstead, Jr.,* and Takayasu Ito**

We begin this proceedings with our brief comments on the significance of each paper (and abstract) that appears in this volume. These papers present a wide range of challenges, opportunities, and accomplishments in parallel symbolic computing. They are arranged into five broad technical areas that are important in this field. *Speculative computation* can increase performance on parallel machines for problems that contain a searching or heuristic component. Innovative *implementation techniques* can yield better systems for future parallel symbolic applications. *Program development tools* can reduce the cost of building such applications and increase their performance. New *languages and conceptual models* can open up new ways of expressing symbolic algorithms so that their inherent parallelism can be exploited effectively. *Systems* for parallel computing put together all of the above technologies so they can be used for real problems and their value can be assessed. Finally, we present the "calls to arms" for the workshop's two panel discussions, which look at some major challenges facing the parallel symbolic computing field today.

Our comments include capsule summaries of each paper's content and its main conclusions, along with our views of what is important about the paper and what future work needs to be done. We also discuss the relationships between the papers that make up each of the five parts of this proceedings. Our comments are like brief abstracts of the papers, but we are not trying to duplicate the function of the papers' own abstracts. Rather, we hope to share some of the perspective on the parallel symbolic computing field that we gained during the workshop and give our point of view, as the editors of this collection, about how the papers fit together and why we have included them.

Part I: Speculative Computation

All three of the papers in this part present techniques for using priorities to control the execution of tasks in speculative parallel computations. Between them, the papers report on a considerable range of applications, including search and artificial intelligence problems, in which these techniques can be used. It appears that the right combination of heuristics, parallel processing, and prioritization can be effective for tackling some quite difficult and important problems, but the opportunities are not yet well understood and the field is still perhaps more

---

* DEC Cambridge Research Lab, Cambridge, MA 02139, U.S.A.

** Department of Computer and Mathematical Sciences, Graduate School of Information Sciences, Tohoku University, Sendai 980, JAPAN

art than science. The accomplishments reported in this section are encouraging, but we still hope for future work to continue deepening and broadening our understanding of speculative computation.

The first paper, by L.V. Kale, B. Ramkumar, V. Saletore, and A. Sinha, discusses several strategies for using priorities for speculative parallel computation in applications such as state-space search, game-tree search, branch-and-bound, and logic programming. One interesting attribute of their priority system is that it has an unbounded number of priority levels. They used the Charm parallel programming system, which supports asynchronous and message-driven execution, to demonstrate the effective use of these prioritization strategies for all the example applications, obtaining excellent speedups in some cases on multiprocessors with up to 512 processors. This is an interesting overview paper explaining prioritization strategies and their application.

Yukio Kaneda, Hideo Matsuda, and Shigeo Suzuka propose a method for OR-parallel execution of Prolog using priorities specified by the programmer. Their system selects the highest-priority Prolog goals at any given time and executes them in parallel. Their system is implemented on a Sequent Symmetry S81 machine,[3] and the authors report their very satisfactory experiences with the problem of molecular phylogenetic tree inference, in some cases even obtaining superlinear speedup of a factor of 40 on 26 processors.

The paper by Randy Osborne explains how to extend his "sponsor model" for speculative parallel computation so that it can be used for computations that include side effects. He discusses two problems. The *relevant synchronization problem* can result when one computation requires a side effect to be performed by another computation. In extreme cases, this problem can even result in *speculative deadlock*: nontermination caused by failure to schedule the task that will perform the required side effect. The *preemptive delay problem* occurs when a computation that will perform an awaited side effect is preempted by computations of lower priority than the computation(s) awaiting the side effect. Osborne shows how to solve these problems by introducing the concept of *classes* which tasks can enter and leave dynamically. In the sponsor model, classes can be used as a "bridge" to transmit sponsorship even when the tasks in the class are not known in advance, allowing a solution to the problems mentioned above. We look forward to the incorporation of these ideas into systems that can be used for substantial applications.

Part II: Implementation Techniques

Dynamic task partitioning is important for the efficient implementation of parallel Lisp systems, and "lazy task creation" has been known as an interesting and efficient technique for that purpose. The first two papers in this part summarize the state of this art, discussing in detail the implementation options for lazy task creation and their impact on performance. The final two papers concern

---

[3] Symmetry and S81 are trademarks of Sequent Computer Systems, Inc.

the PaiLisp parallel Lisp system: the first paper describes in detail a PaiLisp implementation based on P-continuations (a kind of parallel continuation developed by the PaiLisp group and captured using PaiLisp's call/cc procedure) and presents some performance results; the second reports on using PaiLisp for higher-order unification, an interesting application that appears in higher-order logic and typed functional languages. An important question raised by all the papers in this part concerns what kinds of "real-world" applications benefit more from implementation techniques such as lazy task creation and P-continuations than from alternative techniques. We hope future work will address this question, as well as systematically exploring the use of P-continuations for interpreting and compiling parallel Lisp and other parallel languages.

First, Eric Mohr writes about his experiences with grouping tasks dynamically into coarser-grained groups to reduce scheduling costs. He finds that his technique of lazy task creation is the most effective of these techniques. He also distills some rules of thumb about scheduling future-based programs: (1) when choosing between scheduling a child task and its parent, it is better to give preference to the child; and (2) it is good to use double-ended task queues so that processors needing to steal tasks can take the oldest tasks from the queue while the scheduling operations within a processor work with the newest tasks. Mohr also raises an important question for the future: how many applications fall into the range of granularities where dynamic task partitioning is effective?

The paper by Marc Feeley describes a variant of lazy task creation that he has used on large shared-memory multiprocessors. Whereas Mohr's earlier lazy-task-creation implementation relies on efficient shared-memory operations, Feeley's uses a message-passing paradigm. The main advantages of this paradigm are that it is simpler to implement, has a lower cost for locally executed tasks, and allows for full caching of the stack even on machines without coherent caches. Measurements on a 32-processor machine (a BBN TC2000 multiprocessor[4]) show that the message-passing method yields performance improvements of as much as a factor of 2 over the shared-memory method—a significant performance improvement.

The next paper, by Takayasu Ito and Tomohiro Seino, first explains P-continuations, their capture using PaiLisp's call/cc, and PaiLisp's major constructs. It then describes in detail their implementation of a PaiLisp interpreter based on P-continuations. The performance of this PaiLisp interpreter, running on an Alliant FX/80 multiprocessor, is given for several benchmark programs that illustrate various programming styles using PaiLisp's rich set of parallel constructs. An appendix briefly describes an experimental PaiLisp compiler. This paper clearly demonstrates that P-continuations can be used as the basis for a parallel Lisp implementation. We hope future work will shed light on the value of implementation strategies based on P-continuations, compared with other approaches, and will explore the use of P-continuations for implementing other parallel languages. We also hope for a deeper understanding of the most effective programming styles for writing efficient parallel Lisp programs using a rich

---

[4] TC2000 is a trademark of Bolt Beranek and Newman, Inc.

set of parallel constructs such as PaiLisp's.

Finally, Masami Hagiya reports his experience in implementing and running a higher-order unification procedure using PaiLisp. The unification procedure is Huet's higher-order unification procedure as reformulated by Gallien and Snyder and further adapted by Hagiya. The full system is based on the Calculus of Constructions and has applications to the author's research on programming by example and proving by example. The paper reports satisfactory experiences using PaiLisp to implement this higher-order unification procedure using OR-parallelism. Higher-order unification is a challenging problem for parallel computing and the speedup available depends strongly on the particular problem instance; for two problem instances reported in the paper, one was able to use up to 7 processors productively, while the other obtained no further speedup after 3 processors were used.

Part III: Program Development Tools

Recent years have seen several workshops and conference sessions on debugging techniques for parallel and distributed computations, but research activity in these areas is still quite limited compared to the activity in areas such as parallel programming languages, program transformations, run-time systems, and architectures. The papers in this part focus on tools to help with all three major aspects of parallel program development: writing, debugging, and performance tuning. The first of these papers describes a debugging tool, while the second paper presents a tool for both debugging and performance tuning. The third paper describes a "toolbox" of useful subroutines designed to make it easier to write parallel symbolic programs. In the future, we hope to see more research activity in this important area.

The paper by Hidehiko Tanaka and Jun-ichi Tatemura describes Hyper-DEBU, an interative multiwindow debugger for use with parallel logic programs written in Fleng, which is a minimal yet practical committed-choice language designed by the authors' group for writing fine-grained highly parallel programs. Modelling Fleng program executions in a communicating-process style, Hyper-DEBU enables a user to examine and manipulate the many complex control- and data-flow structures that can be created during the execution of programs written in Fleng. HyperDEBU offers the capabilities to view program execution from different perspectives and at different levels of detail, visualize control and data flow, and insert breakpoints for parallel execution. The debugger also includes a source-code browser co-ordinated with the execution visualizations. Examples show HyperDEBU's friendly interface and powerful visualization capabilities. We hope this interesting work will continue to develop and will result in a complete, high-performance, integrated parallel programming environment available to a wide user community. We also hope the ideas presented in this paper inspire improvements in interactive debugging environments for other parallel programming languages.

Robert Halstead, David Kranz, and Patrick Sobalvarro describe MulTVision, a graphical debugging tool for parallel Lisp programs that execute using Multi-lisp and Mul-T. MulTVision features both a graphical display for visualizing program execution histories (useful for performance tuning) and a program replay mechanism. After explaining MulTVision's technical goals as a complete tool for parallel program debugging and development, this paper focuses on MulTVision's graphical display; the replay mechanism, which can trace and replay even a nondeterministic program, is reported elsewhere. Although MulTVision is a working system, many of its goals are only partly achieved by the current implementation. Some important next steps for the MulTVision project are (1) adding a greater variety of displays, incorporating ideas from systems like HyperDEBU; (2) fuller implementation of the interface between the visualization tools and the replay mechanism; and (3) getting MulTVision used by a wider user community. After these steps, we should be able to see which of MulTVision's ideas offer the most valuable support for debugging and performance tuning.

The paper by Kinson Ho and Paul Hilfinger describes a "toolbox" designed to make parallel programming easier by making it look more like sequential programming. The toolbox defines a large number of abstractions, grouped into *parallelism abstractions* and *data-sharing abstractions*. This paper focuses on the data-sharing abstractions, which support common side-effecting operations on shared objects and simplify the construction of parallel programs that modify shared data structures. The paper gives a comprehensive description of the data-sharing abstractions implemented in the toolbox, which include counters, multisets, dictionaries, autolock objects, and many others. A brief example of using this toolbox in a program for finding connected components of undirected graphs is given. The toolbox is now being applied to more extensive applications. It will be interesting to see the toolbox's effect on the ease of programming and on run-time performance; if the results are good, this should become an important technique for parallel programming.

Part IV: Languages and Conceptual Models

Parallel Lisp languages have succeeded for various applications of parallel symbolic computing on small-scale shared-memory parallel machines. The development of distributed-memory and massively parallel architectures has attracted researchers to use these architectures for parallel symbolic computing. At least several parallel Lisp languages and object-oriented languages have been proposed for these emerging architectures. The papers of Part IV discuss some new languages and systems, mostly based on Lisp, for distributed-memory and massively parallel architectures, introducing new language constructs and conceptual tools. We hope to see continued work in these directions, leading to useful parallel languages with efficient implementations on these architectures, contributing in turn to the further development of massively parallel machines.

Christian Queinnec and David De Roure present Icsla, a dialect of Scheme designed to have very simple semantics while also including concurrency, distribution, and sophisticated control features in addition to supporting the variety of programming styles traditionally supported by Lisp. Icsla's added features include a breed function for controlling concurrency, a mechanism for creating tasks in groups using call/de (call with dynamic extent) and its associated predicate within/de?, a different view of continuations that includes protection from premature exits, and a remote function providing a kind of remote procedure call capability. Examples are given of how Icsla can support familiar constructs such as call/cc, either, Qlisp's qlambda, PaiLisp's exlambda, and Multilisp's future and pcall. The paper also provides a semantic definition of Icsla in the form of a metacircular interpreter. A compiler for Icsla is being developed; it will be very interesting to see the results of using it.

An extended abstract by Suresh Jagannathan describes TS/Scheme, a Scheme dialect that includes the concept of *tuple spaces* from Linda. TS/Scheme enhances the concept of tuple spaces in several ways, compared to their Linda incarnation: (1) tuple spaces in TS/Scheme are first-class objects; (2) name-based and content-based access are provided separately by *binding repositories* and *tuple repositories*, respectively; (3) tuple spaces adhere to an object-oriented protocol, hiding their implementation details from their users; and (4) there is no distinction between tasks and data in bindings or tuples. Performance measurements for four applications are given, showing good speedups on a Silicon Graphics multiprocessor[5] with eight 75 MHz MIPS R3000 processors.[6]

A paper by Taiichi Yuasa reports on TUPLE, an extended Common Lisp for a massively parallel SIMD architecture (the MasPar MP-1[7]). Each processing element of the MP-1 supports a tiny subset of Common Lisp and the front end of the MP-1 supports a full Common Lisp (Kyoto Common Lisp). Programs are written in terms of front-end variables which are stored on the front end and PE variables that are stored across the processing elements. Each PE variable may be thought of as a vector of locations containing one location for each processing element, allowing massively parallel computations to be written as simple expressions involving PE variables. This paper explains the syntax and semantics of TUPLE in an intuitive manner, gives an implementation overview of TUPLE, and presents performance data from running a simple application. Unfortunately, TUPLE users have found the 8 KB heap size on each processing element to be too small for many applications. If TUPLE can be implemented on one of the newer massively parallel machines with a larger amount of memory per node, we should have a chance to see which symbolic applications can make good use of TUPLE's SIMD computational model.

Julian Padget, Duncan Batey and Simon Merrall first present a classification of parallel programming models and systems into concurrency abstractions, coordination languages, and architecture-independent ("AI") languages. They then discuss drawbacks of the current models and systems: (1) coordination languages are rarely truly orthogonal to the host language, (2) the concurrency

---

[5] Silicon Graphics is a registered trademark of Silicon Graphics, Inc.

[6] MIPS and R3000 are trademarks or registered trademarks of MIPS Technologies, Inc.

[7] MasPar is a trademark of MasPar Computer Corporation.

abstractions and AI languages embody coordination, and (3) the AI languages are not truly architecture-independent. After these general discussions they outline their Paralation-based model and their plans to implement it on a "virtual multi-computer" including both MIMD and SIMD components. Their success at developing a programming technology allowing such a heterogeneous system to compute efficiently when driven by a single, integrated program would be a significant achievement; we look forward to seeing the results of their future work.

Benny Yih, Mark Swanson, and Robert Kessler designed a store for immutable, persistent data and integrated it into their existing distributed implementation of Scheme. They demonstrated its use by incorporating it into a distributed ray-tracing program. Objects saved in this store could provide a way to pass data between applications that exploits and keeps visible the structure of the data, enabling applications to access the data in a highly parallel way.

The paper by Mario Tokoro and Ichiro Satoh emphasizes the importance of asynchrony and real-time behavior in characterizing the properties of distributed computing. As a starting point for investigating these properties, distributed computations are classified into four types, according to whether communication is synchronous or asynchronous, and whether the objects measure time by the same clock or different clocks. The paper then discusses several of the authors' previous proposals—two formal systems on timed CCS (RtCCS and DtCCS), a real-time object-oriented language (DROL) and Tokoro's proposal for a computational field model—in terms of this framework. In contrast to most of the papers in this proceedings, this paper focuses on distributed computing rather than tightly coupled parallel computing. Although the issues discussed by Tokoro and Satoh are not crucial for tightly coupled computing today, they will increase in importance as we move toward massively parallel computation and the line between "distributed" and "centralized" computing becomes blurred.

The extended abstract by Naoki Kobayashi and Akinori Yonezawa briefly explains ACL—a logic-programming framework based on Girard's linear logic. The authors hope that ACL, because of its ability to model asynchronous communication, will become a formal basis for concurrent computation. We hope that future work will be able to show the applicability and benefit of ACL in the practice of parallel symbolic computing.

Part V: Systems

This part contains six papers reporting on a range of projects involving hardware and software architectures and the implementation of applications on those architectures. Several of these papers report results derived from substantial applications on parallel systems of substantial size; we applaud such experiments and hope to see many more in the future. Beyond that, the range of papers included in this part give clear evidence that there are open questions and interesting possibilities at every level of implementation, from the hardware to the application. We look forward to continued research activity in these areas, and we also hope that as successful ideas at the different levels of implementation emerge, they will be combined into increasingly powerful systems for parallel symbolic computing.

In the first paper, Takashi Chikayama and Ryozo Kiyohara give an overview of the research activities and results on parallel inference systems in the Fifth Generation Computer Systems project, a Japanese national project carried out during 1983–1992 to establish high-performance knowledge information processing systems. Various interesting applications of parallel symbolic computing were developed using their concurrent logic language KL1 and parallel inference machines PIM and Multi-PSI under the operating system PIMOS. These applications include MGTP (a model-generation theorem prover for first-order logic), PAX (a parallel bottom-up parser), Helic-II (a parallel legal reasoning system), a parallel logic simulator, and a genetic information processing system. This project clearly demonstrated that concurrent logic programming can be used to implement a wide variety of applications; unfortunately, the large-scale application of these techniques in production has not yet been demonstrated. Nevertheless, this project's focus on applications has been very important and we hope to see future projects put the same emphasis on application work.

An extended abstract by David Waltz explores the impact of massively parallel symbolic computing on problems involving imprecisely specified operations on large collections of data, such as assigning keywords to newspaper articles, classifying census data, protein structure prediction, and "database mining." Waltz points out that as the cost of computation drops and it becomes economical to assemble very-high-performance, massively parallel systems, larger knowledge bases can be handled and hand-coded algorithms become less effective compared with automated learning and easily programmed brute-force algorithms. The experiments whose results Waltz summarizes illustrate that these effects are already beginning to be felt.

An extended abstract by Anant Agarwal and his collaborators lays out three requirements for processor chips used in large-scale multiprocessing: (1) support for fine-grain synchronization; (2) very lightweight mechanisms for initiating communication and responding to asynchronous events; and (3) ability to tolerate memory, communication, and synchronization latencies without loss of processing throughput. These points are especially important in parallel symbolic computing, where irregular data structures and computation patterns can defeat the compilation techniques used with regularly structured applications to compensate for weaknesses in satisfying these requirements. The authors are building the Sparcle chip, a Sun Microsystems SPARC processor[8] modified to meet these requirements. Working Sparcle chips already exist, and will soon be used to build a multiprocessor called Alewife. It will be very interesting to see how well Sparcle and Alewife perform, especially for irregularly structured applications.

In their paper, Carl Bruggeman and R. Kent Dybvig re-examine the hard-

---

[8] Sun is a trademark of Sun Microsystems Inc. SPARC is a trademark of SPARC International Inc.

ware/software tradeoffs in implementing type-safe symbolic programming languages such as Scheme. In such languages, checks for type errors and out-of-bounds memory accesses can be generated where necessary by a compiler and therefore need not be performed automatically in hardware. The authors argue that if such checks are generated explicitly by the compiler, the need for hardware exception traps disappears. Hardware functional units are then simplified, since all they need to do is process inputs and produce outputs locally—there is no need for "global" control to interrupt functional units and save their state when exception traps occur. Inspired by these observations, Bruggeman and Dybvig propose a new architecture design paradigm based on compiler-enforced memory protection and the elimination of global control. Their work is still in progress and no architecture following these principles has yet been designed and built. The authors acknowledge that their paradigm faces potential pitfalls whose severity needs to be investigated. It will be interesting to see the system designs that emerge from this paradigm and evaluate them as platforms for parallel symbolic computing.

James Philbin writes about customizable policy management in the Sting operating system. Sting is an operating system designed to support programming languages such as Scheme, Smalltalk, and Haskell that require support for parallelism, multiple synchronization models, lazy and eager evaluation, and automatic storage management. Sting is designed with several layers of abstraction where programmers can introduce their own policy modules to control the implementation of these support functions. Philbin's paper focuses on thread policy managers, which control the placement and scheduling of threads. The paper presents performance data for Sting running a parallel sorting benchmark on an 8-processor shared-memory machine using six different thread policy managers, one of which performs about 20% better than the others. The performance differences may be greater on larger-scale and distributed-memory machines; if this is true and if different scheduling policies are best for different applications, the value of Sting's flexibility will have been demonstrated convincingly.

Finally, the extended abstract by Kenjiro Taura, Satoshi Matsuoka, and Akinori Yonezawa describes their efficient implementation scheme for concurrent object-oriented languages on the AP-1000 stock multiprocessor built by Fujitsu. They report a summary of their experiences with this implementation, measuring the costs of intra-node scheduling and inter-node communication. One of their applications achieved a speedup of 440 on 512 processors, which is among the best accomplishments in the area of massively parallel object-oriented computing that has ever been reported.

Part VI: Panel Discussions

The workshop also included two panel discussions, focusing on two research areas—massively parallel computing and parallel symbolic applications—which we believe will need increased attention in the future development of parallel symbolic computation.

The first of these panels, "Massively Parallel Architectures and Symbolic Computation," was chaired by Takayasu Ito and featured Rishiyur Nikhil, Julian Padget, Norihisa Suzuki, and Taiichi Yuasa as panelists. The majority (but not unanimous) view on the panel was that massively parallel symbolic computation is an important direction for future development, but the panelists had many different ideas about how it should be pursued. This diversity is welcome as an indication of a healthy, active field of research, but such disagreement illustrates the difficulty of predicting how the future will develop. We look forward to seeing the results as symbolic computing researchers increasingly focus their attention on large-scale parallel machines.

The second panel, "Applications for Parallel Symbolic Computation," was chaired by Robert Halstead and had a panel composed of Takashi Chikayama, Richard Gabriel, David Waltz, and Akinori Yonezawa. Several panelists presented examples of substantial symbolic applications that have been implemented on parallel machines, but there was a general consensus that progress in using parallel symbolic computing to solve real-world problems has lagged behind the development of implementation technology for parallel symbolic computing. There is a great need to build more bridges between parallel symbolic computing researchers and "real users" with real-world problems to solve. One result of this panel discussion occurred even before the workshop ended: a plan was set in motion for a special journal issue devoted to applications of parallel symbolic computing. While this is a good idea, it is only the beginning. Parallel symbolic computing researchers should continue and increase their efforts to forge links with users in other disciplines.

Final Words

Parallel symbolic computing is a lively discipline with a wide range of ongoing research and an ample supply of difficult and unsolved problems. As the papers in this proceedings attest, there have been exciting results, and we look forward to seeing more such results in the future. As is true in any field of research, some of the important problem areas attract more attention than others. The most solid results in the parallel symbolic computing field are currently of an inward-looking nature (such as programming languages and scheduling techniques) and many of these results have been derived on relatively small-scale parallel machines. We think the continued development of this field will be the healthiest if a high priority is given to extending these results in the direction of larger-scale computing machines and complementing them with greater accomplishments in helping real users solve real problems.

PART I

Speculative Computation

Prioritization in Parallel Symbolic Computing *

L. V. Kale[1], B. Ramkumar[2], V. Saletore[3], and A. B. Sinha[1]

[1] Department of Computer Science, University of Illinois at Urbana Champaign,
1304 W. Springfield Ave., Urbana IL-61801
[2] Department of Electrical and Computer Engineering,
University of Iowa, Iowa City, IA-52242
[3] Department of Computer Science,
Oregon State University, Corvallis, OR-97331

Abstract. It is argued that scheduling is an important determinant of performance for many parallel symbolic computations, in addition to the issues of dynamic load balancing and grain size control. We propose associating unbounded levels of priorities with tasks and messages as the mechanism of choice for specifying scheduling strategies. We demonstrate how priorities can be used in parallelizing computations in different search domains, and show how priorities can be implemented effectively in parallel systems. Priorities have been implemented in the Charm portable parallel programming system. Performance results on shared-memory machines with tens of processors and nonshared-memory machines with hundreds of processors are given. Open problems for prioritization in specific domains are given, which will constitute fertile area for future research in this field.

1 Introduction

The field of Artificial Intelligence — in at least one of its interpretations — sets itself an ambitious goal: that of building computational systems that are capable of intelligent behavior that is on par with the best humans, and better. Building such systems will require a clear understanding of the structure and organization of intelligent systems, and their specific abilities, such as inductive learning, inference, planning and so on. Much research has been carried out (and is going on) on this front. As this work progresses, it is also becoming clear that a significantly large computational power will be required to integrate the strategies derived from the research into a system that can attain a desirable level of performance. Fortunately, recent advances in computer architecture have enabled construction of massively parallel machines with unprecedented levels of performance. Viewed in this light, it seems inevitable that parallel processing technology will be used to build AI systems of the future.

Many research issues must be dealt with before this technology can be used successfully in AI applications. One such issue — the one that we will deal with

---
* Some of the research reported here was supported in part by NSF under the grants CCR-89-02496, and CCR-91-06608.

in this paper — involves scheduling. In a parallel AI computation, there will be many computational subtasks that can be performed in parallel at a given moment. As the number of such tasks can be expected to vastly outnumber the number of processors, one must decide which of the tasks to execute next on which processor. These scheduling decisions have a very significant impact on the performance of many AI applications. This will also be illustrated with examples later in this paper. What mechanism should be used to specify a scheduling strategy? What scheduling strategies are useful in specific contexts? How should the chosen mechanism be implemented on parallel machines?

We believe that an appropriate framework for such applications is one in which subtasks are modeled as medium grained processes that are capable of creating new processes dynamically, and which communicate with each other mainly via messages. In such a framework, we argue that associating *priorities* with messages and processes is a good mechanism for implementing scheduling strategies. Section 2 includes descriptions of some regimes for which effective prioritization strategies are not yet known, and should be areas of active research. In Section 3, we describe *Charm*, a portable parallel programming system that provides such a framework, and supports priorities. This system was used to carry out the experiments described in this paper. In Section 4, we examine several search regimes (e.g. state-space search and game tree search) and describe how specific priority-based scheduling strategies can be used to effectively parallelize them. Section 5 describes techniques for supporting priorities in parallel systems.

2 Alternate Scheduling Mechanisms

Although the scope of AI strategies in general is quite broad, we will focus on a subset that can be characterized as "tree structured computations" or "search computations". This by itself is quite a large class, as illustrated by the list of specific subclasses discussed in Section 4. Such computations can be viewed as a process of developing a tree (starting with a single-node tree, usually), by adding nodes to it, pruning subtrees, and propagating information up and down the tree.

One method for parallelizing such computations is to think of the tree as a shared data structure on which the processors "walk". Such an approach is often used on shared-memory machines with only a few processors. Scheduling strategies can then be expressed as tree traversals. For example, a strategy component might be: "if you are at a leaf node, traverse upward in the tree upto the first node that has an unexplored child". Although this mechanism is sometimes intuitive, it incurs substantial performance penalties on large machines (particularly the ones with nonshared-memory) where pointers between nodes in the tree may often cross processor boundaries. Also, implementation of such strategies is complicated by the intricacies of sharing memory — to avoid deadlocks and race conditions, for example.

A process-based parallelization of such computations is conceptually simple.

Each node of the tree is implemented as a process. New nodes are added to the tree by creating new processes, and propagation of information up and down the tree is implemented via messages.

As the number of nodes in the tree at any moment during its computations may be (and often is) much larger than the number of processors, the underlying system must support multiple processes per processor. In addition, a parallel implementation of such a process-model must deal with the issues of (1) grain size control, (2) dynamic load balancing and (3) scheduling.

Grain size control deals with the problem of amortizing the overhead of process creation and message-passing, typically by combining many processes into a single process. Dynamic load balancing techniques are needed to ensure that processors are effectively utilized, to complete the execution of the overall computation as fast as possible.

Scheduling, in contrast, deals with the question of which messages and processes, among the many available ones, to execute next. It is particularly important for *speculatively* parallel computations, where some of the tasks that can be carried out in parallel may turn out to be futile or unnecessary [29]. Here, the order in which tasks are executed has an impact on the total amount of computations performed — by affecting the number of messages/processes that must be processed before the problem is solved. Speculative computations in parallel functional languages have also been investigated in [1].

What mechanisms can be used to specify and implement scheduling strategies?

1. Assign fractions: In this strategy, each process is given a promise of a certain fraction of the overall CPU-time available in the system. When a process forks sub-processes, it assigns to them fractions of the fraction that was allocated to it. Such a strategy can be implemented in many different ways: for example, a process given 10% of the cpu-time may be given 10% of the processors in the system, or be allowed to run on all the processors in the system for 10% of the time. Many other shades in between are also possible.

2. Assign times: Each process is give a certain fixed cpu-time. It may assign some of its time to its child processes as above. This mechanism is different from the above in that the quanta of cpu-time assigned is a consumable resource — a process is terminated when the quanta assigned to it finishes.

3. Assign priorities to processes and messages. The parallel system must then try to adhere to the priorities to the extent possible.

We will explore the last option, although the first two have their merits in specific situations. In this paper, we will describe (a) how these mechanisms can be used effectively in different search domains, and (b) how priorities can be implemented effectively in parallel systems. First, we will introduce Charm, a portable parallel programming system which supports dynamic creation of small grained processes, and which was used in the implementations described in the paper.

3 Charm: The Parallel Programming Framework

Developing parallel application programs is currently difficult due to (a) the diversity of parallel architectural platforms, (b) the inherent difficulty of parallel programming and (c) the difficulty of reusing parallel software. Due to the diversity, programs written for one parallel machine don't usually run on another machine by a different vendor.

Charm [7] is a parallel programming system that we have developed to address this problem. Charm provides portability and supports features that simplify the task of parallel programming. Programs developed with Charm run efficiently on different shared-memory and nonshared-memory machines without change. It currently runs on Intel iPSC/860, NCUBE, CM-5, Sequent Symmetry, Multimax, Alliant FX/8, networks of workstations, and will be ported to machines including the Intel Paragon in near future.

Charm is one of the first systems to support an asynchronous, message driven, execution model [7]. This allows for maximum overlap between computation and communication and facilitates modular program organization. Recognizing that parallel programs involve distinct modes of sharing information, it supports six modes in which information may be shared between processes. These modes are implemented differently on different machines for efficiency. The system supports (static and) dynamic load balancing and prioritization. Charm was designed to support reuse of parallel software modules and includes specific features for promoting it.

From the point of view of this paper, the important features of Charm are that it supports dynamic creation of processes (called *chares*) and allows multiple processes per processor. A process is activated when a message for it is picked up for execution (or when an initial message containing the "seed" for a new process is picked up for execution). The process is allowed to complete the processing of this message before the system picks up another message — for the same or different process — for execution.

4 Applying Prioritization

In the following subsections, we will describe how we were able to obtain effective speedups by using (specific) prioritization schemes in various search domains. In some of the domains, there still remain open problems signifying the need for better prioritization strategies. The domains discussed include: state-space search, iterative deepening, divide-and-conquer, best-first and branch-and-bound search, AND-OR trees and problem reduction, game trees, and bi-directional search.

4.1 State Space Search

In a state-space search problem, one is given a starting state, a set of operators that can transform one state to another, and a desired state. The task is to find a sequence of operations that transform the start state to the desired goal state. The desired state may be described by a set of properties it must satisfy, and there may be many such states in a given state-space. One can imagine a tree with the starting state as its root, and for any state S in the tree, all the children states that can be obtained by one application of any rule to S. This tree is called the search tree, and is usually implicit, in that it is not explicitly represented in the computer program or data. A state-space search program can be thought of as traversing this tree. A depth-first search strategy is usually implemented using a stack of states in sequential programs. The search begins with the starting state on the stack. From then on a node from the top of the stack is picked up and examined. If it is a goal state, the solution may be recorded. If it is a dead-end state, it can be discarded. Otherwise all possible operators are applied to the state to produce the set of its children states. These are then pushed onto the stack, possibly using some local value-ordering heuristic so that the child most likely to lead to a solution is kept at the top of the stack.

Parallelizing depth-first search may therefore seem simple: instead of searching successor states one after the other, search them in parallel. As the search tree grows exponentially in the depth of the tree, one may also expect to generate a large degree of parallelism. Indeed, if one is looking for all solutions, this is as simple as that, except for the important problems of load balancing and grain size control. Earlier, we worked on the all-solution problem using the Chare-Kernel machine independent parallel programming system [12], which provides dynamic load balancing among other facilities. With this, we were able to obtain very good speedups for many depth-first search problems. Other work on dynamic load balancing for this problem includes that of Kumar and Rao [28, 18], who describe an idle-processor initiated load-balancing scheme which splits (i.e. divides the nodes on) the stack of the donor processors, and [4] which relies on a hierarchical load balancing scheme.

When one is interested in any one solution, such parallelization techniques lead to difficulties. If we search two successors of a state (assume there are only two for simplicity), the solution may lie in the sub-tree of either node. If it lies in the sub-tree of the first node, the work in the second sub-tree will be wasted. Exploring the two subtrees in parallel is thus speculative — we may not need both those sub-computations. This fact, and the resultant speedup anomalies were noted in a branch-and-bound search which is closely related to depth-first search, by Lai and Sahni [19].

One may get deceleration anomalies where adding a processor may actually slow down the search process in finding a solution. This may happen because the added processor may create some "red herring" work that other processors end up wasting their time on. In extreme cases, this may lead to detrimental anomalies, where p processors perform slower than 1 processor performing the search. It is also possible to get acceleration anomalies: a speedup of more than p with p processors. This can happen because the added processor picked a part of the search tree that happened to contain the solution. Kumar $et.$ $al.$ noted this in the context of parallel depth-first search. They reported a speedup varying between 2.9 to 16 with 9 processors for a 15-puzzle problem [28].

We started with the dual objectives of (1) ensuring that speedups are consistent — i.e. do not vary from one execution to another and (2) ensuring that the speedups increase monotonically with the number of processors, preferably being as close to the number of processors as possible. With that objective, it is clear that all the work that is done by the sequential program is "mandatory" whereas all the other nodes not explored by the sequential algorithm are "wastage".

Our scheme, described in [13, 31] is based on bit-vector priorities, and builds upon an idea in [20]. Each node in the search tree is assigned a priority. Priority bit-vectors can be of arbitrary length, and their ordering is lexicographic — the lexicographically smaller bit-vector indicates higher priority. The priority of the root is a bit-vector of length 0. If the priority of a node is X, and it has k children, then the priority of the i'th child is X appended by the $\lceil logk \rceil$-bit binary representation of i. Thus, if a node with priority 01101 has three children, their priorities will be 0110100, 0110101, and 0110110, from left-to-right. It can be shown that lexicographic ordering of these priorities corresponds to left-to-right ordering of the nodes in the tree. To be sure, there is a loss of information in the bit-vector representation: A node with priority 0110110 may be at level 7 of a binary tree, or level 3, with the top-level branching factor of 2, and the next two (grand-parent and parent of this node) with a branching factors of 7 and 5 respectively, among many other possibilities. Fortunately, this loss of information does not destroy the left-to-right ordering in a specific tree, and saves much in storage and comparison costs over a scheme that assigns a fixed number of bits to each level. Figure 1 shows an example of how such priorities are assigned to nodes of a search tree.

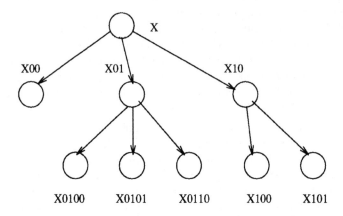

Fig. 1. Illustration of the assignment of bit-vector priorities to nodes. The priority of the topmost node is assumed to be X.

The complete scheme, described in [13], involves a few additional subtle points of strategy. In particular, a technique called *delayed-release* is used to further reduce the wasted work, and reduce the memory requirement to roughly a sum of $D + P$ where D is the depth of the tree, and P is the total number of processors. Most other parallel schemes for depth-first search require storage proportional to roughly $D * P$. Delayed-release works as follows: A process responsible for expanding a node would normally fire a new process for each child node. Instead, it now simply stores the nodes in a list, and goes on to expand the leftmost child. It continues this process until it reaches a node (say N) deemed to be small enough (by the domain specific grain size control heuristic) to search sequentially. At this point, it fires (releases) processes for each of the nodes accumulated in the list, and then goes on to carry out the sequential search under the node N.

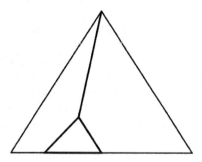

Fig. 2. The prioritization strategy leads to a characteristic broom-stick sweep of the search space.

The scheduling induced by this strategy sweeps the search tree from left-to-right. Moreover, at any moment, the set of "active" nodes — i.e. all nodes being expanded by the processors and their ancestors — form a characteristic shape resembling a broom with a long stick, as shown in Figure 2.

This strategy was implemented and tested with various state-space search problems on shared-memory and small nonshared-memory machines. A sample of the performance data, taken from [29], is shown in Table 1.

This strategy was also applied successfully in obtaining consistent speedups to one solution in test pattern generation for sequential circuits by Ramkumar and Banerjee [27]. In test generation for sequential circuits, we once again have a state space where the nodes in the search space represent assignments to primary inputs or inputs to flip-flops (called *pseudo-inputs*) in the circuit being tested. Typically, in the one processor case, heuristics are used to determine the order in which assignments are made to the inputs. These heuristics were supplemented by our prioritizing scheme for parallel execution. For any given heuristic, our

Table 1. Performance of the prioritization strategy on Sequent Symmetry. All times are in Seconds.

Processors	1	2	4	8	12	16	18
126-Queens	202.0	100.5	51.0	26.3	18.1	14.0	12.7
8x8 Knight's Tour	113.0	52.9	26.5	13.1	8.9	6.6	6.1

scheme was able to consistently speedup the execution time as the number of processors were increased.

The test generator is initially provided with a list of faults in a given circuit for which test vectors need to be detected. A test vector sequence is a solution for a fault if it can successfully propagate the fault to a primary output in the circuit. Whenever a sequence of test vectors is found to detect a given fault, a fault simulator is invoked to determine whether this test vector serves as a solution for other faults in the fault list. All such covered faults are dropped from the fault list. Each fault is assigned a time limit which bounds the computation time that can be devoted to finding a solution for a single fault. If no solution can be found within the time limit, the test generator has failed to find a solution that may exist in the search space. If the entire search space has been explored unsuccessfully, the fault is called a *redundant* fault. The efficiency metric in Table 2 reports the percentage of faults which are redundant or for which test vectors have been detected.

In Table 2, we quote some of the results presented in [27] for an 8-processor Intel i860 hypercube. The test generator, called ProperTEST, was developed using the Charm system and, as a result, ran unchanged on a variety of machines, including a network of Sun Sparc I workstations, a Sequent Symmetry, an Intel i860 hypercube and an Encore Multimax.

In column 1 of Table 2, the benchmark circuits used are identified. In column 2, the number of PEs used in the experiment is listed. In columns 3 and 4, the time spent in test generation and fault simulation phases of the computation is reported. Finally, in column 5, the efficiency of the test generator is presented. The efficiency metric reports the quality of the solution obtained. It is important that speedup is not obtained at the cost of poor fault coverage by the test generator. As can be seen from the results, the use of priorities was instrumental in obtaining consistent speedups *without* significant loss in quality.

There is an interesting postscript to the research on state-space search. As we began experimenting with specific applications, such as the N-queens problem, we attempted to improve the heuristics used in the search, to ensure that the speedups were measured against the "best possible" sequential algorithm. For the N-queens problem, this led to such a good heuristics that it almost always led to a first solution, without much search [11]. This was a true heuristic, as distinct from the well-known closed form solutions to the N-queens problem, in that it can be used continually to generate multiple solutions beyond the first

Table 2. Execution times (in seconds) of the ProperTEST test pattern generator for sequential circuits on selected ISCAS89 sequential benchmark circuits on the Intel i860 hypercube. All reported execution times are in seconds.

Intel i860 hypercube (Message Passing)

Circuit	#PEs	Test gen. time	Fault sim. time	Efficiency
s386	1	184.4	2.7	100
	8	28.8	1.3	100
s713	1	27.0	3.7	98.8
	8	6.6	1.0	98.8
s5378	1	6016.5	184.8	75.3
	8	901.7	38.6	72.7

one. (The 126 queens results quoted in Table 1 is prior to the use of this newly discovered heuristic). A similar experience was obtained for the 3-satisfiability problem [3]. As long as a solution existed, the heuristic we developed was able to find it without much search! We plan to experiment with other heuristics for NP-complete problems.

4.2 Iterative Deepening

Sometimes, one is interested in an optimal solution to a search problem. If an admissible heuristic is available [22] one can use the A* algorithm, which ensures that the first solution found is the optimal one. However, A* requires large memory space on the average, and degenerates to breadth-first search in the worst case. An iterative deepening technique can be used in such a situation: due to admissibility property, we know that the cost of the solution cannot be less than the heuristic value of the root. So, we can conduct a depth-first search, but restrict ourselves to not search below nodes that exceed the bound given by the heuristic value of the root. If no solution is found, we can search for the next possible bound. This can be obtained by keeping track of the heuristic values of the unexplored children (of the explored nodes), and picking the minimum from these. Alternatively, in some problems, the increasing sequence of bounds is clear by the nature of the problem definition itself. For example, in the well-known fifteen puzzle problem, if the cost measure is the number of steps required to produce the goal state, it can be shown that the bound must increase by two in every successive iteration. This process is continued until a solution is found. This algorithm was defined by Korf [17], and is called IDA*, for Iterative Deepening A*. As in A*, the first solution found is an optimal solution in IDA* too. Each successive iteration duplicates all the work done by the previous iteration. However, as the tree-size increases exponentially in the depth of the tree, the cost of the last iteration dominates, and this duplication is not too expensive. Even with a binary branching factor, the duplication cost is at most 100%, which is tolerable considering the significant memory savings.

As each iteration of IDA* is a depth-first search, it can be parallelized using the techniques described above. Kumar *et. al.* in [28] were the first to demonstrate parallel schemes for this problem. Their results did exhibit speedup anomalies for single solutions, and they reported speedups to all solutions (as their primary interest was to demonstrate the efficacy of their load balancing scheme). It is true that all the optimal solutions exist in the last level of the tree (and therefore all the previous layers are completely explored irrespective of the order in which the nodes are explored.) However, the last iteration — complete exploration of the last level — is typically larger than all the previous ones combined. The order in which nodes are explored in the last iteration affects when the first solution is found, and thus the notion of speculativeness prevails in this context too.

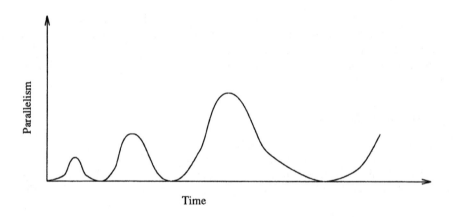

Fig. 3. The nature of inherent parallelism in IDA*.

Our prioritization techniques described in Section 4.1 were successful at obtaining consistent and monotonic speedups for this problem. However, the speedup with these techniques alone are not as high as they could be, although for each *iteration*, we obtained close to the best possible speedups. The difficulty is that the parallelism in this problem increases and decreases in waves with each iteration, as shown in Figure 3. At the beginning of each iteration the parallelism is low. It increases quickly to occupy many processors, and then trails off toward the end of the iteration.

If we knew that $n+1$'th iteration was necessary, we could start it concurrently with n'th iteration, so that by the time n'th iteration finishes, the next iteration is already running full-swing, thereby keeping the processors busy. Even with this knowledge, we would have to make sure that the next iteration did not generate work that kept processors from working on the previous iteration. However, seen from this perspective, this problem seems amenable to prioritization. Just assign higher priority to earlier iterations, and allow multiple iterations to run concurrently. This scheme is described in [32].

The fact that we do not know which iterations are necessary can be handled as follows: We start K iterations in parallel. Whenever any one of them finishes without reporting a solution, we start the next iteration. Whenever a solution is reported from the i'th iteration, we (a) do not start any new iterations, (b) terminate all the iterations larger than i, and (c) wait for all iterations smaller than i to finish, as they may have a better solution. This scheme might seem wasteful, because we are generating a new class of speculative, and potentially wasteful, computations (viz. the iterations beyond the optimal-solution depth). However, with proper use of priorities, our experiments suggest that work on subsequent iterations is done only if no work on the current iteration is available.

To assign higher priorities to earlier iterations, we assign a non-empty bit-vector as the priority of the root node in every iteration, as opposed to an empty one in the baseline algorithm. This priority must be so chosen that every descendant of the root of an iteration has lexicographically smaller bit-vector compared to any node in a subsequent iteration. If the maximum number of iterations is known, this can be accomplished easily by assigning a binary representation of the iteration number as the priority of its root. However, in general, this number is not known. A binary coding scheme we developed solves this problem neatly. The first iteration is given a representation: "0", the second and third one "010" and "011" respectively, the 4'th through 7'th are assigned "00100", "00101", "00110", and "00111", and so on. It can be verified that this representation satisfies the required property — any extension of 011, for example, is lexicographically smaller than all extensions of 00100.

With this scheme we were able to "soak up" the computing resources during the previously idle periods without increasing the wastage, and produce almost perfect speedups even for small-sized problems. The improvement obtained can be seen in Table 3, taken from the data in [29]. The slight superlinearity seen in the data is not surprising, and it occurs because the optimal solution is reported before all the nodes to the left of the solution node are explored — other processors may still be working on such nodes. See [13, 32] for details of this scheme, and additional performance data.

Table 3. Performance of IDA* solving a 15-puzzle instance on Sequent Symmetry. The numbers shown are speedups. The sequential execution time for this instance was 116 seconds.

Processors	1	4	8	12	16	18
Basic Parallel IDA*	1	3.8	6.7	8.9	10.8	11.7
2 Concurrent Iterations	1	4.0	7.9	11.5	15.0	16.5
3 Concurrent Iterations	1	4.0	8.0	12.0	16.2	18.3

4.3 Divide And Conquer: Memory Usage

A divide-and-conquer is a deterministic computation, without any speculative parallelism. A problem is divided into two or more subproblems. This subdivision continues recursively until subproblems are "small enough" to be directly solved. Solutions to the subproblems are "combined" to form a solution to their parent problem. The computation can thus be seen as the process of growing the tree downwards, and then passing information up the tree, combining it at the intermediate nodes, until the root node forms the final solution. In a process-based parallel formulation, each node of the tree is made into a process, with the last few levels of tree being combined into one process for the sake of grain size control (this is just one of many possible methods for grain size control that can be used in tree-structured computations).

Without any speculative parallelism, it may seem to be futile to attach priorities to processes. However, significant savings in memory usage can be obtained by using the left-to-right priorities (as used in state-space search). Because of the broom-stick sweep, the memory used with P processors is proportional to $D + P$, for a D-deep tree, instead of $O(D * P)$, which would have been the memory usage without the use of priorities. The $O(D * P)$ could be obtained by using a LIFO strategy for dealing with new processes and messages. Further reduction in memory usage can be obtained by giving a higher priority to messages carrying solutions to subproblems, in relation to the messages carrying subproblems to be solved. While the former may result in reduction in memory usage by finishing the parent subproblem, the latter often results in creation of more processes. This reduction can be effected by attaching the prefix "0" to the priority of all solution messages, and "1" to that of the new processes. Note that if 1X was the priority attached to a message carrying a subproblem, then the message carrying a solution to it should bear priority "0X".

4.4 Branch-and-bound and Best-First Search

The Traveling Salesperson Problem (TSP) is a typical example of an optimization problem solved using branch-and-bound techniques. In this problem the salesperson must visit n cities, returning to the starting point, and is required to minimize the total cost of the trip. Every pair of cities i and j has a cost C_{ij} associated with it (if $i = j$, then C_{ij} is assumed to be of infinite cost).

In the branch-and-bound computation one starts with an initial partial solution, and an infinite upper bound. New partial solutions are generated by *branching* out from the current partial solution. Each partial solution comprises a set of edges (pairs of cities) that have been included in the circuit, and a set of edges that have been excluded from the circuit. For every partial solution, a lower bound on the cost of any solution that can be found by extending the partial solution is computed. A partial solution is discarded (pruned) if its lower bound is larger than the current upper bound. Two (or more) new partial solutions are obtained from the current partial solution by including and excluding the "best" edge (determined using some selection criterion) not in the partial solution. The upper bound is updated whenever a solution is reached.

Note that the left-to-right tree-traversal strategy that we used for state-space search is inappropriate for this problem. To maximize pruning, we would like to process nodes with lowest lower-bounds first. This leads to a form of best-first search. To parallelize this computation with a prioritized scheduling mechanism, we associate the lower bound of a node with the priority of the corresponding process, with lower values signifying higher priorities. (The parallelization scheme also needs an ability to propagate the cost of the best-known solution at the current time, so that it is accessible from all processors. The *monotonic variable* abstraction supported in Charm provides this capability).

This prioritization scheme was implemented and tested on many versions of the Traveling Salesperson Problem. The major challenge for the priority balancing strategy was to ensure that the number of nodes expanded in a parallel search is not much more than those expanded in sequential search. This implies trying to implement a good degree of adherence to priorities, while still preserving good load balance, and avoiding any bottlenecks. With appropriate choice of priority balancing strategies (described in section 5), we were able to demonstrate good speedups even on 512 processors of an NCUBE machine, as shown in Table 4.

Table 4. The figure shows the execution times and the number of nodes generated for executions of a 60 city asymmetric TSP on the NCUBE/2 with upto 512 processors using the tokens strategy to balance load. In this case the cluster size is 16 processors.

Processors	1 (estimated)	64	128	256	512
Time	19,366	302.6	151.1	86.2	42.1
Estimated Speedup	1	64	128	225	460
Number of Nodes expanded	-	85,165	84,030	93,816	85,420

It should be noted that the lower bounding methods we used are simple, almost naive, methods. Much more sophisticated methods exist today which would cut down the number of nodes generated for this problem by many orders of magnitude. The simple algorithm was sufficient for our purpose here, as we simply wanted to demonstrate how speculative parallelism can be controlled in this context. With better algorithms, one can use our strategies and attempt to solve much larger problems.

As even larger branch-and-bound problems are attempted, we anticipate memory overflow problems. This is because, in the worst case, best-first search can be as bad as breadth-first search for memory usage, and never as good as the depth-first search. As the spread between memory requirements of depth-first and breadth-first varies from a linear to exponential function of the depth of the tree, one can expect memory overflows on many problem instances. Again, a priority based scheme can be used to formulate a solution to this problem. The memory overflows can be avoided by using a prioritization strategy that adapts to the current memory usage. When memory utilization is very high (say more than 90%), one may switch to a depth-first strategy for all new nodes being generated. This can be accomplished with priorities alone as follows: let U be the maximum value the priority make take in the normal strategy, and let D be the maximum depth of the tree. Instead of using a lower-bound x as the priority of a node, we will use $D + x$. When we detect that the memory usage is high, we assign priorities differently. Each node at depth d is assigned a priority $D - d$. Thus, the priority of a node generated after the memory threshold has been reached is always higher (i.e. numerically smaller) than any node generated earlier, as $D - d < D + x$. This will have the effect of finishing off the nodes from the "original" priority queue by completing the depth-first search under each node. Once this strategy reduces memory usage below the preset threshold, we can switch back to assigning the lower-bound based priorities as above (i.e. D+x). The system will thus finish an adequate number of nodes created prior to this point in a depth-first (LIFO) fashion, but then revert back to a best-first pattern. Controlled use of memory has also been used in [35] by combining good features of A* and IDA*.

Another reason for higher memory usage in a prioritized strategy is the potentially large number of low priority nodes that may "rot" in the queue. These nodes represent work that is pruned due to some solution found earlier. However, until they are examined, they won't be discarded; and as we are proceeding in priority order, they will not be examined for a long time. A solution to this problem is to provide a "flush" primitive in the system that would delete all messages below a certain priority level. This can be used whenever a new better solution is found, to clean up the queue. An alternate solution is to switch to a "garbage-collection" mode globally (across all processors) on some trigger — such as high memory utilization on some processor, or as a periodic cleanup phase. Under this mode, all processes simply examine the lower bound of the node they are meant to expand, and discard it (if its lower bound is larger than the current upper bound, as usual), or else simply store it in another repository process. When all the nodes have been cleared in this fashion (and this condition can be detected by the quiescence detection algorithm in Charm), the repository processes on all the processors are awakened, and they create new processes for all the non-garbage nodes.

4.5 Logic Programming: AND-OR and REDUCE-OR trees

A Pure Logic Program is a collection of predicate definitions. Each predicate is defined by possibly multiple clauses. Each clause is of the form: $H : -L_1, L_2 ... L_n$, where the L_i's are called the body literals. (A literal is a predicate symbol, followed by a parenthesized list of terms, where a term may either be a constant or a variable, or a function symbol followed by a parenthesized list of terms). A clause with no body literals is called a fact.

A computation begins with a query, which is a sequence of literals. A particular literal can be solved by using any of the available clauses whose heads unify with the goal literal. In the problem-solving interpretation of a Logic Program, each literal corresponds to a (sub) problem, and different clauses for a predicate correspond to alternate methods for solving the problem. Also, it is possible to have multiple solutions for a given problem. So, again, when one is interested in only one solution, the problem of speculative parallelism arises. This is further complicated by the presence of AND parallelism, which is the parallelism between multiple literals of a clause (or, in problem-solving terminology: that between multiple subgoals of a particular method).

REDUCE/OR Process Model: Our work on speculative computations in Parallel Logic Programming was conducted in the context of the REDUCE/OR process model ($ROPM$), proposed and developed in [9, 14, 8]. The past and ongoing work related to this model in our group includes development of a binding environment [15] and a compiler [26, 25]. The REDUCE/OR process model exploits AND as well as OR parallelism from Logic programs, and handles the interactions of AND and OR parallelism without losing parallelism. It is also designed so that it can use both shared and nonshared memory machines. The compiled system executes on the NCUBEs and Intel's hypercubes, as well as on many shared-memory machines such as: Sequent Symmetry, Encore Multimax, Alliant FX/8, etc. Thus, when we started working on first-solution speedups in Logic Programs (i.e. with speculative computations), it was clear to us that we must work within the framework of $ROPM$ to retain its advantages. This added one more constraint on the possible schemes. Speculative work in OR-parallel Prolog has also been investigated by Hausman in [6].

We first worked on simply improving the first solution speedups in $ROPM$ compared with the then prevalent scheduling scheme, which was a $LIFO$ scheme, with each processor having its own stack. This is described below. The work described in Section 4.1 on pure state-space search came later, and encouraged by those results we set a new objective of consistent and monotonic speedups. The resultant work is described subsequently.

Speedups for a First Solution: The REDUCE/OR process model is based on the REDUCE/OR tree [10], which is an alternative to the traditional AND/OR tree. It overcomes the limitations of AND/OR trees from the point of view of parallel execution. The detailed description of the process model can be found in [9]. What concerns us here is the process structure generated by ROPM. Each invocation of a clause corresponds to a process, called a REDUCE process (with the exception of clauses and predicates explicitly marked sequential: these are used for granularity control). The REDUCE process uses a dependence graph representation of the literals in the clause. It starts with a tuple of initial bindings to its variables, and fires OR processes for each literal that can be fired without waiting for any other literal, according to the graph. Each OR process may send multiple solutions. Each solution results in a new binding tuple, which may trigger firing of other OR processes for dependent literals. For example, consider a clause with four literals, with the dependence graph represented by:

$$h(I, T) \; : - \; t(I, X) \; \rightarrow \; (u(X, Y) \; // \; v(X, Z)) \; \rightarrow \; w(Y, Z, T).$$

When an instance of this clause is activated, an initial binding tuple with variable I bound to some value, and other variables unbound, is created. One OR process for solving p with this initial binding of I is then fired. For every value of X returned by t, one u and one v process is fired immediately. Thus, there may be multiple u (and v) processes active at one time. Each value of Y returned by u is combined with compatible values of Z (i.e. those that share the same X value) returned by the corresponding v process, and for each consistent combination, a w process instance is fired. Each OR process, given an instantiated literal, simply fires off REDUCE processes for each clause that unifies with the literal, and instructs them to send responses directly to the OR-process's parent REDUCE process. Thus, the process tree looks similar to a proof tree, rather than to an OR tree (or SLD tree). This fact is important in understanding (as well as designing) the scheme we proposed.

In the compiled implementation of ROPM, the requests for firing processes were stored and serviced in LIFO fashion. On (small) shared-memory systems, this was done using a central shared stack, whereas on nonshared-memory machines, a separate stack was used on each processor, and a dynamic load balancing scheme moved such requests from one processor's stack to another's. Although this strategy resulted in good use of memory space, it had one drawback (if one is interested in just one solution): all the solutions tended to appear in a burst toward the end of the computation, for problems that involve AND as well as OR parallelism. It is easy to see why, with a different and a simpler example. Suppose there is a clause with two AND-parallel (i.e. independent) literals, p and q. When the clause fires, it pushes p and q process-creation requests on the stack. Assume p is on top, without loss of generality. Literal p may have a large sub-tree, with many solutions, and so all the processors in the system may be busy working on p. This will result in production of all solutions to p before any solutions to q. (Of course, toward the end a few processors will be working on q while others are finishing up p). However, from the point of view of reporting the first solution faster, the system should focus attention on q as soon as one solution from p is obtained. In addition, if there are two alternative computation-intensive clauses for p, we should have the system concentrate its resources on one clause (and its subtree) rather than dividing them arbitrarily among the two.

The solution we proposed used bit-vector priorities, with the root having a null-priority. An OR process with priority X assigned a priority to each of its children, by appending the child's rank to X (as described in the section on state-space search). A REDUCE process uses a more complex method for assigning priorities. If it contains only AND parallel literals, such as p and q in the example above, they receive identical priorities. When the literals form a more complex dependence graph, such as the clause consisting of t, u, v and

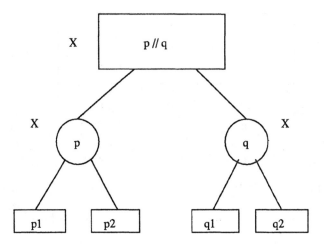

Fig. 4. The Prioritization Scheme applied to a simple and-or tree

w above, priorities are assigned such that the literals closer to the end of the dependence graph receive higher priority than those that precede them in the graph. This is done by assigning "distance bits" to the priorities, which signify the distance from the end of the dependence graph. Thus, for example, the u and v processes receive priority X01, which is higher than the priority of the t process (X10), but lower than that of the w processes (X00). Thus, when there is an s process (and its subtree) available, the system focuses its attention on completing a solution to s (and thereby a solution to the reduce process) instead of finding additional solutions to t (or u or v). In addition, multiple instances of a single literal fired are prioritized so that the one fired earlier has higher priority than the ones fired later. This necessitates addition of "instance bits" in addition to the "distance bits" used above, as shown in Figure 5.

Intuitively, the scheme represents the strategy of supporting the subcomputations that were closer to yielding a solution to the top level goal. ("Support the Leader" strategy). It solved the "all-solutions-in-a-burst" problem mentioned above, because p's and q's subtrees now have identical priority, and so compete for resources with each other, thereby ensuring that some p and some q solutions will be produced in parallel. We were able to demonstrate good first solution speedups for problems involving both AND and OR parallelism, with very little overhead; This was accomplished without affecting the performance on pure AND and pure OR parallel problems, or on all-solution searches. For further information about this scheme, we refer the reader to [30].

Table 5 below shows the performance of our strategy on a benchmark. This program involves finding a prime that can also be expressed as a sum of a Fibonacci number and a perfect number. The first benchmark problem was:

" fib(F,20000) // perfect(P,3000) $\rightarrow$ X is F+P $\rightarrow$ prime(X)."

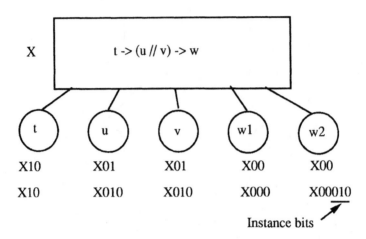

Fig. 5. Prioritization for clauses with dependence graphs. The first row shows priorities with distance bits only, while the second row shows priorities with instance bits appended.

I.e. it first searches for a Fibonacci number and a perfect number (in the specified range) in parallel, and for every pair obtained, checks if its sum is a prime. The second problem increases the problem size and requires that the primes so found be larger than 50,000.

" fib(F,80000) // perfect(P,3000) → X is F+P → X > 50000, prime(X)."

As seen in the table, the time to first solution for the second instance was reduced almost ten-fold, at the cost of a small overhead (as represented by the overall time to completion, which increased from 27.9 to 28.0 to 29.6).

Table 5. Performance of two benchmark problems with AND and OR parallelism on Sequent Symmetry with 16 processors. For each case, time to first solution is shown, followed by the time to completion in parenthesis, in seconds.

	Depth-First	Prioritized: distance bits	distance and instance bits
Problem 1	2.4 (15.0)	1.4 (14)	0.8 (16.0)
Problem 2	23.2 (27.9)	3.5 (28.0)	2.8 (29.6)

Consistent Speedups: The method described above is not free from anomalies. The results from state-space search made it clear to us that consistent non-anomalous and monotonic speedups can be obtained in that domain. We then applied these techniques to the parallel Prolog system, while restricting ourselves to pure OR parallel programs without any AND parallelism. The description of the process structure for ROPM described above should make it clear why the application is not straight-forward. The OR tree (search tree) used in state-space search is now folded into the REDUCE/OR tree.

The scheme we developed in [34] to address the speedup anomaly involves tagging responses with their priorities, and using the response's priority to decide the priority of any processes fired due to it. For example, a REDUCE process with priority X may have two dependent literals p and q, with q being dependent on p. A solution returned for p would have a priority indicating its place in the tree beneath p, say XY. The priority of the q instance fired using this binding returned by p will then be XY also. (Compare this with the scheme described above in which the priority of q would have been X0). If this q instance sends a solution tagged with a priority vector XYZ, the resultant binding is sent as a response to the parent of the REDUCE/OR process with priority vector XYZ attached to it. (As opposed to just X in the previous scheme).

The complete details of this scheme can be found in [29]. We only note that consistent and excellent first solution speedups were obtained for pure OR parallel Logic Programs with this scheme. As an example, the following table shows the performance of the Prolog compiler with priorities, running a Prolog program to find a Knight's tour on a 6x6 board. The speedups observed were very consistent from run to run, and can be seen to increase well with processors. The degree of wastage can be estimated from the number of messages processed, which is proportional to the number of processes created, and is seen to be well controlled.

Table 6. Performance of prioritized Parallel Prolog Compiler on a 6x6 Knight's tour program on Sequent Symmetry.

Processors	1	4	8	12	16	20
Execution Time (Secs.)	1245	337	183	127	97	80
Messages Processed	9348	9464	9526	9617	9624	9694
Wasted Work	0%	1.2%	1.9%	2.8%	2.9%	3.7%

Dealing with AND Parallelism: The first scheme described above improves first solution speedups in AND/OR parallel programs, but suffers from anomalies, whereas the second scheme yields consistent speedups but works only for OR parallel programs. A synthesis of these is needed. We developed a simple scheme [29] that is sufficient to ensure consistent and linear speedups for many (but not all) AND/OR problems. We believe that schemes that involve dynamic changing of priorities are necessary to handle this class of problems.

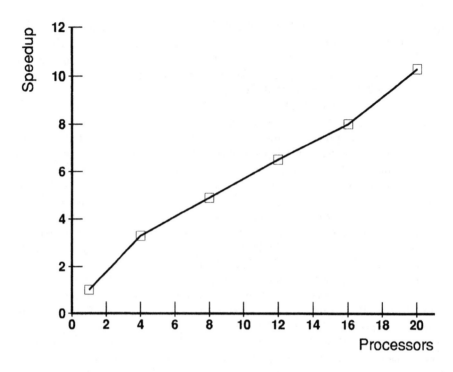

Fig. 6. Performance of a prioritization scheme for game tree search, on Sequent Symmetry. Speedups are relative to one processor speeds.

4.6   Game Trees

Alpha-beta search is an efficient game tree search procedure. However, when trying to conduct the search for the best move in parallel, it imposes a sequential bottleneck, as it requires information generated by left subtrees to be used within right subtrees. Attempts to obviate this bottleneck may reduce the amount of pruning, and thus increase the number of nodes examined, thus undermining potential gains of parallel processing. We investigated a parallel method that is symmetric in the sense of not requiring a strict left-to-right information flow. Each node (process) maintains a lower and upper bound on the value of the position it represents. As these bounds change during computation, their new values are sent to the parent processes. The pruning rule in this context becomes: "any child, for which the best it can do is worse than the worst I can do" is pruned. (For a max node: "Any child whose upper bound is smaller than my lower bound" is pruned.) Notice that this rule may prune children even when none of them have final values, unlike the alpha-beta. So, it is potentially possible that this method, under a proper prioritization strategy, may need to explore fewer nodes than the alpha-beta strategy. Finding such a strategy remains an open problem at the moment. However, we have explored some simple prioritization strategies that lead to reasonably good performances [21]. Figure 6 below shows the performance of a simple strategy from [21] on a game position for the board game Othello, with a 8-ply search.

Notice that the above formulation leads to many different types of messages — those carrying new nodes to be expanded, those carrying updates to lower/upper bounds, those carrying termination messages (telling a child it should terminate its subtree and then itself), etc. Assigning differential priorities depending on the type of messages becomes at least as important as assigning different priorities to messages of the same type. The specific strategies we employed for this purpose are described in [21].

4.7 Bi-directional Search

When the goal state of a state-space search is fixed, and the operators for transforming states are invertible, it becomes feasible to search backwards from the goal state to the start state. Such search is not feasible for the N-queens problem because a goal state is specified only implicitly, by the constraints it must satisfy. It is feasible for the 15-puzzle or Rubik's cube, for example, because the desired state is concretely known.

For such problems, it is then possible to search in both directions - a forward search from the starting state and a backward search from the goal state. This can lead to potentially tremendous reduction in search space, as illustrated in Figure 7. Assuming a uniform branching factor of b and a depth of d for the search tree, the size of the search space reduces from b^d to $2b^{d/2}$. So, with a branching factor 2, and a depth of 30, one can reduce the search space (approximately) from a billion states to only 65,000 states. The promise of such a reduction makes bi-directional search very attractive.

A few details must be dealt with before attempting to realize these gains. Korf et. al. [16, 17] have explored these issues in the past. The forward and backward search must intersect in time, so as to make sure the solution states don't miss each other. This rules out the space-efficient depth-first search for at least one of the two directions. We must store the states in the backward (or symmetrically, the forward) search, and then search in depth-first manner in the forward (backward) direction. Given the memory limitations, it may be necessary to limit the depth of backwards search to less than half of the total depth. Secondly, the depth d may not be known apriori. Again, as suggested by Korf et. al., we can employ an iterative deepening search when d is not known in advance. For simplicity, we can carry out a single backward search up to a depth b from the goal state once, store all the states so generated, and then carry out multiple iterations of the forward search with increasing depth-bounds d (see Figure 8). It suffices to store only the last (top) layer in the backward search, as any solution path must pass through a state in this layer. We will call this layer the "goal layer" in the following.

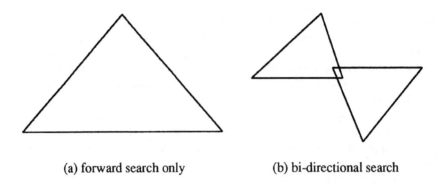

(a) forward search only   (b) bi-directional search

Fig. 7. Potential reduction in search-space with Bi-directional search.

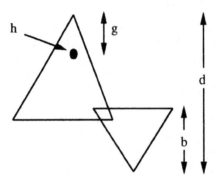

Fig. 8. bi-directional search for an IDA* iteration with depth-bound d

Parallelization of this algorithm requires a decision on how to store the goal layer — it can either (a) be replicated on all processors or (b) distributed across processors. With (a), it uses up more memory and so can store a shallower tree, but avoids message passing overheads for checking the goal layer for every state generated in the forward search. The choice depends on the number of processors — with more processors, you can store more layers with (b) and the gains in reduction of forward search-space start to outweigh the message passing overheads. The crossover point depends on the work done per state, and on the message passing overhead, and so is different for different applications, and possibly on different machines. We chose to use the distributed storage of the goal layer.

The problem we chose for this experiment was the 15-puzzle. We used the Manhattan distance heuristic (the minimum number of moves from any state to the goal state is at least the sum of the distance each tile is away from its "home"). Each node in the forward search has a g value — which is the number of moves from the start state required to reach it — and an h value, which is the heuristic value for the node as defined above. A node in the forward search is checked for occurrence in the goal layer if its g value equals $d - b$. Also, a node a pruned (i.e. discarded) if $g + h > d$, because there is no prospect of finding a solution of depth d under it.

There is an issue of speculative computation in the last iteration, when one is looking for one optimal solution. To understand the issues in bi-directional search, we decided to isolate that issue by assuming that we are looking for all optimal solutions. As we carried out experiments with varying degrees of bi-directional search on 32, 64 and 128 processors of an NCUBE, a surprising result emerged, as seen in Table 7. The performance actually became worse when we used bi-directional search! The variant with no backward-search was the fastest. What happened to the tremendous promise of bi-directional search?

Table 7. Performance is worse with bi-directional search! Timing results for a 15 puzzle instance (Korf Problem #2) on NCUBE/2. All times are in seconds.

Depth of backward search	32 processors	64 processors	128 processors	States Explored
0	461	233	119	81,958,206
12	475	239	125	81,075,244
18	518	266	148	71,819,789

The solution to the mystery can be found by looking at the shape of the forward search tree. By counting the number of nodes at each level in the forward search, it can be seen that this shape is roughly as shown in Figure 9. I.e. the branching factor is not uniform, and it varies with the depth of the tree. It has an expanding phase followed by a "stagnant" phase, followed by a shrinking phase. (Stone & Stone also report similar shapes of search trees in [37].) It turns out that the lower bounding heuristic — the Manhattan distance one — is a strong pruning device, which discards a majority of the new states being generated at deeper levels in the tree. For such problems, backward search is essentially useless, as the size of the search space with bi-directional search is essentially similar to that with forward search alone. This is confirmed by counting the number of states explored (the last column of the table above), which are seen to be reduced from 82 million to 72 million, a much smaller reduction, with a much steeper price to pay in terms of communication.

To confirm the hypothesis further, we explored the 15 puzzle problem further by intentionally weakening the heuristic. The heuristic lower bound on each node was set to be w times the Manhattan distance, with $0 \le w \le 1$. With such weakening, the size of the search space explodes, and we were forced to

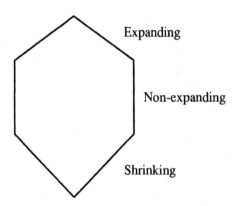

Fig. 9. A schematic view of the shape of the forward search space.

consider a smaller problem instance. With $w = 0.7$, for example, we were able to demonstrate the advantages of bi-directional search, as shown in Table 8. Thus, assuming that there will be other problems where such a strong heuristic is not available, bi-directional search can be still useful.

Table 8. Performance with weakened heuristics — Bi-directional search has its advantages.

Depth of backward search	32 processors	64 processors	128 processors	States Explored
0	952	480	241	177,263,862
12	975	505	270	159,092,443
18	605	301	184	50,810,983

Thus, our aim of exploring first-solution speedups with bi-directional search was beset, at least for 15 puzzle, at this point as even for all solutions, bi-directional search wasn't very promising. For problems (with weaker pruning heuristic) where it is promising, the following steps must be taken for first-solution speedup: First, the forward search must be prioritized, with bit-vector priorities as in simple state-space search. Secondly, to avoid backward search consuming more time than the forward one, the two should be overlapped in time. We plan to explore these issues further with other search problems. Some preliminary results on the "Peg solitaire" game are in [2]. That report also deals with "duplication detection" which is relevant for simple as well as bi-directional searches where states may recur independently in different parts of the search tree.

5 Implementing Priorities on Parallel Systems

Most prioritization strategies for parallel systems can be considered to be variants of either a centralized or a fully distributed scheme. In the centralized scheme, work is allocated to requesting processing elements from a central pool of work, where the work is sorted exactly according to their priorities. In a simple fully distributed scheme, each individual processing element maintains its own pool of work (sorted according to priorities). Any new work generated is sent to a randomly selected processor. The variations in these strategies arise with the differences in schemes used to balance work and balance priorities. In case of the centralized strategies, the central pool of work becomes a source of bottleneck. Fully distributed strategies on the other hand suffer from an inability to adhere to priorities on the global level (low priority work might be done on some processing elements, even though there exist higher priority work on other processing elements).

Our earlier work [29] involved a fully distributed approach to prioritization in a parallel system. The initial distribution of the work onto various processing elements is random. Subsequently, processors periodically exchange information about load and priorities with their neighbors, and attempt to distribute priorities and load by moving work around. These strategies still have the drawback (to a smaller extent) we discussed earlier — priorities are not distributed uniformly over processors, hence low priority (wasteful) work gets done. For additional variants of this strategy and their performance on various machines we refer the reader to [29].

Centralized strategies provide good priority adherence and load balancing. Their weakness is that the central pool of work becomes the bottleneck. We can solve the problem of a bottleneck by splitting the pool of work amongst a few processing elements — essentially creating some sort of a semi-distributed strategy as described in [36, 33]. In the strategy in citeSinhaIPPS93, the processors in the system are partitioned into clusters. One processor in each cluster is chosen as the load manager, the remaining processors in the cluster being its managees. Managees send all new work created on themselves to be queued in a centralized pool (sorted according to priorities) at their corresponding load manager. Each load manager has two responsibilities:

1. It must distribute the work among its managees. The managees inform their load managers of their current work load by sending periodic load information and piggybacking load information with every piece of new work they send to the manager. The load manager uses load information from its managees to maintain the load level within a certain range for all its managees.
2. It must balance both load and priorities over all the load managers in the system. This is accomplished by an exchange of some high priority tasks between pairs of managers. Each manager communicates with a defined set of neighboring managers. An exchange of tasks between a pair of managers occurs in two steps. In the first step, the managers exchange their load information. In the second step each manager sends over some tasks to the

other manager. A fixed number of tasks are always sent — this does the priority balancing. In addition, more (again, a fixed number) tasks depending on the task-loads of the managers involved are sent by the manager with greater load to the manager with the lesser load — this contributes to the load balancing. Note that the tasks exchanged are the highest priority tasks on each manager It might seem that by sending its highest priority tasks to another load manager, the sending manager is not distributing its priorities correctly. However this strategy performed well. We can intuitively explain why exchanging the top priority tasks might be sufficient: the managees of each manager work on the top priority elements on their load managers, so (in some sense) their work represents the top priority elements on the manager. Therefore an exchange of work between managers causes a distribution of the top priorities between two managers and their managees. We experimented further by implementing a strategy in which priorities were balanced by having pairs of managers exchange one-half of their top priority tasks. But this strategy resulted in a degradation in performance. We attribute the degradation in performance to the cost of determining the top half elements.

There is an imbalance in the memory requirements of the load managers and the managees in the hierarchical strategy. The imbalance arises because all newly created work is queued up at the load managers. This poses problems because the amount of new work that can be created becomes limited by the number of managers and their available memory, even though there is a larger amount of memory available on the managees (assuming all processors in the system have an equal amount of memory, and that there is more than one managee for each manager). We can balance memory requirements of processing elements using the following variant of the above strategy, developed in [36].

As in the above scheme, the processing elements in the system are split up into clusters — one processor in each cluster is chosen as the load manager, the remaining processors are its managees. However, now new work created on managees is stored in hash-tables on the processor itself, while only a *token* containing the priority of the new work is sent to the load managers. The load managers balance these prioritized tokens among themselves by exchanging their high priority tokens similar to the above. Each managee informs its manager of its load by (1) piggybacking load information with each token it sends to the manager, and (2) periodically sending load information. When a manager decides that one of its managees (say M) needs work, it selects the highest priority token from its (the manager's) pool of tokens, and sends a request to the processor storing the work corresponding to the token for the work to be sent to M.

6 Discussion

We argued that associating priorities with new processes and messages is an effective method for controlling the "focus" of a parallel symbolic computation. Although integer priorities are sufficient for some domains, other domains are seen to require unbounded levels of priorities specified via arbitrary-length bit-vectors. Priorities are particularly effective for speculatively parallel computations, where part of the parallel work may be wasted, and so it is important to identify and focus on specific parts of the overall computation. Prioritization strategies for several tree-structured computations including state-space search, iterative deepening game tree search, branch-and-bound, and logic programming (which is the same as problem reduction based problem solving and planning from this paper's point of view) were developed and their success demonstrated. There still remain many open problems in prioritization particularly for game-tree search, AND-OR tree search, and bi-directional search.

All the computational experiments were carried out in the framework of the Charm parallel programming system. The system's modular organization allows one to plug different load balancing and queuing strategies without having to re-code the rest of the mechanics of parallel processing including support for message driven execution, portability across shared and nonshared memory machines, etc. Therefore, the Charm runtime system is an excellent testbed for such research. Several prioritization strategies were implemented as Charm modules, including a scalable yet effective variant that balances the three objectives of load balance, priority balance and memory-utilization balance. The modules are now part of the Charm system, where the users can select any one of them to link with their programs.

One of the interesting themes that came up repeatedly in different components of the work described here involves the importance of heuristic. In many state-space search problems, good value ordering heuristics combined with effective pruning strategies were able to obviate the need for parallel processing by essentially homing on to the solution along the leftmost branches of the search tree. This was true for N-queens problem, almost all instances of the 3-SAT problem that we tried, graph-coloring problems, etc. Good pruning heuristics also were seen to nullify the benefits of bi-directional search in many cases (e.g. 15 puzzle). This may seem somewhat discouraging, as it takes away the motivation for parallel processing. However, not all state-space search problems are as easy as the N-queens, and only a right combination of effective heuristics and parallel processing combined with prioritization will allow one to tackle some of the more difficult problems that we may wish to tackle in future. In addition, there are domains, such as game tree search, AND-OR tree search, and branch-and-bound, where the size of the search-space is very large, and which cannot usually be reduced simply by heuristic alone. (Although again lower bounding heuristics do lead to dramatic search-space reduction in branch-and-bound problems.) These problems represent a fertile area for future research, which will have a significant overall impact on real-life applications.

Integration of priorities with *futures* [5] particularly in connection with the *sponsor* model [23, 24] proposed for scheduling futures, represents another interesting problem. Attaching priorities to futures when they are spawned is straightforward; however, the sponsor model requires that when a process touches a future, the future assumes the priority of the touching process. Implementation of this strategy has similarities with the problem encountered in state-space searches in connection with duplication detection [2], and also with the game tree searches, where priorities need to be dynamically propagated [21]. So some of the strategies developed in these works may be applicable in this context.

Acknowledgements: Most of the research reported in this paper was conducted by the first author with different (then) graduate students. One exception is the research by Ramkumar and Banerjee [27], who apply some of our earlier results on priorities to parallel test pattern generation. Much of the research discussed in this paper has been reported in separate papers. This paper should be seen as an overview, which brings together the applications of prioritization from different contexts. In particular, the work on state-space search and IDA was conducted with Vikram A. Saletore, the work on parallel Prolog with B. Ramkumar, and Vikram A. Saletore, the work on branch-and-bound with Amitabh Sinha, and some preliminary work on game-tree searches was conducted with Chin-Chau Low, and additional state-space search problems were implemented and studied by Wayne Fenton. Design and implementation of various priority balancing strategies was carried out earlier with Vikram A. Saletore, and more recently with Amitabh Sinha. We are also grateful to Argonne and Sandia National Laboratories for the use of their parallel machines.

References

1. Burton F. W. Controlling Speculative Computation in a Parallel Functional Language. In *International Conference on Distributed Computer Systems*, pages 453–458, November 1985.
2. Einarsson, Thorr T. Bidirectional Search in Parallel. Master's thesis, Dept. of Comp. Sc., University of Illinois at Urbana-Champaign, July 1993.
3. Fenton, Wayne. Additions to the chare kernel parallel programming system, and its usefulness for parallel state-space search. Master's thesis, Dept. of Comp. Sc., University of Illinois at Urbana-Champaign, 1991.
4. Furuichi, M., Taki, K. and Ichiyoshi, N. . A Multi-level Load Balancing Scheme for OR-parallel Exhaustive Search Programs on the Multi-PSI. In *PPOPP*, pages 50–59, March 1990.
5. Halstead R. Parallel Symbolic Computing. *Computer*, August 1986.
6. Hausman B. *Pruning and Speculative Work in OR-Parallel PROLOG*. PhD thesis, Royal Institute of Technology, 1990.
7. L. V. Kale and W. Shu. The Chare Kernel language for parallel programming: A perspective. Technical Report UIUCDCS-R-88-1451, Department of Computer Science, University of Illinois, August 1988.
8. L.V. Kale. The REDUCE OR process model for parallel execution of logic programs. *Journal of Logic Programming*, 11(1):55–84, July 1991.
9. Kale L.V. Parallel Execution of Logic Programs: The REDUCE-OR Process Model. In *International Conference on Logic Programming*, pages 616–632, Melbourne, May 1987.
10. Kale L.V. A Tree Representation for Parallel Problem Solving. In *National Conference on Artificial Intelligence (AAAI)*, St. Paul, August 1988.

11. Kale L.V. An Almost Perfect Heuristic for the N-Queens Problem. In *Information Processing Letters*, April 1990.

12. Kale L.V. The Chare-Kernel Parallel Programming Language and System. In *International Conference on Parallel Processing*, August 1990.

13. Kale L.V. and Saletore V.A. Parallel State-Space Search for a First Solution with Consistent Linear Speedups. *International Journal of Parallel Programming*, August 1990.

14. Kale L.V. and Warren D.S. Class of Architectures for a PROLOG Machine. In *International Conference on Logic Programming*, pages 171–182, Stockholm, Sweden, June 1985.

15. Kale L.V., Ramkumar B. and Shu W. A Memory Organization Independent Binding Environment for AND and OR Parallel Execution of Logic Programs. In *The 5th International Conference/Symposium on Logic Programming*, pages 1223–1240, Seattle, August 1988.

16. Korf R.E. Depth-first Iterative Deepening: An Optimal Admissible Tree Search. In *Artificial Intelligence*, pages 97–109, 1985.

17. Korf R.E. Optimal Path-Finding Algorithms. In *Search in Artificial Intelligence*, pages 223–267. Springer-Verlag, 1988.

18. Kumar Vipin and Rao V. Nageshwar. Parallel Depth First Search. Part 2: Analysis. *International Journal of Parallel Programming*, pages 501–519, December 1987.

19. Lai T.H. and Sahni Sartaj. Anomalies in Parallel Branch-and-Bound Algorithms. In *Communications of the ACM*, pages 594–602, June 1984.

20. Li G.J. and Wah B.W. Coping with Anomalies in Parallel Branch-and-Bound Algorithms. In *IEEE Transactions on Computers*, pages 568–573, June 1986.

21. Low, Chin-Chau. Parallel game tree searching with lower and upper bounds. Master's thesis, Dept. of Comp. Sc., University of Illinois at Urbana-Champaign, 1991.

22. Nilsson N.J. *Principles of Artificial Intelligence*. Tioga Press, Inc., 1980.

23. R. Osborne. Speculative computation in multilisp. In *Lecture Notes in Computer Science*, number 441. Springer-Verlag, 1990.

24. R. Osborne. Speculative computation in multilisp: An overview. In *ACM Conference on Lisp and Functional Programming*, 1990.

25. B. Ramkumar and L.V. Kale. Machine independent AND and OR parallel execution of logic programs: Part II - compiled execution. *To appear in IEEE Transactions on Parallel and Distributed Systems*, 1991.

26. Ramkumar B. and Kale L.V. Compiled Execution of the REDUCE-OR Process Model on Multiprocessors. In *North American Conference on Logic Programming*, pages 313–331, October 1989.

27. Ramkumar, B., Banerjee P. Portable Parallel Test Generation for Sequential Circuits. In *Proceedings of the International Conference on Computer-Aided Design*, November 1992.

28. Rao V. Nageshwara and Kumar Vipin. Parallel Depth First Search. Part 1: Implementation. *International Journal of Parallel Programming*, pages 479–499, December 1987.

29. Saletore V.A. *Machine Independent Parallel Execution of Speculative Computations*. PhD thesis, Dept. Electrical and Computer Engineering, University of Illinois at Urbana-Champaign, Urbana, IL, September 1990.

30. Saletore V.A. and Kale L.V. Obtaining First Solutions Faster in AND-OR Parallel Execution of Logic Programs. In *North American Conference on Logic Programming*, pages 390–406, October 1989.

31. Saletore V.A. and Kale L.V. Consistent Linear Speedups to a First Solution in Parallel State-Space Search. In *The Eighth National Conference on Artificial Intelligence (AAAI-90), Boston, Mass.*, July 1990.

32. Saletore V.A. and Kale L.V. Efficient Parallel Execution of IDA* on Shared and Distributed Memory Multiprocessors. In *Proceedings of the Sixth Distributed Memory Computing Conference (DMCC6), Portland, OR*, April 1991.

33. Saletore V.A. and Mohammed M.A. A Hierarchical Load Distribution Scheme for Branch-and-Bound Computations on Distributed Memory Machines. Technical Report 93-80-04, Dept. of Computer Science, Oregon State University, January 1993.

34. Saletore V.A., Ramkumar B., and Kale L.V. Consistent First Solution Speedups in OR-Parallel Execution of Logic Programs. Technical Report UIUCDCS-R-90-1725, Dept. of Computer Science, University of Illinois at Urbana-Champaign, April 1990.

35. Sen A.K. and Bagchi A. Fast Recursive Formulations for Best-First Search That Allow Controlled Use of Memory. In *International Joint Conference on Artificial Intelligence*, pages 297–302, August 1989.

36. A. B. Sinha and L. V. Kale. A load balancing strategy for prioritized execution of tasks. In *International Parallel Processing Symposium*, April 1993.

37. Stone Harold S. and Stone Janice M. Efficient search techniques- An empirical study of the N-Queens Problem. *IBM Journal of Research and Development*, pages 464–474, July 1987.

A Priority Control System
for OR–Parallel Prolog
and Its Performance Evaluation

Yukio Kaneda,[1] Hideo Matsuda[1] and Shigeo Suzuka[2]

[1] Department of Computer and Systems Engineering,
Kobe University, Nada, Kobe 657, Japan
[2] Nomura Research Institute, Ltd., Chuo, Osaka 541, Japan

Abstract. In this paper we propose a method for performing priority control in OR-parallel execution of Prolog, with an evaluation function specified by the user as the priority. In the existing OR-parallel Prolog system there was a possibility that the number of goals executed in parallel could increase in combination, but by assigning priorities to the goals and executing in order of priority, the execution can be done in such a way that the search space does not have to be unnecessarily expanded during execution and only goals near the optimum solution are selected. The effectiveness of this method is demonstrated by implementing the processing system on a shared memory multiprocessor machine and showing that so-called super-linear speedup was obtained by applying to molecular phylogenetic analysis.

1   Introduction

As the fields of application of knowledge information processing become diversified and the processing operations become larger in scale, there is a crucial demand for the processing to be speeded up. For this reason, it is believed to be indispensable to introduce parallel processing technology. A number of ways of doing this have been proposed.

There has been particularly active research on a number of methods of parallel processing by using logic programming languages with AND-parallelism and OR-parallelism that use the indeterminacy in logic formulae[1]. In addition, concurrent logic programming languages[2] which explicitly introduce the synchronization mechanisms of suspension and resumption in the language specifications, have been researching in, for example, ICOT.

OR-parallelism, which calls and executes several candidate clauses in parallel, is especially effective with respect to, for example, search problems. However, if all of calls are simply performed in parallel, the degree of parallelism snowballs, and the resulting increase of overhead, such as process switching, limits the speedup. Then, it would be impossible to continue the execution due to lack of enough memory space.

To deal with this problem, in this paper we propose a new mechanism to control OR-parallelism. We introduce the concept of priority among the goals to be executed in parallel; the goals are executed in parallel in order of priority. This way execution can be done in such a way that the search space is not unnecessarily expanded during execution, and only goals near the optimum solution are selected. Priorities are assigned by built-in predicates; arbitrary integers can be assigned as priorities.

The problem of molecular phylogenetic tree inference is raised as an application of OR-parallel Prolog with the priority control mechanism. A molecular phylogenetic tree is a phylogenetic tree of organisms or genes created by using molecular level data such as DNA, RNA or amino acid sequences.

The control mechanism for OR-parallel Prolog, its implementation on a multiprocessor machine, and the result of application to molecular phylogenetic tree inference, are discussed below.

2   Priority Control of OR-parallelism

2.1   Setting of Priorities

The Prolog execution process can be considered to take place in the form of a search tree with the first goal input by the user as the root and the goals at each time during execution as the nodes. An branch extending downward from each node denotes a candidate clause that is unifiable with the goal at that node. Each of the lower-most leaves on the search tree indicates success in reduction of a goal, or failure, with further goal reduction being impossible. The binding values of the variable obtained as the result of success are the solutions of the first goal. OR-parallelism can be expressed as a breadth-first parallel expansion of this search tree from the root.

OR-parallelism is particularly effective in a problem requiring that all solutions that satisfy given conditions be found. When it is required to find an optimum solution that maximizes (or minimizes) an evaluation function, first a set of solutions is found using built-in predicates such as **setof** and **bagof**, as with the regular sequential Prolog system; then the optimum solution is selected from among them. However, in a problem in which the search tree will expand to become very large, the result is a high probability of having to perform a great deal of unnecessary processing, with a danger that the execution time and amount of memory used will become very large.

We propose the use of priority execution control as an efficient means of searching for the optimum solution with OR-parallelism. The priorities are labels conceptually assigned to each branch of the search tree, indicating the priority of execution of the goal below that branch. The overall execution is supervised by the scheduler, starting from the branch having the highest priority, and the goal below that branch is executed. This produces an ideal process in which the expansion of the search tree always proceeds in the direction of the optimum solution, so that unnecessary expansion is avoided.

The priorities are set by the following three built-in predicates.

```
setPriority(a_priority_value)
upPriority(priority_increment)
downPriority(priority_decrement)
```

setPriority sets the argument (an integer value) as the new priority. upPriority and downPriority set the new priority by adding to or subtracting from the present priority value in the argument. The program description using these is generally as follows.

```
head :- calculate_evaluation_function, set_priority, body_goals.
```

Every time a clause is called, the value of the evaluation function at that time is calculated, and the priority is set. Until the priority is reset, the previously set value applies, so it is not necessary to write calculate_evaluation_function and set_priority at each clause; if they are not written, the priority values for the body goals are set to the same as that of the goal which invokes this clause.

2.2 Sample Programs

An example of an OR-parallel Prolog program with a priority control mechanism is shown in **Fig. 1**. This program finds the shortest path between two given nodes on a graph, and consists of the following predicates.

```
:- para searchPath/5, arc/3.

go(From,To,[From|PathList],Cost) :-
    setPriority(10000),
    searchPath(From,To,PathList,Cost,0).

searchPath(From,To,[To],Cost,Cost1) :-
    path(From,To,PathCost),
    downPriority(PathCost),
    Cost is Cost1 + PathCost.
searchPath(From,To,[Via|PathList],Cost,Cost1) :-
    path(From,Via,ViaCost),
    downPriority(ViaCost),
    Cost2 is Cost1 + ViaCost,
    searchPath(Via,To,PathList,Cost,Cost2).

path(From,To,Cost) :- arc(From,To,Cost).
path(From,To,Cost) :- arc(To,From,Cost).

arc(a,b, 5).   arc(a,c,10).   arc(b,c,7).
arc(b,d,13).   arc(c,d,10).   arc(c,e,3).
arc(d,e, 4).
```

Fig. 1. A program for searching the shortest path.

go: Initial priority setting and start of path search.

searchPath: The main search for the path; priorities are changed according to cost as the path search is carried out.

path: The linkage between the nodes given in the arc is followed in both directions.

arc: The two nodes at the ends of the arc and the cost of the arc are given.

In this problem it is permitted to follow the linkage in both directions, so a loop is produced; unless arrangements are made in the Prolog procedure so that the same point will not be passed twice, it will not be possible to find the shortest path.

In addition, even in OR-parallel Prolog, if priority control is not used the paths that includes the fewest nodes ([a,b,d], [a,c,d], etc.) will be found first, so the shortest path will not necessarily be obtained first. However, if there is a priority control mechanism, then, as shown in Fig. 1, every time an arc is followed, by lowering the priority by the amount of the cost, the goal that follows the path having the lowest cost will be executed with the highest priority. In this way,the shortest path is found merely by progressively finding paths between the two arbitrary nodes.

For example, in this program, the results when the goal

```
?- go(a, d, PathList, Cost).
```

is executed in sequence starting from the path having the lowest cost are as follows.

```
PathList = [a,c,e,d],
Cost = 17 ? ;
PathList = [a,b,d],
Cost = 18 ? ;
PathList = [a,b,c,e,d],
Cost = 19 ? ;
        :
```

Note that :- **para** at the start of the program is a **parallel declaration command**; the clauses to be executed in OR-parallel are specified by that head predicate names and the numbers of arguments. Clauses that are not declared with this command are called sequentially by backtracking, just as in the case of a sequential Prolog system. By combining OR-parallel execution and sequential execution, the number of goals executed in parallel is reduced, and the task creation and switching overhead, to be discussed below, is held down.

3 Implementation on a Multiprocessor Machine

3.1 Configuration of a Multiprocessor Machine

This processing system was implemented on a Symmetry S81 multiprocessing machine made by Sequent Corporation. Symmetry is a shared memory multiprocessing machine using Intel 80386 (clock 16MHz) processing elements. There are 28 processing elements in the multiprocessing machine that was used.

In Symmetry, all of the processing elements are equivalent, and are linked by a single bus. Communication among the processors is carried out through a shared memory that is connected to the bus. To suppress contention between the shared memory and the bus, each processor has a 64KB copy-back type cache. The operating system, called DYNIX, is based on UNIX; it supervises the parallel execution, assigning work to processors in units of processes. Functions which are provided include a lock (with dedicated hardware) for mutual exclusion and assignment of shared memory among processes.

3.2 Execution Model

In this processing system, Prolog programs are executed in parallel with the two concepts of the **PE** (Prolog engine) and **tasks.** The PE, like a sequential Prolog processing system, is a software virtual machine that executes programs sequentially in order of depth priority. Seen from DYNIX, the PE is one of the user processes. When the number of user processes is small, the processes and processors are in one-to-one correspondence in DYNIX; in such a case the PE can be regarded as a processor. The PEs of which numbers are many enough for the parallel execution are created before execution starts, and then they process the tasks.

A task is a process of sequentially executing goals. All clauses that have not been declared with parallel declaration, as discussed in section 2.2, are executed by one task. In processing of clauses that have been declared for parallel execution, a number of tasks, one for each clause, are created, and they are connected in a Ready Queue sorted in order of priority. The Ready Queue is only one in the system and shared by all the PEs.

Tasks are assigned to the PEs by each PE itself, not by the global scheduler. Whenever (1) a PE does not have a task assigned to it, (2) a PE completes a task that is assigned to it, or (3) a task having higher priority than one currently assigned to a PE is newly connected to the Ready Queue, the PE acquires a new task from the Ready Queue and executes it. In the case of condition (3), each PE compares both of the task priorities for every reduction (i.e., every time a clause is called) and at the time of the priority setting discussed in section 2.1.

This execution model is practically the same as the SRI model adopted by Aurora[3], but there are some differences, for example: (a) whereas in the SRI model variable binding is a binding array, in this model it is a partitioned stack (to be discussed later); (b) in the SRI model, the timing of task switching is basically at the time of task completion, while in this model it occurs every time a clause is called by priority control.

3.3 Implementation of the Processing System

To implement the tasks, the information needed to execute each task is set as a **TCB** (Task Control Block) as shown in **Table 1**. Task switching occurs with the timing mentioned in the preceding section; the operations involved in this task switching are carried out in the following order: (1) the TCB at the head of the Ready Queue is acquired, (2) PE registers are saved in the register saving area in the current task TCB, (3) the current task TCB is connected to the Ready Queue, and (4) the values in the register saving area of the acquired TCB is set in the PE registers.

Table 1. Fields in a Task Control Block

Pointer to the next task TCB (when this TCB is in the Ready Queue)
Pointer to the parent task TCB
Pointer to a brother task TCB (when executed in parallel)
Base address allocated in the stack area
Number of child tasks
Task execution state
Area for saving PE registers
Priority value

The PE is implemented by extending the WAM[4]. A Prolog program is compiled into an intermediate code that is an expansion of the WAM code. Each instruction in the intermediate code is expressed as a C function and then compiled to an executable object code by the C compiler, linking to the run time module that starts the PE, schedules tasks, etc.

The points of expansion from the WAM are indicated below.

The **para_try** instruction is a WAM **try** instruction expanded for use with the OR-parallelism. This corresponds to clauses declared to be executed in parallel and works as follows. (1) A parallel choice point is created, (2) a number of sub-tasks corresponding to the clauses are created and registered in the Ready Queue, and (3) the current task is disconnected (execution is suspended until all sub-tasks are completed).

The **unite** instruction unites tasks created from the same parent. When one task tries to backtrack over a parallel choice point, it is necessary to check whether the other tasks whose parent is the same exist on not, so it is not possible to simply backtrack. To deal with this problem, this **unite** command does the following: (1) Decrement the number of child tasks, say n, in the suspended parent task TCB, (2) if $n \neq 0$, that means it is not the last child, terminates the task, or (3) If $n = 0$, it is the last child, removes the parallel choice point, then backtracks to the previous choice point.

3.4 Memory Control

Gupta and Jayaraman[5] have proven that there does not exist a memory control method such that all three of (a) creation of a binding environment, (b) variable access and (c) task switching (by means of new task creation) are all performed at a constant order time.

In addition, in this processing system priority control is performed, so besides these three, (d) task switching due to priority change occurs. The processing system is characterized by the manner in which these tradeoffs are chosen[6].

In this processing system, copying using a partitioned stack is used as the means of memory control (**Fig. 2**). The memory is divided into blocks of fixed length, and each task initially acquires only three blocks for trail, heap and local stack areas needed for WAM. With regard to dynamic increase of area during execution, for example by stacking, if it overflows beyond a block boundary a new block is acquired and the area is expanded by linking to it. Figure 2 is simplified by showing only one block acquired for each task.

In the copy method, when a new task is created it is necessary to copy all information on the binding environment, choice points, etc. starting from the root of the search tree, so (c) above cannot be performed within a constant order time, but the other three are performed within a constant order time. It is believed to be important for (d), which is characteristic of this processing system, to be kept within a constant time, so this method was chosen.

4 Molecular Phylogenetic Tree Inference

4.1 Felsenstein's Algorithm

Phylogenetic tree inference was performed as an application of OR-parallelism with priority control. The inference algorithm that was used is Felsenstein's algorithm[7] modified for use in OR-parallel execution.

Felsenstein's algorithm performs inference basically as follows.

Step 1 The given species are combined, and the possible candidate trees are created.

Step 2 Based on a stochastic model, a likelihood value for each candidate tree, which is a confident criteria to select one from the candidate trees, is calculated as the probability that the tree is formed with the sequence data. Then the branch lengths of the trees are calculated so as to maximize that likelihood value.

Step 3 The likelihood values differs depending on the structures of the candidate trees, so the one that gives the largest value among them is selected (this is the final tree).

If the candidate trees in Step 1 are created in a straightforward manner, the number of them, with the number of species n, is given as the following huge value:

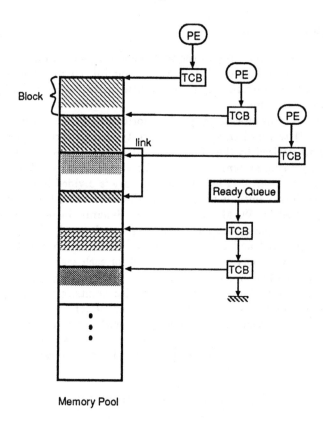

Block

link

Ready Queue

Memory Pool

Fig. 2. Memory control using partitioned stack segments.

$$\prod_{k=3}^{n}(2k-5) = \frac{(2n-5)!}{2^{n-3}(n-3)!} \tag{1}$$

Therefore, in Felsenstein's algorithm, these Steps 1, 2 and 3 are not performed for all of the species at once; instead, the process starts from the tree for three species, that is, $k = 3$ determined uniquely from $2k - 5 = 1$. Then a series of intermediate trees are generated, with one species at a time being added to the branches. For each k, only one intermediate tree, which maximizes the likelihood value, is selected from its $2k - 5$ candidates and the other candidates are suppressed.

Since only one tree, which maximizes the likelihood value, is selected in Step 3, the number of candidate trees that are created can be reduced to:

$$\sum_{k=3}^{n}(2k-5) = n^2 - 4n + 4 \tag{2}$$

However, this is because the possibility of creating the number of topologies given by (1) is constrained by (2); it does not necessarily follow that the tree that maximizes the likelihood value will be obtained in the end since the procedure to obtain the final tree depends on the order of input sequence data.

For this reason, after Step 3, a partial tree check is performed to see whether minor rearrangements lead to a better tree in the case that $k \geq 5$. These rearrangements, called nearest neighbor interchanges, move any subtree to a neighboring branch. This step is repeated until none of the alternatives tested is better than the starting tree. Then return to Step 1 for adding the next species.

The number of local rearrangements is determined at the time of execution to be a value from 1 to (at most) $k - 4$. Also, the number of candidate trees generated in one local rearrangement is $2k - 6$. Thus, in general the time required for local rearrangement for each value of k is proportional to k^2. Consequently, in practice the Felsenstein's algorithm requires processing time proportional to n^3[8] where n is the number of species.

4.2   Tree Inference by OR-parallelism

We have developed a method to accelerate the construction of phylogenetic trees based on the Felsenstein's algorithm. In this method the speedup is obtained by calculating likelihood values for given candidate trees in parallel using OR-parallel Prolog.

In contrast to the Felsenstein's algorithm, our method does neither limiting the candidate trees to one that maximizes the likelihood for each k value nor local rearrangement by nearest neighbor interchanges, but basically processes the trees in the order of their likelihood with a priority mechanism.

The priority control mechanism defers processing of trees having smaller likelihood values until later, so under ideal conditions it would be expected that it would only be necessary to examine a far smaller number of trees than the number given by (1), and that finally the tree having the largest likelihood value would be found first. However, in practice the number of trees generated still snowballs rapidly, so when the priority drops below a certain threshold value that task is forcibly failed and terminated.

Since weighted likelihood values are used as priorities and tasks are forcibly terminated at a certain threshold value, the result obtained from this program is not always globally optimum, like the Felsenstein's algorithm. At present the weights are determined empirically from the input sequence data.

Calculation of the branch lengths in the phylogenetic tree and the likelihood values requires a great deal of numerical computation, so these are written in the C language and used as built-in predicates from Prolog. In writing these built-in predicates a program developed at the University of Illinois[8, 9] based on the Felsenstein's algorithm has been modified for use in a shared memory multiprocessor machine.

Sequence data for 20 species of archaebacteria, 1892 RNA base pairs for each species, were input to the program in the Appendix; the effects on time required for execution and the number of processors used are shown in **Fig. 3**. Using the program developed at University of Illinois[8], it takes about 37700 seconds to obtain a tree for these data in sequential execution on Symmetry.

It can be seen from Fig. 3 that when the number of processors is large, the effect of adding more processors is so-called super-linear (a maximum of 40-fold speedup was obtained on 26 processors).

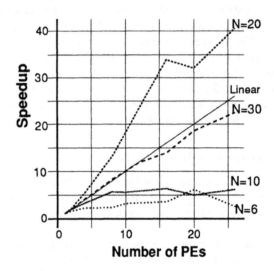

Fig. 3. Speedup for inferring molecular phylogenetic trees.

The relations between number of species and number of generated tasks are shown in **Fig. 4**. It can be seen that as the number of processors increases, the number of tasks decreases. That is, priority control cuts off branches of the search tree, so that the search space itself is contracted and it can readily be seen that the effectiveness is more than linearly proportional to the number of processors.

With regard to the amount of memory used, as the number of processors increases a large amount of memory is necessary on shared memory because areas for keeping phylogenetic trees are allocated on each processor. Reducing the amount of memory required remains as an issue for the future.

5   Conclusion

In this paper a priority control method for OR-parallel execution has been proposed and the implementation of such a processing system on a shared memory multiprocessor machine has been discussed. The molecular phylogenetic tree inference has been taken up as an example, and the programming of this problem in this system and the execution times are shown. The results show that so-called

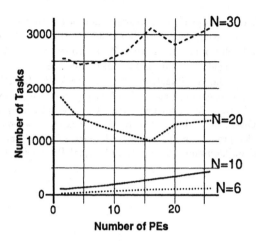

Fig. 4. Numbers of tasks for inferring molecular phylogenetic trees.

super-linear speedup was obtained in some cases. However, when the number of processors becomes large, so does the amount of memory required. Reducing the memory consumption remains as an issue for the future.

Acknowledgments

We thank Prof. Carl Woese and Dr. Gary J. Olsen of the University of Illinois for providing the archaebacteria sequence data. The molecular phylogenetic tree inference program used in this research was based on a program developed by Dr. Olsen. We again thank him for permitting us to use his program. We also thank Dr. Ross Overbeek of Argonne National Laboratory for a great deal of valuable advice in modifying that program for use in parallel processing. This work was supported in part by the Japan Ministry of Education, Science and Culture under Grant in Aid for Scientific Research 05254209.

References

1. Conery, J. S.: Parallel execution of logic programs. Kluwer Academic Publishers, Norwell, MA (1987) 35–61
2. Shapiro, E.: The family of concurrent logic programming languages. ACM Comput. Surv. **21** (1989) 413–510
3. Lusk, E. et al.: The Aurora OR-parallel Prolog system. New Generation Computing **8** (1990) 243–271
4. Warren, D. H. D.: An abstract Prolog instruction set. SRI Tech. Note **309** (1985)
5. Gupta, G., Jayaraman, B.: On criteria for OR-parallel execution models of logic programs. Proc. of NACLP'90 (1990) 737–756

6. Ichiyoshi, N.: Parallel implementation schemes of logic programming languages. J. of Information Processing Society of Japan **32** (1991) 435–449 (in Japanese)
7. Felsenstein, J.: Evolutionary trees from DNA sequences: A maximum likelihood approach. J. of Molecular Evolution **17** (1981) 368–376
8. Olsen, G. J., Matsuda, H., Hagstrom, R., Overbeek, R.: fastDNAml: A tool for construction of phylogenetic trees of DNA sequences using maximum likelihood. Computer Applications in Biological Sciences (1993) (in press)
9. Matsuda, H., Olsen, G. J., Hagstrom, R., Overbeek, R., Kaneda, Y.: Implementation of a parallel processing system for inference of phylogenetic trees. Proc. of Pac. Rim Conf. on Commun., Comput. and Signal Processing (1993) 280–283

Extending the Multilisp Sponsor Model to Deal with Intertask Synchronization Side Effects

Randy B. Osborne
osborne@merl.com

Mitsubishi Electric Research Labs
201 Broadway, Cambridge, MA. 02139

Abstract. Speculative computing is a technique to improve the execution time of certain applications by starting some computations before it is known that the computations are required. A speculative computation will eventually become mandatory (i.e. required) or irrelevant (i.e. not required). In the absence of side effects irrelevant computations may be aborted. However, with side effects a computation which is irrelevant for the value it produces may still be relevant for the side effects it performs. One problem that can result is the *relevant synchronization* problem wherein one computation requires some side effect event (a "relevant synchronization") to be performed by another computation, which might be aborted, before the first computation can make progress. Another problem that can arise is the *preemptive delay* problem wherein a computation that will perform some awaited side effect event is preempted by a computation whose importance (e.g. priority) is less than that of computations waiting for the event. In this paper we show how the sponsor model developed for speculative computation in Multilisp can be extended to provide a novel solution to these two problems. The idea is for the computation awaiting some action, such as the production of a value or the release of a semaphore, to sponsor the computation or set of computations that will perform the awaited action. This sponsorship ensures that the awaited action executes, and executes with at least the waiter's level of importance. We show how to apply this technique to solve the above problems for several producer/consumer and semaphore applications. The idea extends naturally to other synchronization mechanisms.

1 Introduction

Speculative computing is a technique to improve the execution time of appropriate applications by starting some computations before it is known that the computations are required. A speculative computation will eventually become mandatory (i.e. required) or irrelevant (i.e. not required). In previous work [12, 13, 11] we presented a *sponsor* model for speculative computation and demonstrated how this model adds expressive and computational power to Multilisp. However, there were many issues concerning side effects that we did not consider, particularly in the context of aborting irrelevant computations. While we are primarily interested in side effect-free applications (we believe side effects should be used sparingly), there are many applications for which side effects add important expressive power (see, for example, the discussion in Chap. 3 of [1]). Thus it is important to examine the issues with side effects. We restrict our scope in this paper to the issues involved with intertask synchronization side effects by which we mean broadly any side effect that can directly affect the progress of another task. What we choose to call intertask synchronization depends on the granularity that makes sense in the situation at hand. At the finest granularity the only intertask synchronization is that performed by intertask synchronization primitives such as the atomic change in the state of a lock or semaphore. At coarser granularities, it might make sense to regard an object mutation within a critical section (itself guarded by intertask synchronization primitives) as an intertask synchronization. The issues we explore in this paper are similar regardless of the atomicity grain size.

Our sponsor model supports the aborting and preempting of computation. In such an environment two problems arise:

1. The *relevant synchronization* problem: a computation A requires some side effect event (a "relevant synchronization") to be performed by another computation B before A can make progress. However, B might be aborted, preventing progress of A. Thus the synchronization performed by B is relevant with respect to A.

2. The *preemptive delay* problem: a computation C may be preempted by a computation D whose importance (e.g. priority) is less than the importance of other computations $(E, F, G, \ldots)$ that are waiting for C to perform some side effect event. Consequently the waiting computations $E, F, G, \ldots$ may be delayed by a computation of lesser importance.[1] Preemptive delay is a problem in any environment with preemption, and is not restricted to speculative computation or our sponsor model. For example, the preemptive delay problem was first examined by [9] in the context of monitors.

To illustrate the relevant synchronization and preemptive delay problems we examine five different applications, three involving semaphores and two involving producer-consumer synchronization. Three of the examples represent popular synchronization paradigms in parallel computing while the other two illustrate specific points. For each example we demonstrate a novel solution to these problems by extending our earlier sponsor model in a natural way. In each case the idea is for the task waiting for a value or a semaphore to sponsor the task or set of tasks that will produce the value or release the semaphore. This sponsorship ensures that a producer task or a semaphore release task executes, and executes with an importance which is at least the maximum importance of all the waiters. This sponsorship idea for solving the relevant synchronization and preemption delay problems generalizes to other synchronization paradigms.

---

[1] The preemptive delay problem is often called the priority inversion problem (especially in real time systems) when the importance is described by priorities.

1.1 Overview

Section 2 briefly describes Multilisp and our sponsor model for speculative computation in Multilisp. Section 3 illustrates the relevant synchronization and preemptive delay problems by examining two producer-consumer applications and three semaphore applications. Section 4 solves the problems with the examples in Sect. 3 within our sponsor model. Section 5 discusses related work and Sect. 6 concludes the paper.

2 Background

2.1 Multilisp

Multilisp [4] is a version of the Scheme programming language [6] extended with explicit parallelism constructs. Multilisp is based on a shared memory paradigm and includes all the side effects of Scheme.

(future *exp*) creates a task to evaluate *exp* and immediately returns a placeholder for the result. This placeholder (known as a *future*) may be manipulated just as if it were the result of evaluating *exp*. If a task T attempts a strict operation on such a placeholder (i.e. an operation requiring the value represented by the placeholder), the task suspends until the placeholder is *determined* with the result of evaluating *exp*. Task T is said to *touch* the placeholder. We generalize this notion to say that task T touches the task evaluating *exp*.

(make-future) creates and returns an empty placeholder (*future*) without an associated task. Such a placeholder is sometimes convenient for write-once synchronization.

(determine-future *fut exp*) explicitly determines the undetermined placeholder (*future*) *fut* to the value of *exp*. It returns an unspecified value. Each task created by a future ends with an implicit determine-future. It is an error to determine (explicitly or implicitly) a *future* more than once.

The following atomic operation is an extension of the set-car! mutator in Scheme. It may be used for explicit inter-task synchronization — such as locks — as demonstrated by the example in Sect. 3.3.

(rplaca-eq *pair new old*) performs the following eq check and possible swap atomically: If the car of *pair* is eq to *old*, the car of *pair* is replaced by *new* and *pair* is returned. If the car of *pair* is not eq to *old*, nil is returned.[2]

Multilisp has the following semaphore constructs for explicit intertask synchronization:

(make-sema) makes and returns a free binary semaphore object.

(wait-sema *sema*) makes the semaphore *sema* busy if *sema* was free; otherwise, it suspends and enqueues the executing task on the semaphore *sema*. These operations are indivisible.

---

[2] There is also an analagous rplacd-eq extension of Scheme's set-cdr! mutator.

(`signal-sema` *sema*) makes the semaphore *sema* free if no tasks are queued on *sema*; otherwise, it dequeues and resumes one of the tasks enqueued on *sema*. These operations are indivisible. Semaphore requests are queued for resumption in first-come-first-served (FCFS) order.

See [4] or [11] for additional Multilisp constructs. For the purposes of this paper Multilisp does not include Scheme's `call-with-current-continuation`. In the presence of side effects, continuations pose some difficult problems in Multilisp (see [7]).

2.2 Speculative Computation in Multilisp

In other work [12, 13, 11] we developed a sponsor model for speculative computation in Multilisp. Computation proceeds in this model by specifying both an expression to be evaluated[3] and a sponsorship source (a sponsor). Sponsorship is an abstraction of machine resources. This sponsorship gives a means to control the allocation of resources to computations, to favor *mandatory* computations over speculative ones and promising speculative computations over less promising ones. This is the general sponsor model.

To date we have considered a special sponsor model subset. In this special sponsor model sponsorship is associated with tasks and sponsors are agents which supply *attributes* — such as priority — to tasks. Each task has zero or more sponsors which contribute attributes to that task. The attributes contributed are combined according to a *combining-rule* to yield the *effective attributes* of the task and these determine the resources allocated to that task. Notable types of sponsors are:

1. Toucher sponsors — When one task touches another, the toucher task sponsors the touchee task with the effective attributes of the toucher task. Touch and determine automatically trigger the addition and removal, respectively, of toucher sponsors.
2. Controller sponsors — Controller sponsors receive sponsorship and actively distribute it among the tasks in their control domain according to some built-in control strategy.

See [12] or [11] for further details of this model.

We have extended Multilisp to include an initial subset of the special sponsor model in which the only attributes are priorities. The effective priority at which a task runs is the maximum of all the priorities contributed by the task's sponsors. Scheduling is preemptive based on effective priority, except tasks with effective priority 0 (the minimum priority) are not runnable; they are *stayed*. The computational state of a stayed task is retained (until it becomes inaccessible and is garbage collected). Thus a stayed task may be restarted by re-sponsoring the task so that the task's effective priority becomes greater than 0.

---

[3] The environment for evaluation is the lexical environment in which the expression appears.

Of the many language extensions to Multilisp to implement this sponsor model subset we discuss only those few that are pertinent to the discussion in this paper. See [11, 13, 12] for the full set of extensions.

(**make-sponsor-class** *class-type*) creates and returns a *class* object. A class is a collection of tasks and a controller sponsor. We have implemented three types of classes — distinguished by sponsor policy: *sponsor-all*, in which the class sponsor sponsors all the members of the class, *sponsor-any*, in which the class sponsor sponsors an arbitrary member of the class, and *sponsor-max-priority*, in which the class sponsor sponsors only the top effective priority task in the class.

(**add-to-class** *task class*) atomically adds the task *task* to the class *class* and returns an unspecified value. (**remove-from-class** *task class*) atomically removes *task* from *class* and returns *task*.

(**make-future** . *class*) creates and returns a placeholder (as described in Sect. 2.1) and sponsors the class *class* (if specified) with the maximum priority task blocked on the placeholder. This sponsorship is removed when the placeholder is determined.

3   The Problem

3.1   Example 1: Simple Mutual Exclusion — Serializers

In a semaphore serializer, each task wishing to serialize some action (with respect to other tasks) executes the following simple code sequence:

```
(wait-sema sema)
some action           ; critical section (mutual exclusion region)
(signal-sema sema)
```

In addition to mutual exclusion, the usual requirements for such a serializer (see, e.g. [18]) include bounded waiting which implies bounded access time and fairness (in the sense that no process can wait indefinitely for access while others proceed). We assume that these requirements are met in the absence of speculative computation (i.e. in conventional Multilisp).[4] However, with speculative computation tasks can be stayed (aborted), and thus fail to make forward progress, and tasks have different "importance" levels (i.e. priorities) respected by a preemptive scheduler. Thus with speculative computation such a serializer has the following problems:

1. Speculative deadlock: A task in the critical section can be stayed, leading to unbounded access time.[5] [6] This is an instance of the relevant synchronization

---

[4] These assumptions correspond to assuming that the semaphore serializer application is "correct" in the absence of speculative computation. The FCFS queueing policy of semaphore operations in conventional Multilisp assures fairness.

[5] There is no circular waiting so technically it is not deadlock.

[6] Staying a task in the critical section is only a problem if there are non-stayed waiters since stayed waiters do not attempt to enter the critical section.

problem: speculative deadlock occurs because a task is considered irrelevant and stayed when, in fact, it is relevant for a synchronization event (releasing a semaphore).

2. Preemptive delay: A task in the critical section can be preempted, perhaps indefinitely, by tasks with priority less than the priority of tasks waiting to enter the critical section. For example, suppose that task T_{cs} in the critical section has priority p_{cs} and a waiter task T_w has priority $p_w > p_{cs}$. Then a task T_p, with priority $p_w > p_p > p_{cs}$ can preempt T_{cs}, causing T_w to wait further, even though $p_w > p_p$. In fact, there can be a continual stream of tasks T_{p_i}, preempting T_{cs}, each with priority p_i such that such that $p_w > p_i > p_{cs}$ $\forall i$. Thus the priority assignment of T_w has been subverted: it effectively has priority p_{cs}.

3. Unfair access: An access policy that ensures a bounded wait time (e.g. FCFS) may admit low priority tasks before high priority tasks and thus ignore the relative importance of tasks defined by the priorities.

Critical section-based serializers, whether implemented by semaphores or locks, are the most common of all intertask synchronization paradigms.

Solution Alternatives. One alternative is to avoid critical sections entirely by using an atomic compare-and-swap pointer operation. The idea is to convert the critical section operation to an operation on a copy of the original object and then use the compare-and-swap to atomically install the modified object in place of the original if no updates have occurred to the original in the meantime. Thus there is no critical section in which a task can be stayed or preempted. (This compare-and-swap technique is the basis of "wait-free" synchronization [5].) For example, a semaphore-enforced critical section operation to add an element **element** to the head of a difference list (a list represented by a pair with pointers to the head and tail of the list) can be transformed to a copy-and-compare pointer operation as shown below (we assume the difference list, denoted by **dlist** is non-empty).

```
; Semaphore solution
(wait-sema sema)
(let* ((head (car dlist)))
       (new-head (cons element head)))
   (set-car! dlist new-head)
(signal-sema sema))

; Compare-and-swap solution
(define (add-to-head dlist element)
   (let* ((head (car dlist))
          (new-head (cons element head)))
      (if (not (rplaca-eq dlist new-head head))
          (add-to-head dlist element))))
```

This compare-and-swap technique trades copying and looping (i.e. busy-waiting) for blocking. Thus, while this technique may have low overhead for short critical sections, it can be inefficient for long critical sections with high contention. Compare-and-swap is also not appropriate for synchronized access to objects which cannot or should not be copied, such as reading input from an external device. [7] Finally, the compare-and-swap technique does not ensure fairness.

Within the conventional critical section paradigm there are two main approaches to solving the speculative deadlock/relevant synchronization problem: roll-back and roll-forward. In the roll-back approach a task is prevented from being stayed (aborted) in a critical section by "rolling back", undoing any side effects, until it is outside the critical section, at which point it can be stayed. In the roll-forward approach a task is prevented from being stayed (aborted) in a critical section by "rolling forward" until it is outside the critical section, at which point it can be stayed. The roll-forward approach has the advantage that no side effects have to be undone. In both approaches a critical section task may be rolled whenever it is stayed or just when other non-stayed tasks are waiting to enter the critical section. The former alternative with roll-forward yields a "non-stayable" region. This is a conservative approach since it prevents a task from being stayed even when there are no non-stayed waiters.

There are three approaches to the preemptive delay problem. One approach is to make tasks non-preemptable in the critical section, but like the non-stayable region, this is overkill because it prevents preemptions if there are no waiters of higher priority. A second approach, used by Mesa [9], is to execute the task in the critical section at a priority higher than that of all tasks that could ever attempt to ever the critical section. However, priorities are dynamic in our model for speculative computation, making it possible for any task to have the maximum priority, which is non-preemptable. Thus this second approach reduces to the first approach. The third approach is a "parameterized" non-preemptable region in which only tasks with priority greater than the current maximum priority waiter task can preempt the critical section task. This approach uses the set of *actual* waiter tasks, not potential waiter tasks, in determining the priority of the critical section task. Hence in this parameterized non-preemptable region approach, the critical section task executes at the smallest priority possible to prevent preemptive delay with the actual waiter tasks.

With speculative computation, fairness should be based on the relative priority of tasks, and not, for example, on access order (except for tasks of the same priority). Thus access to the critical section by waiters should be in priority order.

3.2 Example 2: Readers and Writers Problem

In this problem, a variation of the simple mutual exclusion problem, there are two types of tasks accessing a shared object. The first type (the "readers") may

---

[7] One could compare-and-swap on a proxy object but then the operation on the original object and the update to the proxy object could not be done atomically. Thus the proxy object reduces to a lock, and therefore there exists a critical section with the speculative deadlock and preemptive delay problems.

access the object concurrently so long as all tasks of the second type are excluded. The second type (the "writers") require exclusive access to the shared object. This readers and writers paradigm is fairly common, especially in database applications.

Figure 1 shows a solution to a variant of the readers and writers problem. **readcount** indicates the number of current readers and **mutex** is a binary semaphore for updating **readcount** atomically. **wrt** is a binary semaphore for the mutual exclusion of readers and writers. When **readcount** is 0 the next reader to arrive defines the start of a read "epoch". Such a reader enters the **readcount** serializer and blocks on **wrt** (line 3) waiting for a writer (if any) to finish. Any subsequent readers during this time block on **mutex**. When a writer finishes, it releases **wrt** and all the readers may read concurrently. As readers finish reading they decrement **readcount**. The last reader to do so returns **readcount** to 0 which defines the end of read "epoch" and then a writer may proceed (line 7). In this variant of the readers and writer problem a writer must wait until there are no pending readers (thus writers may starve).[8]

Initialization:

(define readcount 0)	

Readers execute:

(wait-sema mutex)	; (1)
(incr1 readcount)	; (2) increment readcount by 1
(if (= readcount 1)	
(wait-sema wrt))	; (3) first reader in epoch waits for writer to finish
(signal-sema mutex)	; (4)
read operation	
(wait-sema mutex)	; (5)
(decr1 readcount)	; (6) decrement readcount by 1
(if (= readcount 0)	
(signal-sema wrt))	; (7) last reader in epoch lets a writer proceed
(signal-sema mutex)	; (8)

Writers execute:

(wait-sema wrt)	; (9)
write operation	
(signal-sema wrt)	;(10)

Fig. 1. An example readers and writers problem

The solution in Fig. 1 contains three serializers: lines 1 through 4 and lines 5 through 8 for updating **readcount** and lines 9 through 10 for writing. Thus

---

[8] We assume that waiters for a semaphore are granted the semaphore in first-come-first-served (FCFS) order, thus readers do not starve.

this solution suffers from the same speculative deadlock and preemptive delay problems as simple serializers.

Figure 1 contains another critical region: from the (wait-sema wrt) in line 3 through (signal-sema wrt) in line 7. This critical region is fundamentally different from the critical regions in the simple serializers so far: there may be more than one task in the critical region simultaneously. Furthermore, only the first and last tasks to enter and exit this critical region in a read "epoch" do so via (wait-sema wrt) and (signal-sema wrt) respectively. No one task necessarily holds the wrt semaphore for the entire duration of a read epoch.

Coupling between the simple serializers and this new critical region introduces three new possibilities for speculative deadlock: 1) if a writer is stayed in the write serializer, all readers blocked (on wrt for the first reader and on mutex for the rest) and the remaining writers are deadlocked; 2) if any reader is stayed between lines 3 and 7, the writers are deadlocked; and 3) if a reader is stayed in either readcount serializer all readers are deadlocked.

We draw the following observations from this example:

1. Roll-back can be far from trivial. If a reader in this example is stayed between lines 4 and 5 it must be rolled back to before line 1, through a readcount serializer. This requires 1) preventing other tasks from entering the serializer and 2) decrementing readcount.

2. Non-stayable/non-preemptable regions can be unacceptable. A reader between lines 4 and 5 is not in any serializer and may be there a long time — much longer than we may be willing to have it unstayable or non-preemptable.

3. It is not always possible to identify the task that releases a semaphore. Here the wrt semaphore is passed from task to task. Thus a reader cannot necessarily identify which task is responsible for its lack of progress (by failing to release the semaphore). We will discuss the consequence of this later.

3.3   Example 3: Multiple Potential Determiners

Multiple potential determiners for a placeholder is an example of multiple-approach speculative computation (see [13] or [12]), a fairly common instance of speculative computing. Figure 2 shows such an example where we are interested only in the first solution to a set of problems. For simplicity, we assume that a solution will be found for at least one of the problems. Unlike in the previous two examples there are no semaphores in this example.

There are two problems with this example. First, a solver task may be stayed or preempted in the interval between obtaining the lock and before determining the placeholder, leading to speculative deadlock or preemptive delay. The roll-forward analog in this case is to ensure that the solver task indivisibly enters a non-stayable and non-preemptable region upon grabbing the lock. Other options such as parameterizing the task by the priority of tasks waiting for the result or roll-back will have too much overhead.

The second problem is that we do not know which solver task will determine the placeholder. The solver tasks are in essence producer tasks and all

```
(define first (cons 0 nil))              ; initialize lock

(define first-solution (make-future)) ; create synchronization placeholder

;; attempt to solve the given problem
(define (solve problem)
   (let ((a-solution (work-on-problem problem)))
      (if (solution? a-solution)           ; was a solution found?
          (if (rplaca-eq first 1 0)   ; if so, is it the first solution?
              ;; if first, determine placeholder to solution
              (determine-future first-solution a-solution)))))

;; attempt to solve all problems simultaneously
(define (find-first-solution problems)
   (map (lambda (prob) (future (solve prob))) problems) ; fork solvers
   first-solution)                        ; return first solution
```

Fig. 2. A placeholder example with multiple potential determiners

tasks which access the placeholder first-solution are consumer tasks. If the
"successful" solver tasks are stayed or preempted before determining this placeholder, speculative deadlock[9] or preemptive delay may occur. Since we do not
know *a priori* which tasks are the "successful" solvers, we must use a roll-forward
strategy and ensure that none of the potential solver tasks is stayed. Rolling-
back stayed tasks does not work since we may roll-back a "successfull" task.
One solution is to make all the solvers non-stayable and non-preemptable until
the placeholder is determined. Not only is this solution too strong but it also is
complicated by the need to re-enable preemption and staying in all the solvers
still running after the first solution is found.

3.4   Example 4: Producer-Consumer Problem

The producer-consumer problem consists of some number of tasks synchronizing
the production and consumption of values via a finite buffer. In this very common synchronization paradigm, a producer task computes a value and inserts it
in the buffer where a consumer task later retrieves it. Figure 3 shows the code
for a producer-consumer problem involving a buffer of size N. mutex is a binary
semaphore for atomic insertion and deletion to/from the buffer. empty is a general semaphore, with initial value N, which counts the number of empty slots
in the buffer. Complementing empty is the general semaphore full. Its initial
value is 0 and it counts the number of full slots in the buffer.[10]

---

[9] This time without involving a critical section.

[10] We take the liberty to generalize the binary semaphores described in Sect. 2.1 to
general semaphores. (Multilisp presently only supports binary semaphores.) This
generalization only requires adding an optional semaphore initial value to make-sema
and changing the semantics of wait-sema and signal-sema appropriately.

Producer		Consumer	
`(wait-sema empty)`	;(P1) wait for an	`(wait-sema full)`	;(C1) wait for a
	; empty slot		; full slot
`(wait-sema mutex)`	;(P2) indivisibly	`(wait-sema mutex)`	;(C2) indivisibly
insert in buffer	; add item	delete from buffer	; delete item
`(signal-sema mutex)`	;(P3)	`(signal-sema mutex)`	;(C3)
`(signal-sema full)`	;(P4) indicate a	`(signal-sema empty)`	;(C4) indicate an
	; full slot		; empty slot

Fig. 3. A solution to a producer-consumer problem

This formulation[11] has the familiar two problems associated with a simple serializer like **mutex**. It also has the additional problem that a consumer could be deadlocked waiting on **full** if every producer is in one of the following three states: 1) stayed before line P1, 2) stayed between lines P1 and P4, or 3) blocked on **empty**. Likewise, a producer could be deadlocked waiting on **empty** if every consumer is in one of the following three states: 1) stayed before line C1, 2) stayed between lines C1 and C4, or 3) blocked on **full**.

These problems are unique among the semaphore examples presented so far: they involve tasks (the producers and consumers) outside the semaphore regions. Therefore methods which concentrate on preventing staying or preemption solely within a critical section won't work. As with the producer-consumer interaction in Example 3, a roll-back strategy does not work here, so we must use a roll-forward strategy where we prevent all potential producers and consumers from being stayed. We could make all potential producers and consumers non-stayable but this would prevent staying the whole producer-consumer interaction if it was embedded in a larger irrelevant computation. Making all the potential producers and consumers non-preemptable has a similar problem plus all the tasks involved would have the same priority, defeating the purpose of the task priorities.

In addition, we would like tasks blocked on **empty** and **full** to enter their respective critical regions in correspondence with their priority order.

3.5   Example 5: Modified Readers and Writers Problem

This example combines the producer-consumer flavor of Examples 3 and 4 with the semaphore flavor of Examples 1 and 2 to illustrate a more complex situation.

Consider a reader/writer problem in which at most one reader or writer may access a database at a time. The database contains some number of units, consumed by readers (one unit per reader) and replenished by writers. The database

---

[11] Streams [1] provide a more elegant way to achieve producer-consumer synchronization. However, buffer-based formulations offer better control over storage use.

thus has two states: ready to read (≥ 1 unit present) and not ready to read (no units present). If the database is not ready when a reader enters the critical section then the reader exits the critical region and joins a queue of readers to wait until the database is ready. Queued readers have priority on admission to the critical region over new readers. When a writer enters the critical section it adds some number of units to the database and makes the database ready to read. Within this problem is a producer-consumer synchronization problem (writers = producers and readers = consumers) which leads to ramifications, similar to those with the producer-consumer problem in Sect. 3.4, which we discuss later.

Initialization:

`(define queuecount 0)`	

Readers execute:

`(wait-sema mutex)`	; (1) enter critical section
`(let loop ()`	
`  (if ready-to-read?`	; (2)
`    (begin`	
`      read operation`	; (3)
`      (if (> queuecount 0)`	; (4) check for any queued readers
`        (signal-sema waiters)`	; (5) start one up & exit critical section
`        (signal-sema mutex)))`	; (6) else exit critical section
`    (begin`	
`      (incr1 queuecount)`	; (7) join queued readers
`      (signal-sema mutex)`	; (8)
`      some action`	; (9) arbitrary operation before queueing
`      (wait-sema waiters)`	;(10) queue to reenter critical section
`      (decr1 queuecount)`	;(11)
`      (loop))))`	;(12) try again

Writers execute:

`(wait-sema mutex)`	;(13) enter critical section
`write operation`	;(14) write and set ready-to-read
`(if (> queuecount 0)`	;(15) check for any queued readers
`  (signal-sema waiters)`	;(16) start one up & exit critical section
`  (signal-sema mutex))`	;(17) else exit critical section

Fig. 4. The modified readers and writers problem

Figure 4 shows an implementation of this readers and writers problem using semaphores.[12] New readers must grab the binary semaphore **mutex** to enter the critical region whereupon the readers determine the state of the database and either read and then exit the critical region or increment a count of the number

---

[12] This contrived example is a simplification of a real problem — the implementation of monitors with semaphores [18]. See [11] for details.

of queued readers and then exit. Queued readers block on the binary semaphore **waiters** until a satisfied reader or a writer exits the critical region, at which time one queued reader can enter the critical region. Writers must grab the **mutex** semaphore before entering the critical region.

A satisfied reader or a writer effectively "passes" permission to be in the database critical section on to a queued reader by (**signal-sema waiters**) in line 5 or 16. Thus a reader task can effectively be in the critical section without "possessing" any semaphores. Suppose, for example, that there is a single reader in the system at line 9 and suppose that before this reader arrives at line 10 a writer enters the critical section, updates the database, and exits the critical section. Since **queuecount** is 1, the writer will **not** release the semaphore **mutex** upon exiting the critical section, but will instead signal the semaphore **waiters**. Consequently the reader can immediately enter the critical section when it gets to line 10 but in the meantime no other task can enter the critical section since the **mutex** is still locked (and will remain so until the reader reaches line 6). Thus there is effectively a critical section beween lines 8 and 10. This leads to an interesting new possibility for speculative deadlock: a reader may be stayed at line 9 while not formally in any critical section and yet no other tasks will be able to enter the database critical section.

Another possibility for speculative deadlock occurs if all the potential writer tasks are stayed: any queued readers will be blocked indefinitely. We saw this sort of speculative deadlock in the two previous examples involving producer-consumer synchronization.

There are also the usual sources of speculative deadlock: a reader or writer could be stayed in the critical section. The Appendix gives a formal state description of this modified readers and writers problem and analyzes all the possible transitions.

Roll-back does not work here for either new source of speculative deadlock. Consider first the case of a reader stayed in the "effective critical section". A reader at line 9 must be rolled back through the database critical section to before line 1 and **queuecount** decremented before the reader can be safely stayed. To perform this roll-back the reader must first enter the critical section by grabbing **mutex**. However, a write may have occurred and locked **mutex** once the reader reached line 9. Thus **mutex** may or may not be locked when we attempt to roll-back the reader and we have no way of telling which (without violating abstraction barriers), so the reader cannot be assured of grabbing **mutex** and roll-back cannot safely proceed. Of course, it may be possible to perform roll-back using some sort of checkpointing scheme (e.g. recovery blocks [16]), wherein the system state is restored to the state at some previous checkpoint. This seems unduly expensive.

Now consider the case of the stayed producers in the producer-consumer synchronization between writers and readers. When the last potential writer is stayed, what task do we roll-back? Rolling-back the stayed writer will not free the queued reader. (Besides, how far do we roll-back the stayed waiter?) Rolling-back the queued readers has the same problem as described above.

A non-stayable region is not an attractive solution either for these two cases. In the "effective critical section" case a non-stayable region between lines 8 and 10 is unattractive because a reader may spend an arbitrary amount of time there (it's not in any real critical section). Thus an irrelevant task in this region would be kept running just because it **might** lead to deadlock if stayed. For the producer-consumer synchronization case a non-stayable region is unattractive for the same reasons as discussed in Sect. 3.4.

3.6 Summary

In Example 1 roll-back, roll-forward with non-stayable regions (if the critical section is short), and roll-forward with parameterized non-preemptable regions are all viable solutions to the speculative deadlock/relevant synchronization problem. Non-preemptable regions (if the critical section is short enough again) and parameterized non-preemptable regions are both viable solutions for the preemptive delay problem. In Examples 2 through 5 roll-back does not work and hence is not a general solution to solving speculative deadlock. (Furthermore, roll-back does not address the preemptive delay problem: roll-back only occurs when a task is stayed.) The non-stayable and non-preemptable region approaches are unattractive for situations where tasks spend a long time in the critical section and for producer-consumer synchronization paradigms.

4 Solutions

In this Section we show how to solve the speculative deadlock/relevant synchronization and preemptive delay problems with each of the examples in Sect. 3. We provide a general solution using roll-forward and parameterized preemption by extending our sponsor model.

4.1 The Sponsor Solution

The speculative deadlock problem and the preemptive delay problems both result from a failure in sponsorship: the critical task — the task which is blocking the progress of other tasks — is either unsponsored or not sufficiently sponsored. The problem in both cases is that the sponsorship of waiting tasks is not transmitted transitively to the task responsible for the lack of progress. Our solution is to generalize the "demand transivity" of sponsorship exhibited by toucher sponsors so that whenever a task blocks (or fails to make forward progress) that task should sponsor the task(s) responsible for ensuring its forward progress. In the case of semaphores this means that a blocked task should sponsor the task(s) responsible for releasing the semaphore. Since the blockee task then has at least the sponsorship level of the blocker, the blockee cannot be stayed (unless all the blockers are stayed) and cannot be preempted by a task with priority less than the blocker's priority. Thus the sponsor model provides an elegant framework in which to provide a unified roll-forward solution to both the speculative deadlock and preemptive delay problems.

In the case of simple serializers we can always implicitly identify the task responsible for a waiters lack of progress: it is simply the task holding the semaphore. However, as we saw with the two readers/writers problems and the producer-consumer problems it is not always possible to implicitly identify the responsible task: it might be any task in some collection. Thus we have to conceptually sponsor all the tasks in the collection. The sponsor solution now becomes: Ensure that any critical task (such as a task in the critical section) is the member of a class and ensure that any task requiring some action of the critical task (such as exiting the critical section or producing a value) sponsors that class (e.g. by waiting on a semaphore for access to the critical section). This class in turn sponsors the critical task until it performs the necessary action (such as releasing a semaphore). In general, we have to define a set of classes for tasks and the transitions between these classes, reflecting each task's possible trajectory through the system. In the case of a critical section, the critical task is the task in the critical section: tasks blocked waiting to enter the critical section should sponsor a class containing the task in the critical section. In the case of producer-consumer synchronization, consumers waiting for a producer should sponsor a class containing potential producers. Then at least one producer must remain active while a consumer waits. This sponsoring idea generalizes beyond the synchronization methods of semaphores, locks, and placeholders in the five examples in Sect. 3.

4.2 Extensions to the Sponsor Model

To solve the problems with semaphores, we introduce the following extensions to the sponsor model. The *-sema constructs below are modifications of the respective constructs in Sect. 2.1.

(make-sema *class*) creates and returns a binary semaphore object which contains a priority queue for tasks waiting to enter the critical region, and a class for waiting tasks to sponsor, which we call the **sema class** (or semaphore sponsor class).[13] The maximum priority task in the priority queue sponsors the sema class. The sema class is initialized to *class* and is accessible for a binary semaphore **sema** via the construct (get-sema-class *sema*) and may be set via (set-sema-class *sema class*). Thus, the class that waiting tasks sponsor may change dynamically.

(wait-sema *sema entry-thunk*) is a standard semaphore wait operation augmented with a "entry thunk". *entry-thunk* must be a procedure with zero arguments.[14] wait-sema performs the following operations indivisibly: if *sema* is

---

[13] In Sect. 4.6 we generalize the semaphore constructs in this Section to general semaphores. make-sema then takes an optional second argument which specifies the initial value of the general semaphore.

[14] Such a parameterless procedure is known as a "thunk". By wrapping a section of code in such a parameterless procedure, the code can be passed as an argument to a procedure such as wait-sema but not evaluated until the thunk argument is explicitly applied.

free it makes *sema* busy and makes the executing task non-stayable and non-preemptable; and if *sema* is busy it suspends and priority enqueues the executing task on *sema*. If the task was not queued (i.e. *sema* was free and became busy), the executing task evaluates *entry-thunk* and becomes stayable and preemptable again before **wait-sema** returns. Otherwise, *entry-thunk* is evaluated when the task is finally dequeued as the result of a (**signal-sema** *sema*) (as described below).

(**signal-sema** *sema . exit-thunk*) is a standard semaphore signal operation augmented with an optional "exit thunk". *exit-thunk* must be a procedure with no arguments. **signal-sema** performs the following operations indivisibly: if no tasks are queued on *sema*, it makes *sema* free; otherwise it dequeues the top priority task and resumes its continuation. Doing so causes that task to evaluate *entry-thunk* (the *entry-thunk* captured by the **wait-sema** originally invoked by that task).

Thus *entry-thunk* and *exit-thunk* execute in a non-stayable and non-preemptable region. This enables *entry-thunk* and *exit-thunk* to perform critical operations, such as changing the sema class of **sema** or adding the task to the sema class of *sema*, without danger of being stayed.

Fig. 5 and Fig. 6 show a pseudo-code implementation of **wait-sema** and **signal-sema** respectively. Bold typeface highlights differences from the original Multilisp implementation. Two points regarding the **wait-sema** implementation in Fig. 5 merit elaboration. First, to capture the continuation for blocking on a semaphore the implementation only needs to access the representation of a task in order to enqueue and dequeue the task. Thus the full power of continuations, such as Scheme's **call-with-current-continuation** is not required. Second, the enter and exit non-stayable/non-preemptable region operations are operations on the state of a task and not operations on the state of the processor (such as enabling and disabling interrupts[15]) upon which a task executes. Thus there is no need to exit the non-stayable/non-preemptable region after enqueueing a task continuation on a semaphore.

(**enter-class** *class*) adds the evaluating task to the given class. (**exit-class** *class*) removes the evaluating task from the given class. These can be built out of the **add-to/remove-from-class** constructs described in Sect. 2.2.

No additional extentions are required to solve the problems with Example 3, the single non-semaphore example. The sponsor model constructs described in Sect. 2.2 are sufficient.

---

[15] Though controlling interrupts remains a possibility for implementing non-stayable and non-preemptive regions, in which case interrupts must be enabled before enqueueing a task continuation on a semaphore and disabled before continuing the task continuation.

```
(define (wait-sema sema entry-thunk)
    check arguments
    enter non-stayable/non-preemptable region
    lock sema
    capture current continuation (and save it in c)
    if sema state not free
        priority enqueue task continuation c on sema
        unlock sema
        quit                        ; find another task to run
    make sema state busy        ; start of task continuation
    unlock sema
    apply entry-thunk
    exit non-stayable/non-preemptable region
    )
```

Fig. 5. Pseudo-code implementation of **wait-sema**

```
(define (signal-sema sema . exit-thunk)
    check arguments
    enter non-stayable/non-preemptable region
    apply (car exit-thunk)
    lock sema
    if sema task queue empty
        make sema free
        unlock sema
        exit non-stayable/non-preemptable region
    else
        dequeue top priority task from sema
        resume dequeued task continuation                ; continue queued task
        exit non-stayable/non-preemptable region ; continue signaller
    )
```

Fig. 6. Pseudo-code implementation of **signal-sema**

4.3   Solution for Simple Mutual Exclusion — Serializers

The problems with simple semaphore serializers are solved straightforwardly:

```
(wait-sema sema (lambda () (enter-class cr-class)))
some action
(signal-sema sema)
(exit-class cr-class)
```

where **cr-class** is initialized by (**make-sponsor-class 'sponsor-all**) and **sema** is initialized by (**make-sema cr-class**). The exact timing of exitting the **cr-class** is unimportant as long as it happens after the task exits the critical section. Thus it is not necessary to evaluate the **exit-class** in the exit thunk of `signal-sema`.[16]

Each task enters and exits `cr-class` as it enters and exits the critical section respectively. The maximum priority task blocked on `sema` sponsors the task(s) in the critical section via its membership in `cr-class`. `wait-sema` maintains a priority queue of tasks waiting to enter the mutual exclusion region and admits them in priority order.

The following interface hides the notion of classes from the user.

```
(define (make-serializer)
  (let* ((mutex-class (make-sponsor-class 'sponsor-all))
         (sema (make-sema mutex-class)))
    (lambda (thunk)
      (wait-sema sema (lambda () (enter-class mutex-class)))
      (thunk)
      (signal-sema sema)
      (exit-class mutex-class))))
```

This makes and returns a "serializer" procedure which takes an thunk argument and evaluates the thunk in a mutual exclusion region.

4.4   Solution for the Readers and Writers Problem

The readers and writers problem in Sect. 3.2 may now be solved as shown in Fig. 7. The additions and modifications to Fig. 1 are marked to the right of each line. The main idea is to have two classes: one for the readers or writer in the read/write critical region (i.e. with access to the shared object) — we call this the `accessor-class` — and one for the mutual exclusion region of the `readcount` serializer — we call this the `mutex-class`. Any tasks blocked awaiting access to the critical region sponsor the readers or writer in the critical region. Any readers blocked awaiting entry to the `readcount` mutual exclusion region sponsor the task in that region. These sponsorships prevent speculative deadlock and preemptive delay. The semaphores admit tasks to the critical and mutual exclusion regions in priority order. This solution does not, however, guarantee this priority access order to the critical region across readers and writers.

We now give a line by line description of the solution in Fig. 7. Readers blocked on the `mutex` semaphore region in line 1 sponsor `mutex-class`.[17] As a reader enters this `mutex` mutual exclusion region in line 1, line 2 adds the reader to `mutex-class`. If this reader is the first in a read epoch, it tests the

---

[16] However, doing so might lead to a more efficient implementation since one could then show that there can never be more than one task in the `cr-class` and thus use a simpler and cheaper `sponsor-any` sponsor policy.

[17] When we say that the waiting tasks blocked on a semaphore sponsor a class, we mean that the maximum-priority waiter task sponsors the class.

Initialization:

```
(define accessor-class (make-sponsor-class 'sponsor-max-priority)) ; new
(define wrt (make-sema accessor-class))                            ; modified
(define mutex-class (make-sponsor-class 'sponsor-all))             ; new
(define mutex (make-sema mutex-class))                             ; modified
(define readcount 0)
```

Readers execute:

```
(wait-sema mutex                                          ; (1)
           (lambda () (enter-class mutex-class)))         ; (2) new
(incr1 readcount)                                         ; (3)
(if (= readcount 1)                                       ; (4)
    (wait-sema wrt                                        ; (5)
            (lambda ()
                (enter-class accessor-class)))            ; (6) new
    (enter-class accessor-class))                         ; (7) new
(signal-sema mutex)                                       ; (8)
(exit-class mutex-class)                                  ; (9) new
read operation
(wait-sema mutex                                          ; (10)
           (lambda () (enter-class mutex-class)))         ; (11) new
(decr1 readcount)                                         ; (12)
(if (= readcount 0)
    (signal-sema wrt))                                    ; (13)
(exit-class accessor-class)                               ; (14) new
(signal-sema mutex)                                       ; (15)
(exit-class mutex-class)                                  ; (16) new
```

Writers execute:

```
(wait-sema wrt                                            ; (17)
           (lambda ()
               (enter-class accessor-class)))             ; (18) new
write operation
(signal-sema wrt)                                         ; (19)
(exit-class accessor-class)                               ; (20) new
```

Fig. 7. Sponsor solution to the readers and writers problem

wrt semaphore in line 5 for entry to the read/write critical region. If successful, line 6 adds the reader to accessor-class. If unsuccessful, the reader blocks on the wrt semaphore and sponsors accessor-class via the sema class of wrt. In this case, note that any readers blocked on mutex (in lines 1 or 10) sponsor this reader, which in turn sponsors accessor-class. This transitivity ensures that the maximum-priority waiting reader always sponsors accessor-class. If the reader is not the first in a read epoch, line 7 simply adds it to accessor-class. Finally, the reader exits the mutex mutual exclusion region and mutex-class in lines 8 and 9 respectively. The reader, now in the read/write critical region, remains in `accessor-class`.

When we sponsor tasks in `accessor-class`, we are careful to only sponsor the maximum-priority task in this class (by virtue of the `sponsor-max-priority` class type). This ensures that the relative order of readers established by their priorities in line 1 is not subverted when `accessor-class` is sponsored. (Note that there is never more than one writer in `accessor-class`, except possibly momentarily after a writer exits the critical region in line 19 but before it exits `accessor-class` in line 20.) For example, if `accessor-class` had class type `sponsor-all`, all the readers between lines 9 and 10 could have the same priority (from a high priority writer blocked on `wrt`) and thus readers would gain access to the second `mutex` mutual exclusion region in FCFS order rather than in the order of their original priorities.

The exit of readers from the read/write critical region is straightforward. Readers blocked on `mutex` in line 10 again sponsor `mutex-class`. Readers finally exit `accessor-class` in line 14.

Writers blocked on `wrt` in line 17 sponsor `accessor-class`. Lines 19 and 20 are straightforward.

Note the two parts of this solution as described earlier. We defined a set of classes — `accessor-class` and `mutex-class` — so that each task in a critical/exclusion region is in one or more classes and we defined transitions between these classes to match the trajectory of tasks through the semaphore system. Then we ensured that the tasks blocked on a semaphore always sponsor the class of tasks responsible for releasing the semaphore.

The use of `mutex` and `mutex-class` in Fig. 7 mirrors in every way the previous serializer example, and thus we could use the `make-serializer` abstraction here.

As before, we can easily define an interface that hides the notion of classes from the user. Figure 8 shows one possibility which incorporates our earlier `make-serializer` abstraction. `make-rw-serializer` makes and returns a pair consisting of a reader serializer and a writer serializer. Each of these serializers takes an argument thunk to evaluate in the read/write critical region. Figure 9 illustrates their use.

4.5 Solution for the Multiple Potential Determiners Problem

To solve the problem with the multiple potential determiners example, we sponsor all the solver tasks until the placeholder is determined, i.e. the first solution is found. Thus we need the tasks blocked on a placeholder to sponsor a defined class of potential determiner tasks. This is the reason for the optional class argument to `make-future` in Sect. 2.1. Figure 10 shows how to solve the problem with the multiple potential determiners example in Sect. 3.3 using classes.

The line numbers indicate lines with changes from Fig. 2. Line 1 creates a class for all the potential determiners. Line 2 creates a placeholder which sponsors these potential determiners. Thus any task blocked on this placeholder sponsors

```
(define (make-rw-serializer)
  (let* ((accessor-class (make-sponsor-class 'sponsor-max-priority))
         (wrt (make-sema accessor-class))
         (serialize (make-serializer))
         (readcount 0))
    (cons
      (lambda (read-thunk)
        (serialize
          (lambda ()
            (incr1 readcount)
            (if (= readcount 1)
                (wait-sema wrt (lambda () (enter-class accessor-class)))
                (enter-class accessor-class))))
        (read-thunk)
        (serialize
          (lambda ()
            (decr1 readcount)
            (if (= readcount 0)
                (signal-sema wrt))
            (exit-class accessor-class))))
      (lambda (wrt-thunk)
        (wait-sema wrt (lambda () (enter-class accessor-class)))
        (wrt-thunk)
        (signal-sema wrt)
        (exit-class accessor-class)))))
```

Fig. 8. A user interface for the readers and writers problem

Initialize:

```
(define rw-serializer (make-rw-serializer))
(define reader (car rw-serializer))
(define writer (cdr rw-serializer))
```

Readers execute:	Writers execute:
...	...
; perform a read:	; perform a write:
(reader (lambda () *read-operation*))	(writer (lambda () *write-operation*))
...	...

Fig. 9. Applying the user interface for the readers and writers problem

```
(define determiners
   (make-sponsor-class 'sponsor-all))      ; or sponsor-max-priority  ; 1

(define first (cons 0 nil))               ; initialize lock

;; create synchronization placeholder
(define first-solution (make-future determiners))                    ; 2

;; attempt to solve the given problem
(define (solve problem)
   (let ((a-solution (work-on-problem problem)))
      (if (solution? a-solution)          ; was a solution found?
         (if (rplaca-eq first 1 0)
            ;; if first, determine placeholder to solution
            (determine-future first-solution a-solution)))))

;; attempt to solve all problems simultaneously
(define (find-first-solution problems)
   (map (lambda (prob)
          (add-to-class (future (solve prob)) determiners))          ; 3
        problems)                         ; fork solvers
   first-solution)                        ; return first solution
```

Fig. 10. Sponsor solution for multiple potential determiners problem

the potential determiners and thereby propagates the demand for the place-holder result to the potential determiners. Line 3 creates and adds each problem solver to the potential determiners class. With these additions any demand for the placeholder value sponsors all the potential determiners and thus prevents speculative deadlock and preemptive delay. Conveniently, this sponsoring also solves the speculative deadlock and preemptibe delay problems associated with a solver task being stayed or preempted in the interval between obtaining the lock and determining the placeholder.

4.6 Solution for the Producer-Consumer Problem

To solve the problems with the producer-consumer problem in Fig. 3 of Sect. 3.4 we would like:

1. The consumers blocked on **full** to sponsor any producers before the signal of **full** in line P4.
2. The producers blocked on **empty** to sponsor any consumers before the signal of **empty** in line C4.

Figure 11 shows such a solution. There are two classes: **producer-class** for all the potential producer tasks and **consumer-class** for all the potential consumer tasks. Producer and consumer tasks must be added to these respective classes as soon as the tasks are generated. We use the **make-serializer** abstraction defined earlier in Sect. 4.3 to ensure proper sponsorship of tasks in the mutual exclusion region and priority access to this region. If all the producer (consumer) tasks continually cycle producing (consuming) items from the buffer, then line P4 (C4) to exit the **producer-class (consumer-class)** is not necessary — the tasks can remain in the class for the next iteration. Consumers blocked on **full** sponsor **producer-class** until an item is added to the buffer and its availability is indicated to the consumer by signalling **full** in line P3. Similarily, producers blocked on **full** sponsor **consumer-class** until an item is added to the buffer and its availability is indicated to the producer by signalling **empty** in line C3. **producer-class** and **consumer-class** have class type **sponsor-max-priority** so that we do not disrupt the priority ordering of tasks in these classes. To make progress we only need to sponsor a task in each of these classes, not all the tasks.

Initialization

```
(define producer-class
    (make-sponsor-class 'sponsor-max-priority)) ; producer class
(define consumer-class
    (make-sponsor-class 'sponsor-max-priority)) ; consumer class
(define empty (make-sema consumer-class N))     ; buffer size is N
(define full (make-sema producer-class 0))
(define serialize (make-serializer))            ; serializer from Sect. 4.3
```

All potential producers

```
(enter-class producer-class)                    ; all potential producers
```

All potential consumers

```
(enter-class consumer-class)                    ; all potential consumers
```

Producer

```
(wait-sema empty)                               ; (P1) wait for an empty slot
(serialize (lambda () add to buffer ))          ; (P2) indivisibly add an item
(signal-sema full                               ; (P3) indicate a full slot
        (lambda ()
            (exit-class producer-class)))       ; (P4) optional
```

Consumer

```
(wait-sema full)                                ; (C1) wait for a full slot
(serialize (lambda () delete from buffer ))     ; (C2) indivisibly delete an item
(signal-sema empty                              ; (C3) indicate an empty slot
        (lambda ()
            (exit-class consumer-class)))       ; (C4) optional
```

Fig. 11. Sponsor solution for the producer-consumer problem

4.7 Sponsor Solution for Modified Readers and Writers Problem

The problems identified earlier with the modified readers and writers problem may now be solved as shown in Fig. 12. Although the solution looks complicated, it is fairly easy to explain (most of the apparent complexity is in the initialization). First we describe the class definitions, then the class transitions, and finally the sponsorship.

Class definitions: The solution has a class `accessor-class` for any reader or writer task in the critical sections, a class `waiter-class` for all queued readers, and a class `writers-class` for all potential writer tasks.

Class transitions: A writer is initially in `writers-class`. On entry into the critical section via lines 6 or 22 a reader or writer (respectively) enters the `accessor-class` (line 3). If the task is a writer, it then exits the `writers-class`. If the task is a reader and the database is not ready for reading, the reader enters the `waiter-class` in line 14 and then exits the `accessor-class` in line 16. Note the overlapping class membership here — there is no need for an atomic transition between the writer and accessor classes or the accessor and waiter classes. Readers and writers otherwise exit `accessor-class` in lines 16 and 27 respectively. Queued readers remain in the `waiter-class` until admitted into the critical section in line 18 where they transit to the `accessor-class`. Although not shown, any tasks that may potentially become writers after leaving the critical section must enter the `writers-class`.

Task state	Task sponsors
Blocked on `mutex`	Task in critical section (i.e. task in `accessor-class`), if any. Otherwise, queued readers (i.e. tasks in `waiter-class`)
Blocked on `waiters`	Task in critical section (i.e. task in `accessor-class`), if any. Otherwise, potential writers (i.e. tasks in `writers-class`)

Critial section state	Sponsorship
Critical section occupied	Tasks blocked on `mutex` and `waiters` sponsor reader or writer in critical section
Critical section empty	Tasks blocked on `mutex` sponsor queued readers. Tasks blocked on `waiter` sponsor potential writers

Table 1. Sponsorship invariants

Sponsorship: Table 1 lists the sponsorship invariants. Tasks blocked on `mutex` sponsor `accessor-class` if it contains a task and `waiter-class` otherwise. We implement this by updating the sema class indirection cell for `mutex` in line 1 when a task enters `accessor-class` and in line 4 when a task exits

Initialization:

```
(define accessor-class (make-sponsor-class 'sponsor-all))
(define mutex (make-sema accessor-class))
(define writers-class (make-sponsor-class 'sponsor-all))
(define waiter-class (make-sponsor-class 'sponsor-max-priority))
(define waiters (make-sema writers-class))
(define enter-thunk
   (lambda ()
      (set-sema-class mutex accessor-class)      ; (1) enter class and have
      (set-sema-class waiter accessor-class)     ; (2) remaining tasks sponsor it
      (enter-class accessor-class)))             ; (3)
(define exit-thunk
   (lambda ()
      (set-sema-class mutex waiters-class))      ; (4) redirect sponsorship
(define exit-thunk2
   (lambda ()
      (set-sema-class waiter writers-class))     ; (5) redirect sponsorship
(define queuecount 0)
```

Readers execute:

```
(wait-sema mutex enter-thunk)                    ; (6)
(let loop ()
   (if ready-to-read?                            ; (7)
       (begin
           read operation                        ; (8)
           (if (> queuecount 0)                  ; (9) check for queued readers
               (signal-sema waiters exit-thunk)  ;(10) start one up
               (signal-sema mutex exit-thunk2))  ;(11) else exit
           (exit-class accessor-class))          ;(12) exit class
       (begin
           (incr queuecount)                     ;(13) join queued readers
           (enter-class waiter-class)            ;(14)
           (signal-sema mutex exit-thunk2)       ;(15)
           (exit-class accessor-class)           ;(16)
           some action                           ;(17) arbitrary operation
           (wait-sema waiters enter-thunk)       ;(18) queue
           (exit-class waiter-class)             ;(19)
           (decr queuecount)                     ;(20)
           (loop))))                             ;(21) try again
```

Writers execute:

```
... writers initially in writers-class ...
(wait-sema mutex enter-thunk)                    ;(22)
(exit-class writers-class)
write operation                                  ;(23) write & set ready-to-read
(if (> queuecount 0)                             ;(24) check for queued readers
    (signal-sema waiters exit-thunk)             ;(25) start one up
    (signal-sema mutex exit-thunk2))             ;(26) else exit
(exit-class accessor-class))                     ;(27) exit class
```

Fig. 12. Sponsor solution for the modified readers and writers problem

`accessor-class` (but passes `mutex` to a queued reader task). Queued readers blocked on `waiters` sponsor `accessor-class` if it contains a task and `writers-class` if it does not (to ensure that writers are sponsored to eventually free the queued readers). We implement this functionality by updating the sema class indirection cell for waiter in line 2 when a task enters the critical section and line 5 when a task exits the critical section. The transition into the `accessor-class` and the update of `mutex`'s and `waiter`'s sema classes (lines 1 to 3) must be atomic since these must happen simultaneously to avoid speculative deadlock. Finally, `waiter-class` has class type `sponsor-max-priority` so that we do not disrupt the priority ordering of queued readers.

We give a formal derivation of correctness of this solution in another paper [14].

4.8 Summary and Discussion

Through our five examples, we have illustrated the relevant synchronization and preemptive delay problems and shown how to extend our sponsor model to solve these problems in each case. Each example makes a different point. The simple serializer example is an extremely common and important paradigm in parallel computing. We showed how to solve the relevant synchronization and preemptive delay problems with it in the most general sense by sponsoring the critical section task. In many cases, the duration within the critical section of a simple serializer will be short enough that alternative methods such as compare-and-swap, roll-back, or non-stayable/non-preemptable regions will be more efficient than the overhead associated with sponsoring. The point of the remaining examples is that such alternatives do not work in more complicated situations.

In the readers/writers example — also a fairly common paradigm in parallel computing — it is no longer possible to implicitly determine the task that will release a semaphore, so roll-back and non-stayable/non-preemptable regions are not acceptable. We exhibited a more general solution using classes and our extensions of `wait-sema` and `signal-sema`.

The producer-consumer example (Sect. 3.4 and Sect. 4.6) takes this one step further: it is only possible to identify a set of tasks responsible for lack of progress, and none of them may even be in a critical region. Thus solutions oriented towards simple serializer critical regions, such as roll-back and non-stayable/non-preemptable regions either simply won't work or are reduce the ability to stay or preempt tasks to such a degree as to be totally unacceptable. In contrast, our sponsor-based method using classes and our extensions of `wait-sema` and `signal-sema` solve the problems with this popular synchronization paradigm in a simple and elegant fashion.

Although the modified readers and writers problem is artificial, it does represent a simplification of a real problem (the implementation of monitors). This example demonstrates the need, in general, to have the flexibility to have tasks transit between classes and the ability to modify the class a semaphore's waiters sponsor since the class responsible for releasing a semaphore may change with time. Figure 12 illustrates this last point rather dramatically where two classes (`waiter-class` and `writers-class`) are outside any region guarded by semaphores. This observation motivated the `set-sema-class` construct.

The multiple potential determiner example represents a common paradigm in speculative computation wherein one is pursuing multiple approaches simultaneously where the first successful result will suffice (e.g. disjunction). The main point of this example was to illustrate that the relevant synchronization and preemptive delay problems arise even in non-semaphore situations.

We have presented a general solution to the relevant synchronization and preemptive delay problems. Such a general solution is important because special case solutions cannot always capture all the complicated ways people might perform synchronization. For example, special case solutions based on simple serializer use of semaphores cannot solve the problems that might arise with more complicated use of semaphores, such as in the modified readers and writers problem. However, general solutions can be expensive. In some cases the mechanisms we are proposing here are likely to have worse performance than with simple unstayable/non-preemption regions. Many real uses of semaphores involve short critical sections, for example. However, we expect that our sponsor model extensions are viable alternatives for producer consumer synchronization problems, such as in our multiple determiners and producer-consumer examples, where choices other than parameterized roll-forward are unsuitable.

Our extended sponsor model approach can also be expensive in terms of complexity, as in the modified readers and writers problem. It becomes difficult in such non-trivial applications to determine if the solution is correct. Of course, one could accept less performance — by accepting long non-stayable/non-preemptable regions for example — in exchange for reduced complexity. Another possibility is to amortize the complexity and alleviate the burden on the programmer by having a library of solutions for common paradigms. Finally, perhaps the correct viewpoint to have is that dealing with side effects is rarely easy.

We have implemented these semaphore operations and tested them on the examples (except for the producer-consumer example) discussed in this paper with suitable "driver" stubs specifying task activity inside and outside the critical sections. We have not investigated performance issues since at this time we have only implemented these operations in an interpreted version of Multilisp (running on top of a sequential Scheme) which does not provide accurate performance data.

5 Related Work

The simultaneous presence of both relevant synchronization and preemptive delay problems is unique to a situation with both aborting of tasks and prioritization of tasks, as in our approach to speculative computation. We are not aware of any other work which solves both problems in one framework like ours.[18]

---

[18] Kornfeld and Hewitt proposed the idea of sponsors in [8] but to our knowledge neither they nor anyone else has used sponsors to solve the relevant synchronization and preemptive delay problems.

There has been much work dealing with the aborting of tasks, though in most work aborting is a rare, exceptional event so conservative solutions like "no-abort" regions are frequently acceptable. In contrast, aborting is a common event in speculative computation so more liberal solutions are necessary. The works closest in spirit to ours are MultiScheme [10] and Qlisp [2, 3] which both have some support for speculative styles of computation. Both provide support for aborting tasks and thus suffer from the speculative deadlock/relevant synchronization problem. MultiScheme uses "finalization" to solve this problem. One garbage collection cycle before an object (e.g. a task object) is collected, user-supplied code can be invoked to "finalize" the object, releasing locks and cleaning up. This finalization amounts to a roll-back mechanism and thus is not powerful enough to solve the problems with Examples 3, 4, and 5. Qlisp has a unwind-protect form. (unwind-protect *form cleanup*) evaluates *form* and always evaluates *cleanup* before returning, even if the task evaluating unwind-protect is aborted. The normal use of unwind-protect is as a roll-back mechanism. However, it may also be used as a roll-forward mechanism by putting everything in the cleanup form, thus providing an "no-abort region". Thus Qlisp offers a choice between underpowered roll-back and conservative roll-forward.

The real-time system and Ada communities have been concerned with the preemptive delay problem (which they call the priority inversion problem) for some time. Sha *et al* suggested priority inheritance protocols in which a task in a critical section executes at the priority of at least the maximum priority task waiting to enter that region [17, 15]. Sha *et al* considered only simple applications, such as the semaphore serializer in Example 1, for which the tasks producing a synchronizing event (the synchronizer tasks) are implicitly well-defined. They did not consider how to solve the preemptive delay problem in more complicated synchronization problems, such as Examples 2 and 5, for which the synchronizer task may not even be in a critical section. Solving the preemptive delay problem for producer-consumer synchronization requires more than priority inheritance for instance.

6 Conclusions

In the context of speculative computation side effects, particularly intertask synchronization side effects, can lead to speculative deadlock/relevant synchronization and preemptive delay problems. We demonstrated these problems in five different examples. These examples covered a range of different synchronization types (serializer, readers and writers, producer-consumer), different primitive synchronization mechanisms (semaphores and placeholders), and different complexities (simple serializer vs. the modified readers and writers problem). For simple cases like the critical sections of serializers, there are several alternatives such as roll-back, roll-forward, non-stayable, and non-preemptable regions for preventing the speculative deadlock/relevant synchronization and preemptive delay problems. Such a choice of alternatives exists for such simple cases because it is possible to implicitly identify task the responsible for the lack of progress causing speculative deadlock or preemptive delay: it's always the task in the critical section. For other cases there are much fewer alternatives: difficulties arise because there is no task in the critical section or there is no critical section. In four examples we saw that roll-back did not work and non-stayable and non-preemptable regions were unattractive.

To solve the speculative delay/relevant synchronization and preemptive delay problems demonstrated by these examples we proposed a natural extension of our sponsor model. The basic idea of this novel approach is for a task waiting for some side effect event, such as the release of a semaphore or the production of a value, to sponsor the task or set of tasks responsible for performing the event. The key is to ensure the transivity of sponsorship from tasks whose forward progress is impeded to the task(s) responsible for the impediment.

We introduced language constructs to implement this sponsor model extension and showed how to use them to solve the speculative delay/relevant synchronization and preemptive delays problems for each of the five examples mentioned above. For semaphores, the solution is for the tasks blocked on a semaphore to sponsor the task(s) responsible for releasing the semaphore. To handle complicated applications where it may not be possible to implicitly identify the responsible task(s) we developed a model in which tasks belong to explicitly identified classes and tasks transit through these classes, redirecting the sponsorship of blocked tasks as necessary. The result is a parameterized roll-forward approach that can solve problems roll-back approaches cannot easily solve, such as with producer-consumer synchronization, and is potentially more attractive performance-wise than non-parameterized roll-forward (i.e. non-stayable) approaches for some applications. We introduced

The sponsor model provides a general technique for solving the speculative deadlock/relevant synchronization and preemptive delay problems. One only needs to provide the appropriate language constructs so that the demand for some action can be transmitted into the sponsor of some task that will perform the action.

7 Appendix: State Description of Example 5

This Appendix gives a formal state description of the modified readers and writers problem presented in Sect. 3.5 and analyzes all the possible transitions. For space reasons the presentation is terse. For more expansive details see [14].

We only model the state with respect to whether or not tasks are inside the critical section, waiting to get inside the critical section, or outside the critical section. We are not concerned with task activities otherwise. This amounts to modeling the state at the points of entering and exitting semaphores.

The state tuple for Example 5 is:

$$S = (n_{cr}, mutex, m_q, q, waiter, w_q)$$

where:

n_{cr} is the number of tasks in the database critical region. $n_{cr} = \{0, 1\}$. There are three entry points to the database critical region: (wait-sema mutex) in lines 1 and

13 and (wait-sema waiters) in line 10. Likewise, there are three exit points from the database critical region: line 5 or 6, line 8, and line 16 or 17.

mutex denotes whether the mutex semaphore guarding the database critical section is in the locked state or free state. $mutex = \{locked, free\}$.

m_q is the number of tasks blocked on the mutex semaphore. $m_q = \{0, 1, 2, 3, ...\}$.

q is the number of queued readers that have exitted the critical section in line 8 but have not yet entered the critical section at line 10 (these readers are either at line 9 or blocked at line 10). $q = \{0, 1, 2, 3, ...\}$.

waiter denotes whether the waiters semaphore is in the locked state or free state. $waiter = \{locked, free\}$.

w_q is the number of tasks blocked on the waiter semaphore. $w_q = \{0, 1, 2, 3, ...\}$.

The possible events that can cause a change in the state are:

1. A reader arrives at line 1 and executes (wait-sema mutex)
2. A reader exits the critical section via line 5
3. A reader exits the critical section via line 6
4. A reader exits the critical section via line 8
5. A reader arrives at line 10 and executes (wait-sema waiters)
6. A writer arrives at line 13 and executes (wait-sema mutex)
7. A writer exits the critical section via line 16
8. A writer exits the critical section via line 17

Since for the purposes of the state description we do not distinguish readers and writers we can fold events 6, 7, and 8 involving writers into events 1, 2, and 3 respectively.

The five remaining events lead to the following possible state transitions (a * means "don't care"):[19]

1. A reader or writer executes (wait-sema mutex) in line 1 or 13:
   There are two possibilities. Either a reader (writer) gains immediate access to the critical section (hence $mutex = free$, $m_q = 0$, and $n_{cr} = 0$) as below:

   $$(0, free, 0, *, *, *) \rightarrow (1, locked, 0, *, *, *)$$

   or mutex is locked and the reader (writer) is queued (hence $mutex = locked$):

   $$(*, locked, m_q, *, *, *) \rightarrow (*, locked, m_q + 1, *, *, *)$$

2. A reader exits the critical section via line 5 or a writer exits the critical section via line 16:
   Since the reader (writer) is in the critical section, we must have $n_{cr} = 1$ and $mutex = locked$. In order to make the transition we must have $q + w_q > 0$. *waiter* may either be *locked* (the normal case) or *free* (if waiters has been previously signalled but no task has yet entered at line 10). Thus we have:

   $$(1, locked, *, q, locked, w_q), q + w_q > 0 \rightarrow \begin{cases} (0, locked, *, q, free, 0) & \text{if } w_q = 0 \\ (1, locked, *, q, locked, w_q - 1) & \text{if } w_q > 0 \end{cases}$$

---

[19] All transitions obey the implicit constraints that all state variables are within their legal ranges as defined above.

The top clause on the right corresponds to the queued reader task(s) not having made it to line 10 yet. The bottom clause corresponds to a task waiting on waiters and immediately entering the critical section when reader (writer) exits. And we could also have:

$$(1, locked, *, q, free, 0), \; q > 0 \rightarrow (0, locked, *, q, free, 0)$$

However, some thought reveals that it is not possible to get to the state on the left and thus this transition cannot occur. *waiters* can only become *free* as the result of some reader (writer) executing line 5 (16). Once this occurs, mutex is still locked and thus no other read (writer) can enter the critical section to signal waiters until some queued reader enters the critical section at line 10 and exits at line 6. And as soon as a queued reader enters at line 10, waiters becomes locked. Therefore $n_{cr} = 1$ and $waiter = free$ are in conflict.

3. A reader exits the critical section via line 6 or a writer exits the critical section via line 17:
Since the reader (writer) is in the critical section, we must have $n_{cr} = 1$ and $mutex = locked$.

$$(1, locked, m_q, *, *, *) \rightarrow \begin{cases} (0, free, 0, *, *, *) & \text{if } m_q = 0 \\ (1, locked, m_q - 1, *, *, *) & \text{if } m_q > 0 \end{cases}$$

The result is either mutex is free with no tasks blocked on it or mutex is locked and one of the tasks previously blocked on mutex is now inside the critical section.

4. A reader exits the critical section via line 8:
Once again, since the reader is in the critical section, we must have $n_{cr} = 1$ and $mutex = locked$. Thus:

$$(1, locked, m_q, q, *, *) \rightarrow \begin{cases} (0, free, 0, q + 1, *, *) & \text{if } m_q = 0 \\ (1, locked, m_q - 1, q + 1, *, *) & \text{if } m_q > 0 \end{cases}$$

5. A reader executes (wait-sema waiters) in line 10:
There are two possibilities in this case. Either waiters is free and the reader gains immediate access to the critical section or waiters is locked and the reader is queued. In the former case we must have $q > 0$, mutex locked, and $n_{cr} = 0$ (since waiters can only be made free by a reader (writer) when queuecount > 0 and thereafter mutex stays locked until a queued reader reenters the critical section and unlocks it). Thus:

$$(0, locked, *, q, free, 0), \; q > 0 \rightarrow (1, locked, *, q - 1, locked, 0)$$

In the latter case we must have $q > 0$, but mutex could be either free (if the reader just arrived from line 8) or locked (if some other reader or writer then enters the critical section).

$$(*, *, *, q, locked, w_q), \; q > 0 \rightarrow (*, *, *, q - 1, locked, w_q + 1)$$

The following table summarizes all the possible state transitions:

$(0, free, 0, *, *, *) \rightarrow (1, locked, 0, *, *, *)$
$(*, locked, m_q, *, *, *) \rightarrow (*, locked, m_q + 1, *, *, *)$
$(1, locked, *, q, locked, w_q), \ q + w_q > 0 \rightarrow \begin{cases} (0, locked, *, q, free, 0) & \text{if } w_q = 0 \\ (1, locked, *, q, locked, w_q - 1) & \text{if } w_q > 0 \end{cases}$
$(1, locked, m_q, 0, *, *) \rightarrow \begin{cases} (0, free, 0, 0, *, *) & \text{if } m_q = 0 \\ (1, locked, m_q - 1, 0, *, *) & \text{if } m_q > 0 \end{cases}$
$(1, locked, m_q, q, *, *) \rightarrow \begin{cases} (0, free, 0, q + 1, *, *) & \text{if } m_q = 0 \\ (1, locked, m_q - 1, q + 1, *, *) & \text{if } m_q > 0 \end{cases}$
$(0, locked, *, q, free, 0), \ q > 0 \rightarrow (1, locked, *, q - 1, locked, 0)$
$(*, *, *, q, locked, w_q), \ q > 0 \rightarrow (*, *, *, q - 1, locked, w_q + 1)$

Legal states obey the following constraints: 1) $m_q > 0$ if and only if $mutex = locked$, and 2) $w_q > 0$ if and only if $waiter = locked$. These two constraints correspond to assuming that the semaphores "work".

In addition, an important invariant that must be preserved to avoid deadlock is that **mutex** and **waiter** must not be locked at the same time unless there is no task in the critical region: i.e. we must have

$$mutex = locked \text{ and } waiter = locked \text{ only if } n_{cr} = 0$$

Otherwise, no task can enter the critical region and no task can exit the critical region to change the state of the two semaphores.

The initial state is $(0, free, 0, 0, locked, 0)$. See [14] for a picture of the state transition diagram.

Note that all tasks in Example 5 are in one of five states:

1. in the critical section
2. blocked on **mutex**
3. blocked on **waiters**
4. loitering between lines 8 and 10, or
5. somewhere outside the critical section uninvolved with the modified readers and writers problem.

Speculative deadlock can arise if a task in the critical section is stayed. Staying tasks blocked on either semaphore causes no immediate problem. Such a stayed task may eventually enter the critical section when the semaphore is signalled and then cause speculative deadlock, but this is just state 1 again. As discussed in Sect. 3.5, staying a task in state 4 can also lead to speculative deadlock for reader tasks blocked on **waiters** if the stayed task would otherwise enter the critical section and signal **waiters**. The fifth state gives rise to the producer-consumer form of speculative deadlock noted in Sect. 3.5 caused when a task that will signal **waiters** is stayed outside any critical section.

Staying tasks thus causes speculative deadlock in Example 5 under the following conditions:

1. when a task in the critical section is stayed,
2. when a task loitering between lines 8 and 10 is stayed, and
3. when a **waiters** signaler task is stayed.

References

1. H. Abelson and G. Sussman. *Structure and Interpretation of Computer Programs.* M.I.T. Press, Cambridge, MA., 1984.

2. R. Gabriel and J. McCarthy. Qlisp. In J. Kowalik, editor, *Parallel Computation and Computers for Artificial Intelligence.* Kluwer Academic Publishers, 1987.

3. R. Goldman and R. Gabriel. Qlisp: Parallel processing in Lisp. *IEEE Software,* pages 51–59, July 1989.

4. R. Halstead. Multilisp: A language for concurrent symbolic computation. *ACM Trans. on Prog. Languages and Systems,* pages 501–538, October 1985.

5. M. Herlihy. Wait free synchronization. *ACM Trans. on Prog. Languages and Systems,* January 1991.

6. IEEE Std 1178-1990. *IEEE Standard for the Scheme Programming Language.* Institute of Electrical and Electronic Engineers, Inc., New York, NY, 1991.

7. M. Katz and D. Weise. Continuing into the Future: On the interaction of Futures and First-class Continuations. In *ACM Conference on Lisp and Functional Programming,* 1990.

8. W. Kornfeld and C. Hewitt. The scientific community metaphor. *IEEE Trans. on Systems, Man, and Cybernetics,* pages 24–33, January 1981.

9. B. Lampson and D. Redell. Experience with Processes and Monitors in Mesa. *Communications of the ACM,* pages 105–117, February 1980.

10. J. Miller. MultiScheme: A parallel processing system based on MIT Scheme. Technical Report TR-402, Laboratory for Computer Science, M.I.T., September 1987.

11. R. Osborne. Speculative computation in Multilisp. Technical Report TR-464, Laboratory for Computer Science, M.I.T., November 1989.

12. R. Osborne. Speculative computation in Multilisp. In T. Ito and R. Halstead, editors, *Parallel Lisp: Languages and Systems, Proceedings of U.S./Japan Workshop on Parallel Lisp.* Lecture Notes in Computer Science, Springer-Verlag, Number 441, July 1990.

13. R. Osborne. Speculative computation in Multilisp: An overview. In *ACM Conference on Lisp and Functional Programming,* 1990.

14. R. Osborne. Details on Extending the Multilisp Sponsor Model to Handle Semaphore-based Intertask Synchronization. *Mitsubishi Electric Research Labs, Technical Note,* October 1992.

15. R. Rajkumar, L. Sha, and J.P. Lehoczky. Real-Time Synchronization Protocols for Multiprocessors. In *Proceedings of Real-time Systems Symposium,* December 1988.

16. B. Randell. System Structure for Software Fault Tolerance. In *International Conference on Reliable Software,* pages 437–449, 1975.

17. L. Sha, R. Rajkumar, and J.P. Lehoczky. Priority inheritance protocols: An approach to real-time synchronization. Technical Report CMU-CS-87-181, CMU, November 1987.

18. J. Silberschatz, A. Peterson and P. Galvin. *Operating System Concepts, 3rd Edition.* Addison-Wesley, 1991.

PART II

Implementation Techniques

Distillations
of Dynamic Partitioning Experience

Eric Mohr

Archetype Inc., 100 Fifth Ave., Waltham, MA, USA

Abstract. *Lazy task creation* (LTC) has proven to be an effective dynamic partitioning strategy for parallel Lisp systems. I describe here a key to the success of LTC (always package the parent instead of the child task at potential fork points) and two optimizations whose value extends to standard scheduling strategies (give scheduling preference to the child task, and use double-ended task queues). I also argue that research on real-world applications is strongly needed at this point as opposed to further system optimizations.

1 Introduction

The goal of efficiency in parallel Lisp programs has led to the investigation of dynamic task partitioning strategies for parallel Lisp systems. [6] and [7] introduced the concept of *lazy task creation* (LTC), where tasks are only created retroactively as processing resources become available. [5] gives a full presentation of LTC, a comparison with other partitioning strategies, and a detailed performance analysis using an implementation of the Mul-T language [4] on a 20-processor Encore shared memory computer. The purpose of this paper is to present some important points from [5] that weren't covered in any of the earlier papers, and to argue that research on real-world applications is strongly needed at this point as opposed to further system optimizations.

The well-known `future` construct declares that two branches of a computation *may* proceed in parallel, but leaves open the scheduling decision of whether a separate task should actually be created in any given instance. This decision is determined by a scheduling policy, of which we shall be concerned with three. With *eager task creation* (ETC), executing `future` always creates a separate task. With *load-based partitioning* (LBP), a separate task is created only if the system's load level is below a given threshold. With *lazy task creation* (LTC), a separate task is never created by the processor executing `future`, but idle processors may impose a retroactive fork by *stealing* the continuation to the `future` call. The reader who is unfamiliar with these strategies will find a full explication in any of [6, 7, 5].

In the expression (`future` X) we shall say that the *child* branch computes X while the *parent* branch computes the continuation to the `future` call.

2 Why LTC Eliminates More Task Creation Overhead than Related Methods

Lazy task creation takes advantage of two observations. First, executing a task remotely requires a large number of bookkeeping operations but executing a task locally needn't require any bookkeeping operations (as for example with inlining). Second, when parallelism is abundant most tasks can be executed locally. The essence of lazy task creation is to do as few of the bookkeeping operations as possible when processing a potential fork point while preserving the option to do them later if executing the task remotely becomes desirable.

Several other researchers (e.g. [9, 3, 8]) have derived a similar philosophy based on similar observations and have pared down somewhat the set of book-keeping operations performed at potential fork points, but none has reduced the set quite as far as is possible with LTC. The key difference between LTC and these other approaches lies in which branch of a potential fork (the parent or the child) is continued immediately and which is packaged up for possible migration—with LTC the parent is packaged while with the other systems the child is packaged.

When the child is packaged (recall that this is the X of (future X)) certain bookkeeping operations just cannot be eliminated. First, a closure (or similar object) must be allocated and initialized to contain the code pointer and free variables (or procedure arguments) for the child task so that a remote processor will have the information necessary to run it. Next, the existence of the child must be publicized by placing some "task" object (usually also newly allocated and initialized) on a queue. Finally, even when the child is ultimately executed locally the task must still be dequeued and the information necessary to run the child must be extracted from the closure.

Actually, similar operations are required when packaging the parent. But the key difference is that in most cases, even if the potential fork point were completely ignored, the parent would have to be packaged up anyway. In the programs I have studied, as well as those studied by other researchers, potential fork points invariably occur at calls where the parent's context must be saved, for example by saving the return address and live variables in a stack-allocated closure. When such calls are made with LTC no additional packaging is necessary so only the queuing and dequeuing bookkeeping remain. With LTC as implemented in Encore Mul-T this is accomplished by storing a single pointer, resulting in very low overhead in the common case when tasks are executed locally.

The three systems cited above all have a flavor of lazy task creation and succeed in reducing task creation overhead somewhat, but all require substantially more bookkeeping operations than LTC for the common case when tasks are executed locally. This is because all these systems incur the cost of packaging the child computation at potential fork points.

3   LTC Leads to Optimizations in Standard Scheduling Strategies

In the performance measurements of [6] and [7], LTC was observed to outperform LBP by a small but significant margin. However, further analysis of the two methods (reported in [5]) showed that LBP (and ETC as well) could be modified to take on some of the desirable features that come automatically with LTC. The result of implementing these optimizations is that, in the performance measurements of [5], LTC and LBP actually show similar results. (Despite this comparable performance, LTC is still the preferred method because of its desirable properties regarding deadlock, load balancing, and freedom from programmer involvement.)

As LBP and ETC are easy to implement and will likely see continued use, I would like to report on two of these optimizations. It is interesting to note that although these design changes actually *lengthen* the task creation sequence for LBP and ETC, they do in fact lead to better performance results for benchmark programs. Each is outlined below, with performance measurements summarized in Table 1.

(a) **Give scheduling preference to the child computation**. The first and most important improvement was motivated by the observation that blocked tasks are rare with lazy task creation but common in standard Mul-T. For every benchmark program run with either ETC or LBP, the number of blocked tasks was nearly the same as the number of tasks created; by contrast only a small percentage of tasks created with LTC would block. Because blocking is fairly expensive, reducing the number of blocked tasks is important to good performance.

The important observation in analyzing the frequency of blocked tasks is that typically the parent task can block waiting for the value of the child task, but not the other way around. If the child finishes executing before its value is needed by the parent, the parent will not block. Thus, giving scheduling preference to the child by starting it immediately is likely to lead to fewer blocked tasks.

As discussed earlier, this desirable scheduling behavior of favoring the child rather than the parent is an automatic feature of lazy task creation, since the producer begins executing the child code immediately after making a lazy future call. The parent code only begins to run later, after a steal operation or after the child code has completed. This "head-start" for the child explains the observed behavior that few tasks block with lazy task creation.

Halstead has discussed the desirability of favoring the child task [2, 1]; in the Concert Multilisp implementation of eager task creation the processor executing **future** always suspends the parent task and begins executing the child immediately.

However, because suspending the parent task at this time is more expensive than suspending the nascent child task, the opposite policy of queuing the child and continuing the parent was chosen for the original Mul-T implementation. As detailed in [5], favoring the parent in this way lowers task creation overhead by 13 instructions.

Experience has shown, though, that favoring the parent carries a high price tag in task blocking overhead. Because blocking a task costs 84 instructions and most tasks block, it makes more sense to pay the overhead of 13 instructions to queue the parent. The performance measurements detailed in [5] and summarized in Table 1 support the conclusion that favoring the child leads to greater efficiency; these experiments provide the first direct evidence I am aware of for this conclusion.

| | ETC | | | LBP | | | | |
| | Elapsed Time | | | Elapsed Time | | | Tasks Created | | |
Program	Old	New	(saved)	Old	New	(saved)	Old	New	(saved)
allpairs	1.39	1.33	(4%)	1.35	1.30	(3%)	11616	10964	(6%)
mst	10.22	9.43	(8%)	7.64	7.18	(6%)	151319	154216	(−1%)
tridiag	1.86	1.44	(23%)	.85	.75	(12%)	6671	4637	(30%)
abisort	3.35	2.49	(26%)	1.08	.92	(15%)	17862	16241	(9%)
rantree	.55	.41	(25%)	.18	.13	(28%)	3934	2564	(35%)
queens	1.10	.85	(23%)	.41	.29	(28%)	6318	2673	(58%)
fib	3.28	2.30	(30%)	.47	.27	(43%)	11291	3021	(73%)

Table 1. How scheduler changes improve performance for benchmark programs.

(b) Use double-ended task queues. Many researchers have noted the desirability of what I have called a BUSD (*B*readth-first *U*ntil *S*aturation, then *D*epth-first) partition, achieved by expanding the task tree breadth-first by spawning tasks until all processors are busy and then expanding the tree depth-first within the task on each processor. With ideal BUSD execution single processors execute task subtrees which are as large as possible. Besides allowing fewer tasks to be created, BUSD execution decreases communication costs by executing tasks locally rather than remotely. Thus BUSD execution is beneficial even with ETC, where all possible tasks are created.

With LTC, *oldest-first stealing* helps maximize BUSD behavior: picking the oldest task to steal leads to breadth-first expansion. With the conventional task queues used by ETC and LBP, oldest-first stealing corresponds to a FIFO queuing discipline. But FIFO operations have the drawback of higher expense compared with LIFO operations, leading to higher task creation overhead. Performance measurements reported in [5] and summarized in Table 1 show that the increased cost of FIFO operations for remote dequeuing are more than compensated by the advantage of executing larger subtrees locally.

Table 1 shows the combined effect of these optimizations for several benchmark programs, presenting the statistics for running each program in both "old" Mul-T (without the optimizations) and "new" Mul-T (with the optimizations), for both ETC and LBP. The parenthesized figures show the percent improvement in the new system compared to the old—performance of every program is improved for both partitioning strategies; between 4–30% with ETC and 3–43% with LBP. *([5] has more details.)*

4 A Look Ahead

These optimizations and analyses of partitioning strategies are all well and good, but where are the applications that can make use of them?

Much of the driving force behind the development of parallel hardware and software has come from the scientific computing community, where numerous applications exist which take too long to execute on even the fastest sequential processors. Parallel versions of many such applications have been built and executed, showing real speedup over sequential versions on uniprocessors. In some cases parallel machines are now being used for everyday execution of such problems.

In contrast, demanding symbolic applications have been much less visible. Usable, efficient parallel Lisp implementations have existed for at least a few years, yet I know of no examples where application developers have used them successfully for real problems. People tend to sniff out systems that fill a need they have; my conclusion is that parallel Lisp systems don't yet fill any existing needs.

Unless parallel Lisp is to be a solution looking for a problem, a real need must be demonstrated. A crucial challenge for future parallel Lisp researchers is to demonstrate useful speedup on an important problem. Specifically, can we find a compute-intensive symbolic application (or 5? or 10?) which is important enough that speeding it up would make a qualitative improvement in the ability to solve some problem? Many such scientific applications exist. If so, can we write a program in parallel Lisp which executes 20-50 times faster on a multiprocessor than an optimized sequential version on a top-of-the-line scientific workstation?

Another very important question is whether "real-world" symbolic applications are amenable to large-scale parallelism. The programs described in [5] are a step more realistic than the usual `fib`/`tak`/`boyer` group, but still do not reflect all the demands of real applications. For example, symbolic applications often use large DAGs to represent data, *e.g.* representing program code in compilers or representing relationships between objects in artificial intelligence programs. Typically sequential programs will repeatedly traverse the graphs, destructively modifying the nodes during each traversal. Performing such traversals in parallel requires the careful addition of explicit inter-task synchronization, making program development and debugging much more difficult. Also, the partitioning methods discussed here work much less well when programs contain explicit synchronization.

On small-scale machines such complications may sometimes be avoided by coarse-grained partitions, as for example by compiling several files in parallel or compiling all procedures within a file in parallel, but on larger machines the partition must become finer-grained and the complications will be less easily avoidable.

A specific example of these problems is the **speech** benchmark used to measure Mul-T performance in [6, 7]. The initial version of this program had a lot of parallelism but ended up doing much more work than necessary. Subsequent re-implementations reduced the work required substantially but also resulted in a more complex control structure. The latter version required explicit synchronization and was not at all amenable to dynamic partitioning.

My personal conclusion after being immersed in this research is that to achieve good performance of real applications on large-scale multiprocessors the programmer will tend to need code for explicit partitioning and explicit synchronization. If the parallel Lisp version of our hypothetical application can in fact be made to execute 20-50 times faster than its sequential competition, we must then evaluate what price has been paid in coding it.

I believe that the challenges outlined in this section should be the primary focus of future research in parallel symbolic computing.

References

1. R. Halstead, "An Assessment of Multilisp: Lessons from Experience," *Int'l. J. of Parallel Programming* 15:6, Dec. 1986, pp. 459–501.
2. R. Halstead, New Ideas in Parallel Lisp: Language Design, Implementation, and Programming Tools," in T. Ito and R. Halstead, eds., *Proceedings of U.S./Japan Workshop on Parallel Lisp* (Springer-Verlag Lecture Notes in Computer Science 441), Sendai, Japan, June 1989, pp. 2–57.
3. S. Jagannathan and J. Philbin, "A Foundation for an Efficient Multi-Threaded Scheme System," *Proceedings of ACM Symposium on Lisp and Functional Programming*, June 1992, pp. 345–357.
4. D. Kranz, R. Halstead, and E. Mohr, "Mul-T, A High-Performance Parallel Lisp", *ACM SIGPLAN '89 Conference on Programming Language Design and Implementation*, Portland, OR, June 1989, pp. 81–90.
5. E. Mohr, "Dynamic Partitioning of Parallel Lisp Programs," Ph.D. Thesis, Yale University Technical Report YALEU/DCS/RR-869, May 1991.
6. E. Mohr, D. Kranz, and R. Halstead, "Lazy Task Creation: A Technique for Increasing the Granularity of Parallel Programs," *Proceedings of ACM Symposium on Lisp and Functional Programming*, June 1990, pp. 185–197.
7. E. Mohr, D. Kranz, and R. Halstead, "Lazy Task Creation: A Technique for Increasing the Granularity of Parallel Programs," *IEEE Trans. on Parallel and Distributed Systems* 2:3, July 1991, pp. 264–280.
8. J. Pehoushek and J. Weening, "Low-cost process creation and dynamic partitioning in Qlisp," in T. Ito and R. Halstead, eds., *Proceedings of U.S./Japan Workshop on Parallel Lisp* (Springer-Verlag Lecture Notes in Computer Science 441), Sendai, Japan, June 1989, pp. 182–199.
9. M. Vandevoorde and E. Roberts, "WorkCrews: An Abstraction for Controlling Parallelism," *Int'l. J. of Parallel Programming* 17:4, August 1988, pp. 347–366.

A Message Passing Implementation of Lazy Task Creation

Marc Feeley

Dépt. d'informatique et de recherche opérationnelle
Université de Montréal
Montréal, Québec, CANADA
feeley@iro.umontreal.ca

Abstract. This paper describes an implementation technique for Multilisp's `future` construct aimed at large shared-memory multiprocessors. The technique is a variant of lazy task creation. The original implementation of lazy task creation described in [Mohr, 1991] relies on efficient shared memory to distribute tasks between processors. In contrast, we propose a task distribution method based on a message passing paradigm. Its main advantages are that it is simpler to implement, has a lower cost for locally run tasks, and allows full caching of the stack on cache incoherent machines. Benchmarks on a 32 processor BBN TC2000 show that our method is more efficient than the original implementation by as much as a factor of 2.

1 Introduction

Multilisp [Halstead, 1985] extends the Scheme [IEEE Std 1178-1990, 1991] programming language with a simple and elegant parallel programming paradigm. Parallelism is specified explicitly in the program by the use of the `future` special form. The expression

$$(\texttt{future } expr)$$

is called a *future* and *expr* is its *body*. Parallelism follows a tasking model. When a task evaluates a future, it spawns a *child* task to evaluate the future's body. The *parent* task then starts executing the future's continuation. Thus, concurrency exists between the evaluation of the body and the continuation.

Conceptually, the value returned to the continuation is the value eventually computed for the body by the child task. This paradox is usually avoided by using a *placeholder* object to represent the body's eventual value. The placeholder is initially empty and is assigned a value (is *determined*) only when the child is done. When a placeholder is passed to a strict operation, such as `car` and the predicate position of an `if`, the placeholder must be dereferenced (*touched*) to obtain the desired value. If the placeholder is not yet determined, the current task is suspended until the placeholder is determined by the child.

In addition, Multilisp uses a shared-memory model. This means that tasks can directly access any piece of data regardless of where it was created.

Eager task creation (ETC) is a straightforward implementation of futures which has been used in several parallel Lisp systems [Halstead, 1984; Steinberg et al., 1986; Goldman and Gabriel, 1988; Miller, 1988; Zorn et al., 1988; Swanson et al., 1988; Kranz et al., 1989]. The evaluation of a future immediately creates a heap allocated task object to represent the child task and makes it available to all processors by enqueuing it on a global queue of runnable tasks: the work queue. Task objects are essentially composed of a continuation which represents the task's state. This continuation is initially set up to evaluate the future's body and then determine the appropriate placeholder with the result. When a processor becomes idle it removes a task from the work queue and resumes it by invoking its continuation. To reduce contention and improve locality, the work queue is usually distributed across the machine and by default processors spawn tasks and resume tasks from their local work queue. When an idle processor has an empty work queue, it must obtain the task to resume from some other processor's work queue. This task transfer between the thief and victim processors is called a steal. ETC is illustrated in Fig. 1 (the dark circles represent tasks).

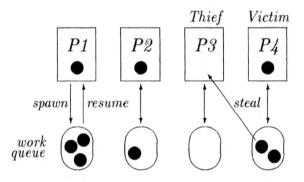

Fig. 1. Eager task creation.

The main drawback of ETC is the high task management overhead. Assuming that each task created eventually runs and terminates, the following task management operations are required for every task:

At task spawning:
1. Creating the task object and the placeholder.
2. Creating a closure for the future's body.
3. Enqueuing the task on the work queue (which requires locking and then unlocking the queue).

At task resumption:
4. Dequeuing the task from the work queue (again locking and unlocking the queue).
5. Invoking the task's continuation.

At task termination:

6. Determining the placeholder (which must also be locked and then unlocked to avoid races with tasks touching the placeholder).

7. Transferring the tasks suspended on the placeholder to the work queue.

The total cost of these operations can easily be in the hundreds of machine instructions. The performance of existing implementations of ETC seem to confirm this. The Mul-T system was carefully designed to minimize the cost of ETC [Kranz et al., 1989] and it takes roughly 130 machine instructions per task on the Encore Multimax (the actual cost depends on the number of closed variables, their location etc.). Other systems have an even higher cost (both portable standard Lisp on the BBN butterfly GP1000 [Swanson et al., 1988] and QLisp on an Alliant FX/8 [Goldman and Gabriel, 1988] take roughly 1400 instructions).

Due to this high cost, the overhead of exposing parallelism (i.e. of adding futures to a sequential program) will depend strongly on the task granularity. The performance of fine grain programs will be poor due to the relatively small proportion of the total time spent doing useful work.

2 Lazy Task Creation

Lazy task creation (LTC) is an alternative implementation of futures proposed in [Kranz et al., 1989] and subsequently implemented and studied by Eric Mohr on an Encore Multimax [Mohr, 1991]. The implementation of LTC described in this section is essentially that used by Mohr and will be called the *shared-memory* (SM) protocol because it assumes the existence of a global shared memory. LTC reduces the cost of evaluating a future by postponing, and in many cases completely avoiding, the creation of the task. In essence, a task is only created when some other processor needs work. LTC achieves this by adopting a stack-like scheduling policy which, in the absence of idle processors, produces the same order of execution as the sequential version of the program (i.e. with the futures removed). The evaluation of the future's body is immediately started and the future's continuation, which logically corresponds to the parent task, is suspended. As shown in Fig. 2, each processor maintains its suspended continuations in a stack-like data structure called the *lazy task queue* (LTQ)[1]. When the body's evaluation is done, the most recently suspended continuation on the LTQ is removed and invoked. This is necessarily the continuation of the future corresponding to the body. Note that there is no need to create and determine a placeholder since the continuation can directly consume the value returned by the body.

In LTC, a steal is performed by first removing the oldest continuation from the victim's LTQ and then constructing the corresponding task object and placeholder, and transferring the task to the thief. For proper linkage between the stolen task and its child, the thief must invoke the stolen task's continuation

---

[1] This structure is really a double-ended queue which supports push, pop, and steal operations.

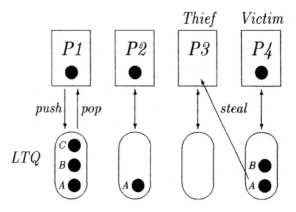

Fig. 2. Lazy task creation.

with the newly created placeholder. The placeholder must also be stored in the stolen task's child so that it can get determined correctly. Referring to Fig. 2, the placeholder created by *P3* when it steals continuation *A* must be "attached" to continuation *B*. A reference to this placeholder, which is called the child's *goal* placeholder, can be stored at a location preallocated for the victim because there is exactly one goal placeholder per LTQ. When the child's continuation (i.e. *B*) returns, the goal placeholder must get determined with the returned value. Note that attaching the placeholder to the child's continuation is important to allow subsequent steals.

Stealing the oldest rather than the youngest task has the following benefits:

1. It tends to reduce the number of steals because the older tasks generally contain more work (the thief will thus stay busy longer before its next steal). This is especially true in programs using divide-and-conquer parallel algorithms. If the algorithm is well balanced, the amount of work in the stolen task will be comparable to the total work left on the victim's LTQ.
2. Access to the LTQ is more efficient because the two ends of the LTQ can be accessed concurrently. The victim can push a continuation to its LTQ while a thief is simultaneously stealing a task.

The stack-like scheduling policy of LTC permits an inexpensive implementation of the continuation push and continuation pop operations. The key idea is that the continuations do not have to be copied or moved from the stack. The LTQ is really a double-ended queue of pointers into the continuation stack. Figure 3 shows the state of the stack and LTQ for *P4* before and after the steal (note that the links between the stack frames are purely conceptual). Initially, the LTQ's head and tail pointers (i.e. HEAD and TAIL) are equal and a pointer to the bottom of the stack is put under HEAD. A useful invariant is that a pointer to the bottom of the LTQ's oldest continuation is always under HEAD. The procedure linkage mechanism pushes and pops activation frames from the stack in the normal way. Each frame contains a return address to be jumped to when the frame is deallocated from the stack. When a future is evaluated, the continuation is pushed by simply pushing a pointer to the current activation frame on the LTQ (this increments the **TAIL** pointer). Popping a continuation, which is performed after the execution of the future's body, needs to be done carefully because another processor may be simultaneously stealing the same continuation. If the LTQ is not empty (i.e. **TAIL** $\neq$ **HEAD**), **TAIL** is decremented and the continuation on the stack invoked with the body's value. If the LTQ is empty, it means that the future's continuation was stolen so the body's value is used to determine the task's goal placeholder and the processor goes idle. Figure 4 gives the C-flavored pseudocode for the evaluation of (**f** (**future** (**g x**))) when the SM protocol is used. The boxed section represents a critical section that must be performed atomically with respect to the steal operation.

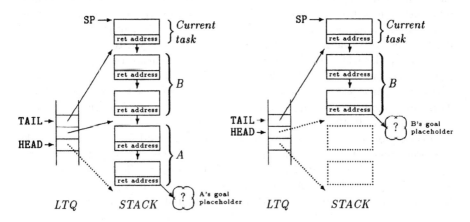

Fig. 3. The lazy task queue before and after a steal.

```
*++TAIL = SP;              Push future's continuation
val = g( x );             Execute future's body
if (TAIL != HEAD)
   {                      Attempt to pop the continuation
   TAIL--;
      f( val );           Execute future's continuation
   }
else
   determine( goal, val ); Determine goal placeholder and go idle
```

Fig. 4. SM protocol's pseudocode for the evaluation of (f (future (g x))).

The thief processors must similarly test the LTQ for an available continuation. If one is available the thief takes a copy of the appropriate frames directly into its stack (**HEAD[0]** and **HEAD[1]** are the boundaries of the section to copy), stores the goal placeholder with the child, and then increments HEAD. Before it can proceed the thief must figure out how to resume the frames it has obtained, in other words where is the code of the continuation. The code that needs to be executed is the one following the continuation pop sequence. The simplest approach is to save this address on the LTQ when the continuation is pushed. Note that this address could be computed from the return address passed to the future's body (for example, the end of the continuation pop sequence could be a constant offset away). Unfortunately, the thief has no way of finding this return address unless severe restrictions are put on the procedure calling convention, the format of frames, and the locations where return addresses can be stored[2].

The total overhead (in number of memory operations) of a non-stolen future is thus the cost of one continuation push and one successful continuation pop: 4 memory writes (2 to the LTQ and 2 to TAIL), 4 memory reads (1 of HEAD and 3 of TAIL), and 2 lock operations. The lock operations, which are expensive on some machines, can be avoided by using "software lock" algorithms such as [Peterson, 1981]. Algorithms specially tailored for LTC are described in [Mohr, 1991] and [Feeley, 1993a]. In addition, TAIL can be cached in a register since it is only mutated by the LTQ's owner. Another trick is to indicate that a continuation is no longer available by clearing the corresponding entry in the LTQ. This allows thief processors to check if the LTQ is empty by testing HEAD[1] = 0. These optimizations bring down the cost to: 3 memory writes to the LTQ and 1 memory read of HEAD.

Because of its special nature, the LTQ can't be used for reactivating tasks that were suspended on placeholders. For this purpose it is better if each processor has a separate ready queue that holds task objects. Both the ready queue and the LTQ must be searched by thief processors but it is preferable to check the ready queue first since less work will be required to obtain a task.

3   Hidden Cost of Sharing the Stack

An unfortunate requirement of the SM protocol is that all processors must have access to the LTQ and stack. Making these structures accessible to all processors has a cost because it precludes the use of the more efficient caching policies on machines that do not have coherent caches. The stack and the LTQ only need to be read by thief processors so they can be cached (by their owner) using the write-through caching policy. This however is not as efficient as the copy-back caching policy normally used in single processor implementations of Lisp. For typical Lisp programs, caching of the stack will likely be an important factor since the stack is one of the most intensely accessed data structures.

But how large is the performance loss due to a suboptimal caching policy? To better understand the importance of caching on performance, the memory access behavior of a few benchmark programs was analyzed (the Gabriel benchmarks were used in addition to a few medium to large sequential programs and 12

---

[2] For example, return addresses can't be put in a register, even temporarily, because the thief could not access them.

parallel programs). The run time of a program can be broken down into the time spent accessing data in memory and the time spent on "pure computation". Memory accesses can further be broken down into: accesses to the stack and accesses to the heap. Thus, a program is described by the three parameters S (stack), H (heap), and C (pure computation) which represent the proportion of total run time spent on each category of instructions ($S + H + C = 1$).

The measurement of S, H, and C was done by running the programs on a cache-incoherent NUMA shared-memory multiprocessor (the BBN butterfly TC2000) with the Gambit system [Feeley and Miller, 1990]. All these programs were run on a single processor. The run time of each program was measured in three different settings. The first run was with the stack and heap located in non-cached local memory. The second run was with the stack located in remote memory (on another processor) so that each access to the stack would cost more. The final run was with the heap in remote memory. The three run times are respectively T, T_S, and T_H. The relative cost of a remote access with respect to a local access is 4.2 on the TC2000 so we obtain the following system of linear equations

$$
\begin{aligned}
S &+ H &+ C &= 1 \\
4.2S &+ H &+ C &= T_S/T \\
S &+ 4.2H &+ C &= T_H/T
\end{aligned}
$$

This system is easily solved to find the value of S, H, and C. The results are given in the plot in Fig. 5. Each program is a point in S-H space. The value for pure computation is $C = 1 - S - H$.

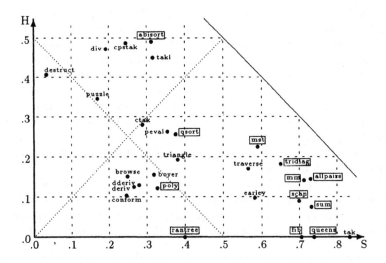

Fig. 5. Relative importance of stack and heap accesses on TC2000.

A few interesting observations can be made from this figure. Firstly, the proportion of time spent accessing memory is high. Most programs spend more time accessing memory than doing pure computation (i.e. all the programs above the $S + H = .5$ line). This is reasonable since symbolic applications typically do a lot of data movement. Secondly, most of the programs access the stack more often than the heap (i.e. all the programs below the $S = H$ line). This tendency is even more pronounced for the parallel benchmarks (the boxed names in the plot). This is to be expected since the majority of these parallel benchmarks are based on recursive divide-and-conquer algorithms.

The high S value of the programs is a sign that the access time to the stack is an important factor in overall performance.

4 The Message Passing Protocol

The message passing (MP) protocol implements LTC in such a way as to allow full caching of the stack and LTQ. In the MP protocol, the thief initiates a steal by sending a *steal request* message to the victim. The victim eventually gets interrupted and calls its *steal request handler*. This handler checks the LTQ and, if a continuation is available, recreates the oldest task and sends it back to the thief. Otherwise a failure message is sent back to the thief which must then try stealing from some other processor. The victim then resumes the interrupted computation.

There are several advantages to this protocol. Firstly, it relies less on an efficient shared memory. The stack and LTQ are private to each processor and can be cached with copy-back caching since only one processor can access them.

Secondly, it is possible to handle the race condition between the continuation pop and steal operations more efficiently than the SM protocol because all operations on the LTQ are performed by its owner. Preventing the race is as simple as inhibiting interrupts for the duration of the continuation pop sequence. This can be achieved by adding a pair of instructions around the sequence that disables and then reenables interrupts. The method used by Gambit is to detect interrupts via polling and to never poll for interrupts inside the continuation pop sequence. There are other methods that have no direct overhead. For example, in the *instruction interpretation* method [Appel, 1989] the interrupt handler checks to see if the interrupted instruction is in an "uninterruptible" section (i.e. a continuation pop sequence). If it is, the rest of the section is interpreted by the interrupt handler before the interrupt is serviced. Other zero cost techniques are described in [Feeley, 1993b].

Thirdly, it is no longer necessary to save the future's return address on the LTQ. Instead, the return address can be found in the first stack frame above the stolen continuation[3]. For this to work properly, it is important that the interrupt handler be called as a subproblem (so that the return address will have been

---

[3] This is done by scanning the stack upwards until the first return address is found. This assumes that return addresses are specially tagged or at least can be distinguished from other object pointers.

moved to the stack if it was in a register at the moment of the interrupt). This is fairly easy to do when the system detects interrupts through polling because the call to the handler is a subproblem call. For a system that uses hardware interrupts it is more complex but still possible.

Finally, the check for an empty LTQ in the continuation pop sequence can be avoided. The trick is to have the victim change the return address of the stolen task's child at the moment of the steal so that the child will branch directly to the right place when it returns. Locating this return address on the stack was described in the previous paragraph. In its place is put the address of a stub that determines the goal placeholder and causes the processor to go idle. The continuation pop sequence is only executed if the LTQ is not empty.

The pseudocode for the MP protocol for evaluating (f (future (g x))) is given in Fig. 6. The cost per non-stolen future is thus only 2 memory writes to copy-back cached memory.

```
*++TAIL = SP;      Push future's continuation
val = g( x );      Execute future's body
TAIL--;            Pop the continuation
f( val );          Execute future's continuation
```

Fig. 6. MP protocol's pseudocode for the evaluation of (f (future (g x))).

5   Potential Problems

The most serious problem with the MP protocol is that the thief must busy wait for the reply to its steal request. The total time wasted, the *steal latency*, is the sum of the time needed by the victim to detect the steal request (T_{detect}) and the time to create the stolen task and send it back (T_{steal}). Little can be done to decrease T_{steal} but if interrupts are detected with polling, T_{detect} can be decreased by polling more frequently. However, this increases the cost of polling so in practice some balance must be found between these two costs.

A related problem is that the speed at which work gets distributed to the processors is dependent on the steal latency. Distributing work quickly is crucial to fully exploit the program's parallelism. It is especially important at the beginning of the program (or more precisely a transition from sequential to parallel execution) because all processors are idle except one.

Finally, the cost of failed steal requests is a concern because the victim pays a high price for getting interrupted but this serves no useful purpose. The victim might get requests at such a high rate that it does nothing else but process steal requests. For example, a continuous stream of steal requests will be received by the victim if it is executing sequential code and all other processors are idle. The problem here is that processors are too "secretive". No indication of the

LTQ's state is shared with other processors so the only way for a thief to know if the victim has some work is to send it a steal request. A simple solution is to have each processor regularly save out HEAD and TAIL in a predetermined shared memory location. Before attempting a steal, the thief checks the copy of HEAD and TAIL in shared memory to see if a task might be available. This snapshot only reflects a previous state of the LTQ but, if it is updated frequently enough, its correlation to the current state will be high. If the snapshot indicates a non-empty LTQ it is thus likely that the steal attempt will succeed. Gambit always keeps HEAD in shared memory so it does not need to be saved out (this does not affect performance because the victim accesses HEAD infrequently). TAIL is saved out on every interrupt poll.

6   Results

To evaluate and compare the SM and MP protocols, some experiments were conducted on the BBN butterfly TC2000. This shared-memory multiprocessor has incoherent-caches and a non-uniform memory access cost. Accesses to the cache are 3.8 times faster than to local memory and accesses to local memory are 4.2 times slower than local memory.

Each parallel benchmark program was compiled with Gambit[4] with each protocol and then the run time was measured for several executions with 1 to 32 processors. Polling was done at a rate sufficient to make T_{detect} roughly comparable to T_{steal} (the instructions added for polling caused an average overhead of 12%). The stack and LTQ were write-through cached for the SM protocol and copy-back cached for the MP protocol. A description of the programs and some comments about their performance can be found in Appendix A.

Figure 7 contains the speedup curves for these programs. Speedup is expressed relatively to the sequential version of the program (i.e. with futures and touches removed) run with a copy-back cached stack. This means that the value of the speedup on one processor is the inverse of the overhead of exposing parallelism with futures (O_{expose}). For the MP protocol, the highest overhead (21%) is for **queens**. The overhead is much higher for the SM protocol which has a run time larger by a factor of two. This big difference is due mostly to the caching policy but, because this program is fine grained, the cost of the continuation push and pop operations is also an important factor. Note that the cache on the TC2000 is really slow when compared to the caches of modern processors (which are easily 20 to 50 times faster than main memory). We expect a much larger difference between the SM and MP protocols on future processors.

The speedup of the SM protocol is consistently lower than that of the MP protocol. For each protocol, the speedup curve starts off at $1/O_{expose}$ on 1 processor (for their respective O_{expose}) and as the number of processors increases the curves tend to get closer. Programs with good speedup characteristics (such as **fib** and **sum**) maintain a roughly constant distance between the speedup curves.

---

[4] A back-end generating C code was used.

In other words, the ratio of their run time stays close to the ratio of their O_{expose}. On the other hand, programs with poor speedup characteristics (e.g. mst and qsort) have speedup curves that become colinear at a high number of processors. This can be explained by the progressive increase of administrative work being performed by the program. Suboptimally caching the stack and LTQ does not affect the administrative costs. The relative importance of suboptimally caching the stack will thus decrease as the programs spend more and more time being idle and/or accessing remote memory.

A more detailed analysis of the SM and MP protocols, including experiments on a 90 processor BBN GP1000, can be found in [Feeley, 1993a].

7 Conclusion

We have proposed a message-passing protocol for implementing lazy task creation. The performance of this protocol was compared with the original protocol which relies on an efficient shared memory. Experiments on a 32 processor cache-incoherent machine show that the overhead of exposing parallelism with the future construct is typically less than 20% when using the message-passing protocol. This is much better than the shared-memory protocol which can have an overhead as high as a factor of 2. This difference is mostly due to the fact that the message-passing protocol can cache the stack in the most efficient way (copy-back caching) whereas the shared-memory protocol must use write-through caching. The experiments also indicate that the latency for detecting steal request messages is not critical. A latency comparable to the task creation cost is sufficient to get good performance.

105

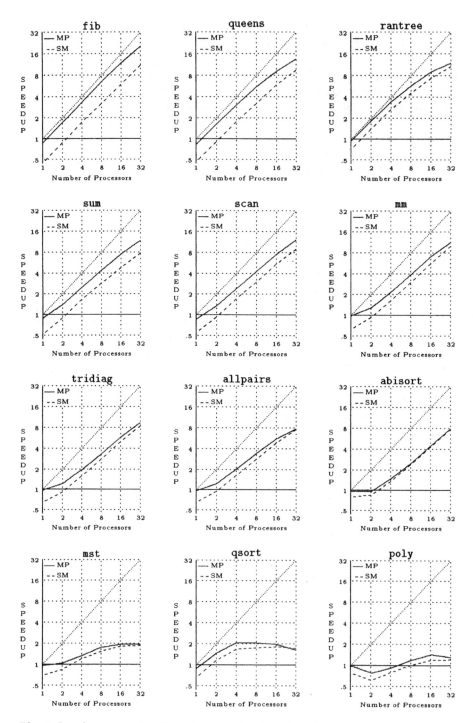

Fig. 7. Speedup curves for MP and SM protocols on TC2000.

A   Description of Parallel Benchmarks

The benchmark programs can be roughly classified in three groups, according to their speedup characteristics.

1. **Parallel and compute bound.** These programs do not access memory. The speedup curve is initially close to linear speedup, and gradually distances itself from it as the number of processors increases (in other words the first derivative of the curve starts at 1 and the second derivative is negative). The flattening out of the curve as the number of processors increases is consistent with Amdahl's law.

   - fib – Compute (fib 25) using the doubly recursive algorithm.
   - queens – Compute the number of solutions to the 10-queens problem.
   - rantree – Traverse a random binary tree with 32768 nodes.

2. **Parallel and memory accessing.** These programs access memory to various extents. The speedup curves for these programs is "S" like (i.e. the second derivative is initially positive and then negative). A good example is abisort. The initial bend in the curve is explained by the increase in cost for accessing shared user data which is distributed evenly across the machine. A memory access has a probability of $\frac{n-1}{n}$ of being to remote memory (where n is the number of processors), so the average cost of an access to shared user data is $\frac{L+R(n-1)}{n}$, where R is the cost of a remote memory access and L is the cost of a local memory access. The bend in the curve is consequently more pronounced for programs which spend a high proportion of their time accessing the heap (e.g. abisort, allpairs, mm, and tridiag).

   - abisort – Sort 16384 integers using the adaptive bitonic sort algorithm [Bilardi and Nicolau, 1989].
   - allpairs – Compute the shortest path between all pairs of 117 nodes using a parallel version of Floyd's algorithm.
   - mm – Multiply two matrices of integers (50 by 50).
   - scan – Compute the parallel prefix sum of a vector of 32768 integers (in place).
   - sum – Compute the sum of a vector of 32768 integers.
   - tridiag – Solve a tridiagonal system of 32767 equations.

3. **Poorly parallel.** These are programs whose algorithms don't contain much parallelism or that contain a form of parallelism that is not well suited for LTC. The speedup curves for these programs are mostly flat. The curve generally starts going down after a certain number of processors because no more parallelism can be exploited but other costs, such as contention and memory interconnect traffic, increase.

   - mst – Compute the minimum spanning tree of a 1000 node graph using a parallel version of Prim's algorithm.
   - poly – Compute the square of a 200 term polynomial of x (represented as a list of coefficients) and evaluate the resulting polynomial for a certain value of x.
   - qsort – Sort a list of 1000 integers using a parallel version of the Quicksort algorithm.

The source code for these programs is available via anonymous FTP as the file /pub/parallele/multilisp-bench.tar on the FTP server ftp.iro.umontreal.ca.

References

[Appel, 1989] A. W. Appel. Allocation without locking. *Software Practice and Experience*, 19(7):703–705, July 1989.

[Bilardi and Nicolau, 1989] G. Bilardi and A. Nicolau. Adaptive bitonic sorting: An optimal parallel algorithm for shared-memory machines. *SIAM Journal of Computing*, 12(2):216–228, April 1989.

[Feeley and Miller, 1990] M. Feeley and J. S. Miller. A parallel virtual machine for efficient Scheme compilation. In *Proceedings of the 1990 ACM Conference on Lisp and Functional Programming*, Nice, France, June 1990.

[Feeley, 1993a] M. Feeley. *An Efficient and General Implementation of Futures on Large Scale Shared-Memory Multiprocessors*. PhD thesis, Brandeis University Department of Computer Science, 1993. Available as publication #869 from département d'informatique et recherche opérationnelle de l'Université de Montréal.

[Feeley, 1993b] M. Feeley. Polling efficiently on stock hardware. In *Proceedings of the 1993 ACM Conference on Functional Programming Languages and Computer Architecture*, 1993.

[Goldman and Gabriel, 1988] R. Goldman and R. P. Gabriel. Preliminary results with the initial implementation of Qlisp. In *Conference Record of the 1988 ACM Conference on Lisp and Functional Programming*, pages 143–152, Snowbird, UT, July 1988.

[Halstead, 1984] R. Halstead. Implementation of Multilisp: Lisp on a multiprocessor. In *Conference Record of the 1984 ACM Symposium on Lisp and Functional Programming*, pages 9–17, Austin, TX, August 1984.

[Halstead, 1985] R. Halstead. Multilisp: A language for concurrent symbolic computation. In *ACM Trans. on Prog. Languages and Systems*, pages 501–538, October 1985.

[IEEE Std 1178-1990, 1991] IEEE Std 1178-1990. *IEEE Standard for the Scheme Programming Language*. Institute of Electrical and Electronic Engineers, Inc., New York, NY, 1991.

[Kranz et al., 1989] D. Kranz, R. Halstead, and E. Mohr. Mul-T: A high-performance parallel Lisp. In *ACM SIGPLAN '89 Conf. on Programming Language Design and Implementation*, pages 81–90, June 1989.

[Miller, 1988] J. S. Miller. Implementing a Scheme-based parallel processing system. *International Journal of Parallel Processing*, 17(5), October 1988.

[Mohr, 1991] E. Mohr. *Dynamic Partitioning of Parallel Lisp Programs*. PhD thesis, Yale University Department of Computer Science, October 1991.

[Peterson, 1981] G. L. Peterson. Myths about the mutual exclusion problem. *Information Processing Letters*, 12(3):115–116, 1981.

[Steinberg et al., 1986] S. Steinberg, D. Allen, L. Bagnall, and C. Scott. The Butterfly Lisp system. In *Proc. 1986 AAAI*, volume 2, Philadelphia, PA, August 1986.

[Swanson et al., 1988] M. Swanson, R. Kessler, and G. Lindstrom. An implementation of portable standard Lisp on the BBN Butterfly. In *Conference Record of the 1988 ACM Conference on Lisp and Functional Programming*, pages 132–141, Snowbird, UT, July 1988.

[Zorn et al., 1988] B. Zorn, P. Hilfinger, K. Ho, J. Larus, and L. Semenzato. Features for multiprocessing in SPUR Lisp. Technical Report Report UCB/CSD 88/406, University of California, Computer Science Division (EECS), March 1988.

P-Continuation Based Implementation of PaiLisp Interpreter

Takayasu Ito and Tomohiro Seino

Department of Computer and Mathematical Sciences
Graduate School of Information Sciences
Tohoku University [Aobayama Campus]
Sendai 980, JAPAN

Abstract. P-continuation is an extension of Scheme continuation into concurrency, which was introduced in PaiLisp. This paper explains in details the implementation of PaiLisp interpreter based on P-continuations. PaiLisp is a parallelized Scheme based on shared memory architecture, and it is a superset of Multilisp with many concurreny constructs. One of the major contributions of PaiLisp efforts is in extraction of its kernel language PaiLisp-Kernel, which is defined to be Scheme plus four concurrency constructs spawn,suspend,call/cc,exlambda, where "call/cc" is an extended call/cc to create P-continuation,a parallel continuation introduced in PaiLisp. [Ito-Matusi 90] shows that all the PaiLisp constructs can be defined using PaiLisp-Kernel.This paper explains the PaiLisp interpreter implemented on a shared memory machine Alliant FX/80 with eight processor elements.The PaiLisp interpreter is featured in use of P-continuation to realise the concurrency constructs of PaiLisp. Experimental results to evaluate the performance of PaiLisp system are also given using several Lisp benchmark programs. Appendix contains a brief description of an experimental PaiLisp compiler.

1 Introduction

PaiLisp is a parallelized Scheme based on shared memory architectures. PaiLisp has been designed to include all the major parallel Lisp constructs of Multilisp [Hals84] and Qlisp[GabM84] in addition to some parallelized Lisp constructs which come from our theoretical studies[ItoW83,ItoTW86] and our experiences of parallel Lisp interpreter on a shared memory machine PAI-68K[ItoMK87]. The language specification of PaiLisp is given in [ItoM90], in which it is shown that the meanings of all the concurrency constructs of PaiLisp can be described using PaiLisp-Kernel, a small kernel language of PaiLisp. The extraction of PaiLisp-Kernel has been one of the major contributions of PaiLisp efforts. PaiLisp-Kernel is defined to be Scheme plus four concurrency constructs $\{spawn, suspend, call/cc, exlambda\}$, where call/cc is an extended call/cc to capture and create P-continuation, a parallel continuation. The expressive power of PaiLisp-Kernel comes from the additional expressive power of P-continuation and PaiLisp call/cc, which enable us to describe how to kill and resume executions of PaiLisp processes. In the sequential Scheme it is known that Scheme continuation and its call/cc provide very powerful control structures to express semantics of various control structures in traditional sequential programming languages like jump, non-local exits, coroutine, backtracking,etc. The P-continuation and PaiLisp call/cc, which are natural extension of Scheme continuation and call/cc into concurrency, also provide powerful control structures to express various control structures in parallel Lisp processes, as is shown in [ItoM90]. In sequential programming languages the continuation-passing style (CPS) has been applied in various implementations of their interpreters and compilers successfully. The P-continuation based implementations of PaiLisp interpreter of this paper may be taken as a first step of interpreting and compiling parallel languages with P-continuations, though a systematic and theoretical study is needed to justify this hope. In Section 2 we explain an overview of PaiLisp and P-continuation, including PaiLisp-Kernel, PaiLisp call/cc and its lightweight version call/ep. Section 3 gives the details of PaiLisp-Kernel interpreter, after explaining an overview of the PaiLisp interpreter. Section 4 explains the details of P-continuation based implementations of various PaiLisp constructs to support concurrency and parallelism. Section 5 presents some experimental results to evaluate the performance of PaiLisp interpreter on Alliant FX/80 with eight processor elements,and the effects of introducing several concurrency constructs into PaiLisp are evaluated. Section 6 concludes with some remarks. Appendix contains a brief description of PaiLisp compiler being developed.

2　PaiLisp and P-Continuation

In this section we explain about the constructs of PaiLisp-Kernel, major constructs of PaiLisp, and P-continuation and its stack mechanism.

2.1　Outline of PaiLisp

PaiLisp is a parallelized Scheme based on shared memory architectures. The the extended constructs of PaiLisp to support concurrency and parallelism were originally introduced from the following standpoints:

1) parallelized basic Lisp constructs
   Initially one of the major aims of parallel Lisp languages and systems was in parallel executions of Lisp programs in artificial intelligence and symbolic computing to achieve high execution efficiency through parallel computation. The simplest and most straightforward approach was to parallelized all the basic Lisp functions and mechanisms which were considered theoretically in [ItoW83] and [ItoTW86]. From this standpoint there were introduced the parallelized Lisp constructs such as parallel evaluations of functional arguments, parallel and/or, parallel conditional expressions, parallel mapcar, etc..

2) constructs for concurrent Lisp programming
   Multilisp [Hals84] is well-known by intruducing the 'future' construct as an

attractive and useful construct in parallel Lisp programming. Qlisp [GabM84], which is a queue-based multiprocessing Lisp, introduced several concurrency constructs such as QLET, QLAMBDA and QCATCH into Common Lisp, among which QLAMBDA is the most important construct introduced in Qlisp. To support concurrent and parallel Lisp programming PaiLisp introdues 'future' of Multilisp, 'exlambda', which is an adaptation of Qlisp's qlambda, and several new constructs like 'par','spawn','suspend' and an extended 'call/cc' to capture P-continuations.

Scheme was favored over Common Lisp as a base language of a concurrent and parallel Lisp language, since it is a compact and static language with clear semantics. The current PaiLisp has been designed as a superset of Multilisp to include all the major parallel Lisp constructs in Multilisp and Qlisp in addition to some parallelized Lisp constructs mentioned above. One of the major contributions of PaiLisp research efforts is in extraction of its kernel language PaiLisp-Kernel, which is a small kernel of PaiLisp to be defined as Scheme plus four concurrency constructs {*spawn, suspend, call/cc, exlambda*}, where "call/cc" is an extension of Scheme's call/cc into concurrency. We call this extended call/cc as PaiLisp call/cc, and the parallel continuation created by PaiLisp call/cc as P-continuation. In [ItoM90] it is shown that PaiLisp-Kernel is actually a kernel language of PaiLisp, that is, all the PaiLisp constructs can be described using PaiLisp-Kernel. PaiLisp is a parallel Lisp language for a parallel machine with shared memory architecture, and we may understand that in PaiLisp sequential Lisp programs which share data and environments for variables communicate each other through those shared data and environments to perform computation in parallel. In PaiLisp a parallel process may be considered as a collection of individual sequential Lisp processes. Each PaiLisp process can be specified by

1) its process identity (Process-ID)
2) its execution state {*Run, Killed, Suspended, Waiting*}
3) its current value, that is, the value computed up to the current point
4) its continuation, that is, the rest of computation following at the current point of the computation.
5) its status of exclusive resources.

PaiLisp should possess the abilities to create, suspend, resume and kill PaiLisp processes. PaiLisp-Kernel is an extension of Scheme with spawn, suspend, call/cc and exlambda, and it possesses these abilities to control PaiLisp processes. PaiLisp with these abilities is actually shown to be universal as a parallel Lisp language in the sense that all the PaiLisp constructs can be defined by PaiLisp-Kernel. Roughly speaking, we may say as follows:

```
{PaiLisp-Kernel} =    {Scheme}
                  + {spawn,suspend,call/cc,exlambda}
{PaiLisp} =    {PaiLisp-Kernel}
            + {pcall,par,future,par-or,par-and,pcond,pmap,...}
```

The four concurrency constructs of PaiLisp-Kernel will be explained below, and a concrete description of PaiLisp using PaiLisp-Kernel is given in [ItoM90].

2.2 PaiLisp-Kernel

PaiLisp-Kernel is a small kernel language of PaiLisp, which is defined as Scheme plus four parallel constructs $\{spawn, suspend, call/cc, exlambda\}$. The four concurrency constructs have the following meanings:

[1] (spawn e)

(spawn e) creates a process to compute e. and the parent process that invoked this 'spawn' statement will be executed concurrently with the newly-created child process for e, without waiting for termination of this new process. The execution of (spawn e) must be realized in the way that the expression e will be evaluated and after its completion the process created by (spawn e) will fall into the killed state, returning only the side-effects caused by evaluating e.

[2] (suspend)

(suspend) is a procedure to suspend execution of a process that invoked this 'suspend' statement. That is,the execution of a process that encountered this 'suspend' statement will be suspended, and the suspended process will resume its execution when the continuation created by this statement is invoked by another process.

[3] (call/cc e)

This is an extended 'call-with-current-continuation' construct in PaiLisp. e must be a procedure of one argument. (call/cc e) creates a procedure of one argument to denote its current continuation with its process-id. This current continuation with its process-id will be called P-continuation, where the process-id is the name of the process that created the continuation. When a P-continuation is invoked by the same process that captured it, the resulting behavior is same as in Scheme and Multilisp. But when a P-continuation is invoked by a different process, the process to execute the rest of computation is the process that captured the P-continuation, and the process that invoked the continuation continues its execution without any disturbance. Thus when a P-contunuation is invoked by a process diffrent from one that captured it, it can be used to give an effect to other processes. Actually it can be used to kill and resume other processes. The details of P-continuations will be explained in Section 2.4.

[4] (exlambda $(x_1 ...x_n)$ e_1 ... e_m)

This is a statement to create an exclusive function closure together with a new queue. When this exclusive function closure is used by a process, other processes that invokes this closure will be suspended in the FIFO queue until this closure is released.

In order to describe concurrent processes like parallel Lisp processes we must know how to 'initiate','suspend','resume' and 'kill' processes.

* The initiation will be realized by (spawn e) which creates a process to compute e and initiates its execution.
* The temporary suspension of a process will be realized by use of (suspend).

* In order to resume a process suspended by (suspend) its continuation must be captured by call/cc, and it must be passed to other processes before their suspension.
* Killing a process created by (spawn e) will be done by invoking the continuation of e.

With these descriptive power of $\{spawn, suspend, call/cc, exlambda\}$ it is shown in [ItoM90] that PaiLisp-Kernel, is universal to describe all the PaiLisp constructs.

2.3   Concurrency Constructs in PaiLisp

PaiLisp is a rich parallel Lisp language to contain all the major parallel Lisp constructs of Multilisp and Qlisp together with parallelized Lisp basic functions. Roughly speaking we can say as follows:

```
{PaiLisp} =  {PaiLisp-Kernel}
              +{future,pcall,par,par-and,par-or,pcond,pmap,...}
```

It is shown in [ItoM90] that all the extended concurrency constructs future, pcall,par,... can be described using PaiLisp-Kernel. Since in this paper we are going to explain P-continuation based implementations of these extended concurrency constructs we explain here the meanings of major PaiLisp constructs among them. For the meanings of other PaiLisp constructs the readers should consult [ItoM90].

[1] (future e)

This is an interesting construct introduced by Halstead[Hals84] into a parallel Lisp language Multilisp, and it is a convenient construct to express and introduce concurrency of functional objects. (future e) returns a special virtual value for e, called the future value of e, and it creates a new process which computes e. This newly-created process for e will be executed concurrently with the parent process that invoked the future statement. The parent process will continue its execution ,using the future value for e, but when an operation on the future value of e requires its true value the parent process will be be suspended until the value of e is obtained. The action to get the true value for the future value will be called 'force', and the state that a process is waiting for the true value will be called 'touching'.

[2] (pcall f,e_1,...,e_n), (eager f,e_1,...,e_n)

(pcall f,e_1,...,e_n) means that after completion of parallel execution of e_1,...,e_n the function f will be evaluated, and the (functional) value of f will be applied to the values of e_1,...,e_n. (eager f,e_1,...,e_n) means ((future f), (future e_1),...,(future e_n)).

[3] (par-or e_1,...,e_n)

e_1,...,e_n will be executed in parallel, and if one of them (say,e_k) yields non-NIL then the non-NIL value for e_k will be returned as the result of par-or,terminating all the executing processes among e_1,...e_n. If none of e_1,...,e_n yields non-NIL the the result of par-or will be false.

[4] (par-and $e_1,...,e_n$)

$e_1,...,e_n$ will be executed in parallel, and if one of them (say,e_k) yields false then the result of par-and will become false,terminating all the executing processes among $e_1,...,e_n$. If none of $e_1,...,e_n$ yields false then the value of en will be returned as the result of par-and.

[5] (pcond $(p_1\ e_1)\ (p_2\ e_2)\ ...\ (p_n\ e_n)$), (pcond# $(p_1\ e_1)\ (p_2\ e_2)\ ...\ (p_n\ e_n)$)

In case of pcond the predicates $p_1,...,p_n$ will be evaluated in parallel, and if $p_1,...,p_{k-1}$ are false and p_k is true then the value of e_k will be returned as the value of pcond, terminating the executing processes among $e_{k+1},...,e_n$. In case of pcond# the predicates $p_1,...,p_n$ and the bodies $e_1,...,e_n$ will be executed in parallel, and if $p_1,...,p_{k-1}$ are false and p_k is true then the value of e_k will be returned as the value of pcond#, terminating all other executions for the predicates and bodies. During this evaluation, whenever the value of p_i is determined to be false the evaluation of e_i will be terminated.

[6] (signal cvar e), (wait cvar)

These constructs will be used for synchronizing during application of an exclusive function closure. 'cvar' is a condition variable to hold an exclusive queue. A PaiLisp process that executed 'wait' releases the innermost exclusive function closure being applied, and it will be suspended entering into an exclusive queue of cvar. A PaiLisp process that executed 'signal' will resume the execution of a process queued by cvar, but if there is no such process queued by cvar the value of e will be returned from the exclusive function closure after releasing the innermost function closure being applied.

2.4   P-Continuation and PaiLisp call/cc

The notion of P-continuation was introduced in [ItoM90] as an extension of Scheme continuation into concurrency. The 'call/cc' construct of PaiLisp is a construct to capture and create P-continuations. In this section we explain on this P-continuation, after explaining breifly about Scheme continuation.

[Scheme Continuation]

The notion of continuation was originally introduced to model the rest of computation following from a point of the computation. In Scheme the procedure 'call-with-current-continuation' causes the current continuation to be captured as a first class object of Scheme. This Scheme continuation will be called S-continuation. Scheme's call-with-current-continuation will be abbreviated as 'cwcc' in this paper to distinguish from PaiLisp's 'call/cc'. The Scheme's 'cwcc' has the following syntax:

(cwcc e)

where 'e' must be a procedure of one argument to denote its current continuation. A continuation created by 'cwcc' packages up the current continuation as an escape procedure of one argument and passes it as an argument to e. When the escape procedure is applied to its argument its current continuation will be discarded,and instead the continuation that the escape procedure was created will become in effect. In the style of denotational semantics we may write

$$\rho \ [\text{cwcc}] = \lambda \ \text{ek.e}(\lambda \ \text{e'k'.ke'})\text{k}$$

where ρ is an environment such that $\rho \ \varepsilon \ \text{Env:I} \rightarrow \text{Val}$. From an implementational standpoint a continuation may be viewed as the stack and register contents that express the current state and the rest of computation. 'cwcc' captures the current stack and register contents, and it copies them into a continuation object to behave as a Scheme procedure of one argument. 'cwcc' passes the continuation object to its argument, which must be a procedure of one argument. Multilisp adopted S-continuations as follows:

a) It packages up as a first class object the continuation (rest of computation) of the task that captured 'cwcc',

b) The content of the control stack that executes 'cwcc' will be kept in the continuation closure, and when its continuation closure is invoked the content of the control stack will be copied into the control stack of the process that invokes the continuation,

c) The continuation captured by Multilisp's cwcc will be executed by a process that invoked the continuation.

When a Multilisp continuation is invoked by the same process that captured it, the resulting behavior is same as S-continuation. When a Multilisp continuation is invoked by a different process that captured it, the continuation will be executed by the different process (that invoked it). Hence in case of Multilisp continuation there is no chance that an invocation of a continuation closure gives any effect to other processes.

[P-Continuation]

The P-continuations are an extension of S-continuations into concurrency in PaiLisp. A P-continuation is defined as follows:

a) it packages up as a first class object the continuation of a PaiLisp process that captured 'call/cc' and the process-id (PID) that identifies its PaiLisp process.

b) When a P-continuation is invoked by the same process that captured it, the resulting behavior is same as S-continuation. When a P-continuation is invoked by a different process, the process to execute the rest of computation is the process that captured the continuation,discarding its current continuation, and the process that invoked the continuation continues its execution without any disturbance.

With this definition of P-continuation a PaiLisp program that uses PaiLisp call/cc but no other concurrency constructs produces the same results as in a sequential Scheme program. But when a P-continuation is invoked by a process different from one that captured it, it can be used to give an effect to other processes. Actually it can be used to kill a process. For example,

```
(let ((kill (call/cc (lambda (resume)
                       (spawn (call/cc (lambda (k) (resume k)
                                         ...)))
                       (suspend)))))

...

(kill 'dummy))
```

The following program is an example to suspend and resume a process:

```
(let ((c 0))
    (call/cc (lambda (resume)
                (spawn (resume (set! c (+ c 1))))
                (suspend)))
    (print c))
```

Fig.2.1 shows an example of stack behaviors of the PaiLisp interpreter for the following simple PaiLisp program:

```
(print (cons 'a (call/cc (lambda (k) (spawn (k 'e)) 'b))))
```

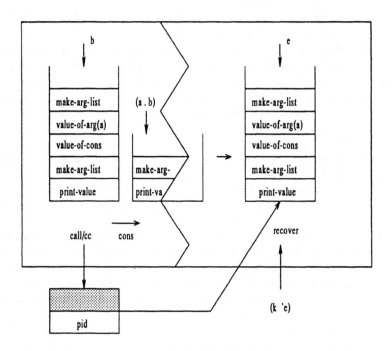

P-continuation

Fig.2.1 Behavior of P-continuation

[Comparisons of P-Continuation and Multilisp continuation]

(1) Continuations on distributed memory architectures

In case of P-continuations the process that executes a P-continuation is the process that captured it, and it cannot be executed by a process different from one that captured it. This means that in a distributed memory architecture the cost of invoking P-continuations will be less than the cost of invoking Multilisp continuations, since Multilisp continuations will be executed by other processes different from a process that captured the continuations.

(2) Halstead test

In [Hals90] Halstead proposed three criteria to test a continuation mechanism in semantics of parallel Lisp programs. The difficulty of semantics of 'call/cc' can be observed in interactions between 'future' and 'call/cc'. Halstead applied his test–say,'Halstead test'–to various proposed mechanisms. Consider the following example in [Hals90]:

```
(future (call/cc (lambda (k)
                 (cons (future (k 0))
                       (future (+ 1 2)))))))
```

This is an example that the future values will be decided twice by interactions of 'call/cc' and 'future'. This kind of multiple decisions of the future values may cause errors. Katz-Weise[KatW90] resolves this problem for Multilisp, slightly changing meanings of 'future'. In case of P-continuations our implementation works as follows:

(a) When the determination of the future value is before the invocation of P-continuation, the corresponding PaiLisp process disappear immediately after determination of the future value, and the invocation of P-continuation will be ignored.

(b) When the invocation of P-continuation is before determining the future value, the future value will be decided as 0 given at its invocation.

For safety of the action (a) P-continuations are actually ignored since the beginning of determining the future value. Hence in case of P-continuations there will be no danger that the future values will be decided multiple times.

2.5   call/ep–A Construct for Single-Use and Light-Weight P-Continuation

Concurrent interactions between continuations and concurrency constructs yield some semantic difficulties in multiple-use continuations as is discussed in [Hals90] and [ItoS92]. Also, in most actual programming practices, the continuations are used only for non-local exits. A single use continuation is enough to realize non-local exits. 'call/ep' is the construct for the single-use continuations in PaiLisp ([ItoM90],[ItoS92]), that is, a restricted version of PaiLisp call/cc for non-local exits. 'call/ep' may be considered to be the procedure to package up

P-continuations as the first class objects to perform only non-local exits. From a standpoint of implementing a continuation as a control stack call/ep may be implemented as follows:

the position of the stack-pointer will be marked at application of call/ep, and the stack contents below the mark denote the continuation at the point.

The exceution of a continuation for call/ep becomes an action to move the stack-pointer to the marked position of the stack. Hence the cost of capturing and invoking call/ep is less than those of call/cc.

Consider the following program:

```
(print (cons 'a (call/cc (lambda (k) (spawn (k 'e)) (suspend)))))
```

'call/cc' in this program may be replaced by 'call/ep'. In case of call/cc it requires the action of copying the stack contents and of recovering it into the stack at invocation of (k 'e). But in case of call/ep the marking information 'tag' will be put on the stack, and the light-weight P-continuation with 'tag' and the process-id PID will be created as in Fig.2.2. Upon invocation of P-continuation the rest of computation will be executed, moving the stack-pointer to the point denoted by 'tag'.

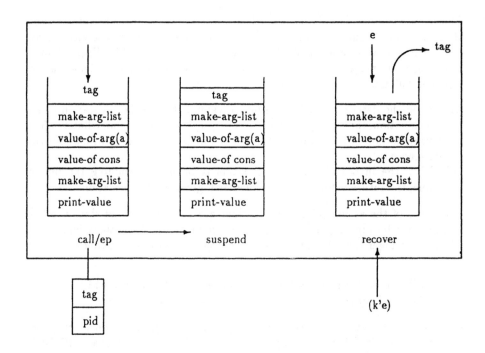

Fig.2.2 Light-weight P-continuation and its stack behavior

3 PaiLisp Interpreter and PaiLisp-Kernel Interpreter

In this section we explain an organization of the PaiLisp interpreter implemented on a shared memory machine Alliant FX/80 with eight computing elements. Then we explain the details of the PaiLisp-Kernel interpreter, which forms a core part of PaiLisp interpreter.

3.1 Outline of PaiLisp Interpreter

The PaiLisp interpreter on Alliant FX/80 is implemented using its real-time concurrent OS called CONCENTRIX-OS, and it is built as an extension of Scheme interpreter to execute PaiLisp concurrency constructs in parallel. Fig.3.1 shows an organization of PaiLisp interpreter.

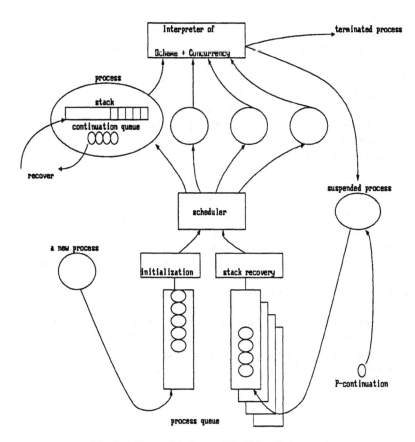

Fig.3.1 Organization of PaiLisp Interpreter

Initialization means the creation of shared memory regions and the creation of processes by forking.

Scheduler gives executable PaiLisp processes to the interpreter, which executes a PaiLisp process and gets other executable PaiLisp processes when it becomes impossible to execute.

Evaluation of PaiLisp concurrency constructs will be performed by an extended Scheme interpreter, and the GC is adapted for parallel Lisp processes.

3.2   On Implementation of PaiLisp Processes

PaiLisp processes will be executed in parallel with shared data under shared environments. Each PaiLisp process will be specified by

```
        its process name,
        its current state,
        its current value,
        its current continuation
    and its current access to the exclusive resources.
```

Each PaiLisp process is actually realized as the following process object:

```
        < [pointer to the stack region],
        [pointer to the continuation queue],
        [pointer to the access state of exclusive resources],
        [current state],
        [lock-byte] >
```

The pointer to the process object will be used as the process-id PID. We assume the following five states for PaiLisp processes:

'Running': state that a PaiLisp process is being executed,

'Killed' : state that the execution of a PaiLisp process is terminated,

'Suspended': state that the execution of a PaiLisp process is suspended,

'Waiting' : state that a PaiLisp process is being waited for execution of an exclusive function closure,

'Queued' : an executable state that no PaiLisp process is allocated.

A P-continuation of a PaiLisp process is realized by the contents of the control stack and the continuation queue. The current value of a PaiLisp process is stored in the val register realized by a global variable expressed in C.

The state transition of a PaiLisp process is shown as Fig.3.2.

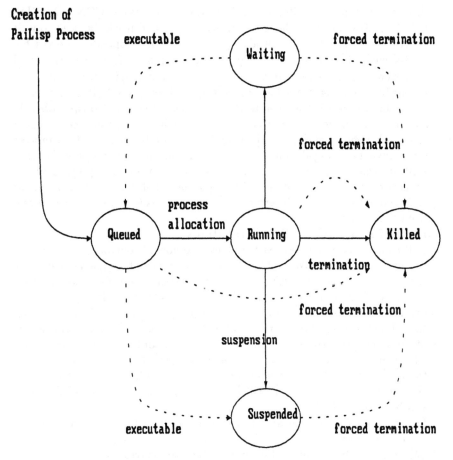

Fig.3.2 State Transitions of PaiLisp Processes

A PaiLisp process will be in the Queued state at its creation. The Running state is a state that a PaiLisp process is actually being executed. A PaiLisp process will be suspended in the Suspended state, and the Waiting state is a state that a process is waited for use of an exclusive function closure. The Killed state is a state that the execution of a Pailisp process is terminated. In Fig.3.2 the arrow lines mean state transitions to be caused by actions of PaiLisp processes, while the dotted arrow lines mean state transitions that will be caused by invocation of P-continuations.

[Scheduling of PaiLisp Processes]

PaiLisp scheduling employs a mixed strategy with the FIFO queue and the LIFO queue. The FIFO queue is the so-called global process queue shared by all the PaiLisp processes, and a newly-created PaiLisp process will be queued in this FIFO queue until it will be allocated a process of CONCENTRIX-OS. The LIFO queue is the local process queue, and it will be used to wait process allocation for a suspended process until its suspended process becomes executable. The scheduler gets a PaiLisp process from the LIFO local process queue and gives it to the interpreter, changing its process state from Queued to Running. If the local process queue is empty, a PaiLisp process in the global queue will be given to the interpreter. Since a PaiLisp process in the global queue is not allocated its stack region yet, it should be allocated the stack region before it is given to the interpreter. The PaiLisp process state must be changed from Queued to Running in this case, too. When a PaiLisp process is created or resumes its execution, the interpreter gives its process to the scheduler. When a PaiLisp process falls into the Killed state or the Suspended state, the interpreter gets another executable PaiLisp process from the scheduler.

[Control of Processes by P-Continuations]

A P-continuation can be used to change the flow of control of a process, as was explained in 2.4. We explain how this control can be implemented. Each process object has an invoking flag and a continuation queue to get invocations of P-continuations created by its process. When a P-continuation is invoked by a process, the invoking flag will be turned on and the continuation object will be added to the continuation queue. The continuation queue of the FIFO style stores the continuations in the order of their invocations. The invoking flag of the current process will be examined at each return from the evaluator. When the process detects an invocation of P-continuations, the execution of the process will be interrupted, and the following actions will be taken:

(1) get a continuation or an escape procedure from the continuation queue of the process,

(2) restore the contents of the control stack to express the continuation,

(3) turn off the invoking flag when the continuation queue becomes empty.

After executing these actions the process with the restored control stack will continue to be runned. If the continuation queue of a process contains a continuation to make it terminate, the continuations invoked after the continuation will be ignored, and the process will terminate immediately. If there remains any continuation in the queue, the above actions will be performed again at the next return from the evaluator.

3.3 Implementation of PaiLisp-Kernel Interpreter

PaiLisp-Kernel is an extension of Scheme with four concurrency constructs $\{spawn, suspend, exlambda, call/cc\}$, as was explained in 2.2. The PaiLisp-Kernel interpreter was implemented by extending a sequential Scheme interpreter to interpret 'spawn' and 'exlambda' and to add 'suspend' and 'call/cc' as procedures.

[1] Implementation of 'spawn'

Upon interpreting (spawn e) there will be created a new process object, equipped with the pointers to the expression e, its environment and the execution routine for 'spawn', and then it will be entered into a global process queue, changing its PaiLisp process state into the Queued state. When a PaiLisp process read from the global process queue is executed, its PaiLisp process execution routine will be called.

[2] Implementation of 'suspend'

Upon execution of 'suspend' the continuation queue of the current PaiLisp process will be checked. If it is called by P-continuation, its P-continuation will be executed. If it is not called by P-continuation, the current process state will be switched into Suspended and another executable PaiLisp process must be obtained from the scheduler.

[3] Implementation of 'exlambda'

'exlambda' creates an exclusive function closure, which contains a closure created by (lambda $(x_1 \ldots x_n)$ $e_1 \ldots e_m$) and a FIFO queue. The exclusive function closure also has the name of the process being called. The queue is used to save escape procedures, which resume processes being waited to enter the closure.

An exclusive function closure is available whenever it is not executed by any process. When a process calls the closure during another process call under progress, it creates an escape procedure which resumes itself and adds this procedure to the tail of the closure's queue, and then it falls into the Waiting state. The forms in the exlambda body are executed by a newly-created process so that the invocations of continuations cannot make the process escape from the critical region.

The queue of an exclusive function closure is a list of escape procedure objects. The process in the Waiting state has a pointer to the cell in the list whose car points the escape procedure to resume the process. When any continuation other than that escape procedure is invoked, the waiting process stores the null pointer to the car of that cell and executes the continuation, When the process completes the execution of the forms in the exlambda body,

if the queue is empty, it releases the closure by removing that process name from the closure;

if the queue is not empty, it resumes one of the waiting processes by invoking an escape procedure in the queue. Notice that Qlisp's process closure is executed by the process that belongs to the closure, while PaiLisp's exclusive function closure is executed by the process being called.

[4] Implementation of PaiLisp 'call/cc' and P-contonuation

PaiLisp's call/cc is an extension of Scheme's cwcc as was explained in 2.4. On application of call/cc it is necessary to obtain its current continuation as in Scheme. A procedure call/cc creates a continuation object shown in Fig.3.3. This object contains a copy of the current contents of the control stack and the name of the current process. The contents of the control stack is transformed into a list of the contents, and the argument of call/cc will be applied to the continuation object. If the continuation is not invoked, the result of this application returns from this call/cc.

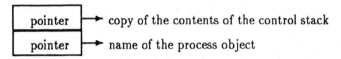

Fig.3.3 A continuation object

The invocation of P-continuation can be done by giving its arguments, and the pair of the continuation and the value of its argument will be entered into the continuation queue of the PaiLisp process recorded in the continuation object. If the state of its PaiLisp process is Suspended, it will be switched to Queued and the PaiLisp process will be entered into the local process queue.

The restoration of continuation can be done by stacking each element of the data list from the bottom of the stack and by placing the stack pointer to point the data on the top element. The execution of this restored continuation will be done by jumping to the address contained in the top of the stack. Hence the cost of application of call/cc is propotional to the depth of the current PaiLisp process in the stack. The cost of restoration of continuation is also propotional to the stack depth.

[Remark]
As was mentioned in 2.5 the call/cc construct is used only for non-local exits in most practical programming. The call/ep construct is introduced as a restricted call/cc to support a light-weight and single-use continuation. As will be explained in 4.9 it is possible to implement the call/ep construct in a really light-weight fashion. However we sometimes need the call/cc construct to support a multiple-use continuation. These issues of P-continuations and PaiLisp call/cc are discussed in details in [ItoS92]. The following program is an example which employs the multiple- use continuation.

```
(let ((c 0) (tag '()))
  (set! c (call/cc (lambda (k) (set! tag k) 3)))
  (print c)
  (if (zero? c) 0 (tag (- c 1)))))
```

That is, "call/cc" in this program cannot be replaced without changing the meaning of the program. However it is an open question to give an algorithm to detect which call/cc can be replaced to call/ep.

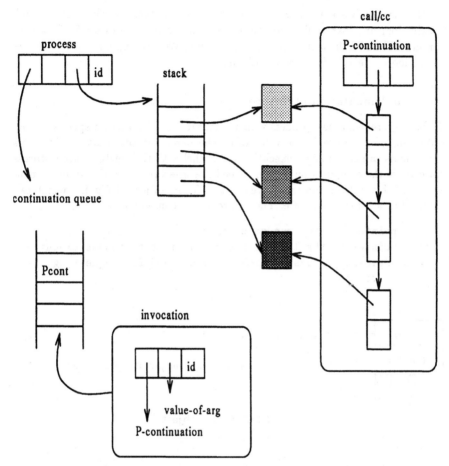

Fig.3.4 Creation and invocation of P-continuation

4 P-Continuation Based Implementations of PaiLisp Concurrency Constructs

Since the meanings of PaiLisp concurrency constructs are given using PaiLisp-Kernel in [ItoM90], it is possible to implement each PaiLisp concurrency construct as a macro definition in PaiLisp. However, if we take such an implementation an interpreter for PaiLisp will be slow in its execution, so that our PaiLisp interpreter is implemented in the language "C". In this implementation of PaiLisp interpreter the P-continuation will be fully used for killing and resuming executions of PaiLisp processes, so that our PaiLisp interpreter is called "P-continuation based".

In this section we explain P-continuation based implementations of 'future', 'pcall', 'par-or', 'par-and', 'pcond', 'signal' and 'wait'. The other PaiLisp constructs will be implemented in a similar fashion. We also explains how to implement 'loop', 'delay', 'force' and 'call/ep'.

4.1 Implementation of 'future'

(future e) creates a new process which computes e and returns a special virtual value for e, called the future value of e. The parent process that executes this statements can continue its execution in parallel with the newly-created process for e while the computation does not need the true value of e. For an implementation of this 'future' construct, we create a future object of Fig.4.1, which can be used as a future value of e. The future object consists of

> **a pointer to the true value of e,**
> **and a pointer to the list of P-continuations to resume executions of PaiLisp processes which are suspended for requesting their true values.**

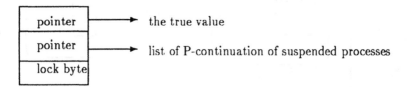

Fig.4.1 A future object

A PaiLisp process, equipped with 'e', its environment, its future object and a pointer to the execution routine of future, will be created, and then it will be entered into the global process queue. A PaiLisp process to compute e will be created in this way.

The execution routine of future will compute e under the environment inherited from its parent process and it will return the resultant value to the future object. The resultant true value of e will be given to each corresponding element of the list of P-continuations recorded in the future object, and the PaiLisp processes which are suspended for requesting their true values will be resumed their executions. When "force" will take place,

if the future value is obtained,

the processes that requested it will continue their executions,

and if it is not obtained yet,

the P-continuation formed by a list of the current continuations will be created and it will be added to the list of P-continuations recorded in the future object, and then the execution of the PaiLisp processes will be suspended as in case of 'suspend'.

Fig.4.2 shows a situation that two PaiLisp processes are suspended by forcing the future value and they will be resumed their executions after determination of the future value.

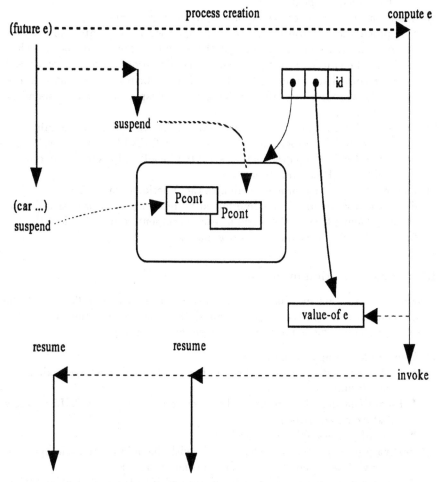

Fig.4.2 Behaviors of PaiLisp processes to force the future value

4.2 Implementation of 'pcall'

'(pcall f e_1 ... e_n)' means that after parallel evaluation of e_1,...,e_n the fuctional value of f will be applied to the values e_1,...,e_n. This is implemented in the following way:

1) form an environment with

* COUNTER which counts the number of arguments whose evaluations have terminated,
* P-continuation which resumes the excution of the parent PaiLisp process that executed 'pcall'

2) create PaiLisp processes corresponding to the arguments.
* A process object will be created, equipped with the pointers to each argument e_i, its environment and the execution routine of 'pcall'. Then it will be entered into the global queue. The process object created will be recorded into the argument list. The PaiLisp process that executes 'pcall' will terminate after creating the PaiLisp processes corresponding to the arguments.

3) The execution routine of 'pcall' will evaluate its arguments e_i, recording their values into the process object, decreasing COUNTER. When COUNTER becomes 0 the PaiLisp process that executed 'pcall' will resume its execution by invoking its P-continuation.

4) The resumed PaiLisp process evaluates the functional part 'f', and the list of the arguments will be determined by replacing each process object at the argument place to the value of each argument recorded. Then the the function 'f' will be applied to its arguments.

4.3 Implementation of 'par-or'

'(par-or e_1 ... e_n)' means that e_1,...,e_n will be executed in parallel and if one of the them returns non-NIL then this non-NIL value becomes the value of the par-or expression. This is implemented in the following way:

1) form the following environment:
* COUNTER which counts the number of arguments whose evaluations have terminated,
* P-continuation which resumes the execution of the parent PaiLisp proces that executed 'par-or'
* a list of process objects created

2) create a process object for each argument with the pointers to each argument e_i, its enviroment and the execution routine of 'par-or'.
* The created process object will be entered into the global queue. Then the parent process that executed PaiLisp process will be suspended as in case of 'suspend'.

3) The execution routine of 'par-or' will evaluate its arguments e_i, decreasing COUNTER.

When the evaluation of e_i returns non-NIL, the parent process that executed 'par-or' will resume its execution by invoking its P-continuation, and in order to force to terminate PaiLisp processes to evaluate the rest of arguments the kill continuation will be invoked for each element of the list of process objects. The kill continuation enables any PaiLisp process to force to terminate by its invocation.

When the evaluation of e_i returns NIL and COUNTER becomes 0, the value of 'par-or' will become NIL, and the parent PaiLisp process that executed 'par-or' will be resumed its execution by invoking its P-continuation.

4.4 Implementation of 'par-and'

'(par-and e_1 ... e_n)' means that $e_1,...,e_n$ will be executed in parallel and if one of them returns NIL the value of the par-and expression will become NIL. When all of the argument expressions return non-NIL the value of the last argument (e_n) will be returned as the value of the par-and expression. The implementation of 'par-and' is similar to that of 'par-or'. We only remark here how the execution routine of 'par-and' will work when the value of e_1 becomes NIL. When the evaluation of e_i returns NIL the parent PaiLisp process that executed 'par-and' will resume its execution by invoking its P-continuation stored in the environment, and in order to force to terminate the other running PaiLisp processes to evalute the rest of arguments the kill continuation will be invoked for eack element of the list of process objects.

4.5 Implementation of 'pcond

'(pcond $(p_1 \ e_1)$ ... $(p_n \ e_n)$)' means that the test predicates $p_1,...,p_n$ will be executed in parallel and if $p_1,...,p_{k-1}$ return NIL and p_k returns non-NIL then e_k will be computed, terminating the executions of processes for $p_{k+1},...,p_n$, and the value for e_k will be returned as the value of the pcond expression. This is implemented in the following way:

1) form an enviroment with
   * P-continuation which resumes the execution of the parent process that executed 'pcond'
   * a list of process objects to evaluate the PaiLisp processes for the test predicates $p_1,...,p_n$
2) create a process object for each test predicate with the pointers to each predicate p_i, its environment and the execution routine of 'pcond'.
   * The created process objects will be entered into the global queue, and the parent process that executed 'pcond' will be suspended as in case of 'suspend'.
3) The execution routine of 'pcond' will evaluate each p_i, recording its result into the process object. If the results of $p_1,...,p_{i-1}$ are NIL and the result of p_i is non-NIL then the pararnt PaiLisp process that executed pcond will

be resumed its execution. This resumption will be done by invoking the P-continuation of the parent process mentioned above. Moreover, in order to force to terminate PaiLisp processes for $p_{i+1},...,p_n$ the kill continuation will be invoked for each element of the list of process objects stored in the environment. For the test predicate p_i which returns non-NIL, its body part e_i will be obtained and executed.

4.6   Implementation of 'signal' and 'wait'

'(signal cvar e)' and '(wait cvar)' are the synchronization primitives to synchronize during application of an exclusive function closure, where cvar is a condition variable with an exclusive queue.

The condition variable will be made by the function 'make-cond-var', which is a function with no argument and returns an exclusive FIFO queue. In case of '(wait cvar)' the current continuations will be packaged up as an object to form P-continuation, and it will be entered into the exclusive queue of the condition variable 'cvar'. Then the right to use the exclusive function closure will be released. When the exclusive queue of the function closure is empty the suspended PaiLisp process will resume its execution. Otherwise the fuction closure will be released, and the PaiLisp process that executed 'wait' will fall into the Waiting state and it will be suspended.

In case of '(signal cvar e)' the argument expression 'e' will be executed and the suspended process will be resumed its execution by invoking P-continuation at the head of the FIFO queue of the condition variable cvar. The PaiLisp process that executed 'signal' will be resumed by invoking P-continuation which returns a value from the exclusive function closure and gets the value of 'e'.

4.7   Implementation of 'loop'

'(loop e_1 ... e_n)' means that the evaluations of $e_1,...,e_n$ will be done in this order repeatedly until escape by invocation of P-continuation. The invocation of P-continuation will be checked every time after evaluating an argument expression. The looping of the parallel execution of $e_1,...e_n$ will be written as
(loop (par e_1 ... e_n)).

4.8   On implementation of 'delay' and 'force'

'(delay e)' is the Scheme construct for delayed evaluation. This construct returns a virtual value called the 'promise' value without an immediate evaluation of 'e'. The true value for the promise value will be obtained by the function 'force' as in case of the future value. The evaluation of e as the argument of 'delay' will take place at the first time that its true value is needed. On implementing 'delay' and 'force' the following considerations have been taken into account in order to match with the implementation of 'future':

* when a non promise value is given to the 'force' function, it will be simply returned,

* a promise value will not be distinguished from its true value; for example, (eq? (delay #f) #f) returns true.
* a promise value will be implicitly forced; for example, "+" will implicitly force the promise value in the following expression so that it will return the value normally. For example,
(+ (delay (* 2 3)) 4)

[1] (delay e)

To implement the delay construct we create a promise object of Fig.4.3, which will be used as the promise value of 'e'. The promise object consists of the pointers to

     1) the true value of e,
     2) a list of P-continuations to resume executions of PaiLisp proceses which are suspended for requesting their true values,
and 3) a process object to compute the value of e.

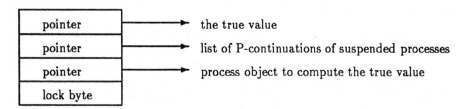

Fig.4.3 A promise object

We create a process object with the pointers to the expression e, its promise object and the execution routine of the delayed evaluation. Unlike 'future' the process object will not be entered into the global queue; instead, its process object will be recored into the promise object. When the promise value is forced at the first time, the process object to compute e will be entered into the global queue and the corresponding PaiLisp process will be created. When the true value of the promise value is obtained the PaiLisp process which forces the promise value will continue its execution with its true value. When the true value of the promise value is still being computed a list of current continuations will be packaged up to form P-continuation, and it will be added to the list of P-continuations of the promise object. After then the execution of the PaiLisp process will be suspended as in case of 'suspend'. The execution routine of the delayed evaluation evaluates 'e' under the inherited environment and records its value into the promise object, and it will invoke the suspended processes by giving the true value to each element of the list of P-continuations of the promise object to resume the executions of the suspended processes requesting the true value of the promise value.

131

[2] (force e)

The future value and promise value will not be distinguished from their true value and they will be implicitly forced if necessary, as was mentioned above. Some extensions of Scheme basic functions are required in this account. They are the following:

(1) the test predicates for objects

eq?, eqv?, equal?, boolean?, pair?, symbol?, number?, char?, string? procedure?, null?, list?

(2) basic functions

car, cdr, set-car!, set-cdr!, length, append, reverse, =, <,>, <=, >= zero?, max, min, +, *, −, abs, quotient, remainder, apply, map

(3) conditionals

if, cond, and, or

(4) function evaluation at function application

The functions of (1) and (4) can be extended without any overhead in executions that do not contain any 'future' construct.

4.9 Implementation of 'call/ep'

'call/ep' is the procedure that captures the lightweight continuation,as was explained in 2.5.

'call/ep' creates a tag object and pushes it on the control stack and also creates an escape procedure object shown in Fig. 4.4. That is, the escape procedure object contains the tag object and the name of the current process. When an escape procedure is invoked, the control stack of the creator process will be scanned and checkd to find the tag object specified by the escape procedure. This method of implementing call/ep enables us to check easily whether the escape procedure is valid or not. The invocation of an escape procedure is implemented similarly to that of 'call/cc'. When call/ep returns a value, the tag object is removed from the control stack. Then the escape procedure becomes invalid, but a continuation invocation validates the escape procedure again. 'call/ep' will be sometimes called a construct for singleuse continuation.

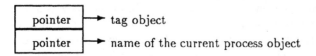

Fig. 4.4 Light-weight continuation object created by call/ep

4.10 On implementations of parallel GC

The garbage collection of PaiLisp has been implemented by the mark-and-sweep method. When the free cells are exhausted the GC actions will take place, interrupting list processings. The local data owned by each process is marked at termination of the process by itself. Then we introduced two parallelizations into GC:

(1) parallelization of marking the global data

(2) parallelization of sweep actions

It is easy to parallelize sweeping by dividing the heap area into the sub-areas relative to the number of processors. By this subdivision and parallelization the interruption of list processings by GC will be significantly reduced.

In the next section we will give some experimental results to compare these parallelizatons of GC. A more dedicated parallel GC that parallelize GC and list processings is left for future study. This method means that GC actions will be activated before the free cells are exhausted so that no interruption of list processings will occur. An implementation algorithm is explored by the author and his former student Norio Irie, but it is not implemented in PaiLisp. This algorithm requires simultaneous actions of marking actions and rewritings of linking cells under list processings, so that the implementation requires some significant changes in implementation of the current PaiLisp.

5 Running PaiLisp Interpreter for Benchmark Programs

The PaiLisp interpreter based on P-continuations was implemented by the second author (T. Seino) on a shared memory computer Alliant FX/80 with eight processor elements, using its real-time concurrent OS called CONCENTRIX-OS. The interpreter itself is written in the language "C". In this section we explain and discuss some basic evaluation results of running PaiLisp interpreter for a variety of benchmark programs. With this benchmark results and experiences the PaiLisp interpreter has been used for various applications of parallel symbolic computing at the authors' laboratory. The purposes of this evaluation by the benchmark programs were mainly

* to see the effects of improving 'execution timing' in terms of the number of processor elements

and

* to see the effects of using PaiLisp concurrency constructs to parallelize Lisp programs.

Thus our major performance index to evaluate the interpreter is:

speedup = TP(1)/min{TP(k) | k=1,...,n}

where TP(k) is the execution time when k processors were used, and n is the maximum number of processors used for evaluations. Notice that n is less than 8 in our case.

[Evaluation Environment]

The PaiLisp interpreter is running on Alliant FX/80 under its real-time OS, so that the 'execution timing' will be measured with its real-time scheduler. The execution time of a program is defined as

```
(the time between program-input and value-return of the
 interpreter)
- (the time required for GC)
```

The following timing construct was implemented to measure the execution time of programs:

```
(time e)
```

This construct returns and displays

```
     the time required to evaluate the expression e (say Tev),
     the time required for GC during evaluation of e (say Tgc),
and (Tev - Tgc).
```

From the standpoint of Operating System the number of processors means the number of OS processes by forking at the beginning of PaiLisp interpreter executions. Since we allocate one processor to each OS process we may identify the number of processors as same with the number of OS processes. This processor allocation to OS processes comes from reducing the cost of process switching under Alliant FX/80 CONCENTRIX-OS. The paralelization of program executions often causes some overheads on process creation and scheduling. The overhead of parallelization may be defined as

```
overhead = (TP(1) - TS)/ TS
```

where TS is the execution time of a sequential program, and TP(1) is the execution time of the parallel program (that corresponds to the sequential program) with one processor element.

[Benchmark Programs]

The benchmark programs that we used are as follows:

(1) Parallelizations of sequential Lisp benchmark programs
   Fibonacci function
   The tarai function
   Sorting
   TPU (Theorem Prover with Unit Binary Resolution)

(2) Parallel programs for N-Queen problem and Travelling Salesman problem

(3) Parallelization of Pure Prolog

Moreover, we gave some experimental results of parallelizing GC.

5.1 Parallelizations of sequential Lisp benchmark programs

The contests of sequential Lisp systems were held three times in Japan[Tak78]. Among the contest programs we used the following functions to evaluate the performance of PaiLisp interpreter.

Fibonacci function, which computes the Fibinacci sequence recursively,

The tarai function, which is sometimes called as the Takeuchi function,

Sorting, which is a sorting program based on 'count-up-sorting',

TPU, which is a simple resolution theorem prover based on unit resolution.

5.1.1 Parallelizations of Fibonacci functions

A sequential Lisp program of the Fibonacci function can be given as follows:

```
(define fib
  (lambada (n) (if (< n 2)
                   n
                   (+ (fib (- n 1)) (fib (- n 2)))))))
```

Using 'future' and 'pcall' we can give several parallel versions of this Fibonacci function. We consider the following three cases.

```
(define ffib
  (lambda (n) (if (< n 2)
                  n
                  (+ (future (ffib (- n 1))) (ffib (- n 2)))))))
(define ffib2
  (lambda (n) (if (< n 2)
          n
          (+ (future (ffib2 (- n 1))) (future (ffib2 (- n 2))))))))
(define ffib3
  (lambda (n) (if (< n 2)
          n
          (+ (if (< n 8) (ffib3 (- n 1)) (future (ffib3 (- n 1))))
             (ffib3 (- n 2)))))))
(define pfib
  (lambda (n) (if (< n 2)
                  n
                  (pcall + (pfib (- n 1) (pfib (- n 2)))))))
```

The table in Fig.5.1 compares 'execution timing' of these programs in case of "n = 16".

T_s	3.16				(sec)
N_p	ffib	ffib2	ffib3	pfib	
1	4.26	5.19	3.75	4.87	(sec)
2	2.20	2.67	1.93	2.51	
3	1.53	1.85	1.33	1.74	
4	1.21	1.46	1.04	1.39	
5	0.99	1.23	0.85	1.21	
6	0.88	1.14	0.74	1.10	
7	0.80	1.02	0.68	1.02	
8	0.76	1.04	0.62	1.05	
speedup	5.61	5.09	6.05	4.64	

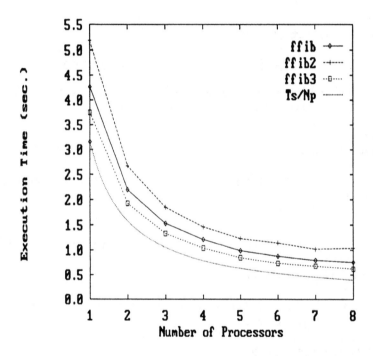

Fig. 5.1 Comparisons of parallel Fibonacci functions

The overheads of process creation and creating the future values in 'ffib2' are twice than those of 'ffib'. This is the reason why 'ffib2' is slower than 'ffib'. 'ffib3' restricts creation of processes when n is less than 8. In this case we obtained the best result. This kind of considerations to reduce overheads caused by parallelizations will be required to achieve high performance with parallel constructs and machines. 'pfib' may be compared with 'ffib2' because of its parallel computation behaviors. The overhead of 'ffib2' is higher than that of 'pcall', so that the parallelization based on 'pcall' is slightly better in this case. But 'future' allows finer control of parallelizations as was seen in 'ffib3'.

5.1.2 Parallelizations of the tarai function

The tarai function was invented for evaluations of recursion of Lisp system during the course of making up the Lisp contest programs in Japan[Tak78]. The word 'tarai' comes from 'taraimawashi', which originally means 'rotation of political power'. The tarai function is defined as follow:

```
(define tarai
  (lambda (x y z) (cond ((> x y) (tarai (tarai (- x 1) y z)
                                        (tarai (- y 1) z x)
                                        (tarai (- z 1) x y)))
                        (else y))))
```

We consider the following three parallelized versions of the tarai function.

```
(define ftarai
  (lambda (x y z) (cond ((> x y) (ftarai (future (ftarai (- x 1) y z))
                                         (future (ftarai (- y 1) z x))
                                         (future (ftarai (- z 1) x y))))
                        (else y))))
(define ptarai
  (lambda (x y z) (cond ((> x y) (pcall ptarai (ptarai (- x 1) y z)
                                               (ptarai (- y 1) z x)
                                               (ptarai (- z 1) x y)))
                        (else y))))
(define ftarai2
  (lambda (x y z) (cond ((> x y) (ftarai2 (future (ftarai2 (- x 1) y z))
                                          (future (ftarai2 (- y 1) z x))
                                          (ftarai2 (- z 1) x y)))
                        (else y))))
```

The inputs to the PaiLisp interpreter were given as follows:

```
(time (force (ftarai 8 4 0)))
(time (ptarai 8 4 0))
(time (ftarai2 8 4 0))
```

The evaluation results of Fig.5.2 shows that 'ftarai' looks much better than 'ptarai' and 'ftarai2'. This is because the tarai function can return its value without getting the true values of the arguments. This means that in case of 'ftarai' there remain some running PaiLisp processes even after returning the value of the tarai function. This may not be good since some computing resources are wastedly used. In case of 'ptarai' all the executions are terminated when it returns the value. In case of 'ftarai2' the future value will not be given to z, so that the result will be returned after terminating all the executions. In case of the tarai function the best result will be obtained, by using 'delay' instead of 'future', as follows:

```
(define dtarai
   (lambda (x y z) (cond ((> x Y) (dtarai (delay (dtarai (- x 1) y z))
                                          (delay (dtarai (- y 1) z x))
                                          (delay (dtarai (- z 1) x y))))
                         (else y))))
```

(time (dtarai 8 4 0)) gave only 0.0775 sec.

T_s	13.66			(sec)
N_p	ftarai	ptarai	ftarai2	
1	2.159	18.21	17.45	(sec)
2	0.247	9.43	9.03	
3	0.209	6.62	6.31	
4	0.118	5.32	5.04	
5	0.247	4.56	4.31	
6	0.157	4.17	3.93	
7	0.179	3.96	3.66	
8	0.288	3.81	3.54	
speedup	18.3	4.78	4.93	

Fig.5.2 Comparisons of parallel 'tarai' functions

[**Remark**] In case of "ptarai" its computation is completely terminated when it returns the result, since the function application will take place after computing the values of three arguments, and its parallelization overhead is about 33In case of "ftarai2" the number of created PaiLisp processes is 2/3 of the number of the processes created in "ptarai", so that we can expect the reduction of overheads in parallelization. Actually the parallelization overhead of Q "ftarai2" is about 28than that of "ptarai".

5.1.3 Parallel Sorting

We use so-called the parallel 'count-up-sorting'[Akl58]. The PaiLisp construct 'spawn' will be used to create a process to count up the elements of a given list to identify an element's position. The following 'psort' is the parallel sorting program based on this count-up-sorting. Fig.5.3 shows the results of applying this 'psort' to sort 50 integers and 100 integers in parallel.

```
(define psort
  (let ((1 '()) (m '()) (c 0) (k 'dummy))
    (let ((term (exlambda () (if (= c 1) (k m) (set! c (- c 1))))))
      (letrec ((count
                (lambda (l r n a i)
                  (cond ((null? l) r)
                        ((> a (car l)) (count (cdr l) (cdr r) (+ n 1) a i))
                        ((= a (car l)) (if (> n i)
                                           (count (cdr l) (cdr r) (+ n 1) a i)
                                           (count (cdr l) r (+ n 1) a i)))
                        (else (count (cdr l) r (+ n 1) a i)))))
               (copy-rec
                (lambda (a n)
                  (cond ((null? a) (suspend))
                        (else (spawn (begin (set-car! (count l m 0 (car a) n) (car a))
                                            (term)))
                              (copy-rec (cdr a) (+ n 1)))))))
        (lambda (x)
          (set! l x)
          (set! m (null-copy x))
          (set! c (length x))
          (call/cc (lambda (r) (set! k r) (copy-rec l 0))))))))
```

psort program

N_p	psort 50	psort 100	
1	6.68	26.26	(sec)
2	3.45	13.53	
3	2.39	9.48	
4	1.89	7.35	
5	1.57	6.27	
6	1.43	5.60	
7	1.33	5.23	
8	1.25	5.15	
speedup	5.34	5.10	

Fig.5.3 Results of parallel Sorting

5.1.4 Parallelization of Theorem Prover with Unit Resolution

We use TPU (Theorem Proving with Unit Binary Resolution) in [Tak78], [ChaL73]. The 'future' construct was inserted at the point to resolve an unit clause to parallelize the unit resolution. The algorithm of TPU is basically sequential in nature, and it contains many aspects that its parallelizations are hard. Our experimental results shown in Fig.5.4 also show this fact of TPU. In Fig.5.4 Th1,Th2,...,Th9 means theorems to be proved by the prover. These theorems are prepared in the contest program [Tak78]. Notice that the parallelization of unification was not implemented here, since it is too fine-grained to parallelize in a parallel Lisp language.

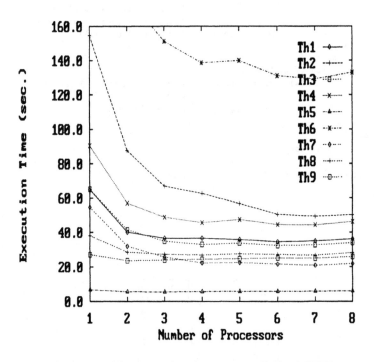

Fig.5.4 Results of evaluationg a parallelized TPU

5.2 Results for N-Queen Problem and Travelling Salesman Problem

The N-Queen Problem was considered in [MasPT90] to evaluate Qlisp. We use the following parallelized version of N-Queen, whose parallelism is introduced by 'future'. In this program an excessive creation of processes is suppressed, since the 'future' construct which creates new processes appears within the 'cond' expression. The table of Fig.5.5 shows the results when the number of queens is 6, 7, and 8.

```
(define columnf
  (lambda (column row-state left-diag right-diag n)
    (letrec (
      (rec-queen
        (lambda (row)
          (cond ((= row n) 0)
                (else
                  (if (and (free-p row row-state)
                           (free-p (l-diagonal column row) left-diag)
                           (free-p (r-diagonal column row n) right-diag))
                      (cond ((= column (- n 1)) (+ 1 (rec-queen (+ row 1))))
                            (else
                              (+ (future
                                   (columnf (+ column 1)
                                   (add-attack row row-state)
                                   (add-attack (l-diagonal column row) left-diag)
                                   (add-attack (r-diagonal column row n) right-diag)
                                     n))
                                 (rec-queen (+ row 1)))))
                      (rec-queen (+ row 1)))))))))
      (rec-queen 0))))
```

N-Queen program

No. of Queens	6	7	8	
T_s	12.95	55.6	256.8	(sec)
N_p				
1	13.03	56.0	259.6	(sec)
2	6.69	28.7	133.3	
3	4.64	19.9	92.5	
4	3.65	15.6	72.9	
5	3.09	13.2	67.5	
6	2.75	11.7	58.8	
7	2.54	10.8	50.6	
8	2.41	10.1	48.0	
speedup	5.41	5.54	5.41	

Fig.5.5 Results of parallel N-Queen program

The travelling salesman problem was used in [Osb90], whose program was adapted with a slight change, creating parallel search processes using the 'par' construct of PaiLisp. Fig.5.6 shows the results when the number of cities is 8, 12, and 16.

NO.of cities	8	12	16	
T_s	8.03	137.0	5482	(sec)
N_p				
1	4.19	51.8	1745	(sec)
2	2.86	28.4	901.7	
3	3.54	20.8	633.6	
4	2.22	17.1	503.8	
5	2.25	15.1	422.7	
6	2.27	13.8	411.5	
7	2.42	14.1	378.1	
8	2.34	12.7	360.5	
speedup	1.89	4.08	4.84	

Fig.5.6 Results of parallel Travelling Salesman program

5.3 Parallelization of Pure Prolog interpreter

In sequential Prolog the conjunction of goals is executed from left to right, and the disjunction of Horn clauses is unified from top to bottom. There are two ways to execute Prolog programs concurrently. One is the or-parallel execution, in which a system tries each Horn clause in parallel. This or-parallelism can be easily realized, handling the multiple environment of logical variables. Another is the and-parallelism, in which Prolog executes goals in parallel, keeping the consistency among the proofs of goals on the shared logical varables with parallel unification. Since an efficient implementation of and-parallelism is hard we implemented here only the or-parallelism for Pure Prolog. We used a tiny Pure Prolog originally written by Ken Kahn and modified by David Betz, transforming it into a PaiLisp version with or-parallelism and implementing the multiple environment with the association list. The syntax of Pure Prolog is as follows:

```
+(f1 p1 ...):                      assert a fact
+(f1 p1 ...)-(f2 p2 ...) ...-(fn pn ...):  assert a theorem
-(f1 p1 ...) ...-(fn pn ...):      query
-(end):                            end of prolog
(? variable)                       a variable
-(eval f clause)                   unify val(f) with clause
```

This Prolog does not support the cut operator and removal of a clause from a database. The Prolog interpreter has three main procedures: reader, prover and unifier. Since a parallel unification requires fine-grained parallelization we consider only a simple or-parallelization of the prover program. A simple parallel prover is given below.

```
(define (prove list-of-goals environment database level)
  (cond ((null? list-of-goals)
         (print-bindings environment environment))
        (else (try-each database database
                 (cdr list-of-goals) (car list-of-goals) environment level))))
(define (try-each database-left database goals-left goal environment level)
  (let ((assertion '()) (new-environment '()))
    (cond
      ((eq? (car goal) 'eval)
       (set! new-environment (try-sys (cdr goal) environment))
       (if (null? new-environment)
           #f
           (prove goals-left new-environment database (+ level 1))))
      ((eq? (car goal) 'end) 'epilog)
      ((null? database-left) #f)
      (else (set! assertion (rename-variables (car database-left) (list level)))
            (set! new-environment (unify goal (car assertion) environment))
            (cond ((null? new-environment)
                     (try-each (cdr database-left) database
                               goals-left goal environment level))
                  (else
                   (par (prove (append (cdr assertion) goals-left)
                               new-environment database (+ 1 level))
                        (try-each (cdr database-left) database
                                  goals-left goal environment level)))))))))
```

Parallel Prolog program

This prover proves the conjunction of the list-of-goals under the current environment. If there is no goal to prove, the procedure 'prove' prints the current environment. The procedure 'y-or-n-p' always returns true in order to search all the solutions in parallel. The try-each tries to expand each goal under an enviroment. If the unification of the 'goal' succeeds, we spawn two processes with 'par'. One of the processes continues to search a solution under the new environment, and another attempts to prove other Horn clauses under the current environment. The parallelism is introduced and expressed using 'par'. We executed two Prolog programs: 'append' and 'queen'.

```
(1) 'append'
+(append () (? x) (? x)):
+(append ((? a) . (? x)) (? y) ((? a) . (? z)))-(append (? x) (? y) (? z)):

(2) 'queen'
+(extract (? x) ((? x) . (? y)) (? y)):
+(extract (? x) ((? w) . (? y)) ((? w) . (? z)))
                           -(extract (? x) (? y) (? z)):
+(queen (? l) (? w) (? r))-(extract (? x) (? l) (? ll))
                  -(checklist 1 (? x) (? w))
                  -(queen (? ll) ((? x) . (? w)) (? r)):
+(queen () (? r) (? r)):
+(checklist (? n) (? x) ((? h) . (? t)))
      -(eval (+ (? x) (? n)) (? x+n))-(eval (= (? x+n) (? h)) #f)
      -(eval (- (? x) (? n)) (? x-n))-(eval (= (? x-n) (? h)) #f)
      -(eval (+ (? n) 1) (? m))-(checklist (? m) (? x) (? t)):
+(checklist (? n) (? x) ()):
```

The "append" program means that the concatenation of the first two lists becomes the last list. The "queen" program solves the N-Queen problem. We executed the following queries to the parallel Pure Prolog interpreter.

```
-(append (? x) (? y) ( 1 2 3 4 5 6 7 8 9 )):
-(queen ( 1 2 3 4 5 ) () (? x)}:
```

Fig.5.7 shows the results. The 'append' contains little parallelism since its search tree is asymmetric

[**Remark**] The results of TPU and Pure Prolog show some good applicabilitiy of PaiLisp for OR-parallelization in theorem proving and logic-based reasoning. An interesting application of PaiLisp was done by M. Hagiya, who used PaiLisp to run Higher-Order Unification in a typed 'λ-calculus. His experience of "Running Higher-Order Unification in PaiLisp" is reported in this proceedings. We have no experience of running AND-parallelization in logic-applications yet. It will be interesting to see what kind of results can be obtained in running some applications of AND-parallelization.

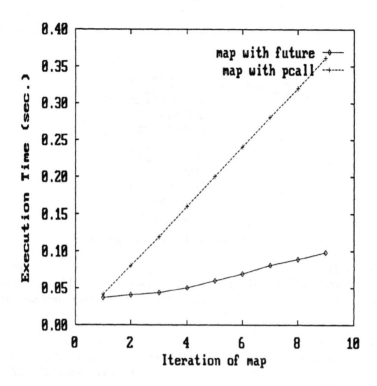

Fig.5.7 Results of running parallel Pure Prolog for 'append' and 'queen'

5.4   Effects of Parallelizing 'map' and 'and'

[parallel map]
We can parallelize the map function which iteratively applys a function on each element of a list. 'fmap' is the one parallelized using 'future', and 'pmap' is the one parallelized using 'pcall'.

```
(define fmap
  (lambda (f l) (if (null? l)
                 '()
                 (cons (future (f (car l)))
                       (future (fmap f (cdr l)))))))
(define pmap
  (lambda (f l) (if (null? l)
                 '()
                 (pcall cons (f (car l)) (pmap (cdr l)))))))
```

We executed these two programs for the case that
f = add1
l = (0 1 2 3 4 5 6 7 8 9 10 11 12 13 14 15 16 17 18 19)

The table of Fig.5.8 shows the evaluation timing results for fmap and pmap with 8 processors.

No. of iterations	fmap	pmap
1	0.0369	0.0412	(sec)
2	0.0406	0.0805
3	0.0437	0.1192
4	0.0504	0.1603
5	0.0600	0.2005
6	0.0694	0.2407
7	0.0812	0.2810
8	0.0892	0.3201
9	0.0982	0.3612

Fig.5.8 Results for 'fmap' and 'pmap'

[parallel and]
The parallel-and is coded in the language "C" as was explained in 4.4. As an example of using 'par-and' we consider to parallelize the following function 'equals'.

```
(define equals
  (lambda (l m)
    (cond ((and (pair? l) (pair? m)) (and (equals (car l) (car m))
                                          (equals (cdr l) (cdr m))))
          (else (eq? l m)))))
```

We can parallelize this function using 'par-and' as follows:

```
(define equalp
  (lambda (l m)
    (cond ((and (pair? l) (pair? m)) (par-and
                                       (equalp (car l) (car m))
                                       (equalp (cdr l) (cdr m))))
          (else (eq? l m)))))
```

As was mentioned in 5.1.1 the restriction of creating the number of processes suppress overheads caused by process creation. The following 'equalc' does this kind of restriction by the parameter d.

```
(define equalc
  (lambda (l m d)
    (if (zero? d)
        (equals l m)
        (cond ((and (pair? l) (pair? m))
               (par-and
                 (equalc (car l) (car m) (- d 1))
                 (equalc (car l) (car m) (- d 1))))
              (else (eq? l m))))))
```

The table of Fig.5.9 gives the results of comparing equalp and equalc, where equalc 3 and equalc 5 means the cases for $d = 3$ and $d = 5$, respectively.

T_s	2.71		
N_p	equalp	equalc 3	equalc 5
1	3.98	2.73	2.80	(sec)
2	2.06	1.39	1.43
3	1.42	1.06	1.00
4	1.11	0.74	0.76
5	0.93	0.74	0.67
6	0.82	0.75	0.59
7	0.76	0.77	0.51
8	0.72	0.43	0.44
speedup	5.53	6.35	6.36

Fig.5.9 Results for parallelized EQUAL using 'par-and'

[**Remark**] The above results for "equalp" and "equalc" are the results of comparing the same lists. When we compare the lists with different elements at several points we obtain rather diffrent results. An increase of the number of different elements in a list gives a better execution result for "equalp" than "equalc", since "equalc" suppresses creation of PaiLisp processes.

Notice that the list difference can be more quickly found with more different elements in the lists compared.

However, since "equalp" creates more processes than "equalc", "equalp" will produce more processes which may exhaustedly use resources and cause much overhead for the computation afterwards.

5.5 Effects of Parallelizing Garbage Collection

As was explained in 4.10 parallel GCs have been implemented. Fig.5.10 shows the results of running the parallel program of N-Queen Problem with N=7 for the sequential GC, the GC with parallel sweeping, and the GC with parallel marking and sweeping. Since the local parallel markings are implemented in nature in our system the parallel markings of Fig.5.10 mean the parallel global markings (that is, the parallel markings for the global data). This results show that the parallel sweeping is more effective than the parallel global markings.

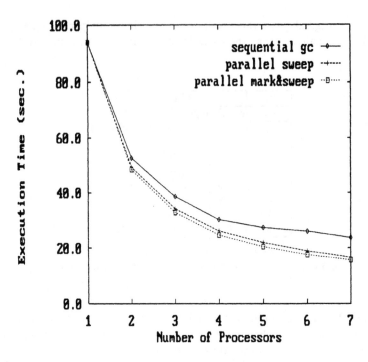

Fig.5.10 Results of parallel GC

6 CONCLUDING REMARKS

In this paper we explained the details of PaiLisp interpreter and its P-continuation based implementations, together with their experimental results of evaluating the system and parallelizing Lisp programs. We would like to give several remarks on various aspects of PaiLisp in this section.

Remark 1: In this paper we showed how P-continuations can be used for implementations of a parallel Lisp interpreter PaiLisp. PaiLisp is a superset of Multilisp, and PaiLisp without side-effects may be considered as a powerful parallel functional language. This means that P-continuation based implementation of this paper will be used for "interpreting and compiling parallel functional languages and other parallel languages with P-continuations". In order to clarify and develop this hope of P-continuation based implementation strategy it will be necessary to explore some systematic and theoretical frameworks for P-continuations and P-continuation passing style in parallel programming.

Remark 2: The PaiLisp interpreter reported here is practically used at the authors' laboratory for various applications to develop parallel alogorithms in parallel Lisp languages. In order to promote PaiLisp applications a parallel object-oriented system called PaiObject was proposed in [Ito91], and the PaiObject system was also implemented on top of PaiLisp interpreter with its slight extensions. The current PaiObject system is slow in its execution so that some improvements have been taken. A debugging system of PaiLisp programs has been also implemented, with developing a system of recording parallel computation histories and a visualization tool.

Remark 3: According to the benchmarking results of Section 5 we could achieve fairly good performance by parallelizing sequential Lisp programs through parallelizations of all the basic Lisp functions in the given sequential programs. The examples that used pcall, pmap and par-and belong to this category of parallelization. With 8 processors they gave more than 4 times better execution results in time, compared to executions with a single processor. Many Lisp programs are written using McCarthy's conditional expression, so that the parallelization of the conditional expression by "pcond" is an easy and simple way to parallelize Lisp programs. However, this parallelization by use of "pcond" gave only 1.2 - 2.5 times better results with 8 processors, compared to the case of a single processor execution. This is because of sequential nature of "pcond" and the overhead of process creation. In order to achieve better performance over the above-mentioned simple minded parallelizations it is necessary to develop and explore some methodologies of concurrent PaiLisp programming
* using "future", "par", "spawn", "call/cc", "call/ep", "delay" and other PaiLisp concurrency constructs,
and
* restricting and suppressing process creation in a proper manner.
The examples of the benchmarking examples and results shows how these aspects of PaiLisp programming are useful to improve execution performance. However, no systematic programming strategies are known yet. In order to achieve high execution performance in a practical situation it is strongly desired to have a good compiler for PaiLisp instead of the PaiLisp interpreter. The issue of the compiler is discussed in more details in APPENDIX.

Remark 4: Parallel Lisp systems have been implemented on some special parallel machines with shared memory; for example, Multilisp on Concert and Enore-Multimax, Qlisp on Alliant and Encore-Multimax, PaiLisp on Alliant FX/80, Top-1 Common Lisp on IBM TOP-1. In order to achieve high execution performance it is necessary and essential to use high- performance parallel machines to execute parallel Lisp programs. Unfornuately parallel machines have been expensive and their OS are not compatible each other, so that parallel Lisp systems have not been used widely and parallel Lisp programming has not been popular. Since we have obtained lots of experiences in parallel Lisp languages and systems it may be interesting to provide more usable parallel Lisp programming environments for Lisp programmers to access parallel Lisp languages and to acquaint parallel Lisp programming to various applications. Otherwise it is rather hard for AI researchers and engineers to use parallel Lisp languages and systems for their applications. From this standpoint to popularise parallel Lisp programming it may be interesting to implement parallel Lisp languages on high performance UNIX workstations such as SPARC system 10, NEXT and the workstations based on MIPS chip and DEC-ALPHA chip. Among them the workstations to support lightweight multitreads like MACH of NEXT and SOLARIS of SPARC System 10 are interesting since their light-weight multithreads architectures support implementations of shared aspects of parallel Lisp languages like Multilisp and PaiLisp. An implementaion of PaiLisp has been taken on SPARC system 10 with SunLWP (Light-Weight Process) mechanism of SUN-OS. According to our preliminary experiments the performace achieved by a single SPARC system 10 corresponds to the performance obtained by Alliant FX/80 with two processor elements. So the SPARC system 10 with 4 processors will corresponds to Alliant FX/80 with 8 processor elements. We hope a wider distribution and development of this kind of systems based on general purpose UNIX workstations to popularize parallel symbolic programming with parallel Lisp systems.

Acknowledgements

The first enthusiastic user of the PaiLisp interpreter was S. Kawamoto, who implemented an interactive Petri net analyser and manipulator using the PaiLisp interpreter. He found many bugs and helped debugging the initial system. Without his efforts to use the system the PaiLisp interpreter could not come to the present practically usable system. Also, other students in our laboratory have become users of the PaiLisp interpreter to implement an object oriented language POOL, parallel CYK parser, a simple ATMS, an equation solver, Concurrent TRS, etc. These attempts helped to improve the system in various ways. Special thanks go to T. Tamura who is implementing PaiObject, A. Koyanagi who is implementing an interactive debugger for PaiLisp programs, and T. Asai who is implementing PaiLisp interpreter using SunLWP mechanism on SUN Sparc System 10. We also would like to express our sincere thanks to M. Ohtomo who helped prepare this manuscript in Springer LaTeX style.

$$\left[\begin{array}{l} \text{This work on PaiLisp was supported by Grant - in - Aid} \\ \text{for Scientific Reseach (A) 01420029, under The Ministry of} \\ \text{Education, Science and Culture, Japan} \end{array} \right]$$

References

[AbeS85] H.Abelson,G.J.Susmann: Structure and Interpretation of Computer Programs, The MIT Press (1985)

[Akl85] S.G.Akl: Parallel Sorting Algorithms,Academic Press(1985)

[ChaL73] C.Chang,R.Lee: Symbolic Logic and Mechanical Theorem Proving, Academic Pressi(1973)

[GabM84] R.Gabriel,J.McCarthy:
Queue-based multiprocessing Lisp,Conference Record of 1984 ACM Symposium on Lisp and Functional Programming,25-44(1984)

[Hals84] R.H.Halstead,Jr.: Implementation of Multilisp:Lisp on a multiprocessor,Conference Record of 1984 ACM Symposium on Lisp and Functional Programming, 9-17(1984)

[Hals85] R.H.Halstead,Jr.: Multilisp:A language for concurrent symbolic computation, ACM Trans.on Programming Languages and Systems,501-538(1985)

[Hals90] R.H.Halstead,Jr.: New ideas in parallel Lisp:Language,implementation, and prog- ramming tools,Springer LNCS,441, 2-57(1990)

[ItoW83] T.Ito,S.Wada: Models of parallel execution of Lisp functions and their evaluations,SIG Report of Symbolic Processing,SYM26-5, Information Processing Society of Japan(1983)<in Japanese>

[ItoT86] T.Ito,T.Tamura,S.Wada: Theoretical comparisons of interpreted/compiled executions of Lisp on sequential and parallel machine models, Information Processing 86, Proceedings of IFIP Congress 86,349-354(1986)

[ItoMK87] T.Ito,T.Matsuyama,H.Kurokawa,A.Kon,M.Ohtomo: An MC68000-based multiprocessor system with shared memory and its applicaton to parallel Lisp interpreter, Proceedings of Symposium on Computer Systems,Information Processing Society of Japan(1987)

[ItoH90] T.Ito,R.H.Halstead,Jr.: Parallel Lisp Languages and Systems,Springer LNCS,441,Springer Verlag(1990)

[ItoM90] T.Ito,M.Matsui: A parallel Lisp language PaiLisp and its kernel specification, Springer LNCS,441,58-100(1990)

[Ito91] T.Ito: Lisp and Parallelism,Artificial Intelligence and Mathematical Theory of Computation,Papers in Honor of John McCarthy, (ed. V.Lifshitz),187-206,Academic Press(1991)

[Ito92] T.Ito,T.Seino: On PaiLisp continuation and its implementation,Proceedings of ACM Workshop on Continuations(ed. O.Danvy & C.Talcott),Stanford (1992)

[MaC60] J.McCarthy: Recursive functions of symbolic expressions and their computation by machine,Communications ACM,3,4,184-195(1960)

[MaPT90] I.A.Mason,J.D.Pehoushek,C.Talcott,J.Weening,:Programming in QLisp, Technical Report STAN-CS-90-1340,Department of Computer Science, Stanford University(October,1990)

[Osb89] R.B.Osborne,: Speculative Computation in Multilisp,MIT/LCS/TR-464 (1989)

[Rees86] J.Rees,W.Clinger(eds): The revised3 report on the algorithmic language Scheme, ACM SIGPLAN Notices,21,37-79(1986)

[SprF89] S.Springer,D.Friedman,: Scheme and the Art of Programming,The MIT Press(1989)

[Tak78] I.Takeuchi(ed): The report of the second Lisp implementation contest,SIDSYM 5-3, Information Processing Society of Japan (1978) [in Japenese]

APPENDIX: On PaiLisp Compiler

A PaiLisp compiler is being implemented, and several benchmark programs have been tested on the compiler. In this appendix we give a brief description on the PaiLisp compiler. Our current PaiLisp compiler relies heavily on the PaiLisp interpreter so that the PaiLisp interpreter which interacts with a programmer will execute the compiled codes of PaiLisp programs. Since our PaiLisp interpreter is implemnnented using Abelson-Sussman's register machine [AbeS85] the PaiLisp compiler is also based on Abelson-Sussman's register machine for ease of implementation. Thus the PaiLisp interpreter plays an essentially important role for managing run-time processor allocations of program executions and invocations of P-continuations since they cannot be handled by the compiler. A PaiLisp process created during execution of compiled codes will be entered into the process queue of its PaiLisp process, and it will be allocated to a processor by the scheduler of the interpreter. The "P-continuation checker" is prepared to check invocation of P-continuations which will be handled by the interpreter.

A.1 About Optimization

The optimizations of codes and executions have been a central and key issue of designing the PaiLIsp compiler. The following optimizations have been taken into account:

* eliminations of unnecessary stack operations relative to the environment registers For example, "save environment" and "restore environment" can be often elimniated on generation of functions and functional-arguments.
* optimizations by static reference of variables Since PaiLisp is based on Scheme and Scheme is a language based on lexical scoping the PaiLisp compiler is also implemented to reflect this nature of static scoping and referencing of Scheme.
* optimizations of executions of Lisp basic functions In case of Abelson-Sussman's Scheme compiler, when it executes (+ 2 3) "+" will be stored into the "fun' register and it will be executed by calling "apply-dispatch" of the interpreter after forming an argument list arg1. However, in this example there is no need to form the argument list and to call "apply-dispatch", since the code like

  "(assign val (add 2 3))"

  suffices in this case. We implemented this kind of optimized executions. When a function takes more than three arguments such a function will be transformed into the corresponding function composed from functions with two arguments. For example, "(+ 2 3 4 5)" ===> "(+ (+ (+ 2 3) 4) 5).
* Other optimizations are contemplated. For example, the costs of call/cc and P-continuations are considered to be relatively high. But according to our PaiLisp programming experiences "call/cc" is used only for non-local exits in most of practical PaiLisp programs, so that it can be replaced by "call/ep". We are trying to characterise the cases where we can safely replace "call/cc" by "call/ep". The use of effect system of D. Gifford is also being examined, but an extension of effect system for P-continuations is an open problem.

A.2 About Extension of PaiLisp Interpreter

In order to implement compiled codes under the PaiLisp interpreter it is necessary to modify and extend the PaiLisp interpreter. The following must be considered:

* Linking compiled codes into the run-time execution routines
  In order to make compiled codes be shared, the following functions which create and kill processes under OS are added to the interpreter.
  (fork n): create n processes and execute them by the interpreter,
  (exit): terminate the interpreter and OS processes when this was applied in PaiLisp processes except looping 'read-eval-print',
  (link filename): read the object-file named by 'filename' into the run-time system, and create a function to execute the object,
  (system command): execute the system command named by 'command'.
* P-continuation checker
  Since compiled codes do not invoke the evaluator it is necessary to add facility to check invocations of P-continuations. The P-continuationchecker which generates an alarm-signal periodically checks the continuation-queue of a PaiLisp process at every alarm-signal; the corresponding continuation will be recovered and applied if it is called. item[*] Modification of garbage collection
  The modification of GC is also done using a 'signal' for GC; that is.when a process exhausted cells a signal for GC will be generated. The GC signal handler interrupts process execution at each GC signal, and the GC marking will take place after terminating all the processes. After completing the GC actions the suspended processes will be resumed and they continue their executions at the time that the GC signal was generated.

A.3 On Compiling PaiLisp Concurrency Constructs

We explain here how to compile 'spawn' and 'future'. The other PaiLisp constructs can be compiled in a similar manner.

[1] Compiling the 'spawn' construct
  We prepare the following codes to create a process object and to enter it into the global process queue.
  * (make_process entry env)
    A newly-created process object will be returned, when 'entry' and 'env' are given, where 'entry' is the jump address to initiate execution of a PaiLisp process and 'env' is the environment for the initiated process.
  * (add_new_process process)
    A process object 'process' will be entered into the global process queue, and the corresponding PaiLisp process will be created. A PaiLisp process must be initialized at the beginning of its evaluation, and a PaiLisp process must be killed at the end of its evaluation. For these purposes we prepare the following codes:

* (initialize_process)
  A PaiLisp process that executed this statement will be initialized.
* kill_process
  This is the label for the subroutine to kill a PaiLisp process. Using these codes (spawn e) can be compiled as follows:

```
    (assign val (make_process spawn_entry (fetch env)))
    (add_new_process val)
    (go_to after_spawn)
spawn_entry
    (initialize_process)
     <<codes to evaluate e>>
    (go_to kill_process)
after_spawn
```

[2] Compiling the 'future' construct

The 'future' construct can be compiled as an extension of compiling the 'spawn' construct, since 'spawn' may be regarded as 'future' without any future value. To handle the future value we prepare the following constructs:

* (make_future)
  This creates a future object.
* determine_future
  This is the label for the subroutine to determine the future value. Using these codes (future e) can be compiled as follows:

```
    (assign val (make_future))
    (assign fun (make_process future_entry (fetch env) (fetch val)))
    (add_new_process fun)
    (go_to after_future)
future_entry
    (initialize_process)
    <<codes to evaluate e>>
    (go_to determine_future)
after_future
```

A.4 On Running PaiLisp Compiler

The first PaiLisp compiler took the following step:

1) create the compiled codes mentioned in A.3,
2) transform them into the C program,
3) execute its C program using the C compiler.

In this approach the compiled-execution was only two times faster than the interpreted execution for the benchmarking programs. This result was worse than we expected, so that we are taking the following approach using Assembler language of Alliant FX/80.

1) transform the compiled codes to the Assembler programs
2) create the object codes by Assembler and execute them.

According to our preliminary experiments of this approach the compiled execution is about five times faster than the interpreted execution. Remark: If we intend to construct a really fast compiler it will be better to construct a stack-machine based compiler rather than a register-machine based compiler of Abelson-Sussman.

Running Higher-Order Unification in PaiLisp

Masami HAGIYA

Department of Information Science, Graduate School of Science
University of Tokyo
Hongo 7-3-1, Bunkyo-ku, Tokyo 113, JAPAN
hagiya@is.s.u-tokyo.ac.jp

Abstract. In this report, I describe an experience in using PaiLisp, a parallel implementation of Scheme, for a reasonably large application in symbolic computation. The application is higher-order unification in a typed λ-calculus, where a unification procedure solves equations containing unknown variables ranging over functions. For a large and balanced unification problem, I could gain almost linear speed-up up to the maximum number of processors.

Background — Higher-Order Unification

A unification problem is called *higher-order* if it contains unknown variables ranging over functions. As higher-order unification is usually formulated under the framework of typed λ-calculi, a solution of a unification problem instantiates a functional unknown with a λ-term.

Higher-order unification problems naturally arise in areas such as the following.

- program transformation
- list processing (by function lists)
- anti-unification
- inductive inference (i.e., programming by example)
- theorem proving
- example-based reasoning (i.e., proving by example)

With these practically important as well as theoretically deep applications, it is vital to develop an efficient implementation of a higher-order unification procedure.

The first practical procedure for higher-order unification was devised by Huet [6]. His idea was to postpone the processing of flexible-flexible equations because they are obviously unifiable but usually have an infinite number of unifiers.

Huet's unification procedure was later reformulated by Gallier and Snyder [2] in the form of a set of transformation rules on equations. Their reformulation followed the series of reformulations of unification procedures for first-order unification, narrowing, E-unification, etc., and made the correctness of the higher-order unification procedure almost self-evident.

As the studies on typed λ-calculi got matured, Huet's procedure, which had been formulated in *simple type theory*, i.e., the weakest typed λ-calculus, was extended to more stronger ones. For example, Elliott [1] and Pym [8] almost simultaneously devised a unification procedure for Logical Framework, a typed λ-calculus with dependent types.

An interesting feature of typed λ-calculi having dependent types, such as Logical Framework, is that proofs in predicate logic can be represented by λ-terms according to the so-called Curry-Howard isomorphism. By this feature, one can do unification or matching between proofs by a unification procedure for those calculi. One can even do proof search, i.e., theorem proving, using the unification procedure almost unchanged [5].

PaiLisp

In this work, I made an experiment in which a higher-order unification procedure was run by PaiLisp. PaiLisp is a parallel extension of Scheme being developed at Tohoku University [7]. At the time of the experiment, PaiLisp was the only implementation of parallel Lisp available in Japan, which could run reasonably large symbolic applications such as mine.

PaiLisp is based on *shared memory model*. This seems important for the parallel program of this experiment because a multiset of equations is a huge data structure shared by or-parallel processes.

The implementation of PaiLisp used in this experiment runs on Alliant FX/80 with 8 processors. Since the compiler was under development, the experiment was made by the interpreter.

Overview of the Program

The program used in the experiment is an almost faithful implementation of Gallier and Snyder's reformulation of higher-order unification. It was originally written in Common Lisp for my research on programming by example and proving by example [3, 4]. Therefore, the typed λ-calculus I use is Calculus of Constructions, which contains Logical Framework as its subsystem. Though the unification procedure is only partially complete for the full system of Calculus of Constructions, it is complete for Logical Framework. The implemented procedure has an optional feature for doing projection on flexible-flexible equations, which makes it work also as a theorem prover [5].

The program consists of a main loop in which an equation is selected and one of the following three transformation operations is applied on it.

- projection transformation
- imitation transformation
- decomposition transformation

A flexible-rigid equation usually allows both the projection transformation and the imitation transformation. Their selection must be nondeterministic. Moreover, in the projection transformation, the selection of an argument to be projected must also be nondeterministic.

The original version of the program was written in Common Lisp. Almost all the coding efforts in this work were spent in converting Common Lisp code into Scheme code. Making the program parallel was relatively easy because it has a simple structure in which transformation operations are iteratively applied on a multiset of equations. It was only necessary to change the program fragment for backtracking control so that it simply spawn new processes instead of preparing for backtracking. Therefore, the resulting parallel program is *or-parallel*.

The unification procedure first checks if there is a rigid-rigid equation. If it finds one, it applies the decomposition transformation on the equation. If there is no rigid-rigid equation, it searches for a flexible-rigid equation and selects one. This selection is arbitrary (currently, some heuristics are used). It then spawns a new process for each selection of the transformation operations and for each selection of an argument in the projection operation. The only parallel constructs used in the program are future and force, which are almost standard in parallel dialects of Scheme.

Environments for variables are implemented by deep binding, i.e., by simple association lists. Each or-parallel process has a distinct association list while multisets of equations are shared by or-parallel processes.

The final program consists of 1206 lines of Scheme code.

Unification Problems of the Experiment

I tried two unification problems in this experiment. The first one is a second-order matching problem in simple type theory. The unification procedure enumerates all the solutions of the following matching problem.

```
f 0 = + (+ (+ 0 0) (+ 0 0)) (+ (+ 0 0) (+ 0 0))
```

In the above equation, + is a constant function of type N->N->N and f is an unknown function of type N->N, where N is the type of constant 0.

The other one is a problem in Logical Framework, where a query on the append predicate of Prolog is simulated. The unification procedure constructs all the terms having the following type.

```
PI x:nlist.PI y:nlist.PI w:nlist.PI w:nlist.
PI answer : (append x y w)->
                 (append w z (cons 1 (cons 1 empty)))->ok.
PI base : PI x:nlist.append empty x x.
PI step : PI n:nat.PI x:nlist.PI y:nlist.PI z:nlist.
                 (append x y z)->(append (cons n x) y (cons n z)).
   ok
```

This problem simulates the following Prolog query.

```
?- append(X,Y,W), append(W,Z,[1,1]).
```

Results of the Experiment

By the experiment, I obtained the following results.

The result of Problem 1 is summarized in Table 1 and Figure 1. The y-axis of the left graph in Figure 1 is the elapsed time for each number of processors, while the

y-axis of the right graph is $1/(t - 11.0)$, where t is the elapsed time and 11.0 is the time for preprocessing (e.g., type checking), which cannot be parallelized (this time was measured by the program). As the right graph shows, I gained almost linear speed-up up to 7 processors.

number of processors	1	2	3	4	5	6	7	8
seconds	122.5	76.5	53.7	47.9	39.8	36.5	35.0	34.7

Table 1. Problem 1

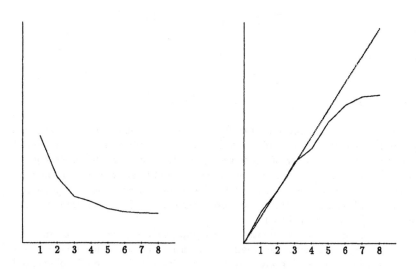

Fig. 1. Problem 1

The result of Problem 2 is shown in Table 1 and Figure 1. I could not obtain any speed-up beyond 3 processors for this problem.

number of processors	1	2	3	4	5	6	7	8
seconds	213.9	139.7	110.8					115.4

Table 2. Problem 2

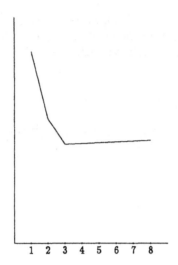

Fig. 2. Problem 2

Discussions

For the first problem, 7 processors could be effectively used. This is because it is a large problem in the sense that it requires a large number of processes (i.e., 263) compared with the number of processors (i.e., 8). Moreover, the process graph is nearly completely binary, i.e., the nondeterminism of this problem is balanced.

For the second problem, on the other hand, only 3 processors were effectively used. This is because the number of processes is small (i.e., 9 processes) and the nondeterminism is not balanced.

At the end of the experiment, I also compared the parallel program running on a single processor with the original sequential one, in which nondeterminism was realized by backtracking and environments for variables were implemented by shallow binding. In general, deep binding by association lists as used in the parallel program is less efficient than shallow binding used in sequential one. In addition to that, the parallel program must have overhead in task switching. Surprisingly, we could not find significant overhead in the parallel program compared with the sequential one. The main reasons are

- Since the experiment was made by the interpreter of PaiLisp, task switching overhead is small compared with interpreter overhead.
- In the higher-order unification procedure, variable access is usually followed by β-reduction, whose cost is much larger than variable access.

Information about the Program

The code used in this experiment is now available by anonymous ftp from

    nicosia.is.s.u-tokyo.ac.jp (133.11.7.151)

on directory

    pub/staff/hagiya/parsym.

Acknowledgements

I deeply thank Prof. Takayasu Ito of Tohoku University for giving me the opportunity
to start this work and for his continuous encouragements. I also thank Mr. Tomohiro
Seino for teaching me about the details of PaiLisp.

References

1. Elliott, C. M.: Some extensions and applications of higher-order unification, Ph.D Thesis, School of Computer Science, Carnegie Mellon University, 1990.
2. Snyder, W., Gallier, J.: Higher-order unification revisited: Complete sets of transformations, *Journal of Symbolic Computation*, Vol.8, Nos 1&2 (1989), pp.101-140.
3. Hagiya, M.: Programming by example and proving by example using higher-order unification, *10th International Conference on Automated Deduction* (Stickel,M., ed.), Lecture Notes in Artificial Intelligence, Vol.449 (1990), pp.588-602.
4. Hagiya, M.: ¿From programming-by-example to proving-by-example, *Theoretical Aspects of Computer Software* (Ito, T., Meyer, A. R., eds.), Lecture Notes in Computer Science, Vol.526 (1991), pp.387-419.
5. Hagiya, M.: Higher-order unification as a theorem proving procedure, *Eighth International Conference on Logic Programming*, 1991, pp.270-284.
6. Huet, G. P.: A unification algorithm for typed λ-calculus, *Theoretical Computer Science*, Vol.1 (1975), pp.27-57.
7. Ito. T., Matsui, M.: A parallel Lisp language PaiLisp and its kernel specification, *Parallel Lisp: Languages and Systems*, (Ito, T., Halstead, R. H. Jr., eds.), Lecture Notes in Computer Science, Vol.441 (1990), pp.58-100.
8. Pym, D.: Proofs, search and computation in general logic, Ph.D Thesis, Department of Computer Science, University of Edinburgh, CST-69-90, 1990.

PART III

Program Development

Tools

HyperDEBU: a Multiwindow Debugger for Parallel Logic Programs

Hidehiko TANAKA, Jun-ichi TATEMURA
{*tanaka, tatemura*}@mtl.t.u-tokyo.ac.jp

Department of Electrical Engineering,
Faculty of Engineering, The University of Tokyo
7-3-1 Hongo, Bunkyo-ku, Tokyo, 113 JAPAN

Abstract. In this paper, a multiwindow debugger HyperDEBU for fine-grained highly parallel programs is presented. The target language of HyperDEBU is Fleng which is one of the committed choice languages. This debugger supports many kinds and levels of views of programs, and helps user to locate bugs efficiently.

Keywords: Programming Environments; Testing and Debugging; Concurrent Programming

1 Introduction

Debugging parallel programs is much more difficult than debugging sequential programs because many processes run simultaneously and interact with each other. While most traditional debuggers only trace each process, they can hardly handle inter-process communication. To comprehend inter-process communication, some prototype systems have been developed : a time-process diagram and an animation of program execution [1]. The time-process diagram represents execution of a program in a two-dimensional display with time on one axis and individual process on the other axis. The animation displays snapshots of processes one after another. However, these are not enough for the debugging of parallel programs.

Though a Committed-Choice Language (CCL), which is a kind of parallel logic programming languages, enables the description of fine-grained highly parallel programs, it is very hard to trace many small processes in a CCL program. The time-process diagram cannot easily display numerous flows of data and control. It is hard to understand an animation which displays many processes created dynamically. To understand execution of a fine-grained highly parallel program such as a CCL program, the relation among control/data-flows is more important than time-sequences of events.

The role of debugger is to present a user the program execution status in the form of model. The user observes and controls the program execution through the model, and finds out bugs through comparing it with his intension.

In this paper, we introduce a communicating process model to represent the execution of a CCL program, and describe a multiwindow debugger HyperDEBU which implements this model on multiwindow interface. This debugger provides flexible views which enable a user to examine and manipulate complicated structures composed of multiple control/data flows of a fine-grained highly parallel program.

2 Committed-Choice Language Fleng

Committed-Choice Languages (CCLs) such as Guarded Horn Clauses (GHC) and Concurrent Prolog are parallel logic programming languages which have a control primitive "guard" for synchronization [4]. Fleng [2] is a CCL designed in our laboratory. We are developing the Parallel Inference Engine PIE64 [3] which executes Fleng programs. Fleng is simpler than other CCLs in the sense that Fleng has no guard goal, though guard mechanism is incorporated in the the head part.

A Fleng program is a set of horn clauses like:

$$H:-B_1, \cdots, B_n. \quad n \geq 0$$

,where H and B_i are predicates called goals.

The side to the left of :- is called the *head part*, and the right side is called the *body part* whose item B_i is called a *body goal*.

Execution of Fleng program is repetition of rewriting a set of goals in parallel. For each goal, one of the clauses whose head can match with the goal, is selected, and then the goal is rewritten by the body goals of the clause. The execution begins when initial goal is given, and is completed when no goal remains. The rewriting operation is called *reduction*, and the matching operation is called *unification*.

Unification is an algorithm which attempts to substitute values for variables such that two logical terms are made equal. To realize communication and synchronization in concurrent logic programs, unification in CCL is divided into two classes : *guarded unification* and *active unification*. Guarded unification is applied in the head part of a clause and variables in the goal are prevented from being substituted. Such unification is *suspended* until these variables have values. Active unification is applied in the body part of a clause and is able to substitute values for variables of goals.

The synchronization mechanism of guarded unification prevents reading a variable before it is bound to a value and eliminates many nondeterministic bugs due to synchronization.

For example, assume that the following program is given :

```
init :- send(X),receive(X).              (1)
receive([D|S])  :- do(D), receive(S).    (2)
send(S) :- S = [0|S1], send(S1).         (3)
```

If an initial goal init is given, this is unified with the head of the clause (1) and two goals send(X) and receive(X) , which have a shared variable X , are generated by reduction. When the goal receive is tried to unify with the head of clause (2), it is found that the argument of receive is required to be a structured data [D|S] (it is called *list cell*) in order to complete the guarded unification. Then this reduction of receive is suspended if its argument is a variable at this time. On the other hand, the goal send is unified with the head of the clause (3), and reduced into two goals S = [0|S1] and send(S1). The goal S = [0|S1] is a system predicate for active unification which unifies two terms S and [0|S1]. After this unification, the guarded unification of the goal receive and the head of (1) can be completed, and then the reduction of receive is resumed and two goal do and receive are generated.

When a Fleng program is executed, many goals are reduced in parallel, synchronizing each other in the way described above.

Fleng is a fine-grained highly parallel programming language in which goals are executed in parallel. Since many goals are created and terminated dynamically, it is very difficult to examine and manipulate execution of a goal.

3 Modeling Execution of Fleng Program

3.1 Requirements of the Model of Program Execution

The role of a debugger is to show users a model abstracted from the execution of a program. A programmer examines and manipulates the execution of the program through this model, compares the model with an intended model, and finds bugs from the difference between them. In this section, some requirements of a model which represents execution of a CCL program are described from the following two aspects.

Parallel Logic Program Since a synchronization primitive "guard" makes a difference of semantics between CCL and a pure logic program language, some operational meaning must be added to the declarative semantics for CCL. The problem with the semantics has been discussed in several works [5] [6]. We must consider the causality relation between input and output of a program. Accordingly, a model which represents execution of CCL program must take account of the input-output causality.

Fine-Grained Highly Parallel Program A model which represents execution of a fine-grained highly parallel program is required to abstract essential data from numerous information on execution of a highly parallel program, and to assist a user, who can deal with only a limited amount of information, to find a bug from it. Such a model is expected to have the following features :

– flexible levels of abstraction
– flexible aspects of abstraction

3.2 Process Model

We model the execution of a Fleng program using processes which communicate each other. In this section we describe the process model for execution of a Fleng program.

Notion of Process for CCL The conventional notion of process for CCL is associated with one goal or one sequence of goals. The process model proposed in this paper is equivalent not to one goal but to all of its subgoals generated by reduction. From outside, the execution of the process is looked upon as the input-output behavior of the process. The substance of the process is a set of goals derived from a goal. Since a goal is reduced to sub-goals, a process can be divided into sub-processes. It corresponds to execution tree which represents a computation of a logic program. The tree has subtrees whose roots are the nodes of the tree. The tree corresponding to the process can be divided into subtrees which corresponds to the sub-processes of the process.

In the process model described above, the definition clause is considered to define a relation between a process and its sub-processes.

Definition of Process The process model described above is formalized as follows. Our debugger provides this model to programmers.

Let G be a goal which is computed in a Fleng program and Q be a set of goals which are derived from G. We call the process P whose substance is Q *"the process with respect to G"*, and call G *"the topgoal of P"*.

The process P with respect to G is represented as follows from outside.

$$\langle G_{skel},\ I/O,\ S,\ G_{ins} \rangle$$

G_{skel} is the skeletal predicate of G whose arguments are replaced by distinct variables like this :
$$p(v_1, \ldots, v_i)$$
, where $v_1, \ldots, v_i$ are the distinct variables which can be regarded as the ports for communication with outer processes.

I/O is I/O data flow which represents the communication of the process P. They show how the variables of G_{skel} are substituted by unifications outside and inside of the process. Details of I/O data flow will be described later.

S is the state of P, which is one of the following states:

- *terminated*
  indicates that all of the goals in P have terminated.
- *suspended*
  indicates that there are no active goals in P and that there are some suspended goals. When one of the suspended goals is activated by input data which is substituted by unifications outside of P, the state turns into *active*.
- *active*
  indicates that some active goals exist in P and that P can be executed.

The above definition makes the model suitable for running programs or a program which runs perpetually, as this model is procedural rather than declarative.

G_{ins} is the *instance* of G. It is regarded as the result of the substitution for G_{skel} by I/O.

Input/Output of a Process I/O data flow of a process is represented as a tree structure which we call an *I/O tree*. This is a tree of causality among active unifications and guarded unifications.

Consider the I/O tree of a process with respect to a goal G. Since the arguments of G_{skel} can be regarded as ports for communication, there are I/O trees corresponding to each port.

The construction of I/O tree O can be represented as follows :

$$O ::= C \ '|' \ O$$
$$| \ U \ 'x' \ O$$
$$| \ O \ '+' \ O$$
$$| \ 'Nil'$$

Each factor has the following meaning respectively :

1. $C|O$

   This indicates input-output causality; O exists if input satisfying the condition C exists. C consists of guarded unifications. It is also graphically represented as:

   ```
   cond(Condition)
      |- O
   ```

2. $U \times O$

   This indicates that the active unification U exists and is followed by O. It is also graphically represented as:

   ```
   T1 = T2
      |- O
   ```

   where T1 = T2 is an active unification and O is the I/O tree which substitutes variables in the term T2.

3. $O + O$

   This indicates that the path of I/O is divided. It is also graphically represented as:

   ```
   |- O1
   |- O2
   ```

An Example of I/O tree A horn clause describes not only the relation between a process and its sub-processes, but also describes the relation between I/O tree of the process and I/O tree of the sub-processes. I/O tree is defined recursively by the clauses committed (selected) in the execution of the program. Detail of the definition is described in [7]. In this paper, we will not explain the details but show a simple example of I/O tree.

Assume that the following program and an initial goal append([1,2],[3],R) are given.

```
append([H|X],Y,Z) :- Z = [H|Z1], append(X,Y,Z1).
append([],Y,Z) :- Z = Y.
```

This program connects a list given in the first argument and a list given in the second argument, and returns it through the third argument. The result will be R = [1,2,3].

Then we will show I/O tree of the process with respect to the initial goal. G_{skel} of the process is represented as $append(A, B, C)$. The output of C is represented as the following I/O tree :

```
cond(A = [D|E]) <= (A = [1,2])
  |- C = [D|F]
       |- cond(E = [G|H]) <= (E = [2])
           |- F = [G|I]
                |-cond(H = []) <= (H = [])
                 |- I = B
```

This meaning is as follows : The active unification C = [D|F] exists on condition that the guarded unification A = [D|E] succeeds. There is the subsequent I/O tree to substitute variable F in the term [D|F]. F is unified with [G|I] on condition that the guarded unification E = [G|H] succeeds.

We can also abstract the I/O tree by replacing its subtree with its subprocesses as follows :

```
cond(A = [D|E]) <= (A = [1,2])
  |- C = [D|F]
       |- F / append(E,B,F)
```

append(E,B,F) is the subprocess of append(A,B,C) and unifies F by the inner unification of it.

3.3 Features of Process Model

The process model proposed in the previous section has the following features :

- hierarchy of processes
  A process consists of some subprocesses.
- multiple views of a process
  A process has three views; a set of goals, an execution tree, and I/O causality.

Figure 1 shows the process model. This model satisfies the requirements for a model of a fine-grained highly parallel program. The other definitions of process such as one goal and one sequence of goals do not seem applicable to debugging a highly parallel program.

Representing input-output causality, the process model also satisfies the requirements for the semantics of CCL. We have applied this model to *algorithmic debugging* of Fleng programs [7].

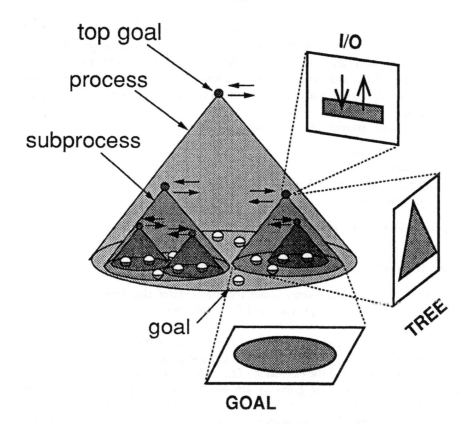

top goal

process

subprocess

I/O

goal

TREE

GOAL

Fig. 1. The Process Model

4 Multiwindow Debugger HyperDEBU

4.1 Design of Debugger for Fine-grained Highly Parallel Programs

A sequential program has only one thread of execution, which can be debugged with a sequential interface. On the other hand, a parallel program has multiple complicated control/data flows which are considered to be high-dimensional information. If a sequential interface is used to debug a parallel program, the bottleneck between a programmer and the program makes it difficult to examine and to manipulate the execution of the program. Therefore, a high-dimensional interface is necessary to debug a parallel program.

Since a user compares a model represented by a debugger with the expected behavior of the program when he/she debugs a program, the debugger must provide a view of the kind he/she wants. Accordingly, the debugger must provide views which have flexible levels and aspects of abstraction.

Most of conventional multiwindow debuggers use many windows, each of which is assigned to one of the processes as a sequential debugger. However, high-dimensional information cannot be handled well in this way. On the other hand, HyperDEBU provides a user with a few kinds of windows he/she wants, through tracing links on a window which displays some information of a program execution.

HyperDEBU consists of the following windows.

1. toplevel-window
2. process-windows
   (a) TREE view (b) I/O tree view (c) GOAL view
3. structure-windows

Figure 2 shows an overview of HyperDEBU.

4.2 Requirements of The Debugger

In this section, we will discuss some requirements of the debugger design in accordance with the concept described in the above section.

Comprehending the Global Situation of the Execution When a program shows unexpected behavior, the first task for the programmer to debug it is comprehending the situation of the execution of this erroneous program. A programmer can debug a sequential program by tracing one thread of execution through some event filters. On the other hand, it is very difficult to trace a complicated structure composed of a large number of control and data flows of a highly parallel program. Even if he tries to trace some threads of these flows through an event filter, it is a hard problem to determine what should be extracted from such an enormous amount of data, and, furthermore, he can not comprehend their relationship with each other. That is to say, it is very much more difficult to comprehend a global situation of the execution of a highly parallel program than of a sequential program.

To solve this problem, a debugger is required to provide a macroscopic view abstracted from the information of the execution in order to help a programmer to comprehend the situation of the erroneous program.

Zooming on the Location of the Bug After the user identifies the area where bugs seem to exist by comprehending the global situation, he must examine this area more minutely and hopes to reach the erroneous points. Since the information of the execution is enormous and complicated, it is necessary to zoom gradually in on the location of the bug with the breadth of a view (that is, a level of abstraction) kept properly.

To zoom in on the location of the bug efficiently, it is important to extract as much useful information from a user as possible, with the amount of data to treat limited to as little as possible. For this reason, a debugger is required to display many kinds of information which the user needs, in abstracted form(with small

170

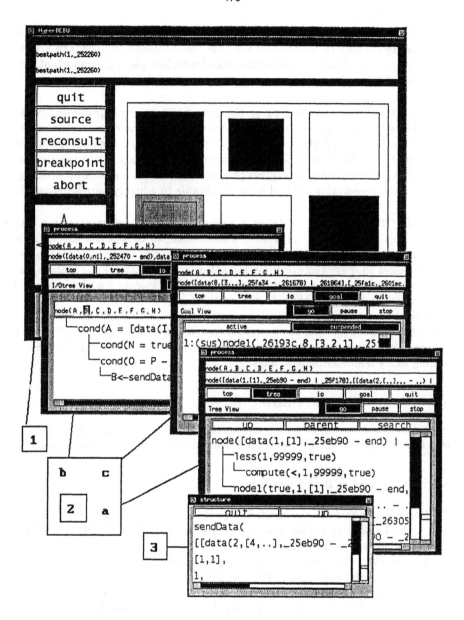

Fig. 2. Overview of HyperDEBU

amount of characters). Moreover, it is essential that the abstracted information on the screen is easy to understand and that the directions the user can give to the debugger are elastic. A high-dimensional interface plays an important role in solving this problem.

Grasping the Static Information of the Program Since a programmer has to grasp the static information of the program to debug it, he refers to the source code if necessary throughout debugging. To debug a concurrent program, he must trace multiple flows in the source code simultaneously. Although most of conventional multiwindow debuggers provide a window as a source level debugger for each process, this method is not applicable to a highly parallel program.

Control of the Execution To debug a program, a programmer examines and manipulates its execution. Therefore, a mechanism to control the execution is needed. For a sequential program, the programmer sets up breakpoints in desirable places to make the execution stop there and to examine the state of the program. However, a new control method is required to debug a highly parallel program which has many threads of execution.

The nondeterminism of a parallel program is also important. To debug such a program, a debugger has to control this nondeterministic behavior. Note that the synchronization mechanism of guarded unification of CCL is helpful in eliminating many nondeterministic bugs.

4.3   Features of HyperDEBU

In this section, we will describe the functions of our debugger HyperDEBU, which is designed to satisfy the requirements described in the above section.

Various Views for Bug Locating

Toplevel-window and Process-windows For the flexibility of levels of views, that is, in order to support global view as well as local view, HyperDEBU provides a toplevel-window and process-windows.

A toplevel-window, which provides a global view, is opened initially, and a user provides initial goals into it. The user can examine and manipulate execution of a program in the global scope with this window. Moreover, the user can get process-windows to examine the details of any processes displayed on the toplevel-window. The toplevel-window manages all of the process-windows.

A process-window, which can be opened for any process, enables examination and manipulation of the process. To locate bugs, a user can get subprocesses as other windows from this process.

Moreover, HyperDEBU has a structure-window which provides a data-level view. A user can get it from any data displayed on windows of HyperDEBU. Since all of the data on HyperDEBU are updated as the program runs, a user can examine state of the program dynamically.

Three Views of Process-window A process-window enables bugs to be located efficiently using the flexible levels and aspects of the process model. The process-window has three kinds of window called views as follows.

- TREE view : This shows an execution tree (control flow relationship of the computation).
- I/O tree view : This shows a tree of input-output causality (data flow relationship of the computation).
- GOAL view : This shows a set of goals (snapshot of the computation).

They enable flexible examination from multiple aspects. A user can get a sub-process as a window from their views.

Program Visualization The global view of the toplevel-window visualizes execution of a Fleng program. Execution of a CCL program is represented by visualizing the following two flows :

- control flow: execution status of goal reduction
- data flow: execution status of guard and unification

Their histories correspond to an execution tree on TREE view, and a tree of input-output causality, respectively. However, visualizing all goals and data is hard to comprehend. The toplevel-window visualizes only processes with respect to some particular goals and only some particular data-flows. A user needs to specify what is *"particular"* , depending on the user's intention. HyperDEBU provides *"breakpoints"* to specify it.

Note that one of the problems of visualization of execution status is the need for locating the display objects dynamically on the screen since the goals and data themselves are created dynamically.

Control-flow The toplevel-window visualizes processes with respect to some particular goals to provide a global view. Figure 3 shows an overview of the toplevel-window. It is regarded as the view from the top of Figure 1. Each process is displayed as a rectangle.

- A color of the rectangle indicates the state of the process (white, light gray and dark gray indicate active, suspend,and terminated respectively)
- A nest of rectangles indicates the relation between a process and its subprocess.
- A topgoal of a process is displayed when the mouse cursor enters the corresponding rectangle.
- Clicking a rectangle generates a new process-window for this process.

Contents of all the windows are updated reflecting the state of the execution dynamically. By observing creations and state transition of processes, and by observing modification of data in the arguments of topgoals, a user can comprehend the execution of Fleng program correctly and easily.

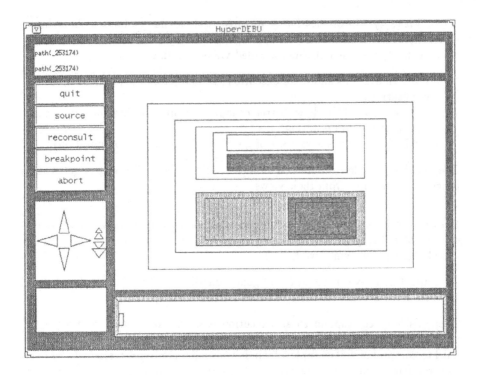

Fig. 3. A Toplevel-window

Data-flow Though data flow is represented as a tree of input-output causality in the I/O tree view, the display of the I/O tree view is too complicated to understand the global data flow of a large scaled program. To solve this problem, the toplevel-window should visualize some particular data flows. We provided a feature of visualizing some particular stream between processes.

Figure 4 shows the 4 forms of stream for visualizing the data flow. They are (1) the generation of stream, (2) the distribution of stream, (3) the data output to the stream, and (4) the data input from the stream(guard).

Breakpoints for Parallel Execution The conventional approach to debugging a sequential program is to stop the program at a breakpoint and to examine the state of execution. However, this approach is not applicable to a parallel program which has multiple control flow.

We extend "breakpoints" as a debugger's knowledge given by a user before the execution of the program. The debugger uses this information to control the execution, visualization and static debugging.

Breakpoints are specified as pairs of "point" and "direction". The following place in a program can be specified as a point :

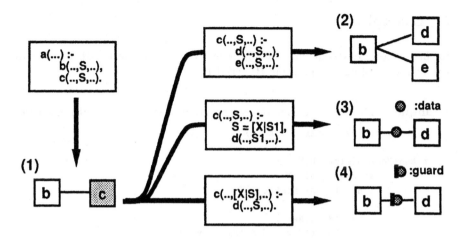

Fig. 4. The Generation, Distribution, IO of Stream

- predicate (a set of clauses which have the same name)
- clause
- body goal
- argument of goal (for dataflow)

There are directions as follows :

- pause : This directs to stop the goal there.
- process : This directs to visualize the process with respect to a goal.
- notree : This directs not to keep execution history.
- stream : This directs to visualize the data as a stream.

Browsing Program Code Since the need to set breakpoints before execution can be a burden to a user, a debugger is expected to aid the user to comprehend static information with which the user decides breakpoints. The program code browser of HyperDEBU is provided for this purpose.

This browser supports the following functions :

- tracing a graph of predicates (procedures) created from cross references caller/callee relations among predicates
- navigating from some execution point of a program to the corresponding point of source program
- searching the history and program code etc. from the name of predicate

These functions are applicable to the following aids to a user :

- setting breakpoints
- static debugging
- correcting a source code

5 Examples

In this section, we will demonstrate the effectiveness of HyperDEBU by showing two examples of debugging using HyperDEBU.

Example 1 The following example is a program to solve "good-path problem".

```
path(A) :- token(start,[],A,[]).

token(Node,History,H,T) :-
        (Node == goal ->
           H = [[goal|History]|T]
        ;
           next(Node,Next),
           checknext(Next,[Node|History],H,T)).

checknext([],History,H,T) :- H = T.
checknext([N|Ns],History,H,T):-
        member(N,History,Result),
        gonext(Result,N,History,H,T1),
        checknext(Ns,History,T1,T).

gonext(true,_,_,H,T) :- H = T.
gonext(false,Node,History,H,T):-
        token(Node,History,H,T).

next(start,Next) :- Next = [a,d].
next(a,Next):- Next = [start,b].
next(b,Next):- Next = [a,c,goal].
next(c,[b,d,goal]).                    %erroneous
%next(c,Next):- Next = [b,d,goal]. %correct
next(d,Next):- Next = [start,c,e].
next(e,Next):- Next = [d,goal].

member(_,[],R) :- R = false.
member(X,[Y|Z],R) :-
        (X == Y -> R = true ; member(X,Z,R)).
```

This program searches the paths on a directed graph and finds all paths from **start** to **goal**. The **next** clauses specify the directed graph; for example, the first clause tells the node **start** has two arrows directed to **a** and **d** respectively. To get the solution, an initial goal **path(X)** is given at first. Then it matches with the first clause of this program and a new goal **token** is generated and spawned. The **token** goals spawn themselves and search the paths from **start** for **goal**. A **token**, which has a node as the first argument **Node**, spawns a goal **checknext** if **Node** is not **goal**. The **checknext** spawns goals **gonext** for the nodes next to the node. Each **gonext** generates a **token** goal if the path from **start** to the node has no loop. If a **token** reaches the node **goal**, it links the solution with the variables **H** and **T** to make the list of the solutions. However, the erroneous definition of **next** makes this program suspend illegally without returning the solutions.

At first, a breakpoint for visualization is placed in order to observe the creation of **token** goals which make the main control flows of this program. Figure 5 shows the visualization of control flow on the toplevel-window. The light-gray rectangles indicate the processes concerned with them are suspended.

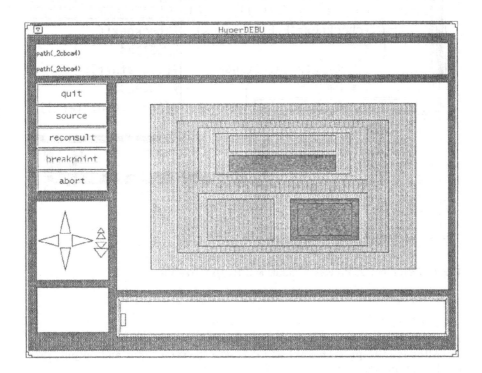

Fig. 5. Example 1-1: Visualization of Toplevel Window

Then, one of these processes, which fails to output results, is opened as a process-window (Figure 6). The third argument of its topgoal is still an undefined variable which must have been fixed. Figure 6 shows the display of an I/O tree view to examine the output of the third argument. It shows that **checknext** is suspended without outputting intended result. The structure-window which displays the instance of **checknext** shows the first argument of **checknext** is an undefined variable. The I/O tree view tells that the input of the first argument E must have come from **next(A,E)** which is suspended illegally. From this part on I/O tree view, we can open a window to display the clauses which defines **next** and get the definition clause which includes a bug as shown at lower side of figure 6.

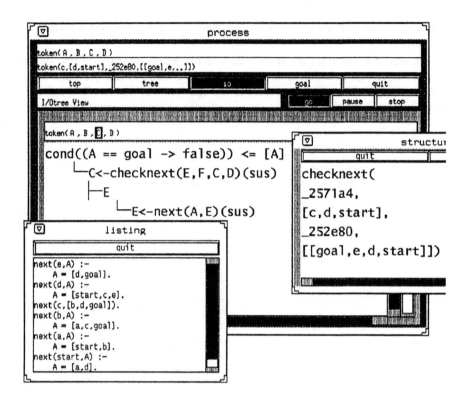

Fig. 6. Example 1-2: Process Window and Its I/O Tree View

Example 2 The next example program has a bug involving input-output causality. Although two programs ex1 and ex2 have the same input and output, their results are different.

```
ex1(A,Z) :-
        multi1([A|X],Y,Z),
        filter(Y,Yout),filter(Z,Zout),
        merge(Yout,Zout,X).
ex2(A,Z) :-
        multi2([A|X],Y,Z),
        filter(Y,Yout),filter(Z,Zout),
        merge(Yout,Zout,X).

multi1([A,B|X],Y,Z) :-
        Y = [A|Y1],Z = [B|Z1],multi1(X,Y1,Z1).
```

```
multi1([],Y,Z) :-
        Y = [], Z = [].

multi2([A|X],Y,Z) :-
        Y = [A|Y1],multi21(X,Y1,Z).
multi2([],Y,Z) :-
        Y = [], Z = [].
multi21([A|X],Y,Z) :-
        Z = [A|Z1],multi2(X,Y,Z1).
multi21([],Y,Z) :-
        Y = [], Z = [].

filter([A|In],Out) :-
        (A > 0 ->
            sub1(A,A1),
            Out = [A1|Out1],
            filter(In,Out1)
        ;
            Out = [A]).
filter([],Out) :- Out = [].

merge([A|X],Y,Z) :- Z = [A|Z1],merge(X,Y,Z1).
merge(X,[A|Y],Z) :- Z = [A|Z1],merge(X,Y,Z1).
merge([],Y,Z) :- Z = Y.
merge(X,[],Z) :- Z = X.
```

Although both of multi1 and multi2 split the input of the first argument into the second argument and the third argument, they are different with respect to input-output causality. While ex2(5,X) returns a result X = [4,2,0,0], ex1(5,X) falls into deadlock and outputs nothing. Figure 7 and Figure 8 show the I/O tree views displaying the results of ex1(5,X) and ex2(5,X) respectively.

Regarding the output of ex1, multi1 is suspended without output to B. It has got input C = [A|F] and waiting for next input from merge which is waiting for inputs of G and E. However, two filter which must output to G and E are both waiting for output of multi1. This loop of input-output causality brings this program into deadlock.

On the other hand, regarding the output of ex2, the output of B exists on condition that C = [D|E] and E = [F|G]. This condition is satisfied by the existence of the output of merge to O which requires the input P. A goal filter can output to P because the input Q = [D|I] exists on condition that C eauals [D|E].

Example 3

Figure 9 shows an example of datafllow visualization. Large rectangles indicate processes, small squares the data generated to the streams, black circle with vertical line the gurds(data is received from the side with the vertical line), and a rectangle with characters a goal. Lines connecting these elements are streams.

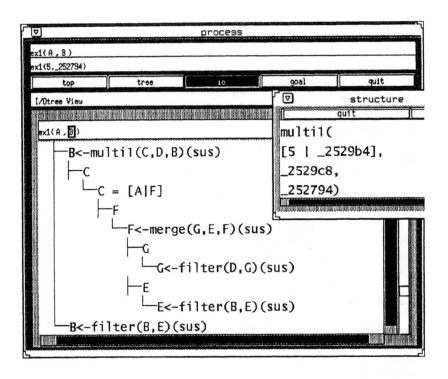

Fig. 7. Example 2-1: I/O Tree View for **ex1**

6 Discussions

6.1 Related Works

PIMOS[8], the operating system on the parallel inference machine PIM, has a tracer for language KL1 which is a practical version of GHC on PIM. It traces a particular thread of execution. However, when we have to deal with many threads of a highly parallel program, it is very difficult to understand them. Moreover, some facilities to trace data flows are required. Although PIMOS can also detect such goals that fall into deadlock, the relation and histories of these goals are not presented to users. On the other hand, HyperDEBU enables to solve this problem since it provides flexible views ranging from global to local view and enables users to examine expected control/data flows and to locate bugs efficiently.

There are some debuggers which visualize the execution of a CCL program as communicating processes. For example, [9] is one of such debuggers. However, they regard one sequence of goals as a process. For this reason, they can hardly visualize execution of a highly parallel program concisely. The flexibility of abstraction, which HyperDEBU has, is required to debug such a highly parallel program.

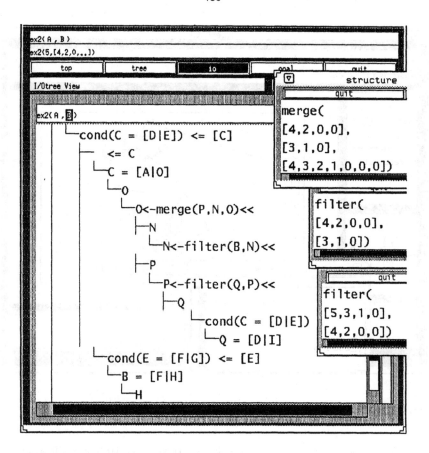

Fig. 8. example 2-2: the I/O tree view for **ex2**

6.2 Nondeterminism

Nondeterminism of a CCL program is caused by the following factors.

1. racing active unifications
2. nondeterministic commitment of clauses

In case 1, a programmer can find a failure of one of these unifications which does not happen in a correct program. Then, using an I/O tree view, the programmer can find the race of outputs to one variable in a tree of active unifications and guarded unifications.

In case 2, introducing some extension such as an OR-tree of input-output causality, an I/O tree view will be able to represent nondeterministic commitment. To analyze how this nondeterminism effects the results of the program execution, some tools need to be developed. However an OR-tree of input-output

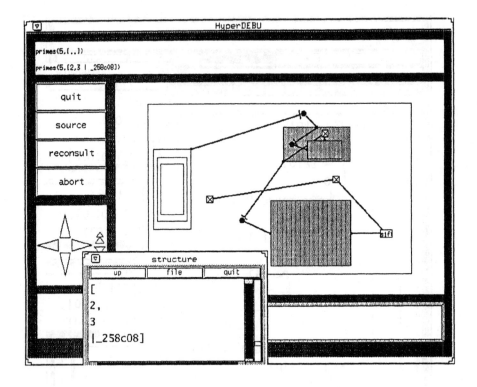

Fig. 9. Example of Visualization of Dataflow

causality is too complex to compute in practical time. Unlike verification, we think that a debugger needs only to report the existence of nondeterminism without computing all possible execution of the program. We are planning to introduce some breakpoints for nondeterministic commitment to enable users to control nondeterminism.

6.3 Costs of Time and Space

When a program is executed with a debugger, there is some overhead such as time to execute codes for debugging and memories for event histories. Although the performance of HyperDEBU is enough for practical use now, more improvement is desired.

HyperDEBU takes much time since it uses meta-interpreter to manage execution of goals. We will design an improved version of the goal management mechanism which is realized by adding some primitives to the interpreter or by modifying the compiled code.

Although event histories are useful to debug parallel programs, it is almost impossible to record whole events. Therefore, HyperDEBU provides a breakpoint to designate such goals (execution tree) that should be recorded. The visualization of program execution through toplevel window helps to identify the erroneous process and results in decreasing the volume of history to store.

7 Future Work

We have realized a realistic debugger for parallel logic programs. For more improvement, we have some subjects as follows:

- support of compiler, operating system, and architecture to debugger
- control of nondeterministic behavior
- static analysis to help debugging
- performance debugging
- total environment for parallel programming

8 Conclusion

In this paper, we introduced a communicating process model to represent execution of a Fleng program, and presented a multiwindow debugger HyperDEBU which represents this model on a high-dimensional interface.

HyperDEBU is written in Fleng and runs on a Fleng interpreter on UNIX workstations and Mach parallel workstations. It is used in the development of application programs including HyperDEBU itself.

References

1. Mcdowell,C.E. and Helmbold,D.P.: *Debugging Concurrent Programs*, ACM Computing Surveys, Vol.21 No.4, pp.593-622 (1989).
2. Nilsson, M. and Tanaka, H.: *Massively Parallel Implementation of Flat GHC on the Connection Machine, Proc. of the Int. Conf. on Fifth Generation Computer Systems*, p1031-1040 (1988).
3. Koike, H. and Tanaka, H. : *Parallel Inference Engine PIE64*, in *Parallel Computer Architecture*, bit, Vol.21,No.4,1989, pp.488-497 (in Japanese).
4. (Ed.) Shapiro, E. : *Concurrent Prolog : Collected Papers* , (Vols. 1 and 2), The MIT Press (1987).
5. Murakami, M. : *An Axiomatic Verification Method for Synchronization of Guarded Horn Clauses Programs*, ICOT Technical Report TR-339, ICOT (1988).
6. Murakami, M. : *A Declarative Semantics of Parallel Logic Programs with Perpetual Processes*, ICOT Technical Report TR-406, ICOT (1988).
7. Tatemura, J. and Tanaka, H. : *Debugger for a Parallel Logic Programming Language Fleng*, Proc. of Logic Programming Conference '89 (1989).
8. Chikayama,T. and Suzaki, K. : *PIMOS 1.5 Introductory Manual*, ICOT Technical Memorandum TM-884, ICOT (1989).
9. Maeda, M., Uoi, H. and Tokura, N. : *Process and Stream Oriented Debugger for GHC Programs*, Proc. of Logic Programming Conference '90 (1990).

MulTVision: A Tool for Visualizing Parallel Program Executions

Robert H. Halstead, Jr.,* David A. Kranz,** and Patrick G. Sobalvarro***

Abstract. MulTVision is a visualization tool that supports both performance measurement and debugging by helping a programmer see what happens during a specific, traced execution of a program. MulTVision has two components: a *debug monitor* and a *replay engine*. A traced execution yields a *log* as a by-product; both the debug monitor and the replay engine use this log as input. The debug monitor produces a graphical display showing the relationships between tasks in the traced execution. Using this display, a programmer can see bottlenecks or other causes of poor performance. The replay engine can be used to reproduce internal program states that existed during the traced execution. The replay engine uses a novel log protocol—the *side-effect touch protocol*—oriented toward programs that are *mostly functional* (have few side effects). Measurements show that the tracing overhead added to mostly functional programs is generally less than the overhead already incurred for task management and touch operations. While currently limited to program executions that create at most tens of thousands of tasks, MulTVision is already useful for an interesting class of programs.

1 Introduction

MulTVision is a visualization tool that supports both performance measurement and debugging by helping a programmer understand what happens during a specific execution of a program. A programmer using MulTVision first runs a program in *trace mode*. Trace-mode execution yields whatever output the program produces when executed in *production* (untraced) mode, but also yields as a by-product a *log* that records the history of the traced computation. A visualization interface offers a way to browse through the log and extract information about the traced execution. MulTVision works for programs written in Multilisp [6], which is the Lisp dialect Scheme [23] extended with the future construct for concurrency. Multilisp's computational model is that of a shared-memory multiprocessor in which tasks interact through shared objects. MulTVision is built on top of Mul-T [14], a Multilisp implementation created by extending the Yale T system [22] with an implementation of the future construct. Mul-T runs on a real multiprocessor, the Encore Multimax.[4]

* DEC Cambridge Research Lab, Cambridge, MA 02139, U.S.A.,
  halstead@crl.dec.com
** M.I.T. Laboratory for Computer Science, Cambridge, MA 02139, U.S.A.
*** M.I.T. Artificial Intelligence Laboratory, Cambridge, MA 02139, U.S.A.
[4] Multimax is a trademark of Encore Computer Corporation.

MULTVISION has two parts: the *debug monitor* and the *replay engine*. Both parts read the log produced by a trace-mode execution of a program, which contains events recording every instance when a task was created, terminated, began to execute on a processor, or became blocked, in addition to the side-effect and side-effect touch events discussed in Section 3. The debug monitor graphically displays the execution of the traced computation and allows the programmer to examine parts of that execution. The replay engine is part of the Mul-T system and allows any data value generated during the traced execution to be regenerated for inspection. Since Multilisp tasks can perform side effects asynchronously on shared objects, program execution can be nondeterministic, making debugging more difficult. The replay engine's ability to reliably replay a prior execution of even a nondeterministic program is thus quite valuable when debugging. However, the replay engine can also assist in performance visualization by identifying the inputs of specific computations shown in the debug monitor's display.

1.1 Multilisp and Futures

By default, execution of Multilisp programs is sequential (and follows the semantic rules of Scheme [23]). Concurrency is introduced using the future construct: if X is a Multilisp expression, (future X) is an expression that evaluates X in a separate *task*. Without waiting for that evaluation of X to terminate, the expression (future X) returns a *future*—a placeholder that stands for the value that X's evaluation will eventually yield. When evaluation of X yields a value, the future *resolves* to that value, essentially losing its identity as a future and becoming the value of X.

Non-strict operations such as passing a parameter to a procedure, returning a result from a procedure, initializing a data-structure element, or storing into a memory location can use an unresolved future as an operand. However, *strict* operations such as addition and comparison (or any operation that requires information about its operand), if applied to an unresolved future, must block and wait for the future to resolve. (If applied to a resolved future, strict operations simply use the value to which the future resolved.) Hence, a strict operation must check each of its operands to see if it is an unresolved future, and if so the operation must block pending the resolution of the future. This check and possible suspension of execution is known as *touching* the operand.

2 The Debug Monitor

Fig. 1 shows a typical debug-monitor display. Time increases as we move from left to right; a scale in microseconds is shown at the bottom. Each task is shown as a horizontal band, filled with a color or stipple pattern that indicates the task's state. The debug monitor usually runs on a color screen, where states can be distinguished using colors: green means that the task is running, yellow means that the task is runnable ("queued") but not currently running, and red means that the task is blocked (waiting for another task to finish). Since we are confined here to monochrome illustrations, we use stipple patterns instead—solid black for running, a halftone gray for queued, and diagonal shading for blocked.

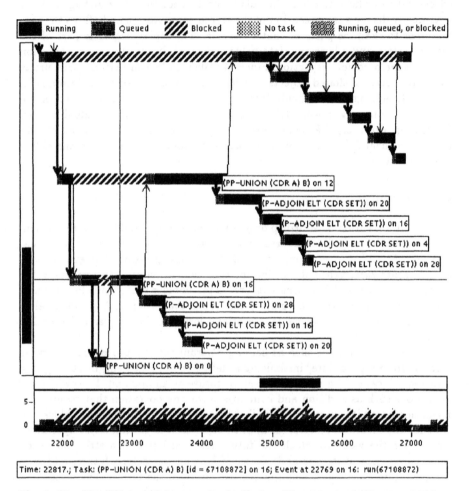

Fig. 1. The MULTVISION debug monitor's display. The program being executed is a parallel set-union algorithm executing on 8 processors and computing the union of two 3-element sets.

Thick arrows point at each task from its parent. Thin arrows point from each running-to-blocked transition to the task computing the value that is awaited; thin arrows also point back from each task completion to those tasks that become runnable as a result. Below the horizontal scrollbar, a summary graph indicates the total number of running, queued, and blocked tasks as a function of time.

MULTVISION uses a heuristic borrowed from ParVis [1] for determining the positions of tasks in the display. Tasks are grouped into a *task-spawning tree* in which each task is a node and each task's parent node is the task that spawned it. Each task is assigned a different vertical co-ordinate in the task display. Each group composed of a task and all of its descendants is assigned a contiguous region of vertical space, with the root task of the group located at the top of this region and the remaining tasks arranged below. Applying this organization recursively throughout the task tree completely determines the vertical ordering of the tasks, except that when a task has more than one child, we need to specify the order to use in arranging the blocks of vertical space that will be assigned to the subtrees headed by each of those children. Here, MULTVISION (following ParVis) makes a counterintuitive choice: the subtrees are ordered so that the subtree headed by the child that was created *last* occupies the highest position, and the subtree headed by the first-created child gets the lowest position. Empirically, this policy usually minimizes the number of arrows that cross over unrelated tasks, but no policy is perfect and one improvement that should be made to MULTVISION is to allow the user to specify alternative task arrangements.

The debug monitor provides several operations for extracting information from or customizing the format of the task display. The user can zoom in on a rectangular area containing a task set and time interval of interest by indicating the corners of the area using the mouse; panning in both dimensions is possible using scrollbars, which also indicate where the currently displayed data fit in the context of the whole execution trace. When the current view is changed by a zooming operation, a description of the previous view is saved in a menu of saved views. This menu makes it easy to return to a previously visited view, but the notation used to represent each saved view in the menu is currently rather cryptic. A good visual representation to help the user understand intuitively the nature of the view represented by each menu entry is badly needed, as is a good way to deal with the clutter that results when dozens of saved views accumulate.

A cursor, indicated by crosshairs, can be moved around to access information about tasks. This information is displayed (currently rather cryptically) in the long horizontal window near the bottom of the display. Information of special importance about a task can be noted by laying down a "signpost" on that task at the time of interest. A signpost shows the expression whose value the task will compute and the processor on which the task is currently running (or most recently ran). Several signposts can be seen in Fig. 1. All the information a signpost contains (and more) can be seen at the bottom of the display by moving the cursor to the signpost's location, but signposts are useful for making annotations on the trace, noting significant facts about the trace so they can all be viewed at once. The cursor can also be used to command the replay engine to perform a replay (to the time indicated by the current vertical crosshair); this capability connects the functions of the debug monitor and the replay engine.

During a MULTVISION session making extensive use of the capabilities described above, quite a bit of state can be built up. It would be frustrating and inconvenient to lose all this state if the MULTVISION session needs to be interrupted, so MULTVISION includes the capabilities to save the current session and to restore a previously saved session. The trace-file name and current view are saved, along with all the saved views and the location and contents of all signposts.

2.1 An Example: Finding a Performance Problem

As Fig. 1 demonstrates, the debug monitor can illustrate the fine structure of a computation in considerable detail. It can also show the source of performance problems. For example, Fig. 2 shows a very simple program sp-union for computing the union of two sets represented as the lists a and b by picking out one element of a, recursively computing the union of b with the remainder of a, and then adjoining the selected element of a with the result, using the sequential procedure s-adjoin. (equal-elt? is a predicate used for testing whether two set elements are equal.)

```
(define (sp-union a b)
  (cond ((null? a) b)
        (else (s-adjoin (car a) (future (sp-union (cdr a) b))))))

(define (s-adjoin elt set)
  (cond ((null? set) (cons elt '()))
        ((equal-elt? elt (car set)) set)
        (else (cons (car set) (s-adjoin elt (cdr set)))))))
```

Fig. 2. Ineffectively parallelized set-union program.

One might suppose that sp-union could achieve some parallelism, owing to the future construct that it contains, but such hopes are quickly dashed by the execution pattern displayed in Fig. 3. It is obvious that sp-union executes quite sequentially, despite its creation of several tasks. Closer inspection of the program reveals the reason: the procedure s-adjoin immediately touches its set argument (by applying the null? test to it), causing s-adjoin to suspend immediately until the future supplied as its set argument resolves. This effectively negates the hoped-for parallelism, as the task display in Fig. 3 shows so clearly.

Fig. 4 shows another set-union program ppr-union designed to avoid the sequentialization encountered by sp-union. This program uses a different strategy: to compute the union of two sets a and b, first pick out an element e of a and remove it (using the procedure p-remove) from the set b, then recursively compute the union of the resulting set with the remainder of a, and finally adjoin e to that result. (e is guaranteed not to be in the set to which it is adjoined in this last step, since we assume that neither a nor b contains duplicates. Therefore, the adjoin operation can be implemented by a simple cons operation, without checking for the presence of e in the set to which it is being adjoined.)

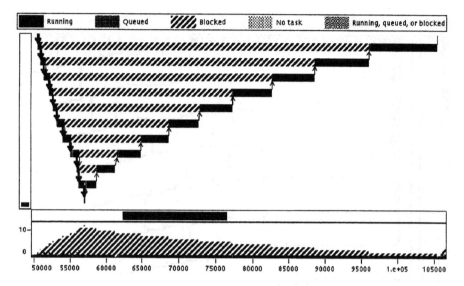

Fig. 3. A MULTVISION debug-monitor display of an ineffectively parallelized set-union algorithm executing on 8 processors and computing the union of two 10-element sets.

```
(define (ppr-union a b)
  (cond ((null? a) b)
        (else (cons (car a)
                    (ppr-union (cdr a)
                               (future (p-remove (car a) b)))))))

(define (p-remove elt set)
  (cond ((null? set) '())
        ((equal-elt? elt (car set)) (cdr set))
        (else (cons (car set)
                    (future (p-remove elt (cdr set))))))))
```

Fig. 4. Better parallelized set-union program.

The use of future in p-remove allows p-remove to return a value while nested calls to p-remove are still executing, leading to an execution pattern in which the elements of the list returned by p-remove gradually appear, from head to tail, as the recursive calls finish. A computation consuming this list can then progress down it, from head to tail, as the elements become available. Thus, parallelism is possible between p-remove (the producer) and a consumer computation. If one unfolds the recursive structure of ppr-union, one finds that the consumer of the list produced by p-remove is generally another instantiation of p-remove, working to remove a different element of the original set a.

This pattern is clearly visible in Fig. 5, where the collection of tasks created

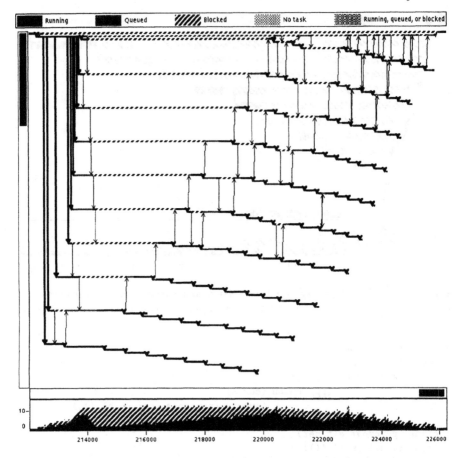

Fig. 5. A MULTVISION debug-monitor display of a better parallelized set-union algorithm executing on 8 processors and computing the union of two 10-element sets.

by each call from ppr-union to p-remove is visible as a downward "staircase" of tasks. When synchronization between producer and consumer results in the blocking of a consumer "staircase" until the producer can catch up, arrows between the "staircases" clearly mark the event. (The task display shown in Fig. 6 is a magnified picture of the upper right-hand corner of Fig. 5, made using MULTVISION's zoom feature. This magnified display shows the details of several cases where a consumer task had to block pending the completion of its corresponding producer task.) While tasks still block some in this version of the set-union program, both the total elapsed time and the height of the running-task graph demonstrate its greater concurrency, as can be seen by comparing Figs. 3 and 5.

MULTVISION makes it easy to see that the additional task creation in Fig. 5 really yields a net benefit, despite the higher overhead cost of managing so many more tasks, but on the whole, MULTVISION simply confirms our intuition about

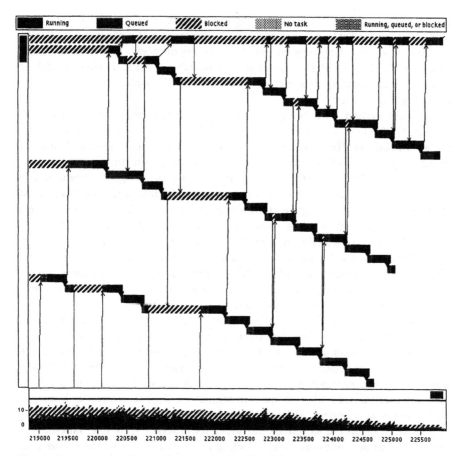

Fig. 6. A zoomed-in display showing the details of the upper right-hand corner of the previous figure.

program behavior in this simple example. The sp-union and ppr-union programs have been kept very simple so they could be discussed fully in this paper. The performance of more complex programs is often governed by interactions between widely separated program sections whose interrelationships may not be obvious. These are the cases in which MULTVISION can really contribute to the program-development process.

2.2 Other Trace-Driven Systems for Visualizing Parallel Execution

Many systems have been built for visualizing data gathered from the execution of parallel programs. MULTVISION's style was influenced most directly by the ParVis system [1], which was an earlier visualization tool developed for use with Multilisp programs. ParVis had the same style of display as MULTVISION's debug monitor, including the intertask arrows, but there are a few differences.

ParVis did not have signposts, the ability to save previous viewpoints, or a replay engine, and it could not use a color display; on the other hand, ParVis did include a query language for specifying events or intervals of interest, which would be highlighted. ParVis also featured movable vertical hairlines useful for marking and measuring time intervals. MULTVISION's display could benefit from including these features.

Another system with many similarities to MULTVISION is the PPUTTs toolkit [4, 18]. Like MULTVISION, this toolkit includes both visualization and replay capabilities. Here, we focus on the visualization tool, "Moviola." Moviola displays the history of each process as a vertical line, with time increasing from top to bottom. Periods during which a process is computing are shown as thin black lines; idle periods are shown as wide gray bands. Interactions between pairs of processes, such as message send/receive event pairs, are shown as slanting lines between the processes involved. Additional information about a particular event can be obtained by selecting it with the mouse. Moviola supports a wide range of display-customization capabilities, including panning, zooming, and selective display of only certain types of events or processes. Additionally, users can extend Moviola by writing Lisp code to compute statistics of interest by traversing the execution graph that Moviola builds.

Upshot [12] is another tool that displays the history of a set of processes based on information in a trace file. The trace file may be created by a logging package that logs events automatically or the user may insert explicit event-logging calls into the program under test. The set of event types in an Upshot trace file is user-defined and extensible: as far as Upshot is concerned, an event's type is just a numerical code with no built-in semantics. Upshot shows the history of each process as a horizontal line, with time increasing from left to right. Each event can be displayed as a little box along its process's time line, labeled with the event's numerical event code. Selecting an event's box with the mouse pops up an information window containing details of the event; this window can be transient or can be left exposed. Upshot also provides a way to define *states* that begin and end with specified event types. When states are displayed, the color of a process's time line is determined by the process's current state. Thus, if a suitable event is logged every time a program under test enters or exits a certain procedure, a state can be defined to indicate that that procedure is active and Upshot can be made to display a distinctive color for all periods of time when a process was executing within that procedure.

Probably the most widely known tool for visualizing parallel program executions is ParaGraph [10, 11], which provides a wide range of tools for viewing trace files produced by message-passing parallel programs that use the Portable Instrumented Communication Library (PICL) [5]. ParaGraph has many advantages:

- Portability. PICL has been ported to a wide variety of platforms, so Para-Graph can be used to study applications running on many different machines. ParaGraph uses X Windows graphics, so it also can run on many platforms.
- A wide variety of data displays. ParaGraph provides more than 20 different

ways of looking at data in a trace file.

- A large user community. ParaGraph has been made publicly available and has been widely used. This experience has helped refine ParaGraph's features and also attests to its practical usefulness.

Although some of ParaGraph's displays resemble MULTVISION's, ParaGraph is based on an animation metaphor: even the displays that resemble MULT-VISION's task display are drawn incrementally from left to right (with occasional scrolling as necessary) as though the execution is occurring in real time as new information is added to the display. One of ParaGraph's features is that it can have many displays open at the same time—some (like MULTVISION's) showing the history of the computation, and some showing an evolving view of the computation's state. All displays are updated in synchrony, so if the user freezes the animation at any point, all displays will show views of the same computation state.

ParaGraph's "processor count" display is very similar to MULTVISION's summary graph. ParaGraph's "Gantt chart" display resembles MULTVISION's main debug-monitor display, except that ParaGraph focuses on the busy/idle states of physical processors, whereas MULTVISION focuses on the running/ blocked states of logical tasks. ParaGraph's Gantt chart does not explicitly show interactions between processors, but ParaGraph also has a "space-time diagram" display that includes slanting lines between matching message send and receive events, similar to the intertask arrows on MULTVISION's display (but again, ParaGraph focuses on processors while MULTVISION focuses on tasks).

The distinction between focusing on physical processors and focusing on logical tasks is a key distinction between ParaGraph and MULTVISION.[5] Some visualization tools, such as Moviola and Upshot, as well as other tools discussed below, adopt an intermediate point on the spectrum by focusing on "processes," which need not correspond one-to-one with physical processors, but which nevertheless are expected to exist throughout the lifetime of the computation. These processes are therefore much more static (and usually many fewer in number) than the dynamically created Multilisp tasks with which MULTVISION deals.

MAD [24] is another system that features a variety of graphical views of program execution. Like MULTVISION, MAD works with dynamically created tasks; like ParaGraph, it offers some displays that are animated pictures of the computation's state and some that show the history of the computation with time as an explicit dimension. MAD's animated displays provide several interesting views of the task-spawning tree. One display shows the spawning tree dynamically expanding and shrinking. Another shows tasks as rectangles that move from left to right as they make progress, with their child tasks similarly shown as smaller

---

[5] ParaGraph also has a concept of "tasks," which are units of computation explicitly marked in the program under test by user-inserted calls to a PICL library routine, but the ParaGraph displays that work with these tasks, while interesting, are quite different from MULTVISION's displays. To give just one example of the difference between ParaGraph's and MULTVISION's concepts of "task," in ParaGraph several processors can be executing the same task at the same time.

rectangles nested within them! MAD's history displays are noteworthy for being able to show the history either from the viewpoint of tasks (as MULTVISION does) or from the viewpoint of processors (as ParaGraph does).

One of the systems that inspired MAD is PIE [25], an integrated system designed to provide all the support needed for parallel program development. PIE's graphical displays include an animated view of the task-spawning tree similar to MAD's, an animated "frame usage view" showing the patterns of access to shared data structures, and a display showing the history of task busy and idle times similar to MULTVISION's display except that it lacks intertask arrows.

Idd [9], like ParaGraph, is designed for debugging distributed-memory message passing programs. Idd combines a language for specifying assertions about correct program behavior with a graphical visualization of parallel program execution that is similar to ParaGraph's space-time diagram. Like ParaGraph, Idd displays the history of a process as a left-to-right progression of events, with time as an explicit dimension in the display. Messages between processes are shown as slanting lines from the (process, time) co-ordinates of the message send event to the (process, time) co-ordinates of the message receive event. Users can customize Idd's display in some interesting ways. Zooming and panning functions similar to MULTVISION's are provided, to allow the user to zero in on a region of interest. The sequence of processes along the vertical axis can be rearranged to bring relevant processes close to each other. Predicates can be specified to select which processes and/or messages will be visible on the display. A final interesting feature is that a user can set a breakpoint in a given process at a given point in time by picking the corresponding (process, time) point on the display with the mouse.

Two other systems, Radar [15] and Belvedere [13], also use trace files to display the execution of distributed message-passing programs, but unlike Idd, they provide animated displays that show processes as boxes laid out on the screen and animate message traffic as it occurs. Radar shows messages as little boxes moving across space from one process to another; Belvedere displays each link between processes as a line, which becomes thicker when there is message traffic on it and is drawn with a number of arrowheads equal to the number of pending messages on that link. In Radar, the speed of the animation is controllable, including freeze-frame and single-step modes; Radar also displays the contents of a message when the user positions the mouse over the representation of that message on the screen. Belvedere includes several ways to select subsets of the messages for display: through specifications like database queries ("add messages with event=READ-MESSAGE and time<61400") or by asking to see a visualization from the perspective of a particular processor, channel, or data item. Belvedere is also able to display system activity in terms of user-defined "abstract events" [2] that represent groups of related lower-level events.

Traceview [17] also displays traces gathered from program executions, but like Upshot, and in contrast to ParaGraph and MULTVISION, Traceview's model of the semantics of traces is very minimal: instead of being specialized for traces generated by message-passing or Multilisp programs, Traceview is designed to be able to process almost any kind of trace and produce a useful display. It is challenging to apply Traceview's general-purpose approach to displays as specialized as most of those discussed in this section, but it would be very attractive to marry such displays to a system with Traceview's flexibility, allowing the displays to be used with data from a range of sources and under a range of interpretations instead of being restricted to use with the one parallel programming system for which they were built.

Some interesting steps in this direction have been taken by the Pablo system [20, 21]. Pablo uses a uniform, self-describing trace-file format called SDDF that can efficiently accommodate a wide range of user-defined trace record types. Pablo also includes a set of generic modules for operating on SDDF files, allowing them to be transformed and displayed in a wide range of user-definable ways. Pablo already offers several displays similar to those provided by ParaGraph; since Pablo's development continues, this set of display capabilities is likely to grow in the future. It would be valuable to make MULTVISION's debug monitor able to work with traces containing a greater variety of information and coming from a greater variety of sources—integration with a flexible trace-manipulation system like Pablo's would be a big step in that direction.

2.3 Discussion

Considering the whole range of visualization tools discussed in this section, we can see some major areas of contrast:

- Focusing on physical processors vs. focusing on logical tasks. Which of these options is preferable depends on the parallel programming model in use. The former option is clearly best for models based on directly controlling the actions of physical processors. The latter option is better for languages such as Multilisp that hide processor management from the programmer. However, even in this case, the physical view can be useful to system implementors and also to application programmers who want to understand how their application's performance is affected by the scheduling of tasks onto processors. Ideally, MULTVISION would make both views available.
- History vs. state display. This choice could also be labeled "static display vs. animation." Currently, MULTVISION offers only a history display, which has the advantage of giving in one diagram a perspective on the evolution of the computation over time, but has the disadvantage of using up one spatial dimension to represent the time axis. There are times when it is better to use both of the screen's spatial dimensions for a more detailed snapshot of a particular computation state. It would be beneficial to add such views (perhaps modeled after those of MAD or PIE) to MULTVISION.
- The display style for intertask interactions. Systems based on message passing naturally display message traffic; systems based on shared memory tend to display synchronization operations. MULTVISION follows the latter style

in its display of intertask arrows, but there are other interactions that MULT-
VISION could also show if good display styles were designed for them: side
effects and references to side-effected values would often be useful to see, as
would synchronization operations on locks and semaphores.

- Interactive use of displays. A display can be more than just a picture: it
  can serve as a map of a computation from which further information can be
  obtained by pointing to an area of interest. MULTVISION's signposts and its
  triggering of a replay by designating a time with the cursor are both examples
  of this metaphor. Idd's setting of breakpoints at locations selected by the
  mouse and Upshot's information windows furnish additional examples. This
  kind of interaction is potentially a great aid in browsing through the vast
  amounts of information that can be collected about a parallel program; its
  aggressive use in future systems should be encouraged.

2.4 Directions for Future Development

MULTVISION's debug monitor still needs development and the illustrations presented in this paper furnish only a preview of what its functionality eventually
should be. Some improvements of great value would be

- Grouping, selection, and rearrangement operations allowing a user to adjust
  the level of detail of the task display to highlight the structural details of
  current interest: thus, for example, a user interested in the overall structure
  of a computation would often like to collapse entire subtrees of tasks into
  single "task bands" to produce a high-level view of the whole computation
  that can fit on the screen. Other ways of selectively highlighting items (as
  offered by ParVis) or hiding them (as offered by Moviola, Idd, and Belvedere)
  would also be valuable.
- The ability to display several views or portions of a trace simultaneously in
  different windows, for easy comparison.
- Additional display formats other than the current task display and summary
  graph formats. It would be useful to have some displays that focus on processors rather than tasks. Some state displays showing tasks, data objects,
  and their relationships would also be useful. Another useful kind of display
  (which could be built with co-operation from the replay engine) would be a
  "data flow" display showing the producer and consumers of a selected data
  value (such as the values returned by p-remove in Fig. 4), illustrating the
  sequence of procedure call/return and memory read/write operations that
  convey the value from the producer to each consumer. Such a display might
  resemble the "data flow" display of the HyperDEBU debugger [26].
- More flexible signposts able to display data other than task names and processor ID's. Ideally, a signpost would be able to display any information
  selected by the user, or even serve as a kind of sticky note that is attached
  at a selected point in a task and displays comments entered directly by the
  user.

- A simple but powerful user model to help the user understand the available display options and remember how they were used to create the currently visible set of displays. As the richness of display options grows, this user model becomes ever more essential.

- User-defined events. It would be useful to be able to insert event-generating calls into a program under test to mark noteworthy events in the program's execution that may not correspond directly to the task creation, task completion, or other events that are logged automatically by MULTVISION. Such events could be displayed using a style like Upshot's. Upshot's notion of states and state transitions would also be a useful addition.

- Alternative trace-file types. Although MULTVISION's replay engine is specialized for Multilisp and similar languages in which mostly functional programs are common, the debug monitor should be useful for almost any model of computing—either shared-memory or message-passing—that is based on tasks and interactions between tasks. Increasing MULTVISION's flexibility in handling alternative trace-file types and adapting its display to their semantics would make MULTVISION useful to a much wider range of users. A self-describing trace format and a set of standard trace-transformation modules such as Pablo's would provide an attractive base for broadening MULTVISION's range and allowing greater flexibility to view traces in many different ways.

- Improving the debug monitor's performance. On a high-performance RISC workstation, the debug monitor begins to be slow when used on a trace consisting of several thousand tasks. Some performance tuning would help here, but another intriguing idea would be to use parallel processing itself to increase debug-monitor performance.

3 Replay

The purpose of generating a log is to "freeze" a particular program execution and preserve it for detailed study: enough information must be logged to answer a wide range of questions from the user. On the other hand, the trace-mode cost of generating the log should be low, to strengthen the resemblance between the timing details of trace-mode and production-mode execution and enhance the system's usefulness for performance visualization. We can reduce tracing cost by logging only enough information to characterize the nondeterministic choices made during the traced execution, instead of explicitly logging all information that may eventually be of interest. The replay engine can then be guided by the log to follow the same path as the traced execution and regenerate the states through which the traced execution passed. P-sequences [3], Instant Replay [16, 18], and PPD [19] all use this approach.

However, the opportunities for nondeterministic choices are so numerous in shared-memory parallel processing that developing a cheap tracing strategy allowing faithful replay of arbitrary programs is difficult, and existing systems make compromises. PPD's logging strategy depends on compile-time identification of variables shared between tasks. Constructs such as pointers or arrays, which preclude identification of a small number of shared variables, will cause PPD's logs to become hopelessly enormous. PPD's strategy is thus unattractive for Multilisp programs, which use pointers heavily.

P-sequences and Instant Replay, by contrast, instrument synchronization objects (semaphores in the case of P-sequences, arbitrary linearizable objects in the case of Instant Replay) to record necessary log information. These systems assume that all nondeterminism in programs comes from the order in which operations are performed on these objects. If a program, perhaps inadvertently, accesses shared variables outside the control of such synchronization objects, replay may be inaccurate.

Most existing Multilisp applications are mostly or wholly functional: they have few *true side effects* (writes to previously existing data structures that are— or may be—shared between tasks).[6] These applications are mostly functional not just because Multilisp and future support this style well, but because it is easier to write a correct, highly parallel program this way. MULTVISION capitalizes on the mostly functional nature of typical Multilisp applications to make a different performance tradeoff than other replay systems for parallel programs. It adds a significant overhead burden to performing side effects[7] and to using values they store (both rare operations in mostly functional programs), but in return, MULTVISION guarantees correct replay for *all* Multilisp programs, not just those written using a certain style.

The essence of MULTVISION's approach is that side-effect operations in trace mode are modified to (1) log a *side-effect event* and (2) store a distinctive *side-effect value* that encapsulates the actual value stored by the side-effect operation. In trace mode, no overhead is added to memory read operations, but every touch operation checks to see if its operand is a side-effect value and, if so, logs a *side-effect touch event* and returns the value encapsulated within the side-effect value. (This check adds little cost because every touch operation already has to check its operand's type code, to see if it is a future.) The resulting log contains enough information to provide a completely faithful replay. Since only side effects and touches of the values they store are subjected to trace-mode overhead, tracing of mostly functional programs is efficient; in particular, *no* overhead is added to ordinary memory reads in trace mode, even if the location read is a shared variable on which side effects could be performed. A justification of this protocol, together with the details of tracing and replay operations using it and directions for future improvement of the replay engine itself, is given in [7, 8].

---

[6] Allocation and initialization of a new data object, although it involves writing to memory, does not involve true side effects, since the data object does not become accessible to other tasks until its initialization is complete, and hence no nondeterminism can result from these writes.

[7] We informally use "side effect" to mean "true side effect."

3.1 Performance of Tracing and Replay

The current implementation of MULTVISION's replay engine still has not been tuned much, so the performance figures presented here are necessarily preliminary. MULTVISION's value as a debugging and tuning tool will not be clear until it has been used on some substantial Multilisp application programs and correctable deficiencies in MULTVISION exposed by that experience have been corrected. Nevertheless, some basic data about MULTVISION's performance when executing primitive Multilisp operations are presented in Table 1. For each of four simple expressions, this table gives the execution time in production mode ("Prod. exec."), trace mode ("Trace exec."), and replay mode ("Replay exec."), and finally the number of log bytes generated by the expression ("Log bytes"). All times were measured on our Encore Multimax[8] multiprocessor, which has eighteen 30 MHz NS32532 processors. (All times are averages over several executions.)

Expression	Prod. exec.	Trace exec.	Replay exec.	Log bytes
1. (touch (future 0))	100	170	146	78
2. (set-car! x 0)	0.27	22	26	18
3. (touch (car x)), side effect	1.0	15	18	18
4. (touch (car x)), no side effect	1.0	2.3	9	0

(Table reproduced with permission from [8].)

Table 1. Preliminary MULTVISION performance measurements (times in microseconds).

The first expression in Table 1 is (touch (future 0)), which serves as a basic benchmark of task management performance: it requires one task creation, one touch operation, one task suspension, one resolution of a future, and one reawakening of a suspended task. The 78 bytes of log data for this expression include one task creation event and several other events used by the debug monitor but not by the replay engine. The expression (set-car! x 0), where x is bound to a pair, is a benchmark of side-effect performance. The cost of side-effect touches is gauged by evaluating the expression (touch (car x)) for the case where the car of the pair bound to x has been side-effected and for the case where it has not.

We can see from line 1 of Table 1 that the tracing overhead for creating a future is less than a factor of 2. (It is lower still in the common case where the

---

[8] Multimax is a trademark of Encore Computer Corporation.

future resolves before being touched.) A touch operation that does not encounter a side effect also suffers tracing overhead of about a factor of 2, so the total tracing overhead for a side-effect-free program will be less than a factor of 2, and even less to the extent that the program emphasizes operations other than task creation and touches. The tracing overhead for side effects is much greater, but a program that averages one side effect or less per future (a reasonable standard for what it means to be mostly functional) will incur a tracing overhead for side effects that is a small fraction of the overhead already present for task creation. Replay execution time is generally longer than trace-mode execution time, but the difference in most cases is not dramatic.

To minimize the timing perturbations introduced by tracing, the log is accumulated by each processor in a private, memory-resident buffer during trace-mode execution. After the traced execution has terminated, the buffers are all dumped to a file on disk. A very long log could obviously fill up one or more of the memory-resident buffers, which in the current MULTVISION implementation would cause the traced execution to fail. This problem could be addressed by halting all the processors whenever any processor's buffer fills up, dumping all buffers to disk, and then resuming the traced execution on all the processors. Properly done, this should not introduce a major perturbation into the traced execution, and the possible user confusion caused by such breaks in the traced execution can be mitigated by logging events that explicitly mark the beginning and end of the break in execution, so the user will know when they occurred.

The time required to dump the log to disk after a traced execution is considerably larger than the tracing overhead itself. It is governed by file-system bandwidth, which in our experience varied over a range of 100–500 kilobytes per second. Fortunately, although the time to dump the log is considerably larger than the tracing overhead itself, it does not distort the timing of the traced execution.

The time to read a log and prepare for a replay is even longer. It is dominated by the computing time used to build a version database [7, 8] in memory. Happily, the log need not be reloaded before each replay—a given execution can be replayed over and over again without reloading the log. Table 2 gives some idea of the log dumping and loading times experienced in practice.

The performance when executing actual programs can be seen in Table 2, which contains some new column labels not seen in Table 1. "Trace dump" and "Replay load" give the times to dump the log file to disk and read the log to build a version database, respectively. "Tasks" counts the number of tasks created. "Side effects" and "Side-eff. touches" count the number of side-effect and side-effect touch events, respectively.

In Table 2, ffib is the familiar doubly-recursive program for computing Fibonacci numbers, written to create one task for each pair of recursive calls. It is given here as an example of a program that creates tasks of very fine granularity. ffib! is a version of ffib modified to use side effects in storing temporary results. The performance of ffib! shows the effect of incorporating modest numbers of side effects into a program. queens solves the familiar 8-queens problem.

Benchmark	Proc-essors	Prod. exec.	Trace exec.	dump	Replay load	exec.	Log bytes	Tasks	Side effects	Side-eff. touches
1. (ffib 18)	1	0.50	0.79	0.66	13.1	0.69	326,123	4180	0	0
2. (ffib! 18)	1	0.56	1.27	1.48	29.6	1.45	702,324	4180	12,540	8360
3. (queens 8)	1	0.55	0.72	0.50	6.4	1.41	160,562	2056	0	0
	8	0.07	0.10	0.53	6.4	0.19	159,000	2056	0	0
4. (seq-union 50)	1	2.68	2.79	0.10	0.04	4.63	251	1	0	0
	8	2.70	2.75	0.16	0.04	4.78	279	1	0	0
5. (par-union 50)	1	2.70	2.77	0.15	0.23	4.63	4151	51	0	0
	8	0.42	0.43	0.14	0.16	0.70	3001	51	0	0

(Data reproduced with permission from [8].)

Table 2. Preliminary MULTVISION performance measurements (times in seconds).

It creates and discards list structure actively, and thus illustrates the performance of a program that emphasizes heap allocation and use of data structures in a functional style. seq-union and par-union are sequential and parallel versions, respectively, of a set-union program, written to have a very large task granularity. These programs do relatively little allocation from the heap, but access heap-allocated data structures quite intensively.

For benchmarks 3–5, the performance of both 1- and 8-processor executions is shown. We see that neither tracing nor replay significantly changes the ratios between 1-processor and 8-processor execution times. Moreover, if a program has usable parallelism, its replay can be speeded up by using many processors even if the original traced execution used fewer: for example, a trace generated by running (queens 8) on one processor still takes only 0.19 seconds to replay on eight processors.

Statistics such as those in Table 2 do not "prove" anything. However, we are encouraged that for all of these programs, the trace-mode and replay-mode execution times are less than 3 times the production-mode execution time.

4 Integration of the Debug Monitor and Replay Engine

As was mentioned earlier, the replay engine can be commanded to perform a replay to a given point in time by indicating that point with the cursor on the debug monitor's display. Additionally, the current MULTVISION prototype makes it possible to print out the value yielded by a task (computed by the replay engine) by designating that task using the cursor.[9]

In a more mature system, it would be possible to designate any point during the lifetime of any task on the debug monitor's display and open up a debugger

---

[9] In the current version, only numerical task values can be printed in this way. Task values that are data structures are also computed correctly by the replay engine, but the means of printing them out have not yet been implemented.

window showing the state of the computation from the point of view of that task at that moment, reconstructed by the replay engine. After examining that state, the user could choose to examine an earlier or later state of the same task, or switch to another task's point of view, just by moving the cursor to the new spot. The replay engine already produces the information needed to implement this vision: the mechanism for extracting the information produced by the replay engine and formatting it attractively for the user is the missing ingredient.

This cursor selection and replay serves many of the purposes of breakpoints in more traditional debuggers, except that breakpoints are a rather blunt instrument by comparison: using breakpoints, it can be tedious to get to the computational moment of interest (such as "the 33rd iteration of the loop in the fifth call to procedure p"), but the point-and-replay style allows the moment of interest to be indicated directly. Thus, the debug monitor's display is useful as more than a picture of a program's performance characteristics: it is useful as a map of the computation on which any point in the execution of any task can be designated unambiguously. This alternative to breakpoint-oriented debugging is especially valuable in parallel computing, where the nearly simultaneous occurrence of breakpoints in many different tasks can create a great deal of confusion, in addition to radically changing timing relationships that may determine the course of the computation.

4.1 Directions for Future Work

Although a complete implementation of the replay engine has been built and it has been integrated with the debug monitor in a preliminary way, much more work on the integration of these two components is needed. Several features would be useful additions to a basic point-and-replay debugger as described above:

- Keeping a record of all interactions between the debug monitor and the replay engine. For example, if a user began a debugging session at a point in task A, then switched to a different point in task B, and then returned to the point in task A investigated earlier, it would be nice for the session to look like simply a continuation of the earlier session involving task A, saving the user from having to ask any previously asked questions again. Perhaps this feature could be integrated with the signpost mechanism.

- Displays showing data structures in the program under test, perhaps offering special formats for lists, trees, and other commonly used data structures. The data to drive these displays would come from the replay engine.

- Enhanced replay modes. To minimize tracing overhead, the log produced by a trace-mode execution is as minimal as possible and is rather cryptic, although it does encode all the information needed to reproduce the traced execution. Replays, however, need not be confined just to regenerating the data values computed during the traced execution; the replay-mode program could be augmented to monitor accesses to specified variables, record entries and exits of specified procedures, or report other information not explicitly recorded in the log, yielding a much more detailed picture of the traced computation without adding any trace-mode overhead. The debug monitor could display the additional information either through an extended signpost mechanism or by displaying additional events in a manner similar to Upshot's [12].

- Increasing the size of the program executions to which MULTVISION can be applied effectively. Not all computations of interest can be performed on the scale of tens of thousands of tasks that the current MULTVISION implementation can handle gracefully. On the other hand, even though it will always be desirable to improve its capabilities, MULTVISION is already powerful enough to handle quite elaborate computations—more than elaborate enough to benefit from the detailed investigation that MULTVISION allows. Moreover, many computations that take longer can be scaled down to smaller problem instances whose investigation using MULTVISION can yield useful insights about the behavior of the larger computations. From our past experiences with Multilisp, we have questions about several problems of this kind that MULTVISION is already a powerful enough tool to answer.

A final and very important comment is that MULTVISION still needs the kind of seasoning that it can only get by being used by a large community of users. Only after use by a wider user community can we put a sensible priority ordering on the many avenues for improving MULTVISION.

5 Conclusion

MULTVISION is already powerful enough to yield valuable information about interesting programs, but it would be improved if it offered a greater variety of visualization tools and could support larger-scale program executions. Further development of MULTVISION must strike a balance between these two goals: (1) improving the visualization tools and their integration with the replay engine and (2) efficiently handling larger program executions. We must now accumulate enough experience with MULTVISION and substantial Multilisp programs to see which directions for improvement will yield the greatest benefit.

References

1. Bagnall, L., *ParVis: A Program Visualization Tool for Multilisp*, S.M. thesis, MIT E.E.C.S. Dept., Cambridge, Mass., Feb. 1989.
2. Bates, P., and J. Wileden, "High-Level Debugging of Distributed Systems: The Behavioral Abstraction Approach," *J. of System Software 3*, 1983, pp. 255–244.
3. Carver, R., and K.-C. Tai, "Reproducible Testing of Concurrent Programs Based on Shared Variables," *6th Int'l. Conf. on Distributed Computing Systems*, May 1986, pp. 428–433.
4. Fowler, R., T. LeBlanc, and J. Mellor-Crummey, "An Integrated Approach to Parallel Program Debugging and Performance Analysis on Large-Scale Multiprocessors," *ACM SIGPLAN/SIGOPS Workshop on Parallel and Distributed Debugging*, SIGPLAN Notices 24:1, January 1989, pp. 163–173.

5. Geist, G.A., *et al.*, *PICL: A Portable Instrumented Communication Library, C Reference Manual*, Technical Report ORNL/TM-11130, Oak Ridge National Laboratory, Oak Ridge, Tennessee, U.S.A., 1990.

6. Halstead, R., "Multilisp: A Language for Concurrent Symbolic Computation," *ACM Trans. on Prog. Languages and Systems 7:4*, October 1985, pp. 501–538.

7. Halstead, R., and D. Kranz, "A Replay Mechanism for Mostly Functional Parallel Programs," Technical Report CRL 90/6, DEC Cambridge Research Lab, Nov. 1990.

8. Halstead, R., and D. Kranz, "A Replay Mechanism for Mostly Functional Parallel Programs," *International Symposium on Shared-Memory Multiprocessing*, Tokyo, April 1991. In N. Suzuki, ed., *Shared Memory Multiprocessing*, MIT Press, 1992, pp. 287–313.

9. Harter, P., D. Heimbigner, and R. King, "Idd: An Interactive Distributed Debugger," *5th Int'l. Conf. on Distributed Computing Systems*, May 1985, pp. 498–506.

10. Heath, M., and J. Etheridge, "Visualizing the Performance of Parallel Programs," *IEEE Software 8:5*, Sept. 1991, pp. 29–39.

11. Heath, M., and J. Etheridge, *Visualizing Performance of Parallel Programs*, Technical Report ORNL/TM-11813, Oak Ridge National Laboratory, Oak Ridge, Tennessee, U.S.A., 1991.

12. Herrarte, V., and E. Lusk, *Studying Parallel Program Behavior with Upshot*, Technical Report ANL-91/15, Argonne National Laboratory, Argonne, Illinois, U.S.A., 1991.

13. Hough, A., and J. Cuny, "Belvedere: Prototype of a Pattern-Oriented Debugger for Highly Parallel Computation," *1987 Int'l. Conf. on Parallel Processing*, August 1987, pp. 735–738.

14. Kranz, D., R. Halstead, and E. Mohr, "Mul-T, A High-Performance Parallel Lisp," *ACM SIGPLAN '89 Conf. on Programming Language Design and Implementation*, Portland, OR, June 1989, pp. 81–90.

15. LeBlanc, R., and A. Robbins, "Event-Driven Monitoring of Distributed Programs," *5th Int'l. Conf. on Distributed Computing Systems*, May 1985, pp. 515–522.

16. LeBlanc, T., and J. Mellor-Crummey, "Debugging Parallel Programs with Instant Replay," *IEEE Trans. Computers C-36:4*, April 1987, pp. 471–482.

17. Malony, A., D. Hammerslag, and D. Jablonowski, "Traceview: A Trace Visualization Tool," *IEEE Software 8:5*, Sept. 1991, pp. 19–28.

18. Mellor-Crummey, J., *Debugging and Analysis of Large-Scale Parallel Programs*, Technical Report 312, University of Rochester Computer Science Dept., Sept. 1989.

19. Miller, B., and J.-D. Choi, *ACM SIGPLAN '88 Conf. on Programming Language Design and Implementation*, Atlanta, June 1988, pp. 135–144.

20. Reed, D., R. Olson, R. Aydt, T. Madhyastha, T. Birkett, D. Jensen, B. Nazief, and B. Totty, "Scalable Performance Environments for Parallel Systems," *Sixth Distributed Memory Computing Conference* (IEEE), April 1991.

21. Reed, D., R. Aydt, T. Madhyastha, R. Noe, K. Shields, and B. Schwartz, "The Pablo Performance Analysis Environment," Technical Report, Dept. of Computer Science, University of Illinois, Urbana, Illinois, November 1992.

22. Rees, J., N. Adams, and J. Meehan, *The T Manual*, fifth edition, (pre-beta draft), Yale University Computer Science Department, October 1988.

23. Rees, J., and W. Clinger, eds., "Revised[3] Report on the Algorithmic Language Scheme," *ACM SIGPLAN Notices 21:12*, Dec. 1986, pp. 37–79.

24. Rubin, R., L. Rudolph, and D. Zernik, "Debugging Parallel Programs in Parallel," *ACM SIGPLAN/SIGOPS Workshop on Parallel and Distributed Debugging*, SIGPLAN Notices 24:1, January 1989, pp. 216–225.

25. Segall, Z., and L. Rudolph, "PIE: A Program and Instrumentation Environment for Parallel Processing," *IEEE Software 2:6*, Nov. 1985, pp. 22–37.

26. Tanaka, H., and J. Tatemura, "HyperDEBU: A Multiwindow Debugger for Parallel Logic Programs," *Parallel Symbolic Computing: Languages, Systems, and Applications* (U.S./Japan workshop, October 1992), Springer-Verlag Lecture Notes in Computer Science, 1993.

Managing Side Effects on Shared Data

Kinson Ho
Paul N. Hilfinger *

Computer Science Division
University of California at Berkeley
{ho,hilfingr}@cs.berkeley.edu

Abstract. We are developing a toolbox for writing symbolic programs
that may be executed on sequential and parallel machines without modification. The toolbox is designed for use by programmers who are not
experienced in parallel programming, and consists of *parallelism abstractions* and *data-sharing abstractions*. Parallelism abstractions represent
common, time-consuming operations that offer good speedup potentials
for parallel implementations. Data-sharing abstractions support common
side-effecting operations on shared objects, simplifying the coding of a
large class of algorithms that modify shared data structures in a parallel
implementation. In this paper we describe the data-sharing abstractions
of the toolbox, and show how the toolbox may be used to construct efficient parallel programs without exposing the programmer to low-level
parallel programming details, which are hidden by the toolbox implementation.

1 Parallel Programming Toolbox

One way to make parallel programming easy is to make it similar to sequential
programming. We are developing a toolbox for writing symbolic (i.e., irregular)
Lisp programs with side effects that can execute without modification on sequential and parallel machines. Each tool provides a *sequential-looking* interface, and
programs that use the tools may be parallelized by using the parallel implementation of the toolbox. These tools may be divided into *parallelism abstractions*
and *data-sharing abstractions*. Parallelism abstractions represent common, time-
consuming operations that offer good speedup potentials for parallel implementations. Data-sharing abstractions support common side-effecting operations on
shared objects, simplifying the coding of a large class of algorithms that modify shared data structures in a parallel implementation. At the moment, we are
concentrating on shared-memory MIMD multiprocessors.

Our toolbox is designed and implemented by parallel programming experts,
and is intended for programmers who need to use their multiprocessing hardware
effectively, but are not interested or experienced in parallel programming. It is
not intended for applications needing optimal performance on a given platform.
Most of the parallel programming issues are hidden from the programmer. This

---

* Ho and Hilfinger are supported by NSF Grant CCR-8451213.

toolbox approach is analogous to the performance-simplicity tradeoff between standard cell and full-custom styles of VLSI design.

To use the toolbox the programmer identifies the sources of parallelism in an application, and expresses them using one or more parallelism abstractions. Instances of accesses to shared data structures are also identified, and are modified to use the data-sharing abstractions. As this approach requires the programmer to rewrite an application to use the toolbox abstractions, it is not applicable to unmodified dusty deck programs.

In this paper we use a case study to give a concrete example of a parallelism abstraction (Fixed-Point), and show how parallelism abstractions and data-sharing abstractions work together on a sample problem. We then describe the data-sharing abstractions of the toolbox in considerable detail. Other parallelism abstractions include graph traversals, heuristic searches, and the mapping of operations over data aggregates. A more detailed discussion of Fixed-Point and other parallelism abstractions of the toolbox is given elsewhere [7].

2   Case Study: A Fixed-Point Computation

Iterative algorithms for finding the fixed point of a computation appear in many different applications, including constraint-satisfaction systems, program-dataflow analysis, and certain graph algorithms. These algorithms are all instances of the following abstract algorithm: "$X \leftarrow X0$; Repeat $X \leftarrow f(X)$ until no change in X". As an example of a fixed-point computation, consider an algorithm for finding all the nodes in a connected component of an undirected graph, starting from a node Root.

Figures 1 and 2 show a typical sequential implementation of the connected-component algorithm. The state X of the abstract fixed-point computation corresponds to Reachable-Nodes and Nodes-to-Visit. The fixed point is reached when no further nodes can be added to Reachable-Nodes, the set of all nodes in the connected component. During execution, all the nodes of the connected component are either in Reachable-Nodes or are reachable from some member of Nodes-to-Visit without traversing Reachable-Nodes. Thus, Nodes-to-Visit represents the outstanding computations to be performed, and corresponds to the *work queue* commonly found in the implementation of fixed-point algorithms. Nodes-to-Visit becomes empty when all the nodes of the connected component are in Reachable-Nodes. In general, a fixed-point computation is usually organized such that when the work queue becomes empty, the fixed point has been reached.

Visit-Node invokes Add-Element to add the node being visited (Node) to Reachable-Nodes, the set of nodes currently known to be reachable from Root. Add-Element adds an element to a set, returning t if it succeeds. If it fails (because the element was already in the set), nil is returned. If the call to Add-Element in Visit-Node returns t (i.e., Node was not previously known to be reachable), Visit-Node is applied transitively to all the adjacent nodes of Node by adding them to Nodes-to-Visit, the set of nodes yet to be visited. As

```
function Connected-Component (Root)
    ;; returns a set of all the nodes reachable from Root
    Reachable-Nodes := Make-Set()
    ;; Invariant: Reachable-Nodes is a subset of the nodes
    ;; reachable from Root

    Nodes-to-Visit := Make-PQ()
    ;; Invariant: All reachable nodes are in Reachable-Nodes,
    ;; or are reachable from some member of Nodes-to-Visit
    ;; without traversing Reachable-Nodes

    PQ-Insert(Root, Nodes-to-Visit)

    while not PQ-Empty-p(Nodes-to-Visit) do
        Node := PQ-Delete(Nodes-to-Visit)
        Visit-Node(Node)

    return Reachable-Nodes
```

Fig. 1. Sequential Connected-Component Algorithm

```
function Visit-Node (Node)
    if Add-Element(Node, Reachable-Nodes)
    then
        foreach Adj-Node in Neighbors-Of(Node)
            if not Is-Element-p(Adj-Node, Reachable-Nodes)
            then
                PQ-Insert(Adj-Node, Nodes-to-Visit)
```

Fig. 2. Operation performed at every node: Add-Element does not add duplicates to Reachable-Nodes, and returns t iff a new element is added. The call to Is-Element-p is merely a *performance* optimization.

a purely *performance* optimization, the call to `Is-Element-p` identifies all the nodes that are known to be reachable (and have therefore been visited). These nodes are not added to `Nodes-to-Visit`, and will not be visited again. If the call to `Is-Element-p` were absent (i.e., all the adjacent nodes of `Node` were added to `Nodes-to-Visit`), an adjacent node `Adj-Node` that is in `Reachable-Nodes` may be added to `Nodes-to-Visit`. When `Adj-Node` is visited by `Visit-Node` again, the `Add-Element` operation will fail, and the traversal from `Adj-Node` will not be repeated.

Figures 3 and 4 show an alternative formulation of the same connected-component algorithm, written using a library for fixed-point computations we have developed. The explicit loop of the sequential implementation in Figure 1

```
function Connected-Component (Root)
    Reachable-Nodes := Make-Set()
    ;; Invariant: Reachable-Nodes is a subset of the nodes
    ;; reachable from Root

    Fixed-Point(Visit-Node, Lifo, Root)

    return Reachable-Nodes
```

Fig. 3. Fixed-Point formulation of Connected-Component Algorithm

```
function Visit-Node (Node)
    if Add-Element(Node, Reachable-Nodes)
    then
        foreach Adj-Node in Neighbors-Of(Node)
            if not Is-Element-p(Adj-Node, Reachable-Nodes)
            then
                FP-Insert-fn(Adj-Node)
```

Fig. 4. Fixed-point version of operation performed at every node

has been replaced by the construct **Fixed-Point**. The implementation of **Fixed-Point** creates the work queue (which is now invisible), and enqueues the initial element **Root** into this work queue. The **Lifo** argument selects a scheduling strategy for the work queue. **Visit-Node**, which is invoked for each element removed from the work queue, has side effects on **Reachable-Nodes**. The call **PQ-Insert(Adj-Node, Nodes-to-Visit)** in function **Visit-Node** of Figure 2 is now replaced by the call **FP-Insert-fn(Adj-Node)** in Figure 4. **FP-Insert-fn** is a function defined by **Fixed-Point**, and is used to add new elements to the work queue. **Fixed-Point** returns when the work queue becomes empty.

The correctness of the connected-component algorithm does not depend on the order of visiting the nodes of the graph (the nodes in **Nodes-to-Visit** in Figure 1). If accesses to global data structures (**Reachable-Nodes**) are synchronized properly, multiple instances of **Visit-Node** can operate on different nodes of **Nodes-to-Visit** concurrently. By providing sequential and parallel implementations of **Fixed-Point**, the connected-component algorithm in Figures 3 and 4 can be executed on sequential and parallel machines without modification. All the low-level parallel programming details concerning process creation, synchronization, scheduling and termination detection are handled by the implementation of **Fixed-Point**.

Reachable-Nodes, the (shared) set of nodes currently known to be reachable, is implemented using a set datatype (data-sharing abstraction) from the toolbox. Concurrent updates of **Reachable-Nodes** are simplified because the datatype is implemented such that concurrent calls to **Add-Element** are atomic, and duplicate elements are not added to the set.

3 Side Effects on Shared Data

Most algorithms implemented in an imperative programming language involve the use of operations with side effects on data structures, and a parallel version of any such algorithm will usually involve concurrent accesses to shared data. For example, multiple threads of control in a parallel unification program may access the unification database concurrently, and may lead to incorrect results if the accesses are not synchronized properly. Ensuring that these concurrent accesses behave correctly without limiting concurrency (i.e., performance) is often a major problem in the parallel port of a sequential program, and the use of complicated schemes such as optimistic concurrency control to achieve good performance is a potential source of errors for parallel programs.

We believe it is the responsibility of the programmer, who has high-level knowledge about the application, to *identify* all instances of data sharing in an application. The programmer then selects an appropriate data-sharing abstraction for each shared data structure, and expresses the accesses in terms of operations provided by the data-sharing abstractions. The parallel programming toolbox assists the programmer by providing a variety of data-sharing abstractions to ensure that common styles of shared accesses are performed correctly and efficiently. These abstractions have sequential-looking interfaces, and may be used by programmers who are not parallel programming experts to achieve reasonable parallel performance. All the low-level parallel programming details are hidden by the toolbox implementation.

4 Overview of Data-Sharing Abstractions

The data-sharing abstractions of the toolbox have sequential-looking interfaces, and support common side-effecting operations on shared objects. They simplify the coding of a large class of algorithms that modify shared data structures in a parallel implementation, and span a spectrum that trades ease of use for performance. We present an overview of them here.

Simple concurrent datatypes are atomic implementations of common datatypes such as counters, sets and priority queues. A simple concurrent datatype has the same interface as its sequential counterpart, and concurrent operations on an object of such a datatype behave correctly (e.g., are linearizable). These datatypes simplify the parallelization of a large class of programs for which mutual exclusion for shared data accesses is a sufficient correctness condition. The implementation of such a datatype may make use of the semantics of the datatype to make the operations highly concurrent, so that shared data accesses do not become performance bottlenecks. No change to an existing (sequential) program is needed to convert it to use concurrent datatypes.

A common high-level operation on an object (say `Obj`) is to destructively modify `Obj` if some test on `Obj` succeeds. For example, a program may add an element `x` to a list `L` if `x` is not in `L` initially. In a sequential program such a high-level operation is usually implemented as two distinct operations on `Obj`, Test and Modify. In a parallel implementation this scheme would fail, even if Test and Modify are individually synchronized. Our solution to this problem is to recognize Test and Modify as logical parts of *one* high-level operation on `Obj`, a *conditional update*. The toolbox provides (parallel implementations of) conditional update operations for common concurrent datatypes such as priority queues, thus eliminating a large class of race conditions in parallel programs. If the side-effecting operations of a sequential program are expressed in terms of conditional update operations, the program may be parallelized by simply using the parallel implementations of the conditional update operations. A small amount of existing code may need to be rewritten to convert an existing program to use conditional update operations.

A *dictionary* is a mapping from *Keys* to *Values*. The dictionary datatype of the toolbox supports a conditional update operation called *conditional insert*, which adds a (`Key`, `Value`) pair to a dictionary `D` if no pair for `Key` is in `D`, and returns the existing value corresponding to `Key` otherwise. The parallel implementation uses fine-grain locks to allow multiple concurrent operations on a dictionary, and uses optimistic concurrency control for better parallel performance. The lookup and insert pairs of an existing program have to be replaced by calls to conditional insert to use this datatype.

Concurrent accesses to shared objects not supported by the toolbox directly (as simple concurrent datatypes) may be synchronized by using mutual exclusion (mutex) locks if the objects are not heavily contended. *Autolocks* are mutex locks that may be associated with arbitrary objects without knowing or modifying the internal representation of the objects. They are useful for synchronizing operations with short critical sections on shared objects, and may be retrofitted to a sequential program relatively easily.

Some mutation operations with long critical sections on shared objects may be rewritten in a stylized functional form using *optimistic read-modify-write* (ORMW), an optimistic scheme that does not lock an object during the entire duration of the operation. The parallel implementation of ORMW uses an application-specific predicate to detect *incompatible* races that may lead to inconsistent results, and retries the operation if such races are detected. ORMW is more difficult to use than autolocks because the programmer has to define what constitutes an incompatible race condition, but has the potential of providing much better performance for heavily contended objects. Substantial changes to an existing program may be necessary to convert it to use ORMW.

False sharing occurs in a parallel program derived from a sequential counterpart when a static global variable is used to hold data logically private to a particular instantiation of a set of procedures. In this context a *variable* is called a *generalized variable* in Common Lisp, and refers to any container for (a pointer to) another object, including a field of a structure. A global variable is one accessible to any thread. In a parallel implementation multiple threads *appear* to conflict at some field of a falsely-shared variable, and the *algorithm* appears to be inherently sequential. For example, in the absence of recursion, a set of procedures may use a global named variable instead of arguments and return values for communication. In a parallel implementation this coding style results in false sharing for the global variable. *Per-thread locations* provide a transparent solution to this problem in the common case where the variable is a field of a structure shared by multiple threads. Through the use of per-thread locations, access and update functions for that field of a shared structure actually refer to different memory locations when invoked from different threads, and only the definition of the structure has to be modified. (If the incorrectly shared variable is a *named* variable at the programming language level, it may simply be replaced by dynamically rebinding the variable in each thread of control in the parallel implementation.)

In the following sections we outline the toolbox approach for handling concurrent data accesses, and examine each data-sharing abstraction for simplifying concurrent accesses.

5 Using the Parallel Programming Toolbox

This section outlines the steps necessary to express an algorithm using the toolbox.

- The sources of parallelism in the algorithm are identified using a parallel abstraction such as `Fixed-Point`.
- Accesses to data structures that would be shared in a parallel implementation of the algorithm are identified.
- False sharing is eliminated from a set of procedures that use global, named variables for communication by converting the set of procedures to use arguments and return values for communication. In general, code with false sharing of named variables is made re-entrant by rebinding these variables dynamically in each thread.
- False sharing of fields in structures are eliminated by using per-thread locations.
- Concurrent accesses to (truly) shared objects are handled by using the simple concurrent datatypes provided by the toolbox. Shared objects not supported by the toolbox may be protected by autolocks.
- Operations on heavily contended objects that are protected by autolocks are rewritten to use optimistic read-modify-write operations to reduce contention.
- Further hints on the performance tuning of shared data successes are given in Section 11.

6 Simple Concurrent Datatype

Simple concurrent datatypes are atomic implementations of common datatypes such as counters, sets and priority queues. A simple concurrent datatype has the same interface as its sequential counterpart, but is implemented to behave correctly (i.e., is linearizable) in the presence of concurrent operations. These datatypes simplify the parallelization of a large class of programs for which mutual exclusion for shared data accesses is a sufficient correctness condition. The implementation of such a datatype may make use of the semantics of the datatype to make the operations highly concurrent, so that shared data accesses do not become performance bottlenecks. No change to an existing (sequential) program is usually needed to convert it to use concurrent datatypes.

6.1 Simple Concurrent Datatype Example: Counter

The toolbox supports the *counter* concurrent datatype with two atomic operations, `Counter-Inc` and `Counter-Value`.

(Make-Counter Init-Value) returns a counter object initialized to `Init-Value`.

(Counter-Inc Counter Delta) atomically increments the value of `Counter` by `Delta`, and returns the new value of `Counter`.

(Counter-Value Counter) returns the value of `Counter`.

6.2 Conditional Update for Concurrent Datatypes

A conditional update operation has a sequential interface, and modifies an object atomically if the existing value of the object satisfies some condition. Two values are returned: the new value of the object and a boolean indicating whether the object has been modified. As a concrete example, consider a multiset datatype with operations (`Make-MultiSet`) and (`Add-New-Element S Elt`). `Add-New-Element` is a conditional update operation that adds `Elt` to `S` if `Elt` is not already in `S`. The use of `Add-New-Element` instead of the usual `Element-of-p` and `Add-Element` pair eliminates a common class of race conditions, and code written in the conditional update style may be parallelized by using a parallel implementation of the multiset datatype from the toolbox. No explicit locking or synchronization by the programmer is required.

The toolbox provides conditional update operations for common concurrent datatypes. If a sequential program is expressed in terms of conditional update operations on these datatypes, it may be parallelized by simply using the parallel implementations of the conditional update operations provided by the toolbox. The implementation of the datatype may use optimistic techniques to achieve good parallel performance without exposing any parallel programming detail to the application programmer. A small amount of existing code may need to be rewritten to convert an existing program to use conditional update operations.

7 Dictionary

A dictionary is a mapping from *Keys* to *Values*, and is used in a large number of application programs. For example, a dictionary may be used in a unification program to record the correspondence between ground and non-ground terms. The dictionary datatype is an important example of a concurrent datatype with a conditional update operation called *conditional insert*. Conditional insert does not modify a dictionary D if a (**Key**, **Value**) pair with the same Key is already present in D, and adds the pair otherwise. The use of this operation instead of separate lookup and insert operations, where insert does not check for the presence of **Key** in D, eliminates a common race condition in the use of dictionaries. As a result, sequential code written using this operation can be parallelized by using a parallel implementation of dictionary, and the programmer is not burdened with synchronization details.

One naive way to implement the dictionary datatype on a parallel machine is to use a single mutex lock to synchronize accesses to a hash table representation. This implementation serializes all accesses to a shared dictionary—even for concurrent accesses with different keys—and leads to poor parallel performance if the dictionary is heavily contended. The toolbox implementation of the dictionary datatype reduces contention for dictionary accesses involving different keys by partitioning the key space into disjoint subspaces, each protected by its own mutex lock. The toolbox implementation provides a general hash function for partitioning the key space, and the programmer may override this by providing an application-specific hash function for better performance. In this way, concurrent conditional insert operations on a dictionary may proceed in parallel if the hash function distributes the keys for the operations to different key spaces. This dictionary interface provides good parallel performance without exposing the internal representation of the dictionary datatype or the low-level locking details to the programmer.

7.1 Dictionary Interface

A dictionary supports the following atomic operations:

(Make-Dict Test-fn Split-fn Buckets) returns an empty dictionary. (**Test-fn Key1 Key2**) is the equality predicate between keys, and returns **t** iff **Key1** and **Key2** are considered identical. (**Split-fn Key Buckets**) is an application-specific function that maps **Key** to one of the integers (subspaces) 0..**Buckets**-1. **Buckets** is a positive integer that specifies the number of subspaces in the internal representation of the dictionary. In a parallel implementation concurrent insert operations of (potentially different) keys with the same **Split-fn** value may take longer to complete than concurrent inserts of keys with different **Split-fn** values. The programmer may use high-level knowledge about the application to provide a faster **Split-fn**, or one that distributes keys more evenly among the subspaces. Assuming that **Split-fn** distributes keys from the key space uniformly among 0..**Buckets**-1, a larger value for **Buckets** may be chosen for faster dictionary operations at the cost of additional storage in a parallel implementation. Defaults for **Test-fn**, **Split-fn** and **Buckets** are provided by the toolbox.

(Conditional-Insert-Dict D Key Value) inserts the pair **(Key, Value)** into **D** if no pair corresponding to **Key** is in **D**, and does not modify **D** otherwise. It returns two values, **Insertedp** and **Value'**. **Insertedp** is **t** if the pair **(Key, Value)** is added to **D** in the current operation, and **nil** otherwise. **Value'** is **Value** if the pair **(Key, Value)** is already in **D**, or is added to **D** in the current operation. **Value'** is *not* **Value** if some pair **(Key, Value')** is already in **D**. **Value** and **Value'** are not tested for equality.

(Lookup-Dict D Key) returns **Value** if some pair **(Key, Value)** is in **D** for some **Value**, and **nil** otherwise.

(Map-Dict Fn D) invokes **(Fn Key Value)** for all **(Key, Value)** pairs in **D** (for side effects). This operation is undefined if **Fn** modifies **D**, or if there are concurrent **Conditional-Insert-Dict** operations on **D**.

7.2 Sample Use of Dictionary

Figure 5 shows a sequential code segment for inserting a **(Key, Value)** pair into a dictionary **D** if no pair corresponding to **Key** is initially in **D**. The two return values correspond to those returned by **Conditional-Insert-Dict**. Figure 6 shows a simple parallel version of the same computation, and Figure 7 is an optimized version that tries not to lock the shared dictionary **D** unless a pair corresponding to **Key** is not found. Note the extra call to **Lookup-Dict** *after* **D** is locked to check for race conditions. Figure 8 is a version that uses **Conditional-Insert-Dict**. This version is much simpler than all of the other alternatives, and may be used in sequential and parallel code without modification. (In Figures 5, 6 and 7, **Existing-Value** and **Insertedp** are local or per-thread variables.) The optimized parallel version in Figure 7 is also inferior to the version in Figure 8 using **Conditional-Insert-Dict** because the toolbox implementation of dictionary provides fine-grain locking without exposing the details of the implementation to the programmer.

```
(let ((D (Make-Dict)))
  ...
  (let ((Existing-Value (Lookup-Dict D Key))
        (Insertedp nil))
    (unless Existing-Value
      (Insert-Dict D Key Value)
      (setf Insertedp t))
    (values Insertedp Existing-Value)))
```

Fig. 5. Sequential Dictionary Insert

```
(let ((D (Make-Dict)))
  ...
  ; Create multiple threads (using some parallelism abstraction)
  ...
  ; In each thread...
  (let ((Existing-Value nil)
        (Insertedp nil))
    (Lock D)
    (setf Existing-Value (Lookup-Dict D Key))
    (unless Existing-Value
      (Insert-Dict D Key Value)
      (setf Insertedp t))
    (Unlock D)
    (values Insertedp Existing-Value)))
```

Fig. 6. Simple Parallel Dictionary Insert

```
(let ((D (Make-Dict)))
  ...
  ; Create multiple threads (using some parallelism abstraction)
  ...
  ; In each thread...
  (let ((Existing-Value (Lookup-Dict D Key))
        (Insertedp nil))
    (unless Existing-Value
      (Lock D)
      (setf Existing-Value (Lookup-Dict D Key))
      (unless Existing-Value
        (Insert-Dict D Key Value)
        (setf Insertedp t))
      (Unlock D))
    (values Insertedp Existing-Value)))
```

Fig. 7. Optimized Parallel Dictionary Insert

```
(let ((D (Make-Dict)))
  ...
  ; Create multiple threads (using some parallelism abstraction)
  ...
  ; In each thread...
  (Conditional-Insert-Dict D Key Value))
```

Fig. 8. Sequential & Parallel Dictionary Insert using `Conditional-Insert-Dict`

8 Autolock

Concurrent accesses to shared objects may be synchronized by using mutual exclusion (mutex) locks. Mutex locks are easy to use, and are appropriate for protecting shared objects that are not heavily contended. The object-lock association is usually maintained by storing the lock as a component of the object. This approach requires knowledge about the internal representation of the object, and is unsatisfactory for abstraction reasons. If the internal representation of the object is not available, or may not be modified without major changes to the code (e.g., the object is a list) some form of composite object—with *data* and *lock* fields— is needed to maintain the object-lock association. This alternative is also unsatisfactory as it requires changes to the way the object is accessed, and may involve changing code that is scattered throughout the application.

Autolocks are mutex locks that may be transparently associated with arbitrary objects without knowing or changing the internal representation of objects with associated locks. They are especially useful for protecting shared data structures with short critical sections that are *not* heavily contended. (Shared data structures that are potential hot-spots should be protected using more sophisticated synchronization protocols to reduce contention.) They are provided for synchronizing accesses to datatypes that are not supported by the toolbox directly as simple concurrent datatypes, and support a programming style of simple critical sections. A trivial change in the source code is required to signify that a section of code modifies a shared object (and hence should be protected by the mutex lock of that object). This programming style is less flexible than the use of explicit lock and unlock operations, but is less prone to programmer errors.

8.1 Autolock Interface

A typical use of autolock is shown in Figure 9.

(Autolock-Init Split-fn Buckets) initializes a mapping from objects to mutex locks. (This mapping is not visible to the programmer.) In a typical program `Autolock-Init` is invoked by the *parent* thread before any *child* thread (which may mutate a shared object `Obj` concurrently) is created, and `With-Autolock` is invoked by each child thread before it attempts to modify `Obj`. (See below.)

A mutex lock is automatically associated with an object `Obj` the first time `Obj` is protected by `With-Autolock` or `With-Autolocks`. This lock is recorded by the object-lock mapping created by `Autolock-Init`.

(With-Autolock Obj Form*) associates a new mutex lock for `Obj` if none exists, acquires the lock associated with `Obj`, and evaluates the enclosed expressions `Form*` while holding the lock. The result of the last evaluated expression in `Form*` is returned, and the lock is released.

```
(Autolock-Init Split-fn Buckets)
...
; Create multiple threads (using some parallelism abstraction)
...
; In each thread...mutate a single object as follows
(With-Autolock  Obj
                ...
                (Mutate Obj)
                ...)
...
; In each thread...mutate multiple objects as follows
(With-Autolocks (Obj1 Obj2 Obj3) #'Obj-<
                ...
                (Mutate* Obj1 Obj2 Obj3)
                ...)
```

Fig. 9. Use of Autolocks: (`Mutate Obj`) is any expression that may modify `Obj` destructively, and (`Mutate* Obj1 Obj2 ...`) is any expression that may modify the objects `Obj1`, `Obj2`, etc.

`With-Autolocks` provides a way to destructively modify multiple objects atomically without the risk of deadlocks:

(With-Autolocks Obj-List Predicate-fn Form*) associates mutex locks with objects in `Obj-List` that do not have locks, sorts the objects in `Obj-List` according to the total order defined by `Predicate-fn`, and acquires the locks of objects in `Obj-List` in this sorted order. The enclosed expressions in `Form*` are then evaluated, and the locks are released. The result of the last expression in `Form*` evaluated is returned. `Obj-List` is not destructively modified. If concurrent invocations of `With-Autolocks` with overlapping `Obj-List`s use the same `Predicate-fn`, the implementation will ensure that no deadlock will occur. `With-Autolocks` is useful for applications that require multiple objects to be mutated atomically.

`Autolock-Init` accepts two optional arguments `Split-fn` and `Buckets` that may be specified by the programmer to improve the performance of `With-Autolock` or `With-Autolocks` for objects that have not been locked before. (See Section 7.1 for details.)

Buckets is a positive integer that determines the number of subspaces in the internal representation of the object-lock mapping created by `Autolock-Init`. A larger value for `Buckets` may lead to better performance at the cost of extra storage in a parallel implementation.

(Split-fn Obj Buckets) maps `Obj` to one of the integers (subspaces) in the range $0 \ldots Buckets - 1$. In a parallel implementation the performance of concurrent attempts to lock objects with the same `Split-fn` value (i.e., a *collision*) may be degraded if the objects have not been locked before. The programmer may provide an application-specific `Split-fn` that may be computed more efficiently than the general one provided by the toolbox, or one that distributes objects to the subspaces more evenly to minimize the frequency of collisions for better performance.

8.2 Sample Use of Autolocks

```
(let ((Obj (Make-Object Init-State)))
...
(Mutate Obj))
```

Fig. 10. Sequential mutation of Obj

```
(let ((Obj (Make-Object Init-State)))
(setf (Obj-lock Obj) (Make-Lock))
...
; Create multiple threads (using some parallelism abstraction)
...
; In each thread...
(Lock (Obj-lock Obj))
(Mutate (Obj-data Obj))
(Unlock (Obj-lock Obj)))
```

Fig. 11. Parallel mutation of Obj without autolock: Obj is now an indirect object with data and lock fields, where (Obj-data Obj) stores what was formerly in Obj. The calling sequence for Mutate, which is scattered throughout the code, is also changed, and explicit Lock and Unlock calls have to be added.

Figure 10 shows a sequential code segment that modifies an object Obj. In a parallel implementation without autolocks (Figure 11), a lock field has to be added to the representation of Obj, and code that mutates Obj may have to modified as well (e.g., from (Mutate Obj) to (Mutate (Obj-data Obj))). This is not necessary when autolock is used (Figure 12).

9 Optimistic Read-Modify-Write

In many applications objects are destructively modified in a sequence of read-modify-write steps. In a read-modify-write operation, values are copied from

```
(Autolock-Init #'(lambda (Obj Buckets)
                   (mod (sxhash Obj) Buckets))
              10)
...
(let ((Obj (Make-Object Init-State)))
  ...
  ; Create multiple threads (using some parallelism abstraction)
  ...
  ; In each thread...
  (With-Autolock Obj (Mutate Obj)))
```

Fig. 12. Sequential and Parallel mutation of Obj with autolock

some parts of the object (read), new values for certain parts of the object are computed in a side-effect-free manner (modify) based on the result of read, and the new values are written to some parts of the object destructively (write).

A simple parallel implementation of a read-modify-write-style operation can be constructed by performing the read-modify-write operations on a shared object in a critical section (say using autolock). If a shared object is heavily contended, this will effectively serialize the accesses, leading to poor parallel performance. As an alternative, the toolbox provides an optimistic protocol, *optimistic read-modify-write* (ORMW), for accessing shared objects concurrently. ORMW does not lock an object during the (potentially time-consuming) modify phase of the computation, and uses an application-specific predicate to detect *incompatible* changes to the object by other threads (during the modify phase) that may lead to inconsistent results. (Not all changes to an object by other threads while the current thread is in the modify phase are necessarily incompatible.) If an incompatible change to the object is detected, the ORMW operation is re-executed. ORMW is more difficult to use than autolocks because it requires the programmer to use high-level understanding of the application to define incompatible race conditions, but has the potential of providing much better performance for heavily contended objects. Substantial changes to an existing program may be necessary to convert it to use ORMW.

9.1 Optimistic Read-Modify-Write Interface

The following is a typical invocation of ORMW:

```
(multiple-value-setq (New-Value Writtenp)
  (ORMW Object Read-fn Modify-fn Write-fn Incompatible-p-fn))
```

ORMW changes the state of (some slots of) Object as specified by the functions Read-fn, Modify-fn, Write-fn and Incompatible-p-fn, and returns two values, New-Value and Writtenp. New-Value is the new value of (the parts of) Object that has been changed, and Writtenp is a boolean that is t iff `Object` is modified by the current `ORMW` operation. (These two values correspond to the two values returned by `Modify-fn` below.) The parameters are as follows.

Object is any arbitrary object. Conceptually it may be thought of as a structure in which a few slots are changed in each `ORMW` operation.

(Read-fn Object) returns the current value of (some slots of) `Object`. The programmer has to lock `Object` explicitly (using `With-Autolock`) if necessary for consistency, based on the semantics of the application.

(Modify-fn Old-Value) is a side-effect-free function that computes the new value of (some slots of) `Object`, `Modify-Value`, based on the value returned by `Read-fn`, `Old-Value`. `Modify-fn` returns two values, `Modify-Value` and `Writep`. If `Writep` is `nil`, `ORMW` is a no-op. `Modify-fn` is invoked by the implementation of `ORMW` without locking `Object`.

(Write-fn Object Modify-Value) changes the state of (some slots of) `Object` destructively based on `Modify-Value` computed by `Modify-fn`. The implementation of `ORMW` invokes this operation in a critical section together with `Incompatible-p-fn`.

(Incompatible-p-fn Object Old-Value Modify-Value) returns t iff the newly computed (but not written) `Modify-Value` based on `Old-Value` is incompatible with the current value of `Object`, based on the semantics of `Object`. The current value of `Object` may be read using `Read-fn` or simply examined in place. If `Incompatible-p-fn` returns t, `Modify-Value` is discarded, and the `ORMW` is re-executed. `Incompatible-p-fn` is not invoked by a sequential implementation of `ORMW` as it corresponds to race conditions that would not occur sequentially, and should return `nil` in a parallel implementation in the absence of concurrent `ORMW` operations on `Object`.

A conceptual parallel implementation of `ORMW` is shown in Figure 13. For a properly chosen `Incompatible-p-fn`, `ORMW` is semantically equivalent to the code segment in Figure 14.

9.2   Sample Use of ORMW

ORMW has been used successfully in the parallel implementation of two large applications based on discrete relaxation. These include CONSAT [3], a general-purpose constraint satisfaction system, and RC [15], a dataflow analysis system. In each application an application-specific predicate `Incompatible-p-fn` ensures that successive states of the system (`Object`) are monotonic with respect to some partial order, as monotonicity is a necessary correctness condition for the discrete relaxation performed by these applications that is not automatically maintained. The performance of the parallel implementation of either application based on ORMW is substantially better than the alternative based on simple critical sections. We describe the use of ORMW for these applications in detail elsewhere [8, 7].

```
(defun ORMW (Object Read-fn Modify-fn Write-fn Incompatible-p-fn)
  (let* ((Old-Value nil)
         (Modify-Value nil)
         (Writep nil)
         (Writtenp nil))

    (setf Old-Value (Read-fn Object))
    (multiple-value-setq (Modify-Value Writep)
      (Modify-fn Old-Value))

    (when Writep
      (With-Autolock Object
        (unless (Incompatible-p-fn Object Old-Value Modify-Value)
          (Write-fn Object Modify-Value)
          (setf Writtenp t))))

    (values Modify-Value Writtenp)))
```

Fig. 13. Conceptual Parallel Implementation of Optimistic Read-Modify-Write: Funcalls have been omitted.

```
(defun ORMW (Object Read-fn Modify-fn Write-fn Incompatible-p-fn)
  (let* ((Modify-Value nil)
         (Writep nil))

    (With-Autolock Object
      (multiple-value-setq (Modify-Value Writep)
        (Modify-fn (Read-fn Object)))

      (when Writep
        (Write-fn Object Modify-Value)))

    (values Modify-Value Writep)))
```

Fig. 14. Semantics of Optimistic Read-Modify-Write (for a properly chosen Incompatible-p-fn)

10 Per-Thread Location

10.1 False Sharing

In some sequential programs data logically private to a particular instantiation of a set of functions is kept in static global variables. In the absence of recursion in a sequential implementation, this logically private data is indistinguishable from static global data. In a parallel implementation this equivalence between logically private data and static global data breaks down. Multiple threads may *appear* to conflict at some field of a shared variable, and the *algorithm* appears to be inherently sequential. This phenomenon is called *false sharing*.

One example of false sharing arises when a set of procedures in a program uses a global (i.e., top-level, or named) variable for communication. One way to eliminate false sharing is to convert the set of procedures to use arguments and return values instead of global variables for communication. Alternatively, code with false sharing of named variables may be made re-entrant by rebinding these variables dynamically in each thread (e.g., by using Common Lisp *special* variables that are dynamically rebound in each thread) in the parallel implementation. Both changes can usually be made with only minimal changes to the program.

10.2   False sharing in Shared Structures

The above transformations do not cover false sharing of individual structure fields, however. Consider the linear time algorithm for finding the union C of two sets A and B in Figure 15, which (only) works for set elements with the property that equivalent elements are identical at the representation level. Each element x of either set A or B has a field x.Mark, which is used by the union algorithm. The algorithm first generates a new unique symbol Mark, and initializes C to contain all the elements of A. Next the a.Mark field of each element a of A is set to Mark. Each element b of B is then examined, and if b.Mark is different from Mark, b is added to C. This algorithm appears to be inherently sequential if an element may belong to multiple sets, as concurrent set operations using this algorithm may conflict at the Mark fields of elements belonging to multiple sets and lead to incorrect results. False sharing also arises in graph algorithms that make use of a mark field in the nodes of a graph structure, say to record that the current node has been visited.

Per-thread locations provide a transparent solution for false sharing in the common case where the object is a structure, and multiple threads falsely-share a field of the structure. Through the use of structures with per-thread locations, access and update functions for that field of a shared structure actually refer to different memory locations when invoked from different threads, and only the definition of the structure has to be modified. In a parallel implementation of per-thread locations a field is just a name, and may refer to distinct memory locations in different threads. The identity of a thread is an implicit argument to the access and update functions of these fields in a parallel implementation, so that different threads may access the same field of a shared structure as if that field were private to each thread. By using per-thread locations, many algorithms with false sharing may be parallelized with minimal changes. The following section describes a specific implementation of per-thread locations for fields in Common Lisp structures.

```
function Union (A, B)
;; Mark and C are local variables

    Mark := Generate-Unique-Mark()
    C := {}

    foreach a ∈ A
        a.Mark := Mark
        C := C ∪ {a}

    foreach b ∈ B
        if b.Mark ≠ Mark
            C := C ∪ {b}

    return C
```

Fig. 15. Linear Time Set Union Algorithm

10.3   Pdefstruct Interface

We extend the Common Lisp structure-defining facility **defstruct** so that certain slots (slot names) of a structure may be specified as *per-thread*. The new structure-defining facility is called **pdefstruct**. Conceptually, a per-thread slot of a shared structure corresponds to a different memory location for each thread in the system.

A typical use of **pdefstruct** has the following form:

```
(pdefstruct Element
    Value
    (Mark Default :private)
    ...
)
```

Pdefstruct defines a Common Lisp structure type that may contain per-thread slots. All valid invocations of **defstruct** are also valid invocations of **pdefstruct**. In the following description a structure type **Element** with a per-thread slot **Mark** is used to illustrate the interface of **pdefstruct**. A structure (type) may have more than one per-thread slot. (Thread creation is *not* part of the **pdefstruct** implementation. Threads are usually created transparently by the implementation of a parallelism abstraction, say **Fixed-Point**.)

(Mark Default :private) denotes per-thread slot **Mark**. **Default** is the expression that evaluates to the default value of (each location of) **Mark**, and is a required argument for the description of per-thread slots. As in Common Lisp **defstruct**, **Default** is evaluated *once* for each instance of type **Element** created, if the corresponding argument is not supplied to the constructor function of the structure type (**Make-Element**). In a parallel implementation all the per-thread locations corresponding to the slot **Mark** of an instance of type **Element** are initialized to the same initial value, which may come from the argument corresponding to **Mark** in the constructor function or from **Default**. (Different instances of the structure type **Element** may have different initial values for the same per-thread slot **Mark** if **Default** has some internal state.)

(**Reduce-**⟨*StructName*⟩**-**⟨*SlotName*⟩ **Fn Struct Identity-Value**) is   a reduction function defined by **pdefstruct** for each per-thread slot of every structure type. For example, **Reduce-Element-Mark** is defined for the structure type **Element** with per-thread slot **Mark**, and reduces the value of *all* the per-thread locations corresponding to **Mark** of a structure instance **Struct** using the binary function **Fn**. **Identity-Value** is the identity value of the reduction operator **Fn**. As the order of applying **Fn** to the per-thread locations corresponding to **Mark** is not specified, **Fn** is usually an associative and commutative operation. The result of the reduction is undefined if the per-thread slot is modified by any thread during the reduction.

A minimum amount of change is necessary to convert existing code to use **pdefstruct**. Structure declarations are converted to use **pdefstruct** instead of **defstruct**, and per-thread fields have the field option :**private**. More importantly, no change is necessary for code that accesses or updates a per-thread field. Through the use of **pdefstruct**, a large class of sequential algorithms can be parallelized relatively easily.

10.4 Sample Use of Pdefstruct: A Unique-Id Generator

The following example illustrates how **pdefstruct** can be used to construct a unique-id (uid) generator of integers that has practically no contention in a parallel implementation, yet does not expose the parallel programming details to the programmer. The generator is a shared structure that consists of a global counter, a subrange size, and a pair of integers for each thread. Each pair of per-thread integers denote a consecutive subrange of uids to be generated by that thread. When the subrange of a thread is exhausted, a new subrange is allocated from the global counter. Uids are generated from each subrange in ascending order.

The structure of the uid generator is defined as follows:

```
(pdefstruct Uid
  Subrange-Step                    ; read-only
  Last-Global-Min                  ; shared atomic counter

  (My-Prev-Uid nil :private)       ; per-thread
  (My-Max-Uid nil :private))       ; per-thread
```

Subrange-Step is the number of uids in each subrange allocated to a thread.

Last-Global-Min is initialized to be an atomic counter shared by all the threads. (`(Counter-Value Last-Global-Min) + Subrange-Step - 1`) is the lower bound of the next subrange to be allocated.

My-Prev-Uid is a per-thread value, and is the *previous* uid generated by this thread.

My-Max-Uid is a per-thread value, and is the last uid in the subrange. If `My-Prev-Uid` is equal to `My-Max-Uid` when a uid is requested, the subrange for the thread has been exhausted, and a new subrange must be allocated by incrementing `Last-Global-Min` (atomically).

The following returns a uid-generator with a minimum uid value of `Start` and a subrange step of `Step` for each thread:

```
(Make-Uid :Subrange-Step Step
          :Last-Global-Min (Make-counter (- Start Step)))
```

In Figure 16 each thread generating unique identifiers in an application takes the *same* (shared) uid-generator `Uid-G`, and invokes `New-Uid` on `Uid-G` to generate unique identifiers. `Last-Global-Min` is an atomic counter, so concurrent accesses (increment operations) are synchronized by the counter implementation. (`(Counter-Inc Counter Inc)` destructively increments the atomic `Counter` by the amount `Inc`.) `My-Prev-Uid` and `My-Max-Uid` are per-thread values, and no locking is required for accessing or updating them.

```
(defun New-Uid (Uid-G)
  (let ((Count (Uid-My-Prev-Uid Uid-G))
        (Step 0))
    (cond ((or ; get first subrange for current thread
               (null Count)

               ; need new subrange for current thread
               (= Count (Uid-My-Max-Uid Uid-G)))

           (setf Step (Uid-Subrange-Step Uid-G))
           (setf Count (Counter-Inc (Uid-Last-Global-Min Uid-G) Step))
           (setf (Uid-My-Prev-Uid Uid-G) Count)
           (setf (Uid-My-Max-Uid Uid-G) (+ Count Step -1)))

          ; normal case
          (t
           (setf (Uid-My-Prev-Uid Uid-G) (1+ Count))))
    (values (Uid-My-Prev-Uid Uid-G) Uid-G)))
```

Fig. 16. New-Uid is called by each thread using a shared Uid-G to generate globally unique identifiers (integers).

Reduce-My-Prev-Uid (defined by pdefstruct) may be used to sum the values of My-Prev-Uid across all the threads:

```
(Reduce-My-Prev-Uid #'(lambda (x y)
                        (+ (cond (x) (t 0))
                           (cond (y) (t 0))))
                    Uid-G 0)
```

11 Performance Tuning of Shared Data Accesses

A programmer may make the following changes to enhance the performance of shared data accesses of an application written using the parallel programming toolbox.

- Datatypes with time-consuming operations (long critical sections using autolocks) should be rewritten as optimistic read-modify-write operations if possible. This involves the derivation of an application-specific definition of incompatible race conditions.
- *Performance*-related false sharing should be eliminated. For example, a global counter used to generate globally unique identifiers (integers) may be replaced by a set of per-thread counters that generates unique identifiers from disjoint parts of the space of unique identifiers. (See Section 10.4.)
- An application using a dictionary should provide an application-specific Split-fn function that is faster and distribute objects more uniformly than the default hash function. A larger dictionary size (Buckets) may also be specified to speed up insert and lookup operations.

12 Related Work on Shared Data Accesses

In the following we examine how other explicitly-parallel languages or systems simplify concurrent accesses to shared data, and survey related work for each data-sharing abstraction of the parallel programming toolbox described in this paper.

12.1 Other Approaches to Concurrent Accesses

Jade Jade is a language designed for coarse-grained parallelism. A Jade program consists of a sequential imperative program (in C) annotated with *task decompositions* and *access specifications* [12]. Task decompositions specify the sources of parallelism in a program, while access specifications identify the shared objects accessed by the tasks, as well as the modes of accesses (e.g., read-only, write-only, read-write). Access specifications are interpreted at runtime, and may contain arbitrary code segments containing access declaration statements that make use of runtime information. If a *conflict* (e.g., two concurrent writes to the same object from different tasks) is detected, the sequential execution order specified in the sequential version of the program is preserved. The Jade implementation handles shared accesses automatically on the basis of access declarations, while the toolbox requires the programmer to select appropriate data-sharing abstractions to ensure that the accesses behave correctly.

M-structures Barth recently proposed the introduction of M-structures (mutable structures) to the functional programming language Id [1]. M-structures are data structures with atomic read-modify-write protocols. An M-structure supports two implicitly synchronized operations, *take* and *put*. Take locks an M-structure and reads its value, while put updates an M-structure and unlocks it. Programs written using M-structures are more declarative (simpler) than their functional counterparts, and are more efficient because the need to copy data is reduced. At the implementation level M-structure is a language-level feature that requires extensive compiler support to implement efficiently, while the data-sharing abstractions of the toolbox may be added to any language by the inclusion of the appropriate runtime library.

Concurrent Aggregates Concurrent Aggregates is an object-oriented language for fine-grained message-passing machines [2]. *Aggregates* allow the programmer to construct multi-access data abstractions that are not serializing. The programmer has explicit control over data repetition, partitioning and consistency. We believe Aggregates are more appropriate as an implementation platform for parallel programming experts to construct high performance abstractions than a user-friendly language for programmers not experienced in parallel programming.

Steele Steele proposed a programming model that combines the flexibility of MIMD programming with the simplicity of SIMD programming [14]. This is a shared-memory MIMD model with severe restrictions on side effects, such that threads may not use shared memory for communication or synchronization. The restriction ensures that the unpredictability of program execution order among threads is not externally observable, so that a given input will always produce the same output. This programming model requires extensive changes to existing sequential or parallel (shared-memory MIMD) programs, and will probably require hardware support to implement efficiently.

Multilisp Multilisp *futures* are placeholders for yet uncomputed values [4]. They may be inserted into sequential programs with no side effects to introduce concurrency relatively easily, but do not simplify the construction of parallel programs with side effects.

12.2   Per-Component Comparisons

Simple Concurrent Datatype Libraries of simple concurrent datatypes have been proposed by Gong and Wing [16], Yelick [17] and for Charm [9]. We plan to build upon the work of researchers in the concurrent datatype area by adapting their highly concurrent implementations of these datatypes to the toolbox as the need arises.

Conditional Update for Concurrent Datatypes Multilisp provides a family of low-level atomic primitives called *replace-if-eq* for the construction of higher-level synchronization operations [5]. For example, the atomic (`replace-car-eq C V V'`) operation tests if (`car C`) is `eq` to V', and if so changes (`car C`) to contain V. A boolean is returned from this operation to indicate if the replacement did occur. Currently this family of operations is only supported for the `car` and `cdr` fields of cons cells, and is not supported for arbitrary datatypes.

*Dictionary*Yelick describes an implementation of the *mapping* (dictionary) datatype based on *multiported objects* [17]. A multiported object is a shared object with per-thread data for each thread that accesses the object, and each thread's version of the state of the object (shared and per-thread data) is called a *port*. The multiported dictionary implementation does not use locks, and uses the full power of sequentially consistent shared memory. It provides much higher throughput for operations on a mapping object than an implementation based on critical sections, at the cost of significant implementation complexity.

Charm *dynamic tables* are dictionaries with integer keys, and support insert, delete and find operations. A variant of the insert operation supports a conditional insert-style operation.

The use of an application-specific (hash) function that partitions the key space into a programmer-specified number of subspaces for improved performance is somewhat similar to state partitioning or domain decomposition techniques used for distributed memory computers, where the state of a data structure is distributed over a number of processors, and each processor is responsible for handling requests for its part of the data structure [13].

Autolock Mesa provides *monitored objects* for associating monitors with individual objects [10]. The lock of a monitored object is passed as an argument to the entry procedure of the monitor, and is automatically acquired and released by the monitor implementation. However, the object-lock association is still left to the application programmer.

Id with M-structures provides *atomic objects*, which are mutable structures that are transparently associated with locks. An *atomic scope* is similar to a critical section provided by **With-Autolock**, except that *only* the operations with side effects in the scope are synchronized. Other operations are allowed to proceed without delay to achieve more throughput. An atomic scope may also be used to perform M-structure operations on multiple objects atomically.

Optimistic Read-Modify-Write Charm provides *monotonic variables* whose values increase monotonically according to some programmer-defined metric. A monotonic variable supports an atomic update operation that is commutative, associative, monotonic and idempotent. This update operation modifies a monotonic variable only if the new value satisfies some partial order predicate with respect to the existing value of the variable. It corresponds to a monotonic, *non-optimistic* read-modify-write operation in which the read, modify, write and monotonicity test operations are lumped into the monotonic update operation. There is no provision for the use of optimistic protocols to reduce contention for concurrent update operations on a monotonic variable.

Herlihy's methodology for implementing *non-blocking* and *wait-free* concurrent datatypes for large objects [6] is somewhat similar to the ORMW abstraction of the toolbox. In both cases only a part of the object is modified, and the programmer uses the semantics of the datatype to minimize the parts of the object that has to be copied. The major conceptual distinction between these two approaches lies in their treatment of concurrent updates to a shared object (race conditions). Under ORMW an *application-specific* test is used to determine if any of the concurrent updates to a shared object are compatible (e.g., linearizable), based on the *semantics* of the object. If so, the concurrent updates will (all) complete successfully. Otherwise, the incompatible updates are aborted and re-executed. Herlihy's approach is a special case of ORMW in which all concurrent updates are considered incompatible. Consequently, concurrent updates are effectively serialized at the implementation level. Herlihy has also mentioned the use of the semantics of the object to increase concurrency as a possible improvement to his methodology. Another difference is that the current implementation of ORMW uses locking, so ORMW operations are neither non-blocking nor wait-free.

Per-Thread Locations Multiprocessing SPUR Lisp provides dynamically-bound *special* variables that may be bound to different values in different processes [18]. A special variable (name) has different bindings in different processes, and a process is unable to access or modify the binding of a special variable rebound by another process. Top-level special variables, however, may be accessed by all the processes in the system. These two cases are similar to the private and non-private (default) slots of structures defined by `pdefstruct` respectively.

Structures defined by `pdefstruct` are very similar to multiported objects as defined by Yelick. However, the ports of a multiported object are much more closely coordinated than the per-thread locations of a shared structure, which are used to eliminate false sharing.

Barth describes the use of M-structures in Id to construct per-thread hash tables for storing per-thread data about the nodes in shared graph structures. However, the use of hash tables for storing per-thread data changes the way the per-thread fields of a node are accessed, and requires substantial changes to the original program.

13 Summary

Various parallel programming languages or systems differ in the amount of programmer effort required to create a parallel program. Automatic program analysis tools or parallelizers represent one end of the spectrum. For example, Curare transforms a sequential Scheme program into an equivalent parallel program automatically [11]. Data dependencies between multiple threads of control in the parallel version are serialized using locks. No programmer intervention is required. As the parallelizer is only given a sequential *implementation* of the underlying algorithm, potential sources of concurrency in the *algorithm* may not be discovered by the parallelizer. For example, the sequential implementation may contain extraneous orderings that are not necessary for the correctness of the algorithm, but would prevent the *sequential implementation* from being parallelized successfully.

Languages or systems for explicitly parallel programs represent the other end of the spectrum of programmer effort required. The programmer may use high-level knowledge or understanding of the *algorithm*—perhaps extracted from a sequential implementation—to create a parallel implementation that has good parallel performance. However, these systems are designed for use by parallel programming experts, and a large amount of low-level parallel programming detail—including the synchronization of concurrent accesses to shared data— has to be specified by the programmer. In general, the sequential and parallel versions of the same program are substantially different, and there are significant software engineering costs in maintaining two versions of a given program. In extreme cases this cost alone may preclude the parallelization effort of a large existing sequential program.

The toolbox approach to parallel programming represents an engineering compromise between these two extremes of programmer involvement. The programmer uses his high-level understanding of the underlying algorithm to introduce parallelism, and is also responsible for *identifying* all instances of data sharing in the parallel implementation. The toolbox provides high-level tools for managing the parallelism and for simplifying concurrent data accesses in the common cases. These data-sharing abstractions include simple concurrent datatypes (including dictionaries), autolocks, optimistic read-modify-writes and per-thread locations. Simple concurrent datatypes and dictionaries are supported by the toolbox directly, and may be used as drop-in replacements for their sequential counterparts. The use of conditional update operations on these datatypes eliminates a major source of race conditions in parallel programs. Autolocks may be used to synchronize concurrent accesses to arbitrary (lightly contended) objects not supported as concurrent datatypes by the toolbox, and very little modification to the source code is required. Optimistic read-modify-write operations may be used to synchronize concurrent updates to heavily contended objects by making use of the semantics of the datatype to achieve more concurrency. They have the potential of providing significant performance improvements over implementations based on simple critical sections, but require some high-level understanding of the operations being performed. Per-thread locations in structures help eliminate false sharing of structure fields in parallel code, and simplify the parallel port of a class of sequential programs (with benevolent side effects) significantly.

The data-sharing abstractions are designed for use by programmers not experienced in parallel programming, and may be retrofitted to existing (sequential) programs easily. In addition, programs written using these tools may be executed on uniprocessors and shared-memory multiprocessors without modification. As most of the low-level parallel programming details are hidden by the toolbox implementation, programs that use these tools are less error-prone than explicitly parallel programs that do not use them. The tools cover a spectrum that trades ease of use with performance, and allow a programmer to use more complicated tools for heavily contended data structures to obtain better performance. This approach has been applied successfully to three significant applications that will be described in detail elsewhere [7]. We are currently examining a large range of application programs to identify other data-sharing abstractions that will be useful for a large class of symbolic parallel programs.

References

1. Paul S. Barth. *Atomic Data Structures for Parallel Computing*. PhD thesis, MIT Laboratory for Computer Science, Cambridge, MA, March 1992.
2. Andrew Andai Chien. *Concurrent Aggregates(CA): An Object-Oriented Language for Fine-Grained Message-Passing Machines*. PhD thesis, MIT Artificial Intelligence Laboratory, Cambridge, MA, July 1990.
3. Hans Werner Guesgen. *CONSAT: A System for Constraint Satisfaction*. Research Notes in Artificial Intelligence. Morgan Kaufmann, San Mateo, CA, 1989.
4. Robert H. Halstead, Jr. Multilisp: A language for concurrent symbolic computation. *ACM Transactions on Programming Languages and Systems*, 7(4):501–538, October 1985.
5. Robert H. Halstead, Jr. An assessment of Multilisp: Lessons from experience. *International Journal of Parallel Processing*, 15(6):459–501, 1986.
6. Maurice Herlihy. A methodology for implementing highly concurrent data objects. Technical Report CRL 91/10, Digital Equipment Corporation Cambridge Research Laboratory, Cambridge, MA, October 1991.
7. Kinson Ho. *High-level Abstractions for Symbolic Parallel Programming*. PhD thesis, Computer Science Division (EECS), University of California, Berkeley, CA, 1993. To appear.
8. Kinson Ho, Paul N. Hilfinger, and Hans W. Guesgen. Optimistic discrete parallel relaxation. In *Proceedings of the 13th International Joint Conference on Artificial Intelligence*, page ??, Chambery, Savoie, France, August 1993. To appear.
9. L. V. Kale. The Chare Kernel parallel programming language and system. In *The Proceedings of the International Conference on Parallel Processing*, volume II, pages 17–25, St. Charles, IL, August 1990.
10. B. W. Lampson and D. D. Redell. Experience with processes and monitors in Mesa. *Communications of the ACM*, 23(2), February 1980.
11. James R. Larus. *Restructuring Symbolic Programs for Concurrent Execution on Multiprocessors*. PhD thesis, Computer Science Division (EECS), University of California, Berkeley, CA, May 1989.
12. Martic C. Rinard, Daniel J. Scales, and Monica S. Lam. Jade: A high-level, machine-independent language for parallel programming. *IEEE Computer*, 26(6):28–38, June 1993.

13. Charles L. Seitz. The Cosmic Cube. *Communications of the ACM*, 28(1):22–33, January 1985.
14. Guy L. Steele Jr. Making asynchronous parallelism safe for the world. In *Conference Record of the Seventeenth Annual ACM Symposium on Principles of Programming Languages*, pages 218–231, San Francisco, CA, January 1990.
15. Edward Wang and Paul N. Hilfinger. Analysis of recursive types in Lisp-like languages. In *Proceedings of the 1992 ACM Conference on Lisp and Functional Programming*, pages 216–225, San Francisco, CA, June 1992.
16. Jeannette M. Wing and Chun Gong. A library of concurrent objects and their proofs of correctness. Technical Report CMU-CS-90-151, School of Computer Science, Carnegie-Mellon University, Pittsburgh, PA, July 1990.
17. Katherine Anne Yelick. *Using Abstraction in Explicitly Parallel Programs*. PhD thesis, MIT Laboratory for Computer Science, Cambridge, MA, July 1991.
18. Benjamin Zorn, Kinson Ho, James Larus, Luigi Semenzato, and Paul Hilfinger. Multiprocessing extensions in SPUR Lisp. *IEEE Software*, 6(4):41–49, July 1989.

PART IV

Languages

and

Conceptual Models

Design of a concurrent and distributed language*

Christian Queinnec**   &   David De Roure***
École Polytechnique   University of Southampton
& INRIA-Rocquencourt

Abstract. This paper presents a new dialect of Scheme aimed towards concurrency and distribution. It offers a few primitives, including first-class continuations, with very simple semantics. Numerous examples are given showing how to program the classical concurrent control operators such as future, pcall and either. The implementation is sketched and presented along the lines of a metacircular interpreter.

This paper presents the idiom of Icsla[1], a language belonging to the Lisp family and more precisely a descendant of Scheme. This dialect has been designed with respect to the following main objectives:

- It should have a very simple and understandable semantics, with few but powerful and unrestrictively combinable concepts;
- It should offer concurrency, distribution and some other modern features such as sophisticated control features while not sacrificing the variety of styles traditionally offered by Lisp.

These goals are rather general and deserve further comment. Following Scheme, the semantics must be kept small and clean; this in turn favors correct implementation, precise documentation and eases learning or teaching. The concepts must be understandable and simple, i.e. providing only one functionality since composition is already offered at various levels by procedures, macros or modules. Existing concurrent features, proved useful in other languages, must be programmable—this demonstrates the power of our concepts as well as providing implementations that can be taught. Having no current user community to protect, some concepts have been freely revised, such as continuations, objects and equality. Currently the idiom lacks an abundance of features, since any feature that can be delivered by a library has been postponed. Finally we view our resulting idiom as a proto-language on top of which other languages can be built such as Scheme, EuLisp or CLOS.

---

* *Revision* : 1.21 presented at the Workshop on Parallel Symbolic Computing: Languages, Systems and Applications, October 1992, Boston (Massachussetts US).

** Laboratoire d'Informatique de l'École Polytechnique (URA 1437), 91128 Palaiseau Cedex, France – Email: queinnec@polytechnique.fr This work has been partially funded by GDR-PRC de Programmation du CNRS.

*** Declarative Systems Laboratory, Department of Electronics and Computer Science, University of Southampton, Southampton SO9 5NH, UK D.C.DeRoure@southampton.ac.uk

[1] Icsla (standing for *interpretation, compilation and semantics of applicative languages*) is the name of a joint project between École Polytechnique and INRIA-Rocquencourt, hence the name of the designed language.

Many concurrent or distributed languages propose (or even impose) a unique model for distribution or concurrency: objects in Emerald [RTL+91], shared objects in Orca [BKT92], threads/objects in Clouds [DJAR91] etc. These models cannot be directly applied to Scheme dialects due to their lack of first-class closures or continuations, which introduce specific problems if added carelessly. Moreover to adopt a unique model would seriously restrict the variety of styles which is traditionally the apanage of Lisp. Purely functional languages offer many opportunities for concurrency and distribution, however they usually reject side-effects, continuations and non-determinacy. Side-effects are necessary since modern computing has to deal with UNIX[2], files, NFS, X-windows: new languages cannot simply ignore the myriad of programs with fixed interfaces they have to cooperate with. Continuations are a very useful concept popularized by Scheme which promoted them to first-class objects. They allow us to program escapes, coroutines and multiple returns. Yet they raise non-trivial problems with concurrency, as shown for instance in [KW90, HD90, Que90]. Finally languages tend to avoid non-determinacy since it makes reasoning about programs difficult, computations rarely reproducible and hence debugging hard. We nevertheless offer non-determinacy and side-effects as basic features (not to be less powerful than the UNIX shells) but expect their use to be encapsulated within appropriate abstractions so to obtain *mostly functional programs.*

The target of the idiom is the development of stand-alone applications that can run on network(s) of workstations[3]. We feel a need for a tool which will extend the usual UNIX shells to offer better support for distribution (compared to rsh). Many attempts already exist for such tools (see [CM92] for such an attempt as well as an excellent overview) but have some limitations. They, for instance, require homogeneous computers or ubiquitous file systems. Considering that Lisp dialects are renowned for providing extension languages, the idiom will be an ideal glue to connect, run, and synchronize programs on a network scale. It does not require that everything be written within the idiom but provides basic services such as global network mutable variables, fork-join synchronization etc. in an easily and interactively programmable way.

Speed has not been considered a major objective but cleanliness of the semantics as well as understandable canonical implementation were preponderant. We believe the result to fit a natural mental model of how programmers conceive their applications. Most of the features that compose the idiom of Icsla are not new and might be found in the abundant literature; they nevertheless constitute further improvements upon CD-Scheme [Que92a].

1 Terminology

Applications (i.e. programs) run on a network of interconnected *processors*. Any processor has its own data space. A processor can be identified with a computer or

---

[2] UNIX is a registered trademark of UNIX Systems Laboratories, Inc. in the USA and other countries.

[3] Networks of workstations usually represent the most powerful multicomputers configuration people have access to.

with a UNIX process running on a computer. The evaluation of a program passes through a series of atomic *computation steps*. Computations are performed by *tasks* gathered into evolving tree-structured *groups* of tasks. Each processor has an evolving subset of *tasks* that it executes *tour à tour*. A task can be represented, at any time, by an expression to evaluate, a *lexical context* and a *dynamic context* that contains a *continuation*.

The implementation manages *entities* that can be first-class *values* or behind-the-scene objects (like tasks). Compound entities have *fields*, the content of which might refer to other entities. Fields can be *mutable* or *immutable*.

2 Philosophy

The idiom of Icsla adopts the Distributed Shared Memory concept which is the rather natural distributed extension of the single data space of Lisp. Distribution of data is transparent to the computation, but for speed: no explicit user-invoked copying operation is required in order to pass a value from one processor to another. The burden of managing replication and coherence is performed by the runtime library. To ease the runtime as well as to protect the user (from a software engineering point of view) the mutability of all fields of all entities is known. Logically a mutable entity (an entity that has at least one mutable field) is never copied from the processor where it was created. Conversely immutable entities can be freely replicated. This logical view does not prevent the runtime system from migrating entities rather than replicating them, to avoid copying huge immutable values, or replicating mutable values with an associated coherence protocol.

Concurrency and distribution are explicit: specialized functions exist that can be invoked where concurrency or migration are required. To offer these features as functions allows us to choose dynamically the computations that will benefit from them. Avoiding the use of these functions confers a sequential semantics on our language as in regular Scheme.

Dynamic extent is a key feature of our language. Dynamic extent already exists in regular Scheme with functions like `with-output-port` or `call-with-input-file` but is not recognized as a basic concept *per se*. In a traditional sequential setting as in COMMON LISP, dynamic extent usually refers to the duration of a computation. In our language, the dynamic extent of an expression encompasses all the tasks that are evaluating (sub)parts of the original expression. When a task makes an expression return a value, it exits the dynamic extent of this expression. The dynamic extent of an expression is not directly related to global time since scheduling interleaves computations.

In our language, many tasks may be running simultaneously. It is then possible that an expression, the evaluation of which is initiated by a single task, returns more than one value if its continuation is used by newly created tasks during the dynamic extent of the original expression. Tasks are thus pervasive but orthogonal to dynamic extent. Tasks are not first class objects in our language, they cannot be suspended, sent signals or have an identity. Computations instead can be controlled. Dynamic extents are well nested or disjoint: they have a tree shape.

Following the usage in Scheme, special functions are preferred over special forms;

this makes some examples rather ugly with numerous thunks, but of course more attractive syntax can be devised.

3 Features

The idiom of Icsla is strongly based on Scheme but adds a few features partially explored in [Que92a, QS91]:

- Assignment atomically exchanges old and new values (it is the only feature that allows data mutation);
- Equality predicates stress instantaneous or eternal substitutability;
- The **breed** function controls concurrency;
- Distribution (data and task migration) is achieved by the **remote** function or **placed-remote** function;
- Groups of tasks can be created and imperatively paused or awakened;
- Dynamic extent is emphasized and **call/cc** is no longer primitive.

We will first introduce these features informally, give some examples in §4 and finally a metacircular interpreter in §5.

3.1 Concurrency

Concurrency is introduced by means of the **breed** function. The **breed** function takes some thunks as arguments and *replaces* the current task by new tasks evaluating these thunks in the same dynamic context.

(**breed** *[thunk...]*)

The effect of **breed** is to create, detach and kill tasks: **breed** is the only function that manages tasks and its sole effect is to change the number of tasks. The different tasks that **breed** creates are independent: they have no synchronization constraint. When a task finishes the evaluation of the thunk it was spawned on, it commits suicide and yields no result at all. Tasks can only return information through continuations (as discussed in §3.3), which explicitly represent causality. The **suicide** utility function which allows the current task to vanish obviously returns no value at all, and can be defined simply in terms of **breed** as:

(**define** (**suicide** . ignored-arguments) (**breed**))

Tasks are not first-class objects but groups of cooperating tasks can be managed as explained in §3.2. Had tasks been first-class objects, many questions would arise about their identity with respect to continuations.

No particular scheduling strategy is actually stressed but a fair one is required. The initial continuation of stand-alone applications (resp. the toplevel loop) waits for all spawned tasks to finish before returning to the operating system (resp. starting a new evaluation cycle). The **breed** function introduces indeterminacy which is already present (but to a lesser extent) in Scheme since the evaluation order of the terms of a functional application is unspecified.[4]

---

[4] The idiom of Icsla has an explicit left to right order of evaluation. For people who want application to be sequential with an unknown order, we offer macros based on **random(3)**.

The **breed** function is equivalent to the existing low-level primitives of some implementations, for example **fork** of MultiLisp [Hal89]. We just unveil it to become the sole concurrency primitive the user can see.

3.2 Groups

Tasks can be created easily by means of **breed** but insufficient control is offered to program the classical parallel-or operator, also known as **amb** [McC63], **either** [Pri80]. The form (**either** $expression_0$ $expression_1$) concurrently spawns two computations to evaluate the two expressions, returns the value of the first one which returns true and kills the other computation since it is no longer useful. We introduced the concept of *group*, inspired from the *sponsor* of [Osb90] and the *controller* of [HDB90] but also related to UNIX's concept of groups of tasks. Groups of tasks can be imperatively controlled, allowing us to program **either** (see section 4).

The **call/de** (for *call with dynamic extent*) function starts a computation under the responsibility of a fresh group.

(call/de (lambda (*group*) *expression*))

This form creates a first-class object called a group, binds it to the variable *group* and evaluates *expression* under its control. Any value yielded by *expression* is a value returned by the **call/de** form.

When a task creates another task, the new task belongs to the same groups as its progenitor task: groups are inherited. The group created by **call/de** initially contains only the current task, i.e. the task that invoked **call/de** then belongs to one more group during the computation of the associated *expression*. All subsequent tasks that will be created by the computation of *expression* will then belong to *group*. When a task makes **call/de** return a value (normally or by premature exit— see **abort** below), the task ceases to belong to the associated group.

A group can be viewed as the set of tasks that participate in the computation of an expression. When a group is empty, the group can be reclaimed since no new task can be created inside this group[5] and no new value can be produced as a result of the associated expression.

A group can pause or awaken the tasks it controls by means of the associated imperative functions **pause!** and **awake!**.

(pause! *group*)   (awake! *group*)

Pausing a group means that all the tasks that belong to this group will be suspended wherever they are geographically and however many there are. Conversely all the tasks of a group can be resumed when wakening the group. The **pause!** and **awake!** functions return unspecified values. A task can determine if it currently participates in a group by using the **within/de?** predicate.

(within/de? *group*)

---

[5] Actually, call/de takes an optional argument, a unary function, that will be called on the group object whenever the group is empty i.e. contains no more tasks. This allows us to specify some (finalization) code that will be run (for its effect) when the computation associated to the group finishes. This effect corresponds to a built-in distributed termination facility.

A group can also be viewed as the reification of the dynamic extent of the associated expression. A canonical implementation for call/de, see §5, is to push a so called group-frame onto the stack of the current task to indicate the creation of the group. It is therefore simple for within/de? to check if a particular group appears in the stack of the current task. breed pushes a suicide frame onto the stack of the current task then creates new tasks, each of which shares that new stack.

The awake! function can simply be implemented as a broadcast that indicates that all tasks of this group must be made runnable. Some protocol must be used to avoid simultaneous overlapping contradicting broadcasts. A naive solution is to dedicate a machine for that task. The awake! function can return as soon as the broadcast is emitted. On the other hand, the pause! function is more subtle. The naive implementation is to broadcast to all processors a message indicating that all tasks belonging to a particular group must be paused, i.e. removed from the list of runnable tasks. These tasks must not be reclaimed since they can be awakened later: they are stored, associated with their group, in the list of paused tasks of the processor. If the group object is reclaimed then its associated tasks are implicitly reclaimed[6]. The pause! function returns when all processors have removed these tasks and sent back an acknowledgment. The precise semantics of pause! makes it return as soon as no task which is to be paused but is still running can causally affect the behavior of the continuation of pause!. This respects causality and leaves room for some optimizations.

3.3 Continuations

The continuation of a task defines at any time what that task has yet to do. Any computation step the task performs either extends its continuation, adding new pending evaluations, or yields a value to its continuation.

Continuations are first-class objects in Scheme. They are created (captured) by means of the call/cc function. Scheme continuations have an indefinite extent which confers upon them numerous usages from escape constructs such as catch/throw à la COMMON LISP, to coroutines [HFW84]. They are very powerful but difficult to compile well [CHO88, HD90, JG89] and they pose complex implementation problems.

We decided to emphasize the concept of dynamic extent and use the primitives of [QS91] known as splitter, abort and call/pc. Furthermore we identify splitter with call/de. call/de marks the current continuation so that it can be referenced by abort and call/pc, but these can only be used while in the dynamic extent of the intended group. This can be checked with the within/de? predicate. The abort function takes a group and a thunk as arguments.

(abort *group thunk*)

When a task invokes abort it replaces its continuation up to *group* by the evaluation of *thunk*. This thunk is still evaluated in the dynamic extent of the group. The aborting of one task does not affect the others, in particular multiple tasks can invoke abort concurrently. Consider for instance the following generator in the spirit of [MH90]:

---

[6] A particular message can be used for this double action.

```
(define (//iota start stop)
  (call/de
   (lambda (return)
     (define (iota start stop)
       (if (< start stop)
           ;;concurrently return a number and continue to generate the others
           (breed (lambda () (abort return (lambda () start)))
                  (lambda () (iota (+ 1 start) stop)) )
           (suicide) ) )
     (iota start stop) ) ) )
```

The task that invokes (//iota 0 4) dies while four new tasks are sequentially
created and each of them appears to return 0, 1, 2 or 3 as the value of the (//iota
0 4) form. For instance (display (//iota 0 4)) prints in some undetermined
order the integers 2, 0, 1 and 3. Although these four new tasks were created under
the sponsorship of the return group, they loose this sponsorship shortly after they
call abort when leaving the group, i.e. when leaving the dynamic extent of //iota.
The enclosing group does not gain four new tasks since they already belong to it (by
set inclusion).

Premature exits à la catch/throw can be easily programmed with the abort
function, which is the sole function (with protect) to have a control effect[7]. The
call/pc function deals with partial continuations which are already described in
[QS91] and will not be discussed further here.

(call/pc *group* (lambda (*partial-continuation*) ...))

A useful feature to detect the end of a computation is the unwind-protect
feature of COMMON LISP. It is simple to know when a computation starts but not
so simple to know when it ends. In fact we do not provide any means to know when a
computation ends; this would break modularity where the implementor of a package
wants to hide the fact that s/he uses (groups of) tasks. It is nevertheless useful to
provide a way to detect when a computation returns a value, i.e. to detect when a
value exits a dynamic extent. Since premature exits restart a task with a thunk, the
protect feature we present uses thunks instead of values.

(protect *thunk thunk-transformer*)

If *thunk* normally returns a value *v* then this value is wrapped into (lambda () v)
which is transformed into a new thunk, the result of (*thunk-transformer* (lambda
() v)); this latest thunk is then applied and its value becomes the final value of
the protect expression. When a premature exit leaves the dynamic extent of *thunk*,
then the second argument of abort is transformed by *thunk-transformer* and the
abort is restarted with its transformed result. For instance:

```
(call/de (lambda (exit)
          (protect (lambda () (abort exit (lambda ()
                                            (display 'meep)
                                            3 )))
                   (lambda (thunk) (display 'mip)
```

---

[7] Ignoring errors such as (car 42) which invokes the error handler and therefore might
induce control effects.

```
(lambda () (* 2 (thunk))) ) )
```
displays mipmeep *and returns 6*

This **protect** mechanism not only provides a control effect triggered by a value returning but also enables the user to intercept and transform the passing thunk.

Let us sum up our continuation model. It stresses dynamic extent (checked by **within/de?**) and offers simple escape forms with **abort**. Sharing continuations with **breed** allows multiple returns that can be detected with **protect**. Finally groups of tasks can be managed. The emphasis on dynamic extent would suffice, in regular Scheme, to prevent expressions from returning multiply since continuations would only be used at most once. This is not the case in our language because of the concurrency: expressions can fork into multiple tasks multiply returning. Alternatively we can develop a new programming style based on multiple returns and, for instance, view a function of the X windows library such as **XNextEvent** as an event generator.

Partial continuations, i.e. **call/pc**, allow us to define **call/cc** as in [QS91]. More precisely they allow us to define multiple versions of **call/cc** depending on the required relation with respect to **protect**. We nevertheless do not retain **call/cc** as a primitive function since it can also be defined solely with **call/de**, **breed**, **abort**, **pause!** and **awake!**, see §4.

3.4 Migration

Computations can migrate using the **remote** function which implements a kind of remote procedure call (RPC) [SG90, GL90].

(**remote** *function arguments...*)

When a form such as (**remote** $F\ A\ B$) is to be evaluated, F, A and B are sequentially evaluated yielding values f, a and b. These values are then possibly migrated onto a neighboring processor (the precise choice is left unspecified using **remote** but can be imposed with **placed-remote** inspired by **placed par** in Occam [Bur88]) where the migrated f is applied on the migrated a and b. This differs from a regular RPC in that the continuation k of the original (**remote** ...) form is also migrated and will be directly resumed, from the neighbor, with the result of the application (if any).

The **remote** function involves some kind of concurrency which is implicit if the computation is really migrated. On a single processor (**remote** *function arguments*) is equivalent to (**call/de** (**lambda** (g) (**breed** (**lambda** () (**abort** g (**lambda** () (*function arguments*))))))) which explicitly reveals the underlying **breed** effect.

We have adopted a very simple "migration" model where entities never move, always residing on the site where they were created. When an entity o on processor μ is to be migrated to the processor μ', a *remote pointer* $< \mu, o >$ is created on the remote processor μ'. This remote pointer can be read as "go to μ and find o". Extra rules can be added to simplify "remote remote" pointers, for example on machine μ'', $< \mu', < \mu, o >>$ is no more than $< \mu, o >$ if processor μ is accessible from μ''.

An effective implementation of this theoretical migration model does not exclude the "real" migration of entities provided the semantics is respected, nor does it exclude multiple duplication of immutable entities such as small integers, booleans, characters, immutable cons cells, function code or universally known primitives like + or cons. To achieve this, the mutability of all user-created data can be taken into account and a specialized migration policy devised. Fortunately, the percentage of mutable data is usually small.

Some primitives are *geographically strict*: to be applied, their arguments must be local. Such strict computations are handled through the following rule:

geographical commutation rule: Applying the geographically strict primitive p on $< \mu', o >$ with continuation k on processor μ is just applying p on o with continuation $< \mu, k >$ on processor μ'.

Examples of strict computations include looking up an identifier in a remote environment (activation record), sending a value to a remote continuation, storing a value in a remote mutable object etc—almost all primitive computations follow this rule. Observe that computations carry their continuation and are therefore not bound to the sites through which they pass. Migration of computations towards data is not unreasonable, especially when the data consists of files or other site-bound resources, but does not exclude moving some data towards computations to lessen communication cost. Adopting the parallel shell view mentioned before, it is sensible to offer another function which achieves migration but towards a precise processor where, for instance, specific resources may be accessed.

Migration can create a subtle problem: a computation can overflow a processor with multiple copies of a single immutable entity. We are studying hash-consing for these values but cannot report more on this topic.

3.5 Assignment

Synchronization is often achieved with a test-and-set operation. Rather than providing additional primitive objects like (some flavors of) semaphores, or offering functions like `replace-if-eq` that only work on pairs, we decided that assignment should play this rôle. The form (`set!` *variable form*) first computes *form* then atomically exchanges the obtained value with the former content of the location bound to *variable*; this former value becomes the value of the assignment form. This value is undefined if the location was previously uninitialized.

Following the spirit of [Per87, §3.4], a busy-waiting loop can be written as[8]:

```
(define-macro (with-mutex bool . critical-section)
  '(let ((local #t))                             ; occupied
     ;; exchanges local and bool and loops until bool is free
     (while local (set! local (set! ,bool local)))
     ;; evaluates the critical section
     (protect (begin . ,critical-section)
       (lambda (thunk)
         (unless (set! local #t) (set! ,bool #f))   ; frees bool
         thunk )) ) )
```

---

[8] To avoid looping until being preempted, the real implementation explicitly calls the task scheduler.

This syntactic form ensures that only one task will enter[9] the `critical-section` expression. The mutual exclusion is ensured by the atomic control of the `bool` variable[10].

If the value of the assignment is not needed, i.e. if it is used for its effect rather than its value, then the former content of the location need neither be returned nor migrated. Nevertheless for causality reasons the continuation of the assignment is resumed only after the assignment is performed, so the implementation cannot avoid sending back at least an acknowledgment. Continuations explicitly represent causality.

The assignment has been banished by the ML family of languages in favor of first-class mutable cells because they are easier to type-check. On the contrary, we restrict side-effects to be performed only by assignment. No power is lost since it is well known that each can be simulated by the other. For local variables, the advantage of assignment is that all mutation sites can be determined statically. The mutability of global variables can be stated by exportation directives associated with modules [QP91]. All variables thus have a known mutability but only the mutable variables might pose an implementation problem if accessed concurrently, since the assignment must be atomic. A static sharing analysis [Deu90] can be performed to determine those variables which might present such conflicting access. A simple-to-compute superset of these "dangerous" variables is those that are mutated and closed. This allows us to use at no cost common idioms where a local variable is only mutated once.

On the other hand, the simplest implementation for mutable locations is to use boxes as popularized by [KKR+86]. The sole mutable entities of our implementation are boxes which can (logically) never be migrated. An assignment to a box is therefore a request for the processor that hosts this box to update it. It is a simple matter for that processor to serialize these updates. After an update is performed, the hosting processor reports it to the requesting processor which can then resume its computation. More elaborate protocols with partially replicated boxes have also been studied [Piq90, Piq91].

3.6 Equality

The old `eq?` predicate comparing addresses of heap-allocated values bears no meaning in a distributed world: a single entity can be replicated on two different processors where the addresses of the replications have no obvious relation. It seems that only two reasons exist to compare values: they can be compared for substitutability or instantaneous similarity. Two values are substitutable one for the other if there does not exist a program able to distinguish them. Two values are similar if at the time of the comparison they have similar structure and content. Substitutable values are always similar. Similarity is known as `equal?` but requires special precautions for

---

[9] *enter* and not *evaluate* since tasks can be created inside the critical section that might return multiply.

[10] The (`unless (set! local #t) ...`) form protects `bool` from being freed more than once when the critical-section returns more than one value, but does not prevent these extra computations from taking place. Also observe that the boolean flag is freed whether a value is normally returned or an escape is performed.

cyclic values. Substitutability is not a computable property but can be safely approximated as follows: two values are substitutable if they are both immutable and the content of their fields are substitutable or if they are the same mutable object [Bak90].

Concerning the geographical commutation rule, binary strict predicates such as substitutable? or equal? require a special implementation. The canonical implementation can be termed as "geographic currying": follow the first argument until reaching the processor where it resides, then send its coordinates to the second argument which will compare it against itself. If data can migrate while being compared, the canonical algorithm has to be refined.

4 Examples

Despite its simplicity, the idiom of Icsla has surprising capabilities and can be used to describe other proposals for concurrent programming. The following examples are mainly syntaxes and are defined with old-style but hygienic macros[11].

Multiple results for an expression might pose problems. The once syntax constrains an expression to return no more than one value. The following definition also ensures that all spawned computations will cease after returning a value. The trick is to pause the group of tasks which computes the expression as soon as it returns a first value. The paused group will be automatically reclaimed once unreferenced. Observe that call/de returns at most one value (the first that toggles the result? variable). The reclamation of the other tasks is done outside the g group.

```
(define-macro (once . expression)
  '(let ((result? #f))                          ; is the result present ?
     (let ((g+v (call/de
                  (lambda (g)
                    (cons g (protect (begin . ,expression)
                              (lambda (thunk)
                                (if (set! result? #t)
                                    (suicide)   ; kills superfluous values
                                    thunk ) ) )) ))))
       (pause! (car g+v))                       ; kills other spawned tasks
       (cdr g+v) ) ) )
```

4.1 qlambda

An effect similar to the qlambda feature of Qlisp [GM84, GG88] or the exlambda of PaiLisp [IM89], is to define a function whose body is in a critical section. The function is associated with a queue of tasks waiting to enter the body of the function. Tasks are reified into groups that will be awakened one by one (in FIFO order)

---

[11] We do not use the new macro proposal in the appendix of [CR91] since the pcall syntax does not seem easily amenable to this model. We nevertheless suppose our macros to be hygienic [KFFD86], i.e. not to introduce name conflicts.

when the critical section is free[12]. Observe that busy-waiting loops are only used for short mutations of shared variables, thus ensuring inexpensive waits. The first expression of the body, a kind of *barrier*, acts as the 'P' primitive on `bool`, considered as a semaphore, whereas the second argument of `breed` mimics the 'V' primitive. Waiting tasks are resumed in a FIFO order; other strategies can be devised. Observe the second `with-mutex` form, which chooses what to do in a critical section but the resulting choice (a thunk) is not critical and can be evaluated without precautions. The `once` syntax imposed `body` to return at most one value or to exit, the first argument of `breed` also respects escaping.

```
(define-macro (exlambda variables . body)
  '(let ((bool      #f)        ; controls body entrance
         (queue-flag #f)       ; controls the queue shared variable
         (queue     '()) )     ; list of waiting tasks
     (lambda ,variables
       (when (set! bool #t)
         (call/de (lambda (caller)        ; suspends caller
                    (with-mutex queue-flag
                      (set! queue (cons caller queue)) )
                    (pause! caller) )) )
       (protect (once . ,body)            ; computes body (once)
         (lambda (thunk)
           (call/de
            (lambda (return)
              (breed (lambda () (abort return thunk))
                     (with-mutex queue-flag
                       (if (null? queue)
                           (begin (set! bool #f) suicide)
                           (let ((client (car (last-pair queue))))
                             ;;FIFO mode
                             (set! queue (remove client queue))
                             (lambda () (awake! client)) )))))))))))))
```

4.2 pcall

Many proposals for concurrency [Hal84] include a `pcall` (for parallel call) special form to introduce concurrency. When a form such as (`pcall` *F A B*) is to be evaluated, the different terms *F*, *A* and *B* are concurrently evaluated by different tasks yielding values *f*, *a* and *b*. When all values are computed, *f* (presumably a function) is applied on *a* and *b*. This is an instance of a classical fork–join model.

The continuation of a term of a `pcall` form is problematic due to the concurrency that exists between the terms and the fact that these terms might multiply return results. At least two solutions seem to be natural. Without restraining the problem, let us only consider the two-term combination (`pcall` *F E*). The first meaning is

---

[12] This does not ensure that at most one single task evaluates the body of the function since other tasks might be created and concurrently return a value. It ensures that only one task enters when another one exits.

nicknamed "multiplicative" where all values of F are applied to all values of E. This requires all values in every **pcall** form to be kept, since to multiply return results is a dynamic (and generally unforeseeable) property. The second meaning is "additive", where the continuation of E is a function that waits for a value e: when invoked the first time and if F already returned some values f_i then all these (presumably) functions f_i are applied on e. If F has not returned any values, then e is memorized as a possible value for E. When invoked later, the last value of F is applied on e and e is memorized as the last value for E. These continuations are symmetrically defined and the number of effective applications is $1 + (n_F - 1) + (n_E - 1)$ where n_F (resp. n_E) is the number of values returned by F (resp. E). This behavior is illustrated in figure 1 and detailed in [Que91, Mor92].

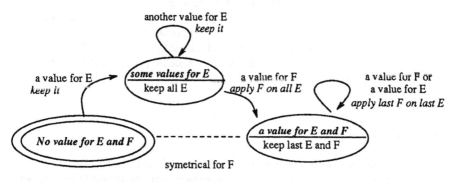

Fig. 1. Continuation of a term of a **pcall** form

The idiom of Icsla allows us to program **pcall** with whatever semantics. The trick appears in the **pcall** syntax: any value produced by a term of the **pcall** form is given with its rank to the "funnel". This funnel can sort, store, or forget the incoming values and thus decide when the application is ready to be performed, with the correct continuation **return**. When the funnel is built, temporary structures can be preallocated on the basis of the number of terms. The code for the additive (or multiplicative) semantics is lengthy and is skipped.

```
(define-macro (pcall . terms)
  '(call/de
    (lambda (return)
      (let ((funnel (make-additive-pcall-handler
                       return ,(length terms) )))
        (breed ,@(map (lambda (i term)
                        '(lambda () (funnel ,i ,term)) )
                      (iota 0 (length terms))
                      terms )) ) ) ) )
```

4.3 either

The **either** syntax can also be defined. Here again the group of tasks computing
the two branches is paused when a true result is produced. When both expressions
return false, the final value of **either** is false.

```
(define-macro (either e1 e2)
  '(let ((group  'wait)    ; the group of tasks
         (last   #f)       ; is it the last task ?
         (result #f) )     ; the default final result
     (set! result
         (call/de (lambda (g)
                     (set! group g)
                     (define (handle v)
                       (abort g (if v (lambda () #t)
                                      (if (set! last #t) (suicide)
                                          (lambda () #f) ) )) )
                     (breed (lambda () (handle (once ,e1)))
                            (lambda () (handle (once ,e2))) ) )) )
     (pause! group)
     result ) )
```

4.4 future

Another example is related to the well-known **future** [Hal84, Hal89]. We can define
it without resorting to magic functions such as **make-future** or **determine-future!**.
These futures must be explicitly **touch**-ed to deliver their value.

```
(define (touch f) (f))
(define-macro (future e)
  '(let ((computed? #f)       ; is the future determined ?
         (queue-flag #f)      ; controls queue and computed?
         (queue    '())       ; waiting touching tasks
         (value    'wait) )   ; future's value
     (call/de
      (lambda (return)
        (breed                ; concurrently (1) and (2)
         (lambda ()
           (abort return      ; (1) returns ...
             (lambda ()       ; ← the future
               (call/de
                (lambda (caller)
                  (if (with-mutex queue-flag
                        (or computed?
                            (begin (set! queue (cons caller queue))
                                   #f ) ) )
                      value (suicide) ) )) ) ) )
         (lambda ()           ; (2) computes the value of the future
```

```
(set! value ,e)
(if (with-mutex queue-flag (set! computed? #t))
    ; Variant: (abort return (lambda () value)) [KW90]
    (suicide)
    (apply breed ; resumes all waiting tasks in parallel
           (map (lambda (caller)
                   (lambda () (caller value)) )
                (with-mutex queue-flag
                (let ((q queue))
                (set! queue '())
                q ) ) ) ) ) ) ) ) ) ) )
```

The difference between a future and a regular Scheme delay is that the computation of the future is performed concurrently with its use. This behavior raises subtle issues (detailed in [KW90]) with different behaviors, all of which can be directly programmed in our language.

4.5 call/cc

The final example we will give is call/cc without using partial continuations. The trick is to encode a continuation into a paused group containing only one task. Awakening the group will achieve the resumption of the continuation once. To allow the continuation to be used more than once, as soon as the group is awakened, it spawns a new task that will pause the group again. Many implementation details concerning access to the shared variable **values** and the race condition between the **abort** and **pause!** effects are not shown here, to avoid encumbering the definition. The interest of this example is to show that call/cc bears no relationship with **protect** or dynamic-wind as would be the case with partial continuations.

```
(define (call/cc f)
  (let ((values '()))
    ((call/de
      (lambda (g)
        (breed (lambda ()
                (abort g (lambda ()
                          (lambda ()
                           (f (lambda (v)
                               (set! values (cons v values))
                               (awake! g)
                               (suicide) )) ) )) )
               (lambda ()
                (let loop ()
                 (if (pair? values)
                     (let ((v (car values)))
                       (set! values (cdr values))
                       (breed (lambda ()
                               (abort g (lambda ()
                                         (lambda () v) )) )
```

```
            loop ) )
      (pause! g) ) ) ) ) ))) ) )
```

Other features like M-structures [BNA91], actors or active objects [AR89] can be programmed in the idiom of Icsla and are left as exercises to the careful reader. Of course, all the previous syntaxes can be combined into higher-level abstractions since users often do not need to know the details of these macros.

5   More formal semantics

In this section, we provide the definition of a metacircular interpreter for the idiom of Icsla. We will depart from the tradition since the expression to be evaluated is first rewritten using a program transformation based on Abstract Continuation Passing Style (ACPS) [FWFD88, Que92b]. The resulting expression is evaluated using any regular Scheme interpreter, see for instance [Dyb87]. We can thus define our language in a very compressed form with only two key points: a program transformation and a library of functions that are defined in Scheme. This presentation is close to the compilation model: control operators are defined in a module which is compiled without ACPS since they are already written according to this style. The resulting compiled module is linked with the regular modules which are ACPS-rewritten.

Abstract Continuation Passing Style is a program transformation that allows us to remove all known control operators such as call/cc, unwind-protect as well as others dealing with partial continuations. It can moreover express the dynamic extent concept, dynamic binding etc. ACPS is based on a non-standard representation of the continuation: a list of frames. We extend ACPS by making the set of runnable tasks explicit. A frame now waits for a value, a continuation and the current list of eligible tasks; it selects one of the latter and runs it in the appropriate context. Our metacircular definition does not take into account distribution which is difficult to reveal due to its transparency (see [Que92a] for a formalization of distribution). We concentrate on the control features that were discussed above and hide the description of error handling, dynamic binding and substitutability, which require us to encode types.

The frames of which a continuation is composed are made apparent by ACPS. Each frame has a behavior which specifies what to do when receiving a value, as well as the list of the frames that are below it. The Extended ACPS program transformation appears in table 1. Sending a value to a continuation is expressed with resume, while pushing a frame is written extend. θ^* is the list of eligible tasks, q is the continuation and v some value.

Some utility functions are needed to encapsulate the representation of continuations. The extend function pushes a frame onto a continuation. When a value is given to a frame, the frame suspends the current computation into a task and calls the scheduler. The scheduler chooses one task, finds its associated behavior and applies it. The oneof operator randomly selects one task among a set and invokes its second argument on this task and the set containing the others[13].

---

[13] The oneof can be given a functional definition with a powerdomain for the final answers, see [Que92a].

$$\begin{aligned}
&\text{ACPS}[\![\nu]\!]\theta^*q \to (\text{resume}\ \theta^*\ q\ \nu)\\
&\text{ACPS}[\![(\text{quote}\ \varepsilon)]\!]\theta^*q \to (\text{resume}\ \theta^*\ q\ (\text{quote}\ \varepsilon))\\
&\text{ACPS}[\![(\text{if}\ \pi_0\ \pi_1\ \pi_2)]\!]\theta^*q \to\\
&\quad \text{ACPS}[\![\pi_0]\!]\theta^*(\text{extend}\ q\ (\lambda(\theta'^*\ q'\ v')\ (\text{if}\ v'\ \text{ACPS}[\![\pi_1]\!]\theta'^*q'\ \text{ACPS}[\![\pi_2]\!]\theta'^*q')))\\
&\text{ACPS}[\![(\text{set!}\ \nu\ \pi)]\!]\theta^*q \to\\
&\qquad \text{ACPS}[\![\pi]\!]\theta^*(\text{extend}\ q\ (\lambda(\theta'^*\ q'\ v')\ (\text{resume}\ \theta'^*\ q'\ (\text{set!}\ \nu\ v'))))\\
&\text{ACPS}[\![(\lambda(v^*)\ \pi)]\!]\theta^*q \to (\text{resume}\ \theta^*\ q\ (\lambda(\theta'^*\ q'\ v^*)\ \text{ACPS}[\![\pi]\!]\theta'^*q'))\\
&\text{ACPS}[\![(\pi_1\ldots\pi_n)]\!]\theta_0^*q_0 \to\\
&\quad \text{ACPS}[\![\pi_1]\!]\theta_0^*(\text{extend}\ q_0\ (\lambda(\theta_1^\star\ q_1\ v_1)\ \ldots\\
&\qquad\qquad\qquad \text{ACPS}[\![\pi_n]\!]\theta_{n-1}^*(\text{extend}\ q_{n-1}\ (\lambda(\theta_n^\star\ q_n\ v_n)\\
&\qquad\qquad\qquad\qquad\qquad\qquad (v_1\ \theta_n^\star\ q_n\ v_2\ \ldots v_n)))))
\end{aligned}$$

Table 1. Extended ACPS rules

```
(define (extend q frame)
  (cons frame q) )
(define (resume tasks q value)
  (schedule (cons (make-task q value) tasks)) )
(define (schedule tasks)
  (if (pair? tasks)
      (oneof tasks (lambda (task tasks)
                     (let ((q (task-q task))
                           (value (task-value task)) )
                       ((frame-behavior (car q))
                        tasks (cdr q) value ) ) ))
      end-of-computation ) )
```

To shorten the presentation we will use object technology and define classes for the entities we will manage. The **define-class** defines a class with a particular super-class and a list of proper fields[14].

```
(define-class Task Object (q value))
(define-class Group Object (running? tasks))
(define-class Frame Object (behavior))
(define-class Group-Frame Frame (group))
(define-class Protect-Frame Frame (cleaner))
```

We can now give the definition of the special functions of the idiom of Icsla. Tasks are created by **breed**, sharing the same continuation with a suicide frame on top of it. The breed function calls **schedule** directly, thus committing suicide.

```
(define (breed tasks q . thunks)
  (let ((q (extend q (make-Frame (lambda (tasks q v)
                                   (schedule tasks) )))))
    (schedule (append (map (lambda (thunk)
                             (make-task
```

---

[14] We use a personal and small object system called MEROON.

```
                       (extend q (make-Frame
                                   (lambda (tasks q v)
                                     (thunk tasks q) ) ))
                   'go ) )
                 thunks )
             tasks )) ) )
```

Groups are created by call/de, where a group frame is simply pushed onto the continuation to indicate that the dynamic extent is entered.

```
(define (call/de tasks q f)
  (let ((new-group (make-Group #t '())))
    (f tasks
       (extend q (make-Group-Frame
                    (lambda (tasks q v) (resume tasks q v))
                    new-group ))
       new-group ) ) )
```

The following function is a utility that, given a continuation and a group, returns #f or a pair cutting the continuation into two parts, the above and below parts with respect to the corresponding group frame. Since partial continuations can make a group-frame appear more than once in a continuation, the deepest one is preferred (see also [HD90]).

```
(define (split q group)
  (define (search left* right*)
    (if (pair? right*)
        (if (and (Group-Frame? (car right*))
                 (eq? (Group-Frame-group (car right*)) group) )
            (or (search (cons (car right*) left*) (cdr right*))
                (cons (reverse left*) right*) )
            (search (cons (car right*) left*) (cdr right*)) )
        #f ) )
  (search '() q) )
```

We can now easily express within/de? and call/pc, which simply use the previous split.

```
(define (within/de? tasks q group)
  (resume tasks q (not (not (split q group)))) )
(define (call/pc tasks q group f)
  (let ((above+below (split q group)))
    (if above+below
        (f tasks q (lambda (tasks q v)
                     (resume tasks (append (car above+below) q) v) ))
        (wrong tasks q "Not in the dynamic extent of" group) ) ) )
```

The abort control operator is more complex since it must respect the protect forms that it has to bypass.

```
(define (abort tasks q group thunk)
  (let ((above+below (split q group)))
    (if above+below
```

```
(let ((q-group (cdr above+below)))
  (define (unwind tasks q q-group thunk)
    (cond ((eq? q q-group) (thunk tasks q))
          ((Protect-Frame? (car q))
           ((Protect-Frame-cleaner (car q))
            tasks
            (extend (cdr q)
                    (make-Frame
                     (lambda (tasks q thunk)
                       (unwind tasks q q-group thunk) ) ) )
            thunk ) )
          (else (unwind tasks (cdr q) q-group thunk)) ) )
  (unwind tasks q q-group thunk) )
(wrong tasks q "Not in the dynamic extent of" group) ) ) )
```

The two functions pause! and awake! have straightforward definitions. We encode them with a side effect on the group object to indicate whether it is running or the set of paused tasks. These are the sole side-effects we use. Due to Extended ACPS, the body of pause! and awake! are implicitly in a critical section.

```
(define (awake! tasks q group)
  (if (Group-running? group)
      (resume tasks q an-unspecified-value)
      (let ((paused-tasks (Group-tasks group)))
        (set-Group-tasks! group '())
        (set-Group-running?! group #t)
        (resume (append paused-tasks tasks)
                q an-unspecified-value ) ) ) )
(define (pause! tasks q group)
  (define (sort-tasks tasks k)
    (define (sort tasks paused others)
      (if (pair? tasks)
          (if (split (Task-q (car tasks)) group)
              (sort (cdr tasks) (cons (car tasks) paused) others)
              (sort (cdr tasks) paused (cons (car tasks) others)) )
          (k paused others) ) )
    (sort tasks '() '()) )
  (if (Group-running? group)
      (sort-tasks
       (cons (make-task q an-unspecified-value) tasks)
       (lambda (tasks-to-pause other-tasks)
         (set-Group-running?! group #f)
         (set-Group-tasks! group tasks-to-pause)
         (schedule other-tasks) ) )
      (resume tasks q an-unspecified-value) ) )
```

Finally the protect control operator just pushes a special frame that abort will consider.

```
(define (protect tasks q thunk thunk-transformer)
```

```
(thunk tasks
        (extend q (make-Protect-Frame
                    (lambda (tasks q v)
                      (thunk-transformer
                       tasks
                       (extend q (make-Frame
                                   (lambda (tasks q thunk)
                                     (thunk tasks q) ) ))
                       (lambda (tasks q) (resume tasks q v)) ) )
                    thunk-transformer )) ) )
```

Other features such as dynamic binding and exception handling can be described with the same framework, implemented through special frames in the continuation. Dynamic binding is achieved through two functions (associate/de *key value thunk*) to associate *key* with *value* in the dynamic extent of *thunk*. The value associated with *key* can be retrieved with (lookup/de *key success failure*). One point worth noting is that the dynamic environment is immutable so it can be migrated easily (this does not prevent binding a mutable value to a key). This dynamic binding facility corresponds to a deep binding implementation.

6   Implementation

This section describes the implementation of a distributed interpreter for the Icsla idiom. The interpreter has been developed in order to gain practical experience of the ideas we have presented, and it is intended that much of the technology will be reusable in the runtime system of the proposed compiler. Some of the techniques are based on experience with development and use of the QPL system [DeR90b] [DeR90a].

Preliminary work involved construction of a small interpreter supporting the breed and remote primitives, embedded in Scheme. This was based on a continuation-passing metacircular evaluator where each task has an associated state consisting of a *(continuation, value)* pair [DeR90c]. A state is selected by the scheduler and the continuation is invoked to advance the state by one computation step, returning a list of states representing the states of tasks to replace the original; in this way a task is replaced by zero or more tasks. To simulate remote, 'geography' is introduced by extending the task state to include a *machine* component, and this aspect can be taken further by introducing distinct environments and implementing the geographical commutation rule. This tool enabled us to explore abstractions using breed and remote.

The current distributed interpreter is closely related to the metacircular interpreter presented in the previous section. There are two versions: a single process version which supports breed using resumptions and a scheduler (as above), and a distributed version which additionally supports remote by a system of *lazy migration* of objects to other processes. The distributed version employs multiple processes on a network of UNIX hosts and enables us to study the migration techniques and to conduct experiments to investigate issues of concurrency, asynchrony and fault tolerance in the Idiom of Icsla.

In the single process version, input expressions are read, expanded, parsed and transformed into an intermediate form consisting of objects. This is then evaluated using a generic **eval** function, under the control of a simple scheduler. The **eval** function is 'pushy' in that it indirectly calls the generic function **resume** which in turn calls **eval**, and ultimately the initial continuation is called whereupon control returns to the top level loop.

The distributed version separates the top level user interaction from the evaluation. A *listener* process performs the read phase, then submits the encoded expression to a separate process called an *evaluation daemon*. The daemon performs the same evaluation as the single process version, supporting multiple tasks (created by **breed**), but it also acts as a client of other evaluation daemons (implementing **remote**) and as a server for incoming remote requests. Eventually the result is returned to the listener and presented to the user. The selection of a neighbor for **remote** can be made by the user (as in the case of a **placed-remote**, which can be used to return a value to the listener and to access specific resources) or by the implementation of **remote**. The latter case must capture the topology of the network, realising the concept of neighbors.

Migration of tasks is achieved by transmitting the various interpreter structures between daemons. Note that this is not a traditional remote evaluation, because the continuation of the remote application migrates too. A lazy strategy is essential, and is achieved through remote pointers: when an object is migrated it may not be fully populated, but rather some of its slots contain remote pointers to entities on the original host. When one of these slots is accessed, the pointer is followed. Remote pointers remain valid when they are migrated provided they point to a site that is accessible from their new site. The communications layer supports serialization and deserialization of arbitrary objects, while the migration strategy addresses the details of replication of immutable data, safe update of mutable data, and heuristics for the extent of transfer of specific data structures.

The listener and the evaluation daemons are implemented as UNIX processes which communicate via the RPC mechanism. This layer was chosen as it provides a suitable level of independence from evolution of the particular machines, networks and operating system versions. In fact we do not adhere to the strict RPC client–server model, because the evaluation daemons are both clients and servers, and we wish to avoid blocking operations in these so that other tasks can be scheduled. Essentially, RPC is used as a message-passing layer.

The object encoding uses the XDR standard [xdr] to facilitate communication with machines on a heterogeneous network and interaction with other software. When sending the same entity more than once in a single message, the algorithm used for serialization generates references to the earlier value, providing an efficient encoding of immutable values (such as strings), preserving substitutability within a transmission and avoiding problems of circularity. Different encoding protocols may be used, indicated by a protocol word which prefixes a message. To preserve equality between entities in different messages it would be necessary to search a large cache during transmission, and to avoid this complexity the protocol includes a mechanism for clearing the caches. Preservation of equality is therefore the responsibility of the remote pointer mechanism built above this lower level of object encoding.

There is a significant 'housekeeping' requirement in the handling of dynamic process creation, multiple daemons per UNIX host, multiple applications per user and multiple users per network. This is achieved through management daemons which run one per host and oversee all these operations. The management daemons perform the combined roles of maintaining the RPC service program numbers (which are transient) and spawning new processes on request (like `inetd`); in addition, they provide diagnostic facilities to aid program development.

7 Related and future work

The pioneer work of Halstead [Hal84] on MultiLisp popularized the `future` concept. As explained in [Hal89], futures are not primitive but defined in terms of lower level functions. The evolution from MultiLisp to MultiScheme, where continuations have an indefinite extent, also makes futures more problematic since they can be multiply determined [KW90].

Our language is simpler than MultiScheme since we promote combinable low-level features and show their constructive power on various examples. We thus do not address the exact nature of futures but provide ways to program variants of them [KW90]. Our language is also cleaner since we propose some solutions to integrate continuations à la Scheme compatible with the dynamic extent concept. On the other hand, our language is actually only simulated on a distributed network of workstations whereas MultiLisp is implemented on a shared memory architecture and benefits from very clever compiling techniques [MKH90].

Concurrent Scheme [KS89] is an implementation of Scheme for distributed memories. It introduces a `future`-like mechanism called `make-thread`. Mutual exclusion is handled through *domains*. No two computations can be simultaneously performed in a same domain. Domains define disconnected data subsets: no data sharing is possible between different domains. Data are thus copied before being passed from one domain to another. Domains are therefore good candidates to be associated to processors.

Since domains and threads can be dynamically created, it seems difficult to control where data are shared or copied. This precludes the use of deterministic side-effects and breaks the tradition of the single workspace of Lisp. On the other hand, our language introduces fewer concepts than Concurrent Scheme.

Qlisp [GM84, GG88, GGS89] offers a huge number of constructs, such as `qlambda` and `catch`, that can be simulated in our language. We depart from this approach since we based our work on Scheme rather than COMMON LISP but reintroduced dynamic extent. We also separate the control effects of Qlisp `catch` into `abort` and `pause!`.

PaiLisp [IM89] is a parallel extension of Scheme whose kernel only comprises four primitives: `spawn` (to create tasks), `suspend`, `exlambda` (similar to Qlisp's `qlambda`) and `call/cc`. The semantics of continuations is extended to handle the concept of tasks. PaiLisp's `call/cc` has a task-killing or task-resuming effect if the caller and the creator of a continuation are different: this permits imperative control of individual tasks which are identified with their unique starting continuation. As in PaiLisp, we tried hard to reduce the number of non primitive features; similarly we altered the semantics of continuations in the presence of concurrency. On the other hand, we chose a different set of primitives offering the simple to learn and useful concept of groups of tasks.

Hieb and Dybvig [HD90] propose a spawn primitive which allows control of *task continuations*, i.e.tree-structured continuations. Spawn and call/de are very close in their effect on groups of tasks. Nevertheless spawn associates a partial continuation with the group of tasks, something we think unrelated to the group but only appropriate to a single task. The group object in our language thus has more properties and can be more tightly controlled.

8 Conclusions

We have presented a language which offers simple concepts allied to a great expressiveness. Distribution relies on a neighborhood topology, making it suitable for running programs on a large number of processors. Lisp dialects are often used as extension languages; the idiom of Icsla is such an extension language. We actually sacrifice speed (compared to a non-concurrent, non-distributed implementation of Scheme) in order to easily program widely distributed algorithms in a mostly functional style. Our language is also a pedagogical tool to describe concurrent features.

A real compiler is actually under progress associated with a distributed and concurrent GC along the lines of [LQP92]. Thorough experiments will be conducted and reported in the future.

References

[AR89]   Pierre America and Jan Rutten. A parallel object-oriented language: design and semantic foundations. In J W Bakker, editor, *Languages for Parallel Architectures: Design, Semantics, Implementation Models*. Wiley, 1989.

[Bak90] Henry G Baker. Equal rights for functional objects or, the more things change, the more they are the same. Technical report, Nimble Computer Corporation, 16231 Meadow Ridge Way, Encino, CA 91436, USA, October 1990.

[BKT92] H E Bal, M F Kaashoek, and A S Tanenbaum. Orca: A language for parallel programming of distributed systems. *IEEE Transactions on Software Engineering*, 18(3):190–205, March 1992.

[BNA91] Paul S Barth, Rishiyur S Nikhil, and Arvind. M-structures: Extending a parallel, non-strict, functional language with state. In John Hughes, editor, *FPCA '91 – Functional Programming and Computer Architecture*, volume Lecture Notes in Computer Science 523, pages 538–568, Cambridge (Mass. USA), August 1991. Springer-Verlag.

[Bur88] Alan Burns. *Programming in Occam 2*. the Instruction Set Series. Addison Wesley, 1988.

[CHO88] William D. Clinger, Anne H. Hartheimer, and Eric M. Ost. Implementation strategies for continuations. In *Conference Record of the 1988 ACM Conference on Lisp and Functional Programming*, page 124 131, August 1988.

[CM92]   Henry Clark and Bruce McMillin. Dawgs – a distributed compute server utilizing idle workstations. *Journal of Parallel and Distributed Computing*, 14(2):175–186, February 1992.

[CR91]   William Clinger and Jonathan A Rees. The revised[4] report on the algorithmic language scheme. *Lisp Pointer*, 4(3), 1991.

[DeR90a]   David C. DeRoure. Experiences with Lisp and distributed systems. In *High Performance and Parallel Computing in Lisp*, November 1990. Also appears as Technical Report CSTR90-21, Department of Electronics and Computer Science, University of Southampton.

[DeR90b]   David C. DeRoure. *A Lisp Environment for Modelling Distributed Systems*. PhD thesis, Dept. of Electronics and Computer Science, University of Southampton, January 1990.

[DeR90c]   David C. DeRoure. QPL3—Continuations, concurrency and communication. Technical Report CSTR 90-20, Department of Electronics and Computer Science, University of Southampton, 1990.

[Deu90]   Alain Deutsch. On determining lifetime and aliasing of dynamically allocated data in higher-order functional specifications. In *POPL '90 – Seventeenth Annual ACM symposium on Principles of Programming Languages*, pages 157-168, San Francisco, January 1990.

[DJAR91]   Partha Dasgupta, Richard J LeBlanc Jr, Mustaque Ahamad, and Umakishore Ramachandran. The clouds distributed operating system. *Computer*, 24(11):34-44, November 1991.

[Dyb87]   R. Kent Dybvig. *The Scheme Programming Language*. Prentice-Hall, Inc., Englewood Cliffs, New Jersey, 1987.

[FWFD88]   Matthias Felleisen, Mitchell Wand, Daniel P. Friedman, and Bruce Duba. Abstract continuations: a mathematical semantics for handling functional jumps. In *Proceedings of the 1988 ACM Symposium on LISP and Functional Programming*, Salt Lake City, Utah., July 1988.

[GG88]   Ron Goldman and Richard P. Gabriel. Preliminary results with the initial implementation of qlisp. In *LFP '88 – ACM Symposium on Lisp and Functional Programming*, pages 143-152, Snowbird (Utah USA), 1988.

[GGS89]   Ron Goldman, Richard P. Gabriel, and Carol Sexton. Qlisp: An interim report. In Takayasu Ito and Robert H Halstead Jr., editors, *Parallel Lisp: Languages and Systems, US/Japan Workshop*, volume Lecture Notes in Computer Science 441, Sendai (Japan), June 1989. Springer-Verlag.

[GL90]   J F Giorgi and Daniel Le Métayer. Continuation-based parallel implementation of functional programming languages. In *LFP '90 – ACM Symposium on Lisp and Functional Programming*, pages 209-217, Nice (France), June 1990.

[GM84]   Richard P Gabriel and John McCarthy. Queue-based multi-processing lisp. In *LFP '84 – ACM Symposium on Lisp and Functional Programming*, pages 9-17, Austin (Texas USA), 1984.

[Hal84]   Robert H. Halstead, Jr. Implementation of multilisp: Lisp on a multiprocessor. In *LFP '84 – ACM Symposium on Lisp and Functional Programming*, pages 9-17, Austin (Texas USA), 1984.

[Hal89]   Robert H. Halstead, Jr. New ideas in parallel lisp: Language design, implementation, and programming tools. In Robert H Halstead, Jr. and Takayasu Ito, editors, *US-Japan Workshop on Parallel Lisp*, volume Lecture Notes in Computer Science 441, Sendai (Japan), June 1989. Springer-Verlag.

[HD90]   Robert Hieb and R. Kent Dybvig. Continuations and concurrency. In *PPOPP '90 – ACM SIGPLAN Symposium on Principles and Practices of Parallel Programming*, pages 128-136, Seattle (Washington US), March 1990.

[HDB90]   Robert Hieb, R. Kent Dybvig, and Carl Bruggeman. Representing control in the presence of first-class continuations. In *Proceedings of the SIGPLAN '90*

Conference on Programming Language Design and Implementation, pages 66–77, White Plains, New York, June 1990.

[HFW84] Christopher T. Haynes, Daniel P. Friedman, and Mitchell Wand. Continuations and coroutines. In *Conference Record of the 1984 ACM Symposium on Lisp and Functional Programming*, pages 293–298, Austin, TX., 1984.

[IM89] Takayasu Ito and Manabu Matsui. A parallel lisp language PaiLisp and its kernel specification. In Takayasu Ito and Robert H Halstead, Jr., editors, *Proceedings of the US/Japan Workshop on Parallel Lisp*, volume Lecture Notes in Computer Science 441, pages 58–100, Sendai (Japan), June 1989. Springer-Verlag.

[JG89] Pierre Jouvelot and David K Gifford. Reasoning about continuations with control effects. In *ACM SIGPLAN Programming Languages Design and Implementation*, volume 24 of *SIGPLAN Notices*, pages 218–225, Portland (OR), June 1989. SIG-PLAN, ACM Press.

[KFFD86] Eugene E. Kohlbecker, Daniel P. Friedman, Matthias Felleisen, and Bruce Duba. Hygienic macro expansion. *Symposium on LISP and Functional Programming*, pages 151–161, August 1986.

[KKR+86] David Kranz, Richard Kelsey, Jonathan A. Rees, Paul Hudak, James Philbin, and Norman I. Adams. Orbit: an optimizing compiler for scheme. In *Proceedings of the SIGPLAN '86 Symposium on Compiler Construction*, pages 219–233. ACM, June 1986.

[KS89] Robert R. Kessler and Mark R. Swanson. Concurrent scheme. In *US-Japan Workshop on Parallel Lisp*, volume Lecture Notes in Computer Science 441, Sendai (Japan), June 1989. Springer-Verlag.

[KW90] Morry Katz and Daniel Weise. Continuing into the future: On the interaction of futures and first-class continuations. In *LFP '90 – ACM Symposium on Lisp and Functional Programming*, pages 176–184, Nice (France), 1990.

[LQP92] Bernard Lang, Christian Queinnec, and José Piquer. Garbage collecting the world. In *POPL '92 – Nineteenth Annual ACM symposium on Principles of Programming Languages*, pages 39–50, Albuquerque (New Mexico, USA), January 1992.

[McC63] John McCarthy. A basis for a mathematical theory of computation. In Braffort and Hirshberg, editors, *Computer Programming and Formal Systems*. North Holland, 1963.

[MH90] Thanasis Mitsolides and Malcolm Harrison. Generators and the replicator control structure in the parallel environment of alloy. In *PLDI '90 –ACM SIGPLAN Programming Languages Design and Implementation*, pages 189–196, White Plains (New-York USA), 1990.

[MKH90] Eric Mohr, David A. Kranz, and Robert H. Halstead, Jr. Lazy task creation: A technique for increasing the granularity of parallel programs. In *LFP '90 – ACM Symposium on Lisp and Functional Programming*, pages 185–198, Nice (France), 1990.

[Mor92] Luc Moreau. An operational semantics for a parallel functional language with continuations. In D. Etiemble and J-C. Syre, editors, *PARLE '92 – Parallel Architectures and Languages Europe*, pages 415–430, Paris (France), June 1992. Lecture Notes in Computer Science 605, Springer-Verlag.

[Osb90] Randy B. Osborne. Speculative computation in MultiLisp, an overview. In *LFP '90 – ACM Symposium on Lisp and Functional Programming*, pages 198–208, Nice (France), 1990.

[Per87] R. H. Perrott. *Parallel Programming*. Addison Wesley, 1987.

[Piq90]   José Piquer. Sharing data structures in a distributed lisp. In *High Performance and Parallel Computing in Lisp*, Twickenham, London (UK), November 1990. a EUROPAL workshop.

[Piq91]   José Piquer. Preserving distributed data coherence using asynchronous broadcasts. In *Eleventh International Conference of the Chilean Computer Science Society*, pages 283–290, Santiago (Chile), October 1991. Plenum Publishing Corporation, New York NY (USA).

[Pri80]   Gianfranco Prini. Explicit parallelism in Lisp-like languages. In *Conference Record of the 1980 Lisp Conference*, pages 13–18, Stanford (California USA), August 1980. The Lisp Conference, P.O. Box 487, Redwood Estates CA 95044.

[QP91]   Christian Queinnec and Julian Padget. Modules, Macros and Lisp. In *Eleventh International Conference of the Chilean Computer Science Society*, pages 111–123, Santiago (Chile), October 1991. Plenum Publishing Corporation, New York NY (USA).

[QS91]   Christian Queinnec and Bernard Serpette. A Dynamic Extent Control Operator for Partial Continuations. In *POPL '91 – Eighteenth Annual ACM symposium on Principles of Programming Languages*, pages 174–184, Orlando (Florida USA), January 1991.

[Que90]   Christian Queinnec. PolyScheme : A Semantics for a Concurrent Scheme. In *Workshop on High Performance and Parallel Computing in Lisp*, Twickenham (UK), November 1990. European Conference on Lisp and its Practical Applications.

[Que91]   Christian Queinnec. Crystal Scheme, A Language for Massively Parallel Machines. In M Durand and F El Dabaghi, editors, *Second Symposium on High Performance Computing*, pages 91–102, Montpellier (France), October 1991. North Holland.

[Que92a]   Christian Queinnec. A concurrent and distributed extension to scheme. In D. Etiemble and J-C. Syre, editors, *PARLE '92 – Parallel Architectures and Languages Europe*, pages 431–446, Paris (France), June 1992. Lecture Notes in Computer Science 605, Springer-Verlag.

[Que92b]   Christian Queinnec. Value transforming style. Research Report LIX RR 92/07, Laboratoire d'Informatique de l'École Polytechnique, 91128 Palaiseau Cedex, France, May 1992.

[RTL+91]   Rajendra K. Raj, Ewan D. Tempero, Henry M. Levy, Andrew P. Black, Norman C. Hutchinson, and Eric Jul. Emerald: A general-purpose programming language. *Software — Practice and Experience*, 21(1):91–118, January 1991.

[SG90]   James W. Stamos and David K. Gifford. Implementing remote evaluation. *IEEE Trans. on Software Engineering*, 16(7):710–722, July 1990.

[xdr]   Rfc 1014: external data representation standard: Protocol specification. Technical report, ARPA Network Information Center.

TS/Scheme: Distributed Data Structures in Lisp (Abstract)

Suresh Jagannathan

Computer Science Research, NEC Research Institute, 4 Independence Way, Princeton, NJ 08540, *suresh@research.nj.nec.com*

1 Introduction

Many parallel dialects of Lisp express concurrency via a lightweight process constructor such as **future**[6], and model process communication via dataflow constraints that exist between a future instance and its consumers. These dataflow constraints may be enforced implicitly via strict operations which are passed a future as an argument (*e.g.,* as in MultiLisp[6] or Mul-T[11]), or explicitly via a primitive wait operation on futures (*e.g.,* **touch** in MultiLisp, or the **future-wait** procedure in QLisp[5]). In either case, task communication is tightly-coupled with task creation: tasks[1] can only initiate requests for the value of an object if the identity of the object is known. Because of this constraint, multiple tasks cannot collectively contribute to the construction of a shared data object without using other explicit (low-level) synchronization primitives such as locks or monitor-like abstractions (*e.g.,* **qlambda**[4] or **exlambda**[8]). Thus, while amenable to fine-grained parallel algorithms in which synchronization is predicated on the values generated by tasks upon termination, future-style process abstractions are not convenient for expressing algorithms in which tasks have no manifest dependencies with one another, but which nonetheless must communicate data.

A distributed data structure[2] is one alternative abstraction for expressing concurrency that addresses some of these concerns. A distributed data structure is a concurrent object that permits many producers and consumers to concurrently access and update its contents via a well-defined synchronization protocol.

We have built a dialect of Scheme called TS/SCHEME that incorporates first-class distributed data structures as a basic data type. TS/SCHEME uses distributed data structures specified in terms of *tuple-spaces* as its main coordination device. Generally speaking, the utility of the tuple-space abstraction derives from a simple interface that usually requires only small perturbations to sequential code to build parallel programs, and an appealing metaphor for parallel programming in which task communication is anonymous, and totally decoupled from task synchronization.

There are four basic operations that can be performed on tuple-space structures: *read* a tuple, *remove* a tuple, *deposit* a tuple, and *deposit* a *process-valued* tuple. (A tuple is a heterogeneous ordered collection of values.) The first two are blocking operations

---

[1] A *task* or *thread* is a lightweight process that executes in the same address space as its parent.

that are permitted to execute only if the desired element exists in a tuple-space. The last defines a task creation operation.

We enumerate the salient aspects of our system below:

1. Tuple-spaces are first-class objects: they can be defined explicitly, bound to variables, passed as arguments to (and returned as results from) procedures.
2. Tuple-spaces are comprised of two distinct components: a *binding repository* that defines a collection of bindings, and a *tuple repository* that defines a collection of tuples. Elements in a tuple repository are accessed by content, not by name; elements in a binding repository are accessed by name only.
3. Tuple-spaces adhere to an object-oriented protocol. Even though the intended use of a tuple-space (*e.g.*, as a vector, shared variable, queue, set, etc.) can be specified by the programmer, the interface to any tuple-space is specified exclusively by the read, write, remove, and spawn operations described above. Thus, all tuple-space instances define the same operations regardless of their internal representation.

   In addition, tuple-spaces can be organized into an inheritance hierarchy. If a tuple-space T is specified to be the parent of another T', a read or remove operation sent to T' that is not satisfiable by T' is resolved by T and its parents. The ability to organize tuple-spaces into hierarchies makes TS/SCHEME a flexible concurrent object-oriented language.
4. There is no distinction between tasks or data in bindings or tuples. Thus, programs can deposit tasks as well as data; processes can match on either. The runtime system uses the uniformity of process and data to implement an efficient dynamic scheduling and throttling policy for fine-grained parallel programs.

2 The Language

Concurrency and coordination is introduced in TS/SCHEME via the make-ts primitive procedure. When applied, this procedure returns a reference to a new tuple-space object.

2.1 Tuple Repositories

Tuple repositories are manipulated via operations that deposit, read, remove tuples as described below. Tuples are defined using the tuple constructor, [...].

(rd TS [*tuple-template*] *body*) reads a tuple t from TS 's tuple repository that matches *tuple-template* and evaluates *body* using the bindings established as a consequence of the match. This operation blocks if no matching tuple is encountered in TS .

For example, the expression:

```
(rd TS [ ?x 2 ?y] (+ x y))
```

reads a tuple from TS whose second field is 2 , binds the first field to x and the third to y and evaluates their sum. X and y are referred to as *formals*.

Tasks reading a tuple from TS have exclusive access to TS only while bindings for a template's formals are being established; all locks on TS are released prior to the execution of *body*.

(get TS [*tuple-template*] *body*) has a semantics similar to rd except that it atomically removes its matched tuple from TS 's tuple repository after establishing all relevant bindings.

(put TS [*tuple*]) deposits *tuple* into TS 's tuple repository; the operation completes only after the tuple is deposited. Blocked rd or get operations that match on *tuple* are resumed as a consequence of this operation. Formals are not permitted in a tuple deposited by put . Tasks have exclusive access to TS until the operation returns.

(spawn TS [*tuple*]) creates a lightweight process for each field in *tuple* and returns immediately thereafter. Thus, the expression:

    (spawn TS [(f x) (g y)])

deposits a two-tuple into TS 's tuple repository. These fields are lightweight tasks computing (f x) and (g y) . Once both tasks complete, the tuple quiesces to a passive (data) tuple containing the values yielded by these tasks. In the above example, both f and g are assumed to be lexical closures and their applications evaluate in the environment in which they are defined, and *not* in the call-time dynamic environment in which they are instantiated.

Rd and get operations can match on process-valued tuples. The mechanism by which this is done is described in [9].

Tuple-spaces are represented as Scheme objects, obey the same storage semantics as any other object, and may be garbage collected if there exist no outstanding references to them.

2.2 Binding Repositories

Binding tuples and templates are defined using the binding constructor, $\{\dots\}$. These objects are manipulated by the same tuple operations described above.

Bindings are orthogonal to ordinary data and reside in a tuple-space's binding repository. When used as an argument to a put or spawn operation, a binding tuple has the form:

    { $(x_1\ E_1)\ (x_2\ E_2)\ \dots\ (x_n\ E_n)$ }

Each of the x_i are labels, and each of the E_i are expressions. When used in conjunction with a put operation, for example, the expressions are first evaluated to yield values $v_1,\ v_2,\ \dots,\ v_n$. Each label/value pair, $(x_i,\ v_i)$ is then deposited into the specified tuple-space's binding repository.

A binding template takes the form,

```
{ ?x ?y ... ?z }
```

where x, y, ... z are labels. When evaluated in the context of a `rd` or `get` operation, *e.g.*,

```
(rd ts { ?x₁ ?x₂ ... ?xₙ } E)
```

each label x_i acquires a value as defined by its binding in `ts`'s binding repository; these bindings are then used in the evaluation of E. E is evaluated only after all formals in the binding template have acquired a value, *i.e.*, only after bindings for all the x_i have been deposited into `ts`.

3   A Simple Example

Fig. 1 shows an implementation of a generalized version of I-structures[1]. I-structures are monotonic write-once arrays; an attempt to read an unwritten element of an I-structure causes the accessing expresssion to block until a value is written.

The implementation provides four operations on I-structures:

1. `(make-I-structure` *size*`)` creates an I-structure vector. An I-structure vector is represented as a tuple-space with two bindings. The first binds `elements` to a tuple-space that will hold I-structure values. The second binds `status` to a tuple-space vector of length `size` used to determine if an I-structure cell has a value.

2. `(I-ref` *rep i*`)` returns the value of the ith I-structure component of *rep*, blocking if the structure is empty.

3. `(I-set` *rep i v*`)` atomically sets the ith element of *rep* to *v* provided that this element has not already been previously written. We use *status* to synchronize multiple writes to an I-structure.

4. `(I-remove` *rep v*`)` is an operation that demonstrates the use of tuple-spaces as content addressable data structures.
   Given a value *v* and an I-structure *rep*, `I-remove` creates a new thread that re-initializes all I-structure elements that contain *v*. The thread repeatedly removes a tuple in *rep*'s *elements* tuple-space that contains *v*, setting the appropriate status field to false. In the implementation shown, these threads run forever, but it is straightforward to augment their functionality such that they terminate upon a user-specified condition.

4   Runtime Support

Efficient runtime implementation of first-class tuple-spaces requires at the minimum (a) cheap creation and management of lightweight tasks, (b) flexible scheduling policies that

```
(define (make-I-structure size)
  (let ((rep (make-ts)))
    (put rep { (elements (make-ts)) })
    (put rep { (status   (make-ts (type/vector size))) })
    (let -*- ((i 0))
      (cond ((= i size) rep)
            (else (put rep [i '#f])
                  (-*- (+ i 1)))))))

(define (I-ref rep i)
  (rd rep { ?elements }
      (rd elements [i ?v] v)))

(define (I-set rep i v)
  (rd rep { ?status }
      (get status [i ?state]
           (cond (state (error "I-structure currently written"))
                 (else (rd rep { ?elements }
                           (put elements [i v]))
                       (put status [i '#t]))))))

(define (I-remove rep v)
  (spawn (make-ts)
    [(rd rep { ?elements ?status }
         (let -*- ()
              (get status [i ?z]
                   (get elements [?i v]
                        (put status [i '#f])))
              (-*-)))]))
```

Fig. 1. A generalized implementation of I-structures using first-class tuple-spaces.

can be dynamically instantiated to support different programming paradigms, (c) support for fine-grained parallel computing via efficient process throttling and scheduling protocols, and (d) storage management capabilities sensitive to tuples and tuple-spaces.

STING is an operating system kernel for high-level symbolic programming languages that provides these capabilities. Details of the system are given in [9, 10]. The system is implemented entirely in Scheme with the exception of a few operations to save and restore thread state, and to manipulate hardware locks. Tuple-space operations translate to operations on threads and ordinary Scheme data structures.

5   Benchmarks

Timings shown in this section were measured on an eight processor Silicon Graphics PowerSeries shared-memory machine; each node consists of a 75 Mhz MIPS R3000 processor. Because of STING's aggressive treatment of data locality, its separation of evaluation contexts from threads which use them, its use of thread absorption to increase dynamically increase thread granularity, and the lightweight costs of tuple operations, we expect these programs to scale well even on larger processor ensembles.

Fig. 2 and Fig. 3 shows timings and relevant statistics for five benchmarks. The tuple operations shown in Fig. 3 gives an indication of how much synchronization and communication occurs in the corresponding benchmark. The benchmarks were chosen to exercise different aspects of both the language and runtime system. All benchmarks are structured not to trigger garbage collection. We expect a slight dropoff from absolute linear speedup in the eight processor timings because we are allocating a STING virtual processor[9] exclusively to run the top-level[2]. The super-linear speedups seen in several of the benchmarks are attributable to significant cache effects in the shared memory system.

N-Queens is a fine-grained parallel solution of the well-known n queens problem. The timings are shown for a 14x14 chessboard with a cutoff depth of $\log n + 1$ where n is the number of processors. The program generates over 11,000 threads; almost of these threads, however, never acquire a separate evaluation context. Instead, they are *absorbed* by other threads that require their value[9, 10].

Alpha-Beta is a parallel implementation of a game tree traversal algorithm. The program does α/β pruning[3, 7] on this tree to minimize the amount of search performed. The input used consisted of a tree of depth 10 with fanout 8; the depth cutoff for communicating α and β values was 3.

Hamming computes the extended hamming numbers upto 1,000,000 for the first five primes. The extended hamming problem is defined thus: given a finite sequence of primes $A, B, C, D, \ldots$ and an integer n as input, output in increasing magnitude without duplication all integers less than or equal to n of the form

$$(A^i) \times (B^j) \times (C^k) \times (D^l) \times \ldots$$

This program is the most communication intensive of the benchmarks presented, and also exhibits the most thread locality.

N-body simulates the evolution of a system of bodies under the influence of gravitational forces using a version of the Barnes-Hut algorithm. Each body is modeled as a point mass and exerts forces on all other bodies in the system. The simulation proceeds over time-steps, each step computing the net force on every body and thereby updating that body's position and other attributes. This benchmark ran the simulation on 3500 bodies over six time-steps. The storage requirements for this program are the highest among all the applications presented.

---

[2] On 8 processors, the maximum real efficiency obtainable is 88%.

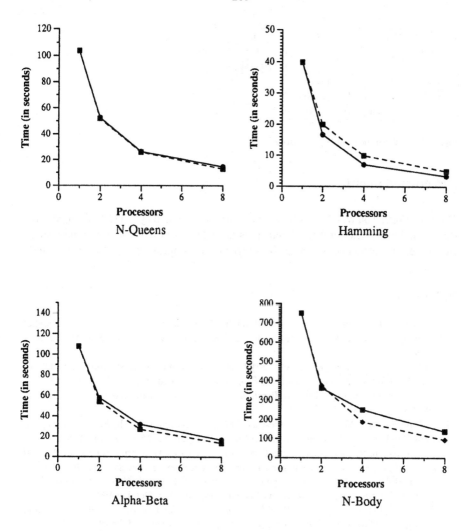

Fig. 2. Timings for N-queens, Alpha-Beta, Hamming, and N-body. Dashed lines indicate ideal speedup based on single processor times; solid lines indicate actual speedup.

267

Benchmark	Put	Get	Rd	Spawn
N-Queens	0	0	11167	11167 11108 (absorbed)
Alpha-Beta	23	20	597	11
Hamming	10367	7417	17405	8
N-Body	198630	191620	1165492	49

Fig. 3. Tuple Operations on 8 processors.

Acknowledgments

The STING kernel on which TS/SCHEME runs was implemented by James Philbin. Monika Rauch implemented several of the benchmarks, and has been a major user of the system; Henry Cejtin contributed several useful suggestions to improve the quality of this paper.

References

1. Arvind, Rishiyur Nikhil, and Keshav Pingali. I-Structures: Data Structures for Parallel Computing. *Transactions on Programming Languages and Systems*, 11(4):598–632, October 1989.
2. Nick Carriero, David Gelernter, and Jerry Leichter. Distributed Data Structures in Linda. In 13th *ACM Symposium on Principles of Programming Languages Conf.*, January 1986.
3. Raphael Finkel and John Fishburn. Parallelism in Alpha-Beta Search. *Artificial Intelligence*, 19(1):89–106, 1982.
4. R. Gabriel and J. McCarthy. Queue-Based Multi-Processing Lisp. In *Proceedings of the 1984 Conference on Lisp and Functional Programming*, pages 25–44, August 1984.
5. Ron Goldman, Richard Gabriel, and Carol Sexton. QLisp: An Interim Report. In *Parallel Lisp: Languages and Systems*, pages 161–182. Springer-Verlag, LNCS 441, 1990.
6. Robert Halstead. Multilisp: A Language for Concurrent Symbolic Computation. *Transactions on Programming Languages and Systems*, 7(4):501–538, October 1985.
7. Feng hsiung Hsu. *Large Scale Parallelization of Alpha-Beta Search: An Algorithmic and Architectural Study with Computer Chess*. PhD thesis, Carnegie-Mellon University, 1990. Published as Technical Report CMU-CS-90-108.
8. Takayasu Ito and Manabu Matsui. A Parallel Lisp Language PaiLisp and its Kernel Specification. In *Parallel Lisp: Languages and Systems*, pages 58–100. Springer-Verlag, LNCS 441, 1990.
9. Suresh Jagannathan and James Philbin. A Customizable Substrate for Concurrent Languages. In *ACM SIGPLAN '91 Conference on Programming Language Design and Implementation*, June 1992.
10. Suresh Jagannathan and James Philbin. A Foundation for an Efficient Multi-Threaded Scheme System. In *Proceedings of the 1992 Conf. on Lisp and Functional Programming*, June 1992.
11. David Kranz, Robert Halstead, and Eric Mohr. Mul-T: A High Performance Parallel Lisp. In *Proceedings of the ACM Symposium on Programming Language Design and Implementation*, pages 81–91, June 1989.

A SIMD Environment TUPLE for Parallel List Processing

Taiichi Yuasa[1]

Toyohashi University of Technology, Toyohashi 441, Japan

Abstract. An extended Common Lisp language and system, called TU-PLE, for massively parallel SIMD (Single Instruction stream, Multiple Data streams) architectures is presented. Unlike other Lisp languages on SIMD architectures, TUPLE supports the programming model that there are a huge number of subset Common Lisp systems running in parallel. For this purpose, each PE (processing element) of the target machine has its own heap in its local memory. In addition, there is a full-set Common Lisp system with which the user interacts to develop and execute parallel programs. This paper briefly introduces the TUPLE language and system, and then reports the current implementation of TUPLE on the SIMD machine MasPar MP-1 with at least 1024 PEs.

1 Introduction

Several computation models have been proposed for the so-called massively parallel computation, in which thousands or more PEs (processing elements) run in parallel. The SIMD (Single Instruction stream, Multiple Data streams) model seems one of the most promising models, though its application area is restricted compared with many other models. In fact, some commercial SIMD machines are available and are being used for realistic applications.

So far, SIMD machines have been mainly used for numeric computation, and thus most languages in use are extensions of Fortran and C. On the other hand, parallel computation is highly required in the application areas of symbolic computation or list processing, where Lisp languages have traditionally been used. As SIMD architectures are getting more popular, several Lisp languages have been proposed for SIMD architectures, including Connection Machine Lisp [10, 11, 15], Paralation Lisp [7, 8], Plural Eulisp [4, 5], and *Lisp [17, 16]. Unfortunately, however, these languages are not seriously used for symbolic applications. Thus, it is still a question whether the SIMD model is suitable for symbol computation.

In this paper, we present TUPLE (Toyohashi University Parallel Lisp Environment), which is a Lisp language and system to develop application programs of symbolic computation on SIMD architectures. By supplying a high performance Lisp system, we would like to see the possibility of employing the SIMD model for symbolic computation.

Most Lisp languages on SIMD architectures, including those listed above, provide new data structures that can be handled in parallel. For example, *xappings* in Connection Machine Lisp are vector-like data structures with parallel operations defined on them. These languages share a same computation model that the front-end processor dominates the entire control flow and the PEs are used for parallel execution of operations on the extended data structures. By taking a different approach, TUPLE allows flexible and efficient programming on SIMD architectures.

In general, a SIMD machine consists of a huge number of PEs and the front-end processor which controls the execution of PEs. Each PE has its own local memory. By operating on the data in the local memory, each PE can run concurrently with the other PEs. PEs do not have their own instruction streams but they simply execute instructions supplied by the front-end. Except for this last point, each PE can be regarded as an ordinary uni-processor. This means each PE has the ability to run a Lisp system. Because of the small size (typically a few kilo bytes) of the local memory in actual SIMD machines, the Lisp system on each PE ought to be very compact, but it should be powerful enough to allow symbolic computation and list processing. The front-end, on the other hand, is a general-purpose machine such as a Unix workstation and thus has the ability to run a modern Lisp system.

The computation model of TUPLE reflects these features of SIMD architectures. That is, there are a huge number of Lisp systems called *PE subsystems* running in parallel. These PE subsystems execute programs in a subset Common Lisp. In addition, there is a full-set Common Lisp system, called the *front-end system*, with which the user interacts to develop and execute parallel Lisp programs. This model of TUPLE has the following advantages.

- Parallel programs can be described in the same notation as ordinary sequential programs.
- Performance of a program can be estimated easily. This increases the possibility of tuning up program performance.
- The programmer can make use of the efficient programming environment supplied by the front-end system.

The TUPLE system is implemented by extending KCL (Kyoto Common Lisp [12]), a full-set Common Lisp system developed by the group including the author. The system is currently running on the MasPar MP-1, a SIMD massively parallel computer with at least 1024 PEs. As the original KCL is written partly in C and partly in Common Lisp, the TUPLE system on the MasPar is written partly in MPL [18], the extended C language on the MasPar, and partly in TUPLE itself. Thus the TUPLE system can be easily ported to other SIMD or SPMD (Single Program, Multiple Data stream) architectures.

In this paper, we first introduce the TUPLE language and system in Section 2 through an example of parallel list processing in TUPLE. The entire language of TUPLE is made clear in Section 3. In Section 4, we present the current implementation of TUPLE on the MasPar MP-1 and finally in Section 5, we report some results of performance measurements of TUPLE.

2 An Overview

This section introduces the language and system of TUPLE, through examples.

2.1 A Simple Example

The first example is a simple function abs which computes the absolute value of the given argument. In ordinary Common Lisp, this function can be defined as follows.

```
(defun abs (x)
  (if (>= x 0) x (- x)))
```

That is, if the argument is greater than or equal to zero, then the function simply returns the argument. Otherwise, the function returns the negative of the argument. By replacing defun with defpefun, the similar function will be defined in the PE subsystems.

```
(defpefun abs (x)
  (if (>= x 0) x (- x)))
```

When this *PE function* is invoked, all PEs receive independent values, one value per PE. Then those PEs that received non-negative numbers return the arguments. The other PEs return the negatives of the arguments.

TUPLE runs on SIMD architectures, where no two PEs can execute different instructions at the same time. What actually happens is the following. When the PE function abs is invoked, those PEs that do not satisfy the condition becomes inactive while the other PEs (i.e., those PEs that satisfy the condition) evaluate the *then* clause. Then the activity of each PE is reversed and the previously inactive PEs evaluate the *else* clause, while the previously active PEs are inactive.

Below is an example interaction between the user and the TUPLE system. The top-level of TUPLE is similar to that of ordinary Common Lisp systems. The user can input any Common Lisp form at the top-level. Then the form is (sequentially) evaluated and the result is displayed.

```
% tuple
TUPLE (Massively Parallel KCL)

>(defun abs (x)
   (if (>= x 0) x (- x)))
ABS
>(abs -3)
3
```

Here, the lines with lower case letters are inputs from the user and the lines with upper case letters are outputs from the system. The symbol '>' at the beginning of a line is the prompt from the system.

In order to start a parallel computation, the user has to supply a form in the extended language of TUPLE.

```
>(defpefun abs (x)
   (if (>= x 0) x (- x)))
ABS
>(ppe penumber)
#P(0 1 2 3 ...)
```

```
>(ppe (abs (- penumber 2)))
#P(2 1 0 1 ...)
```

In this example, the user uses the ppe form that passes a *PE form* to PE subsystems for evaluation and displays the results. This form is mainly used at the top-level of TUPLE to supply a top-level form to the PE subsystems.

The **penumber** in the above example is a built-in constant in PE subsystems which holds the processor number for each PE. The "first" processor has 0 as the value of **penumber**, the "second" has 1, and so on. The second **ppe** form computes the absolute value of **penumber** − 2 by calling the PE function **abs**. Thus, the first processor, for instance, returns 2 as the value.

Note that TUPLE uses distinct name spaces for ordinary sequential functions and PE functions. In the example, **abs** names both the sequential function and the PE function. This is because a PE function is defined in the PE subsystems, whereas a sequential function is defined in the full-set Common Lisp system on the front-end with which the user interacts.

The ppe form in the example displays the values returned by the PEs, but it does *not* return the values. Actually, it returns "no value" in the terminology of Common Lisp. The so-called "parallel values" or "plural values" are not first-class objects in TUPLE. In order to obtain a single value from the values of PEs, the user has to use a *reduction* operation. TUPLE supports a variety of reduction operations, such as the one to choose the value returned by a specified PE, the one to randomly choose a non-**nil** value among the returned values, and the one to sum up all the returned values.

2.2 Parallel List Processing

As a typical example of parallel list processing, we will show how binary search trees can be handled in TUPLE. In Lisp, each node of a binary search tree can be represented as a list of three elements.

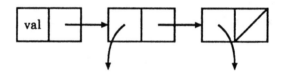

The first element is the value of the node, and the second and the third elements are respectively the left and the right subtrees of the node. Node values in the left subtree are all less than the current node value, and node values in the right subtree are all greater than the current node value. Ordinary binary search function can then be defined so that it recursively descends the given binary search tree, to find the given item in $\log n$ time, with n being the number of nodes in the tree.

In Common Lisp, the binary search function can be defined as follows.

```
(defun binary-search (tree item)
  (if (null tree)
      nil
```

```
(if (= (car tree) item)
    t
    (binary-search
      (if (> (car tree) item)
          (cadr tree)
          (caddr tree))
      item))))
```

When this function reaches at the bottom of the binary search tree, it returns the false value nil to indicate that the specified item is not found in the tree. Before that, the function compares the current node value with the specified item. If they are the same, the function returns the true value t. Otherwise, it goes down to the left or the right subtree depending on the current node value.

In order to parallelize the binary search function, we assume that the entire binary search tree is represented by disjoint *PE trees*, one per PE. Each PE tree of a PE is itself a binary search tree that is constructed with cons cells in the PE subsystem of the PE. If any pair of two PE trees are disjoint (i.e., have no common node value), then we can regard the whole collection of the PE trees as a large binary search tree. We will show later how such PE trees can be constructed in TUPLE.

The parallel version of the binary search function can be defined as follows.

```
(defpefun binary-search (tree item)
  (if (null tree)
      nil
      (exif (= (car tree) item)
            t
            (binary-search
              (if (> (car tree) item)
                  (cadr tree)
                  (caddr tree))
              item))))
```

The point here is that, when one of the PEs finds the item in its PE tree, the other PEs need not go further. Rather, we would like to stop computation as soon as a PE finds the item. Since this kind of processor synchronization is common to many parallel algorithms, we introduce a new construct exif (exclusive if). The exif form

  (exif *condition then-clause else-clause*)

is similar to the ordinary if form, but if some PEs satisfy the *condition*, then the other PEs do not evaluate the *else-clause*. The parallel binary search function above returns immediately if the current node value for some PE is equal to the item, in which case that PE returns the true value t and the rest of the PEs return the false value nil. By computing the logical *OR* of all values returned by the function, we can determine whether the item was found in one of the PE trees. Or, by asking which PE returned the true value, we can determine in which PE tree the item is registered. TUPLE supports reduction operations for these purposes.

In order to construct PE trees, we use the following PE function, which inserts an item into one of the PE trees.

```
(defpefun bs-add (place item)
  (cond ((some-pe (null (car place)))
         (exif (binary-search (car place) item)
               nil
               (when (= (some-penumber
                          (null (car place)))
                        penumber)
                 (rplaca place
                   (list item nil nil)))))
        ((some-pe (= (caar place) item))
          nil)
        (t (bs-add
             (if (> (caar place) item)
               (cdar place)
               (cddar place))
             item))))
```

To simplify the algorithm, we pass to the function the place holders of the current subtrees. Each place holder is a cons cell whose car part points to the current subtree. By replacing the car part of a place holder with a pointer to a new node, we can easily expand a tree. Initially, each PE has an empty tree. This initialization can be done by the following top-level form.

```
>(defpevar pe-tree (list nil))
```

This form defines a *PE variable* named pe-tree, whose initial value is the place holder for the empty tree for each PE. By invoking the PE function bs-add, the specified item will be inserted into one of the PE trees. For example,

```
>(ppe pe-tree)
#P((NIL) (NIL) (NIL) (NIL) ...)
>(ppe (bs-add pe-tree 503))
#P(T NIL NIL NIL ...)
>(ppe pe-tree)
#P(((503 NIL NIL)) (NIL) (NIL) (NIL) ...)
```

By repeatedly invoking the function, we can construct PE trees in the PE local memories.

The difficulty here is that we have to decide to which PE tree the specified item is to be inserted. Perhaps the best choice will be to choose a PE that first reaches a leaf. With this simple choice, the PE trees are kept balanced among PEs. To do this, the PE function bs-add uses two built-in predicates some-pe and some-penumber. The predicate some-pe returns the true value to all PEs if its argument is true for some PE, and some-penumber returns the processor number of such a PE to all PEs. By comparing the value of some-penumber with the processor number of each PE, we can choose one of the PEs that satisfy a given condition. In the definition of bs-add, if some PE reaches a leaf, then the other PEs just search their subtrees. If some PE finds the item, then bs-add returns the false value, meaning that the item is already in some of the PE trees. Otherwise, we choose one of the PEs that has already reached a leaf and expand the leaf with a new node.

3 The Language

In this section, we briefly present the language of TUPLE. Remember that TUPLE is
an extension of Common Lisp. This means TUPLE supports all features of Common
Lisp and any Common Lisp program runs on the TUPLE system, though such a
program runs sequentially.

3.1 Data Objects

All data objects defined in Common Lisp are also defined in TUPLE. In addition,
TUPLE supports the following data objects for parallel computation.

- Cons objects that are allocated in the PE subsystems. We have already seen how
  these objects are handled in TUPLE programs. These objects are distinguished
  from ordinary Common Lisp cons objects and are sometimes called *PE cons* or
  pons for short. Like ordinary conses, a pons can hold any TUPLE object in its
  car and cdr fields.
- *PE vectors* that are one-dimensional arrays allocated in the PE subsystems.
  Like ordinary vectors, a PE vector can hold any TUPLE object as its element.
  In order to simplify the implementation, possible operations on PE vectors are
  restricted, compared with Common Lisp vectors,
- PE function objects. As in Common Lisp, functions are first-class objects in
  TUPLE. PE functions are also first-class objects. This allows TUPLE programs
  to dynamically determine a function to be invoked. In Common Lisp, the function
  funcall is used to dynamically specify the function to invoke. The function to
  invoke is given as the first argument to funcall. In TUPLE, the PE function
  funcall works in the same way. In SIMD architectures, only one function can
  be invoked at a time. Thus the PE function funcall requires its first arguments
  to be identical among all PEs. That is, when the following form is evaluated in
  PE subsystems,

    (funcall f x y)

  all values of f in the PE subsystems must be identical.

Both front-end variables and PE variables can hold any TUPLE objects. In particular, a front-end variable can hold a pons, a PE vector, or a PE function object, and
a PE variable can hold any Common Lisp object.

As in many Common Lisp systems, fixnums, short-floats, and characters are
immediate data in TUPLE. Operations on these objects are performed in parallel
by the PE subsystems. The other Common Lisp data objects, such as symbols, are
represented as a pointer to the data cell in the front-end heap. In SIMD architectures,
no two PEs can access different locations of the front-end memory simultaneously.
Thus, accessing the front-end heap from the PE subsystems is inevitably a sequential
operation, one access at a time. The only parallel operation on front-end objects is
the pointer comparison eq.

3.2 Forms

Forms that are input to the TUPLE top-level are regarded as *front-end forms*, or
FE forms for short. Any ordinary Common Lisp forms are FE forms. FE forms

are evaluated in the front-end system, until TUPLE encounters forms for parallel computation. If a FE form does not contain such a form, then TUPLE behaves in exactly the same way as a Common Lisp system does.

We have already seen the following forms for parallel computation.

(defpefun *function-name lambda-list form* ···)
(defpevar *variable-name form*)
(ppe *form*)

Each of these *forms* is not an ordinary (i.e., front-end) form, but is a form that is intended to be executed by the PE subsystems in parallel. Such forms are called *PE forms.*

Most FE forms can be accepted as PE forms, but some FE forms are not allowed as PE forms. Conversely, some PE forms are not allowed as FE forms. Note that PE forms differ from FE forms only in their interpretation. Since most forms are input to the TUPLE top level, PE forms are usually represented by objects in the front-end heap.

TUPLE supports several front-end functions that accept a PE form as the argument and start parallel computation by evaluating the given PE form. Among these functions are:

(pevoid *form*)
(pesome *form*)
(peselect *form number*)
(pearray *form vector*)

These functions differ in the handling of the values of the PE form. pevoid discards the values and thus is used only for side effects. pesome is used to test if at least one PE subsystem returns a "true" value (i.e., a non-nil value). peselect returns the value that is returned by the PE subsystem specified by the second argument. pearray returns all values from PE subsystems by storing them into the specified (front-end) vector. By using these front-end functions, the user can construct PE forms dynamically (because arguments to functions are obtained by evaluation) and evaluate them.

It is possible to embed FE forms in PE forms by the use of the the PE function fe. This function receives a FE form as its argument and evaluates it in the same way as Common Lisp does. After the evaluation, fe broadcasts the value to all PE subsystems.

3.3   PE Forms

The followings are valid PE forms.

- List forms
  - Special forms
  - Macro forms
  - Function call forms
- Variables
- Self-evaluating forms

This classification of PE forms is exactly the same as for front-end forms (or, Common Lisp forms).

TUPLE is designed so that each PE subsystem be as close to the front-end Common Lisp system as possible. Below is the list of special forms in the PE subsystems, that have counterparts in Common Lisp.

and	function	prog1
case	if	prog2
cond	labels	progn
declare	let	psetq
do	let*	quote
do*	locally	setq
dolist	loop	unless
dotimes	macrolet	when
flet	or	

The syntax of each special form is similar to that of the corresponding Common Lisp special form, and the semantics is also similar, except that execution of these *PE special forms* are performed in parallel by PE subsystems.

There are some additional special forms. We have already seen exif (exclusive if) in the previous section. The number of such special forms is very small. Presumably, exif will be the only one that is frequently used in actual TUPLE programs. In other words, most TUPLE programs can be described by using exif and those PE special forms listed above.

A macro form for the PE subsystems is a list whose first element names a *PE macro*. As usual, a macro form is expanded to another PE form, which is then evaluated. To define a PE macro, the following front-end form is used.

(defpemacro *macro-name lambda-list form*···)

Remember that PE forms are usually represented by front-end objects. This means that macro expansion is an operation of the front-end system. Therefore, PE macros are defined in exactly the same way as ordinary front-end macros defined by defmacro of Common Lisp. The only difference is the name space in which the defined macro is registered. defpemacro defines a macro into the name space of PE subsystems whereas defmacro defines a macro into the front-end name space.

A function call form for the PE subsystems is a list whose first element is either a function name or a lambda list. Arguments to the function are evaluated by the PE subsystems in parallel and then the function is invoked simultaneously by the PE subsystems.

As in Common Lisp, a PE variable is represented by a symbol. By evaluating a symbol, the value of the PE variable named by the symbol is returned to each PE subsystem simultaneously. The PE subsystems do not share PE variables. Each PE subsystem has its own variable named by the symbol, and the value of the variable is returned to the PE subsystems.

Any TUPLE object other than lists and symbols is regarded as a self-evaluating form when evaluated as a PE form. When evaluated, the object is broadcast to the

PE subsystems. If the object is represented as a pointer to a data cell in the front-end heap, then only the pointer is broadcast and the data cell is not copied into the PE subsystems.

4 Implementation

In this section, we will report the implementation of TUPLE on the MasPar MP-1. The MasPar MP-1 is a SIMD machine with at least 1024 PEs. This machine consists of two parts: the front-end UNIX workstation and the back-end called the data parallel unit (DPU). The back-end consists of the array control unit (ACU), which broadcasts instructions to PEs, and the PE array, where PEs are aligned in a two-dimensional array. A program on the MasPar consists of front-end functions and ACU functions. Parallel computation begins by invoking an ACU function from a front-end function. The memory size in each component is relatively small. The size of the data memory in the ACU is 128 Kbytes and the size of the memory in each PE is 16Kbytes. Virtual memory is not supported on these memories.

4.1 Heaps

Before the current version, we implemented a prototype version of TUPLE [3] (see Figure 1). In that version, all PE functions (both built-in and user-defined) were stored in the front-end memory. The parallel evaluator also resided in the front-end. In the prototype version, therefore, several subroutines were implemented on the ACU, which are invoked by the parallel evaluator in the front-end. Since most of the subroutines were responsible for small jobs such as popping up the PE stack, communication between the front-end and the back-end took place frequently. Unfortunately, this communication is very slow and accordingly the performance of the prototype version was not satisfactory.

To improve the performance, the current version of TUPLE stores all PE functions in the ACU and the parallel evaluator runs in the ACU. When the user defines a new PE function, the *downloader* in the front-end puts the function definition into the ACU memory. Some front-end forms such as **ppe** downloads PE forms into the ACU memory before passing control to the parallel evaluator. Thus, in the current version, once triggered by the front-end, the entire parallel computation is performed solely in the ACU and no communication takes place between the front-end and the back-end.

To sum up, the current implementation of TUPLE on the MasPar uses three kinds of heaps:

- the font-end heap where ordinary Common Lisp objects are allocated
- the PE heaps where PE cons cells are allocated
- the ACU heap where those objects common to all PE subsystems, such as PE function objects (including built-in functions, user-defined functions, and function closures) and PE vector headers, are allocated

Any object in one of these heaps can be referenced from any component of the MasPar system. For example, an object in the front-end heap may be referenced

First Edition

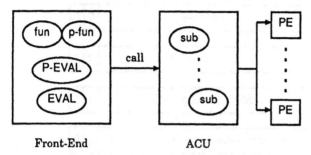

Second Edition

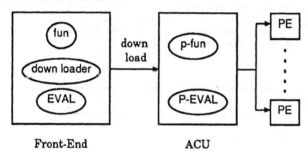

Fig. 1. Two versions of TUPLE

from the ACU (as part of a user-defined function) and PEs (by broadcasting). Also, a cons cell in a PE heap may be referenced from the front-end (by reductions), the ACU, and the other PEs (by PE communications).

4.2 Data Representation and Allocation

Figure 2 illustrates data representation of TUPLE. This representation is common to all components of the MasPar system. By having the same representation, we can avoid data conversion in communications among the components. The first four formats are those used by the original KCL. As indicated in the Figure, the two least significant bits are used to distinguish these four formats. Since the third significant bit of a character object is always 0, we extended the data representation of KCL so that pointers to the ACU and PE heaps are distinguished by the bit pattern 110 at the three least significant bits.

Figure 3 shows the data area of each PE that TUPLE handles directly. The run-time stack of MPL is not shown in the Figure. The first words of the memory area are used to allocate built-in constants nil, t, and penumber. Next to these words is the PE global area, where user-defined global PE variables, constants, and vectors

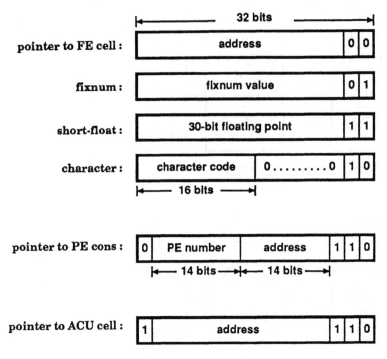

Fig. 2. Object representation of TUPLE

are allocated. This global area expands dynamically as the user defines PE variables etc. Next is the PE stack area where local PE variables are allocated and temporary values (including arguments to PE functions) are stored.

Then there is a heap area where PE cons cells are allocated. Mark bits for PE cons cells are separately stored in the last part of the data area. These mark bits are used by the parallel garbage collector of TUPLE to reclaim unused PE cells (see the next subsection). The total size of the data area is 8 Kbytes for the MasPar system that has 16 Kbytes of local memory per PE. Half of the data area is used as the heap. Since each cons cell occupies 8 bytes (i.e., 2 words), 512 cells are available per PE.

Cells in the ACU heap are homogeneous and each cell occupies four words. The first word of a cell is used as the data tag and the GC mark bit. Use of the remaining three words depends on the tag. For the ACU cell for a PE vector, these words contain the name, the length, and the address of the PE vector in each PE global area. Each user-defined global function is represented by an ACU cell whose three words contain the name, the lambda list, and the body of the function.

Global PE variable bindings and global PE function bindings are represented by ACU cells called *ACU symbol cells*. Each ACU symbol cell corresponds to an ordinary front-end symbol, and no two ACU cells correspond to a same front-end symbol. When a global PE variable is defined (typically by defpevar) or when a global PE function is defined (typically by defpefun), a new ACU symbol cell is

lower address

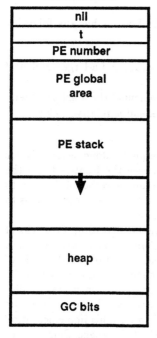

nil
t
PE number
PE global area
PE stack
heap
GC bits

upper address

Fig. 3. The PE data area

created that corresponds to the name of the PE variable or the PE function if and only if there exists no such ACU symbol cell. The downloader converts all references to global PE variables and global PE functions in a PE form, to pointers to the corresponding ACU symbol cells.

Each ACU symbol cell contains the address of the global PE variable in the PE global area, the PE function object (pointer to an ACU cell), and the pointer to the corresponding front-end symbol. The pointer to the front-end symbol cell is mainly used in error messages in case unbound variables and undefined functions are detected. On the other hand, each front-end symbol cell contains a pointer to the corresponding ACU symbol cell, if one exists. This pointer is used mainly by the downloader for conversions from front-end symbols to back-end symbols.

As of the front-end cells, cells other than symbol cells are represented exactly in the same way as in the original KCL. Front-end symbol cells are extended so that they can contain information on parallel computation such as the ACU routine that handles a PE special form, and the pointer to the corresponding ACU symbol cell. Thus modification of the front-end system was surprisingly small.

4.3 Garbage Collection

As already seen, the implementation of TUPLE on the MasPar has the following unique features in relation with garbage collection.

1. It has multiple heaps: the front-end heap, the ACU heap, and a large number of PE heaps.
2. Each cell in a heap may be referenced from any component of the MasPar system.
3. Communication between the front-end and the back-end is relatively slow.
4. PEs can execute instructions in parallel.

The second feature implies that garbage collection cannot be done separately for each heap and that communications are inevitable between the front-end and the back-end during garbage collection. The third feature requires some mechanism to reduce communications during garbage collection. The last feature encourages us to develop parallel algorithm for garbage collection on PE heaps.

The original KCL uses the conventional mark-and-sweep algorithm. Free cells of the same size are linked together to form a free list. Some objects such as arrays are represented by a fixed-length *header cell* which has a pointer to the *body* of the object. For an array, for instance, array elements are stored in the body and the header cell contains various information on the array, such as the dimensions. Bodies are allocated in a special area called the *relocatable area* and are relocated during the sweep phase to make a large free space in the relocatable area. This implementation is closely related with the fact that KCL is written in the C language. Since bodies are always referenced via the header cells, we do not need to change the values of C variables that hold KCL objects, even when bodies are relocated. Note that the address of a C variable depends on the C compiler. Thus, this implementation of the original KCL increases the portability of the system.

Since TUPLE is written in MPL, a data-parallel extension of the C language, we essentially use the mark-and-sweep garbage collector for back-end heaps. Remember that all cells in a back-end heap are homogeneous. This includes that we need only one free list for each heap, and that no relocation is necessary once the size of the heap is fixed.

The garbage collector of TUPLE is invoked when one of the free lists becomes empty or when the relocatable area of the front-end becomes full. As in KCL, the garbage collector consists of two phases:

1. the mark phase, when all cells in use are marked, and
2. the sweep phase, when each non-marked cell (i.e., garbage cell) is linked to a free list and each body whose header cell is marked is relocated.

The sweep phase can be executed for each component of the MasPar, independently of the other components, for the following reasons.

– Each garbage cell in a component is linked to a free list in the same component.
– There is no pointer that points to the body in the front-end directly from the back-end. Even when a body is relocated in the front-end, no back-end pointers need to be changed.

Therefore, we use the sweep phase routine of the original KCL without changes. The sweep phase routine for ACU cells is obvious. It scans the entire ACU heap and simply links non-marked cells to the free list of the ACU. The similar routine works for cells in each PE heap, and this routine can be executed in parallel by all PEs, without overhead such as PE synchronization.

The mark phase, on the other hand, is not so easy because it requires communications between the front-end and the back-end.

SIMD parallel garbage collection has been implemented in the TUPLE system. This garbage collection is a parallel version of the conventional mark and sweep garbage collection. To reduce the time for the communication, we use buffers in PE local memories, where pointers from PEs to the front-end are temporarily stored. Before sending the buffered pointers to the marking routine of the front-end, duplicated pointers are removed by using a parallel sorting algorithm. Then the remaining pointers are block-transferred to the front-end. The similar technique is used for pointers from the front-end to PEs. Refer to [14] for the details of this SIMD parallel marking algorithm.

5 Performance Measurements

We have measured the run time of the function bs-add in Section 2, by supplying several random numbers as the arguments. We used the MasPar MP-1 with 1024 PEs and with the VAXstation 3520 as the front-end. The result is shown in Figure 4. The Figure shows that the parallel version is only five to six times faster than the equivalent sequential version on the front-end. Roughly speaking, each call of bs-add requires $\log_2 n$ time for the sequential version, and $\log_2 \frac{n}{2^k}$ time for the parallel version, with n being the number of items and 2^k being the number of PEs. (According to our experiences with the MasPar MP-1, the performance of the front-end is almost the same as a single PE.) In this experiment, we used 1024 PEs, and thus $k = 10$. If $n = 2^{12}$, for example, the sequential version runs in time 12 whereas the parallel version runs in time 2. Thus the maximum speed up will be 6. This means that the performance of the TUPLE system is very close to the theoretical upper bound. Another reason for this small gain is that each expansion of a tree is performed for only a single PE. Obviously, tree expansion is one of the most time-consuming operations in the program because cons cells must be allocated in the PE heap. On SIMD architectures, all PEs except one have to wait while the selected PE expands its PE tree. We can possibly increase the performance by modifying the program so that tree expansions are deferred until many (or all) PEs become ready to expand their PE trees, as suggested by [2].

Figure 5 shows the result of another test for the same program. This time, we change the number of PEs that join the parallel computation. Note that the program is independent of the number of PEs. When we used only one PE, the performance of the "parallel" program was only a little bit worse than the sequential version. This means TUPLE is well implemented for each PE. As seen in the Figure, the runtime decreases steadily as the number of PEs increases, but the runtime seems to converge. The convergence point indicates the time for the essentially sequential part of the program.

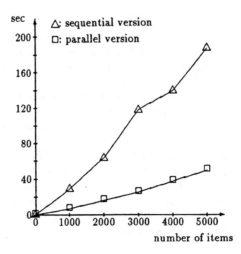

Fig. 4. Adding items with 1024 PEs

To see the performance of the TUPLE system for more popular applications on SIMD architectures, we wrote a TUPLE program to simulate fluid flow by solving Navier-Stokes Equations. Figure 6 illustrates the field that we used for the test. A certain kind of fluid flows into the field from the left side and flows out from the right side. At the lower left corner of the field is a step that causes some irregular flow. As is well known (see [1] for example), the computation is performed by dividing the entire field into small regions and then by repeating a loop body that updates values of the regions. In order to implement the program efficiently on our MasPar system, we divided the entire field into a 32 × 32 matrix of small regions, since this matches the hardware configuration of the PEs in our MasPar MP-1.

In the sequential version of the fluid flow program, the region values are represented by 32 × 32 arrays, and thus the loop body consists of two inner loops, one for the x axis and the other for the y axis. In the parallel version, the matrix of regions is directly mapped onto the physical matrix of PEs. Thus the loop body contains no inner loops. Instead, each PE obtains values from its neighbors to compute the next values for the region that the PE is responsible for. The result of repeating the loop body 200 times is shown in Table 1. Currently, TUPLE does not have a compiler, and thus runs programs interpretively. Compared with the interpreted execution of the sequential version, it is clear that the parallel version runs quite fast. Even if compared with the compiled version on the SPARC, the parallel version is more than five times faster. It is obvious that TUPLE programs are slower than equivalent MPL programs. Nevertheless, the runtime of this TUPLE program is not very far from the runtime of the MPL version.

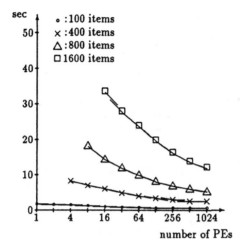

Fig. 5. Adding items with various number of PEs

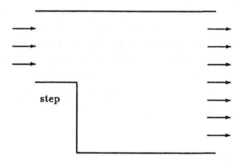

Fig. 6. A fluid field

6 Concluding Remarks

In this paper, we introduced the TUPLE language for SIMD architectures and presented the current implementation of TUPLE on a SIMD machine MasPar MP-1. We have shown that the TUPLE system has a high performance for typical SIMD applications.

TUPLE is currently being used for research purposes to exploit parallel algorithms in some application areas of symbolic computation, such as computer algebra and term rewriting. TUPLE is also used for education. The highly interactive parallel environment of TUPLE helps the students write their first parallel programs. Since we have only one MasPar MP-1 available for education, we have developed a

C version
> VAXstation 3520   108.8 sec
> SPARCstation 1+   32.9 sec

MPL version   3.0 sec

KCL version (interpreted)
> VAXstation 3520   1700.4 sec (49 GCs)
> SPARCstation 1+   390.3 sec (49 GCs)

KCL version (compiled)
> SPARCstation 1+   44.4 sec (no GC)

TUPLE version   8.0 sec (no GC)

Table 1. Time for 200 iterations

TUPLE simulator that runs on Unix workstations. The students prepare their programs by using the simulator and test the performance on the real TUPLE system. This enables efficient use of the computation resource.

In our experience with TUPLE, the heap size (8 Kbytes) of each PE subsystem is too small for real applications, or even for experimentation. This small size is the major obstacle to develop parallel programs in TUPLE. On MasPar MP-1 with 1024 PEs, the total size of 8 Mbytes seems satisfactory in many cases. However, it is hard to distribute the entire data among the PE heaps. The binary tree search program in this paper is one of the few programs that succeeded in balanced data distribution. A SIMD machine with much more local memory is highly expected to solve this inessential problem.

Acknowledgements

Takashi Okazawa implemented the back-end part of the prototype version of TUPLE. Yoshitaka Nagano and Katsumi Hatanaka have been implementing the current version in cooperation with the author. Taichi Yasumoto designed and implemented the mark phase parallel algorithm jointly with the author. Toshiro Kijima joined the design of the parallel algorithm and gave many useful suggestions based on his experiences of designing and implementing his extended C language for SIMD parallel computation. The project of TUPLE is supported partly by Sumitomo Metal Industries., Ltd. and partly by Digital Equipment Corporation.

References

1. Grosch, C.: Adapting a Navier-Stokes Code to the ICL-DAP, SIAM J. SCI. STAT. COMPUT., Vol.8, No.1 (1987)
2. Halstead, R.: private communication with the author (1992)

3. Okazawa, T.: Design and Implementation of a Common Lisp System Extended for Massively Parallel SIMD Computer. Master's thesis (in Japanese), Toyohashi Univ. of Tech. (1992)

4. Padget, J.: Data-Parallel Symbolic Processing. Proceedings of the DPRI symposium, Boston (1992)

5. Padget, J.: Collections and Garbage Collection. Proceedings of the Internal Workshop IWMM 92, St. Maro, Springer Lecture Notes in Computer Science No. 637 (1992)

6. Quinn, M.: Designing Efficient Algorithms for Parallel Computers. McGraw-Hill (1987)

7. Sabot G.: Introduction to Paralation Lisp. Technical Report PL87-1, Thinking Machines Corporation (1987)

8. Sabot G.: The Paralation Model: Architecture Independent Parallel Programming. MIT Press (1988)

9. Steele, G.: Common Lisp the Language. Digital Press (1984)

10. Steele, G., Hillis, D.: Connection Machine Lisp: Fine-Grained Parallel Symbolic Processing. Proceedings of 1986 ACM Conference on Lisp and Functional Programming (1986)

11. Wholey, S., Steele, G.: Connection Machine Lisp: a dialect of Common Lisp for data parallel programming. Proceedings of Second International Conference on Supercomputing (1987)

12. Yuasa, T.: Design and Implementation of Kyoto Common Lisp. Journal of Information Processing, Vol.13, No.3 (1990)

13. Yuasa, T.: TUPLE - An Extension of KCL for Massively Parallel SIMD Architecture - Draft for the Second Edition. available from the author (1992)

14. Yuasa, T.: Memory Management and Garbage Collection of an Extended Common Lisp System for Massively Parallel SIMD Architecture. Proceedings of the Internal Workshop IWMM 92, St. Maro, Springer Lecture Notes in Computer Science No. 637 (1992)

15. Connection Machine Lisp Reference Manual. Thinking Machines Corporation (1987)

16. Introduction to Data Level Parallelism. Technical Report PR86-14, Thinking Machines Corporation (1986)

17. *Lisp Reference Manual. Thinking Machines Corporation (1988)

18. MasPar Parallel Application Language (MPL) User Guide. MasPar Computer Corporation (1991)

Architecture Independence and Coordination (Preliminary Version)

Julian Padget*   Duncan Batey**   Simon Merrall***

School of Mathematical Sciences
University of Bath
BATH, BA2 7AY, United Kingdom
E-mail: {jap, djb, sm}@maths.bath.ac.uk

1 Introduction

In the spirit of a workshop, the work described here is in progress, being a snapshot of the current state on the way towards our goal of constructing a virtual multi-computer. This paper comes in two parts:

- The first (section 2) discusses our dissatisfaction with current programming models claiming to offer either architecture independence or coordination or both and dissatisfaction with the interpretation of these terms. Of course, this is a fairly subjective matter in which generalizations are disputable. In consequence, we would expect proponents of a particular view to take exception on detail points. In return, we suggest this might be a case of not seeing "the wood for the trees". This first part summarizes what has motivated us to attempt the second part.
- In the second part we describe our current work in which we are using and exploring the Paralation model (section 3) as a basis for orchestrating networks of virtual processors to carry out both MIMD and SIMD style computations (section 4) under a modified notion of architecture independence.

2 Analysis of some parallel programming models

Parallel programming languages can be broadly classified into three categories:

1. Those with explicit parallel constructs, which embody a particular style of parallel processing, such as Ada and occam;
2. Those with coordination extensions, better known as coordination languages [16], whose most well-known instances are the many variants of Linda;
3. Those with implicit parallel constructs, such as Gamma [1, 2, 3] and Unity [12], which are often called architecture-independent languages.

---

* This work was partially supported by SERC grants GR/F63183 and GR/G31048.
** Supported by a SERC CASE award in conjunction with Perihelion Software Ltd.
*** Supported by a SERC CASE award in conjunction with ICL Ltd.

We do not specifically make mention of Lisp in the above categories because, due to its extensible nature, it can and does permit instances of all of these ideas. Naturally, each category has its enthusiastic supporters. What we attempt to show in this paper is that these perceived divisions are not as rigid as might be thought and that a synthesis of these approaches offers a useful way forward in the programming of what will most likely become the common workhorse: the multi-computer [6] comprising collections of workstations, SIMD and MIMD processor arrays and shared memory multiprocessors linked by high-speed networks, be they local or wide area.

We begin with a survey of various concurrency abstractions and develop some criteria to categorize them against the above list. The conclusion we draw is that the greatest difference between the categories is their name and that each abstraction has elements of each category depending on the perspective taken. In fact, the distinguishing feature between the abstractions lies in the scale of parallelism that each can handle. Which of architecture independence and coordination has the advantage in the matter of scale is an open question.

In this paper we are recording our attempt to consider what direction language design should be taking if we are to be able to program the kinds of machines that we expect to see in the next few years. While we accept that most work will continue in C and FORTRAN [11], our interest is in making it easier to prototype programs, which behave correctly and repeatably, to utilise these architectures without each new parallel machine imposing its will on the program or programmer.

For the purposes of this discussion we will limit ourselves to the following specific instances of concurrency abstraction, coordination and architecture-independent languages:

concurrency abstractions: futures, communicating sequential processes (or CSP), time-warp;

coordination languages: Linda, Parallel Virtual Machine (or PVM), Virtual Systems Architecture (VSA);

architecture-independent: Gamma, Unity, Paralations, High Performance Fortran (HPF), Connection Machine Lisp (CM-Lisp).

These models have each been placed in a particular category according to what we believe is a widely accepted view of their role. However, it is the latter two that are trying to distinguish themselves from the former by suggesting they have properties which the common abstractions do not. As we proceed, we aim to convince you that the divisions between the three categories are not so clear cut.

2.1 Linda

Inevitably, as the prime example of a coordination language, we consider Linda at length. Also, as the prime example, it is necessarily the prime target for any criticism of this approach. If we take Linda as the *lingua franca* of coordination let us consider each of the abstractions in terms of it:

futures: [17] The process spawning operation can be expressed as an **eval** followed by an **in**; indeed, the similarity is even stronger in the work-crews implementation of futures [30].

CSP: [18, 19] The channel operations can be expressed as **out** of message followed by **in** of acknowledge (send) or **in** of message followed by **out** of acknowledge (receive);

time-warp: [22] The modelling here is rather more complex. However, all is really needed is a means of ordering the tuples using a priority-queue-like mechanism[21]. Otherwise, each time-warp process is like an element in a pipeline which consumes and produces messages.

Lest we be misunderstood, it should be stated that we are not trying to set any of these models above or below one another in a hierarchy, nor are we advancing the view that Linda is a universal model. We simply wish to establish equivalences. The purpose of the above is to show that each of the abstractions embodies a specialised form of coordination which has the virtue of being suited to a particular kind of task (for example, simulation, in the case of time-warp) or offering a convenient model of certain kinds of concurrent activities (futures for divide and conquer problems and CSP for static networks). In this sense, we can regard these abstractions as coordination languages too, except that the user buys into a particular coordination policy when choosing the abstraction.

This brings us to the founding principle of Linda as advanced by Gelernter and Carriero: computation and coordination are orthogonal activities and should be handled by separate languages [16]. However, in practice, the marriage of a computation language and a coordination language, while initially attractive and offering an easy programmer migration path from sequential to parallel programming is not always a happy one. The problems stem from integration with the host language [10] and with Linda itself:

conflicts of abstraction: Linda's tuple space adds another form of data abstraction to its host, but the representation in tuple space may differ significantly from that in the host language's data structures imposing a translation overhead when transferring data between the two. Alternatively the programmer must choose to divide his data between the two classes of storage, which "codes-in" the decision to use Linda. A novel solution to this is proposed in Lucinda [10], a language with a type scheme based on Russell [8], where tuples and tuple spaces are the only general aggregate data structures.

termination: Detecting when a process should terminate often leads to bizarre *ad-hoc* solutions involving special flag tuples, which may then lead to problems in the following two categories.

temporal aliasing: A term to describe the circumstance when two components operate as producer and consumer, but the former generates faster than the latter can accept *and* there is an implied ordering on the tuples. One way to resolve this is by enumerating tuples, but this is neither elegant nor general; another is to use multiple tuple spaces and a process to implement the protocol between the producer and consumer.

unintended aliasing: A term to describe the circumstance when different components of a program interfere with one another as a result of using the same tuple name and structure. This is precisely the same problem as global variable name clashes, such as can arise in large pieces of software. The addition of multiple tuple spaces can resolve this issue in a manner analogous to modules resolving the variable name-clash, but leaves some open problems in cross tuple space visibility (*cf.* import and export operations on modules).

It does not seem unfair to conclude that very rapidly a coordination language can become part of the problem rather than the adjunct it was supposed to be. The real issue with Linda seems to be a choice between orthogonal coordination with attendant conflict of abstraction problems, or hiding the coordination aspects, thus refuting the separation argument. However, there are some advantages to a coordination language, like Linda, in the way it can decouple the producer and the consumer:

space decoupling: The process generating a tuple has no knowledge of the process that will eventually read the tuple—either its name or its location;
time decoupling: The producer and the consumer need not co-exist to communicate.

These benefits are passed on to the programmer by forming an abstraction barrier around each process.

2.2 Parallel Virtual Machine

PVM is significantly more coarse-grain than Linda and should be viewed as a harness to coordinate (heavy-weight) processes distributed across a local or a wide area network [29, 15]. It provides the means—through a daemon process running on each participating node—to create a process remotely and connect its standard-input and output to a socket which is multiplexed for all the traffic between two physical network nodes. Thereafter the programmer may transfer data, after having converted it into a suitable form, which can then be reconstituted by the receiving process. Clearly, this codes in the use of PVM because of the relatively low-level at which the transfer services are accessed. PVM has successfully been applied to numerical (scientific) programming as well as distributed processing in Lisp [9].

2.3 Virtual Systems Architecture

VSA, conversely, is fine-grain, although it claims architecture independence, and is used to specify manipulations of regular collections of data such as occur on data-parallel architectures [23]. VSA has the facility to define the shape of a collection of data and the means to create mappings from one collection to another in ways similar to both Paralation Lisp and FORTRAN D. We believe its only use has been as an intermediate language in a FORTRAN compiler for the ICL DAP.

2.4 Architecture Independent Languages

If we now turn to the architecture-independent (AI) languages we also find stylised forms of communication. A distinguishing feature compared with the abstractions we examined earlier is that the AI languages describe communications between collections of data rather than between one process and another. Thus, they describe many communication operations at once rather than individual ones. The use of collections of "data" is a significant pointer to the orientation of the AI languages since they seem to ally themselves much more closely with the SIMD than the MIMD world.

Gamma: Answers are produced by multi-set transformation, triggered by the guards on condition-action pairs with termination being implementation-defined [3].

Unity: The only form of aggregate data structure is the array and operations upon the elements are controlled by guards. Each statement is executed infinitely often and, like Gamma, termination is implementation-defined [12].

Paralations: A paralation is a collection of (virtual) processors (VPs), and an instance of a paralation (called a field) is a collection of data in which one element is stored in the (local) memory of each virtual processor [27]. These collections of data are manipulated constructively using universally quantified expressions. Data may be transferred from the memory of one virtual processor to another by constructing a map connecting VPs in the source paralation to VPs in the target and then moving the data down the map.

CM-Lisp: This is a direct ancestor of the Paralation model. The basic parallel data structure is the *xapping* (derived from set and mapping) and comprises a set of ordered pairs of keys and values, but the key is actually an integer since it is an element of the enumeration of the processors on which the xapping is stored [28]. The three important operators in CM Lisp are: α, $\bullet$ and β. The first is used to project singular valued expressions into xappings in the manner of a distribution operator (*cf* Backus' FP notation) and $\bullet$ is used to check distribution, in order to be able to place xappings in expressions to which we wish to apply α. The β operator is used to reduce a xapping to a single value as well as rather complicated data movement operations.

Coordination in these languages comes from the selection of certain processing elements: in Gamma and Unity it is specified by the guards and in Paralation and CM Lisp by the mappings or xappings. So, it seems that AI languages can also be viewed as coordination languages of a specialised variety capable of describing communication on a grander scale than at the abstraction level discussed earlier.

It is interesting to note that both Gamma and Unity choose only a single form of aggregate structure and operate on that in parallel, which highlights the question of conflict of abstraction raised earlier. A second observation is that programming is considerably simplified by passing the termination buck to the processor. In fact, it seems that Linda, Unity and Gamma form a family since the underlying concept in each is the transformation of a collection of data as proposed in the Chemical Abstract Machine (CHAM) [7]. The difference lies in the level at which each supports the concept.

Paralation and CM-Lisp form a different family, although they too operate on collections of data, because they are primarily concerned with combining data sets to form new ones. In this sense they are constructive, whereas the others are destructive, but the net result is the same[4].

We finish this section by summarizing that both concurrency abstractions and architecture independent languages offer varieties of coordination and that attempting to divorce computation entirely from coordination is both impossible and undesirable, because the limitations of the coordination language leak back to the host and to the algorithm. On the other hand coordination languages (specifically Linda) can package abstractions, as shown by the equivalences discussed earlier, and can offer a degree of architecture independence as evidenced by the property of space-decoupling. However, the architecture-independence is of a fundamentally different nature to that of the AI languages, being strongly MIMD oriented. In conclusion it seems that none of these models is exactly and only what it claims to be: (i) coordination languages are rarely truly orthogonal to the host language (ii) the concurrency abstractions and AI languages embody coordination (iii) the AI languages are not truly architecture independent.

3   What is Architecture Independence?

When a language is described as being architecture independent, it is usually in the context of some relevant group of platforms. It is then reasonable to expect programs written in that language to run any of these platforms without prejudice. This is done by basing the language on some abstract computing model that applies to each and every one of the processors in the group.

The problem with architecture independence in the context of parallel computing is that the models chosen to base these languages on are often not directly applicable to all parallel architectures. More often the model is based on the operation of some specific machine or set of machines, and then great effort and ingenuity is employed in making the programs written in the resulting language run on machines whose underlying models are radically different to that upon which the language was originally based. This is especially apparent in the attempts to provide efficient compilation of SIMD programs for MIMD machines, and vice versa [13, 14].

We propose a different approach, involving a slightly altered perspective on architecture independence. In fact, the difference in perspective may seem so small as to be insignificant, but perception of it and the standard interpretation is not unlike the two views of Necker's cube. Instead of attempting to coerce algorithms expressed in terms of one model to a different one, we aim to provide one language which, via the same essential constructs, can be used to express

---

[4] However, we do not feel we have explored far enough to assert that they are equivalent.

algorithms appropriate to any of our intended target machines' basic computational model. In the traditional sense of architecture independence, programs written in such a language should still run on any of the target machines, but from our new viewpoint should result in more efficient code if the algorithm expressed by the program is applicable to the operation of the target machine.

3.1 An experimental framework

We have chosen the Paralation model as a starting point for our experiments. Although the Paralation model is SIMD in nature[5], just as Lisp can treat data as program so, in our extended Paralation Lisp, data-parallelism can be treated as control-parallelism. This is best illustrated by a few examples. First, a summary of the Paralation model.

paralations: A contraction of *parallel relations*; sets of virtual processors, or *sites*; the implementation maps these onto the available physical processors, in much the same way that a virtual memory mechanism abstracts physical memory.

fields: Instances of paralations, that is, parallel data structures whose *elements* are allocated on the sites comprising the parent paralation.

elwise: A contraction of *element-wise*; an explicit parallel evaluation mechanism: the code body is executed at each site of the parameter fields' associated paralation, and any references to the parameter fields within the code body are resolved with their local element values at that site.

mappings: Describe transformations between paralations; a field in the source paralation can be *moved* down a mapping to create a new field in the destination paralation.

Code is executed in parallel by **elwise** evaluation with respect to a collection of fields belonging to the same paralation, for example:

```
p                          ;; a field of four elements
=> #F(0 1 2 3)
q                          ;; and another
=> #F(1 2 3 4)
(elwise (p q) (+ p q)))    ;; add them together in parallel
=> #F(1 3 5 7)
```

Such operations are clearly data-parallel and gives the impression that the Paralation model is SIMD only. Now consider the case of an **elwise** form containing a conditional expression:

```
(elwise (p) (if (evenp p) (/ p 2) (* p 2)))
=> #F(0 2 1 6)
```

---

[5] Although [27] asserts otherwise.

There are two ways in which the evaluation of this expression could be implemented: (i) SIMD, where the condition is used to disable the processing elements which do not satisfy it; the consequent expression is evaluated; those processing elements are then disabled and the other set enabled; the alternative expression is evaluated; all processors are enabled; the results are returned. (ii) MIMD, where the conditional expression is evaluated in parallel on each processing element, implying that different processing elements are simultaneously capable of different actions. The choice between these, in this example, is immaterial to the user. However, there is a difference which should be noted: the time taken with SIMD is proportional to the sum of the worst case for each arm, whereas for MIMD it is the worst case for either arm. This situation is potentially more serious with the execution of nested conditional expressions or case expressions.

Since we are programming in Lisp, data can also be program. We can therefore express control parallelism by creating a field of functions, a field of arguments, and then executing code that applies one to the other elementwise with respect to these fields, for example:

```
(elwise (fn arg-list) (apply fn arg-list)))
```

In conclusion, we see that the Paralation model seems readily able to *express* both data and control parallel programs.

However, the semantics of control paralations are not so obvious. The original description of the model [27] calls for barrier synchronization after each **elwise** and leaves some open questions in the treatment of nested paralations (*ie.* nested **elwise** forms). The barrier synchronization is both wasteful of resources under MIMD control and a recognized hard problem in a distributed environment. In consequence, we have discarded this condition in favour of a future or dataflow-like mechanism where attempts to access field values whose computation is not yet completed will cause the accessing process to block. More detailed descriptions of this system can be found in [5, 4]. The matters relating to nested paralations are beyond the scope of this paper, but will be dealt with in detail in [24]. Also, in the interests of brevity we omit a description of mappings, since they are not directly relevant in the present context.

4 A Virtual Multi-computer

We foresee that in the near future the main computing resources available will be networks of a wide variety of computers, the majority of which will be workstations, and many of which will be underutilised while other users have tasks requiring significant computing resources which even specialist machines, should they be available, might not satisfy. The aim is to harness the power of this so-called multi-computer. Such a system will allow multi-user remote manipulation of massively-parallel SIMD machines, transputer arrays, LAN and WAN networks, all from within one application session, using just one language, without detailed user-foreknowledge of the resources they are utilising.

Even given the physical resources, the problem remains as how to program such a machine. The first level is to insulate the programmer from the number of those physical resources, since as was realised long ago in SIMD programming, problems rarely have the same number of components as the actual hardware. Hence, we distinguish a virtual multicomputer from a physical one by analogy with virtual memory: there are as many virtual processors in a virtual multicomputer as the problem requires. The second level is rather more subtle, being to insulate the programmer from their variety: to provide an architecture independent programming model. By this we do not mean universal theoretical models such as Unity or Gamma, both of which are so poor in terms of data structures, modularity and abstraction facilities as to be inappropriate for anything other than pedagogic exercises. What we believe is needed is a universal *programming* model, which these do not offer. The key phrase is "programming model": the programmer is to be able to write in the same terms whatever the variety of architectures, but may assume the existence of facilities for both MIMD and SIMD execution without significant performance penalty for either. We conceive of an environment providing multiple, specializable (in the object-oriented sense) concurrency abstractions which can be organized into hierarchies.

4.1 Implementation Sketch

We are building this networked ensemble of disparate computing resources using the extended Paralation model outlined in the previous section. We envisage an environment offering a client-server model: client programs request paralations suited to each subtask's particular requirements, for example, powerful independent processors or fast inter-process communications, and these requests are then honoured by the most appropriate server. New servers can join the system at any time and are registered by sending their network address and capabilities to an existing server, from where the information will be propagated. Similarly, a server may leave at any time, if, for example, the local load average exceeds a certain threshold. This requires the tasks being run for the virtual multi-computer to be suspended, reified and migrated to another server within the system. Each server is responsible for any computation involving the paralations it creates, and will route computation requests for other paralations to their creators. Migration of data and program from one server (collection of VPs) to another is achieved under user-control by means of Paralation Lisp's general communications constructs—the mappings mentioned earlier. A diagram of the physical components of our envisaged virtual multicomputer appears in Figure 1.

Prototype implementations of Paralation Lisp for traditional sequential and distributed MIMD architectures have been written, as well as a more advanced SIMD implementation for a massively-parallel architecture (Maspar MP-1). A simple server for the latter has also been written, providing remote multi-user support. The network glue for this system is provided by PVM and the underlying dialect of Lisp is EuLisp [26].

On the workstations and shared memory multi-processors, a distributed subsystem, consisting of interconnected Lisp processes (our "virtual computers"),

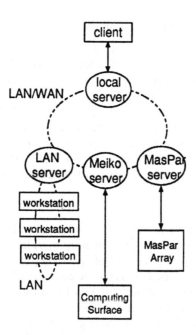

Fig. 1. The structure of a potential virtual multicomputer based on some of the computing resources at Bath: a network of Sun workstations, the Meiko Computing Surface, and the MasPar MP-1.

provides low-level distributed computation abstractions, local object caching to reduce the size of messages, and asynchronous distributed garbage collection. Each of these workstations or multi-processors is potentially the front end to some other parallel machine, running its own specific Paralation Lisp implementation. The paralations and fields from each virtual computer are then built into (potentially) heterogeneous composite objects in a "meta" Paralation Lisp, which coordinates computation and communications between the components making up these distributed objects, and provides the insulating layer between the different architectures.

On the MasPar, which is currently a disjoint system, each processor element executes a global instruction stream broadcast by the Array Control Unit (ACU) applying the instructions to local data. In BLINDPEu, as this implementation of data-parallel EuLisp on the Maspar is called, each element of the processor array contains the state, stack pointer, program counter etc., of a single bytecode interpreter. The ACU repeatedly broadcasts all the instructions of the interpreter and each PE executes the code for its current instruction. Because the state information is local to each PE the interpreter can, and usually does, behave in a MIMD fashion. Hence this approach to implementing a functional data parallel language has also given the opportunity to experiment with MIMD-SIMD duality [20, 25].

Some recent additions to our prototype system have increased its robustness as well as advancing toward the overall goal:

limited fault tolerance: The servers involved in a particular computation are checked regularly (via PVM)—if a server fails before the computation is completed, an error is signalled to the client for the user program to take some suitable remedial action.

dynamic reconfiguration: Upon receipt of a particular condition the supervisor thread of a virtual processor initiates a shut-down procedure and transfers its resident data to another server in the network. It forwards any requests received after it has migrated, until all virtual processors have acknowledged the migration, whereupon the shut-down is completed.

4.2 Future Work

In the near future we plan to integrate the Maspar subsystem with that which runs on the workstations and shared-memory machines. However, we have not yet resolved upon a suitable method of specifying the characteristics of these heterogeneous paralations in a program. A coarse distinction, which we intend using initially, offers specializations of paralations in which the virtual processors simply correspond to the three classes of machine available to us.

In the long-term, a compiler producing non-architecture-specific byte-codes is required, and each target architecture then needs an interpreter that uses or ignores these byte-codes as appropriate. The byte-codes are thus portable within the system, enabling us to transfer compiled code between servers during application execution.

It remains to be seen whether we need paralation-specific byte-codes: the difficulty lies in the interpretation of the paralation operators at each server—we do not necessarily know at compile-time *which* server the code will be executed upon, and so we cannot make the compiled code server-specific. If we use and adapt our current general byte-code compiler, then each interpreter must be loaded with a server-specific module in which the paralation code resides—references to paralation operators can then be resolved by the function definitions in this locally-present module.

5 Conclusion

We believe that existing parallel programming models are insufficiently adaptable for the variety of parallel hardware available and therefore do not make effective use of programmer time and effort. While we do not consider our modest contribution addressing this question to be anything like a final solution, we hope it has provided some food for thought.

6 Acknowledgements

This paper has developed since the original presentation at MIT in September 1992. We particularly wish to acknowledge fruitful discussions with Randy Osborne on the dichotomies present in Linda and with Rishiyur Nikhil in which he pointed out the similarity of the data-flow model to paralations minus barrier synchronization after **elwise**.

References

1. Banâtre, J. P. and Le Metayer, D. *A New Computational Model and its Discipline of Programming.* INRIA Research Report, 566, 1986.
2. Banâtre, J. P. and Le Metayer, D. *Programming by Multiset Transformation.* IRISA, Campus Universitaire de Beaulieu, 35042 - Rennes Cedex, France, March 1990.
3. Banâtre, J. P. and Le Metayer, D. *Introduction to GAMMA,* pages 197–202. Proc. of Workshop on Research Directions in High-Level Parallel Programming Languages, Mont Saint-Michel, France, June 1991. LNCS 574.
4. Batey, D. J. and Padget, J. A. *Towards A Virtual Multicomputer.* Proc. of Workshop on Heterogeneous Processing at the 7th International Parallel Processing Symposium, University of Southern California, Newport Beach, CA, April 1993.
5. Batey, D.J. *DPL - A Distributed Implementation of Paralation Lisp.* Bath Mathematics and Computer Science Technical Report, 92-60, June 1992.
6. Bell, G. *Ultracomputers: A Teraflop Before Its Time,* volume 35(8), pages 27–47. Communications of the ACM, August 1992.
7. Berry, G. and Boudol, G. The Chemical Abstract Machine. In *1990 ACM Conference on Principle of Programming Languages,* pages 81–94. ACM, ACM Press, 1990.
8. Boehm, H-J. Type inference in the presence of type abstraction. In *ACM SIGPLAN Conference on Programming Language Design and Implementation,* pages 192–206. ACM, ACM Press, 1989.
9. Broadbery, P.A. and Burdorf, C. Applications of Telos. *Lisp and Symbolic Computation,* 6(1–2), 1993.
10. Butcher, P.R.A. *Lucinda, General Purpose Programming for Parallel Distributed Systems.* PhD thesis, University of York, 1993. in preparation.
11. Cann, D. *Retire Fortran?,* volume 35(8), pages 81–89. Communications of the ACM, August 1992.
12. Chandy, K. M. and Misra, J. *Parallel Program Design: A Foundation.* Addison Wesley Publishing Company, 1988.
13. Dietz, H. *Common Subexpression Induction.* MasPar Corporation, March 1992. Unpublished.
14. Dietz, H. and Cohen, W. *The MasPar MP-1 Is A MIMD?* MasPar Corporation, 1992. Unpublished.
15. Geist, G. and Sunderam, V. *Network Based Concurrent Computing on the PVM System.* Oak Ridge National Laboratory, 1991.
16. Gelernter, D. and Carriero, N. *Coordination Languages and their Significance,* volume 35, pages 97–107. Communications of the ACM, Feb 1992.
17. Halstead, R.H. Multilisp: A Language for Concurrent Symbolic Computation. *ACM Transactions on Programming Languages and Systems,* 7(4), October 1985.
18. Hoare, C.A.R. Communicating sequential processes. *Communication of the ACM,* 21(11):666–667, August 1978.
19. Hoare, C.A.R. *Communicating Sequential Processes.* Prentice-Hall International Series in Computer Science. Prentice-Hall, London, 1985.

20. Hudak, P. and Mohr, E. *Graphinators and Duality of MIMD–SIMD*, pages 224–235. ACM Conference on Lisp and Functional Programming, 1988.

21. Hutchinson, D.J.C. Lisp meets Linda. In *EUROPAL Workshop on High Performnce and Parallel Computing in Lisp*. 1990.

22. Jefferson, D. Virtual time. *ACM Transactions on Programming Languages and Systems*, 7(33):404–425, 1985.

23. Jesshope, C. R. and Flanders, P. M. *The VSA Definition*. Available from AMT Ltd., Reading, UK, 1990.

24. Merrall, S. *The Art of Memory*. PhD thesis, University of Bath, School of Mathematical Sciences, 1994. in preparation.

25. Merrall, S. C. and Padget, J. A. *Bridging the MIMD-SIMD Gap*. Proc. of BCS Workshop on Abstract Parallel Models, 1991.

26. Padget, J.A., Nuyens, G., and Bretthauer, H. An Overview of EuLisp. *Lisp and Symbolic Computation*, 6(1–2), 1993.

27. Sabot, G. W. *The Paralation Model: Architecture Independent SIMD Programming*. MIT Press, Cambridge, MA, 1988.

28. Steele, G. L., Jr., and Hillis, W. D. *Connection Machine Lisp: Fine-Grained Parallel Symbolic Processing*, pages 279–297. ACM Conference on Lisp and Functional Programming, 1986.

29. Sunderam, V. S. *PVM: A Framework for Parallel Distributed Computing*, volume 2(4), pages 315–339. Concurrency: Practice and Experience, Dec 1990.

30. Wagner, D.B. and Calder, B.G. Leapfrogging: A Portable Technique for Implementing Efficient Futures. In *Fourth ACM SIGPLAN Symposium on Principles and Practice of Parallel Programming*, pages 208–217. ACM, ACM Press, 1993.

Persistent Immutable Shared Abstractions*

Benny Yih, Mark Swanson, and Robert Kessler

Center for Software Science,
Department of Computer Science,
University of Utah,
Salt Lake City, UT 84112

Abstract. A write-once, read-many persistent store has been developed for *Concurrent Scheme*, a distributed-memory parallel Lisp for the *Mayfly* multicomputer. The prototype implementation supports the explicit store and implicit retrieval of instances of the Scheme data types. Items are stored into per node repositories, using a modified form of the original *Concurrent Scheme* "message" format. Potential access concurrency and transaction atomicity of the store are discussed. The efficacy of the prototype is demonstrated via its utilization within a parallel ray tracer, on a network implementation of *Concurrent Scheme*.

1   Introduction

Historically, the ability to retain data beyond a single program invocation has not been well supported within conventional programming languages. Some languages, such as Lisp and APL, offer this in a very coarse grain manner via snapshots of the running program's entire data state. The typical approach has been for individual applications to incorporate *ad hoc* solutions, such as custom translators to some disk file format, or translators to some backend database system. The mismatch between the application and traditional databases can be significant[31, 6]. Persistent languages offload this burden from the application, by offering a standard mechanism for retaining data.

This standard mechanism can introduce additional benefits, such as data sharing between applications and access to a store larger than the available virtual address space. This access to large stores was one impetus for adding a backing store to *Concurrent Scheme*[30, 13] (*CS*). The *CS* port of a public domain ray tracing program, Rayshade, is currently restricted to rendering simple scenes due to limited heap size. The *CS* model of encapsulating computation within *domains* restricts the number of graphic primitives (e.g., triangular surface patches) to only a few thousand within each domain, while complex scenes typically require orders of magnitude more primitives.

Rayshade and many similar applications do not require the ability to change the shared graphic primitives after their creation. Thus, we chose a simplified

---

* This work was supported in part by Hewlett-Packard Corporation, and by DARPA Contract No. N00014-91-J-4046.

write-once form of persistent store. This *immutability* offers the potential of better cache performance and increased concurrency, over a store incorporating a *multiple copy update* protocol. Such a protocol, however, could be supported on top of the current implementation, if deemed necessary. These *Persistent Immutable Shared Abstractions* (PISA) provide a solid foundation for persistence in *Concurrent Scheme.*

A second impetus for providing a persistent object base is a consequence of the performance characteristics of Scheme input in a distributed system. The original Rayshade database is textual in representation. Even in a sequential version of Scheme, reading the database and converting it into an internal Scheme representation is time consuming and, without restructuring of the database itself and of the reading process, inherently sequential. Thus, the reading process makes poor use of the resources available to a distributed concurrent system. Furthermore, in such a system, the reading process is even more expensive, as input functions carry a greater overhead imposed by synchronization mechanisms built into the input and output facilities. Taking advantage of the immutable nature of the objects allows for off-line, sequential creation of the persistent object base for repeated use by subsequent distributed instances of the Rayshade program.

2 Related Work

Related work on persistence added to programming languages is quite varied. Languages like Pascal, Algol, Prolog, ML, Ada, C++, Lisp, and Smalltalk have all been the target of persistence work. As far as Scheme is concerned, there have been no notable systems. We discuss several Lisp-based systems below; the list is not exhaustive, simply representative. Most of the systems surveyed emphasize persistent *objects* rather than a more general concept of persistent data. As we shall see, PISAs take the more general approach,[2] although a primitive object system is supported. The references on immutability help to demonstrate some of the nuances in constructing immutable systems.

2.1 OBJFADS

The OBJFADS[26] system, was designed on top of the Postgres[29, 28] relational database. This is based on the Common Lisp Object System[27, 17] (CLOS), and intended for multimedia applications. Instances are created as classes derived from a DBClass metaclass. Common Lisp datatypes are mapped to native Postgres types, or to a string which is evaluated. Specific instances are externally referenced by string names composed of their class name and integer object identifier, and within the database by just the object identifier.

Different grain consistency modes are supported: direct-update sends every change to the database, deferred-update batches changes between a begin

---

[2] Largely because Scheme does not enjoy the benefit of a rich and widely accepted standard object system as does Common Lisp.

transaction and commit, and `object-update` uses exclusive write locks. The cached object is invalidated by a database alerter, when changed by another application. Per class methods are stored in binary form, and class hierarchy information is stored in OBJFADS system catalogs.

2.2 PCLOS

PCLOS[20, 21] utilizes a virtual database interface, and implements persistence via the CLOS Meta-Object Protocol[14] (MOP). Protocol adapters map requests from the virtual, relational interface to any of the three specific databases currently supported. A `pclos-class` metaclass is used to include the extra mechanism for persistence. Object slots may be declared transient when the class is defined. Individual instances may switch between a transient and persistent state dynamically.

By default, instances initially retrieved from the database are represented by a *husk* which passes slot accesses back to the appropriate database. Within explicit transactions, caching of slots, or objects, locks those values from other processes. Write-through caching, as expected, sends slot updates onto the database.

Persistent slots do not support the more complex Lisp datatypes (e.g., methods), and most supported data types are stored within the databases as strings. An optional `after-retrieve` method is invoked for custom initializations, when instances are first retrieved. Data structure sharing between slots is lost when written to the database, or if transactions are rolled back. In-place modifications of cached data must explicitly notify PCLOS by rebinding the slot, or only be used inside transactions.

2.3 OXS

The Object eXchange Service[22], OXS, also provides a Common Lisp persistent store, as part of the Zeitgeist project. This store is targeted toward the computer aided design environment. Persistent items are internally referenced by a 64 bit identifier, with a number of global items, such as *nil*, predefined. Items are stored in a self-describing EXTernal Object Representation (EXTOR), which is intended as the language independent transmission format for distributed computing.

An Object Management System contains the OXS translation routines and policy rules. These govern behavior such as which are global items, the prefetching of indirectly referenced items, datatypes which constitute separate items, etc. Due to the likelihood of sharing, Lisp symbols are considered separate items. Within Lisp, items are represented by a *surrogate* which faults in the actual item if accessed. No concurrency control is presently specified.

2.4 CLiDE

CLOUDS Lisp Distributed Environments[23], *CLiDE*, offer very large-grained persistent objects, as part of CLOUDS object-oriented operating system project.

Each object emulates a traditional single-user Lisp environment, and can communicate with other CLOUDS system[24, 33, 9, 8] objects developed in CC++ or C-Eiffel. Objects are referenced via a *sysname* registered with CLOUDS. Each CC++ object contains conventional C++ objects, and C-Eiffel objects contain Eiffel objects. Both CC++ and C-Eiffel objects can contain multiple threads. Within these other languages, two thread types, *s-threads* (standard threads) and *cp-threads* (consistency-preserving threads), are supported. Automatic locking and recovery features are provided with *cp-threads*. Normal Unix executables are post-processed into a text *segment* and multiple data *segments* under programmer control. Each *cp-thread* applies read and write locks to the *segments* it uses.

A form of the *future*[12] construct for concurrent evaluations is provided in CLiDE, by a group of functions dealing with *future set* structures. These allow for the asynchronous remote evaluation of series of expressions by other objects (passed in the form of a string), and return of their values. For object integrity, Lisp symbols within the CLiDE environment have access control lists, governing local and remote evaluations.

2.5   Jasmine

Immutable versions are used in the Jasmine[32] software description model. User authentication and per database access control lists are employed for object protection. Objects are saved through a five phase protocol to support the atomic creation of replicas. The phases consist of the following:

location Find required number of live sites.
negotiation Request to store at the sites.
transfer Pack from volatile to compact form, and send to sites.
write Sites conditionally write the object.
commit Collect required successful writes for total operation to succeed.

Conversions between the volatile form for use, and the compact storage form, are specified as part of the class definition, using Xerox's Courier RPC language. Changes in the object class are supported via **version** clauses in the Courier descriptions. Instances are removed by manually deleting the individual replicas at the storage sites with that database. Each site maintains a mapping table of locations for each database, to assist object location. Lazy replication of requested objects by each database site is planned, based on access frequency, item size, and future usage hints.

3   Design of PISAs

The design of the PISA facility was inspired by the observation that the format of data within messages in the Concurrent Scheme implementation possessed many of the characteristics required for a persistent data representation. Data within messages is relocatable–it can be re-instantiated within the heap of any

Concurrent Scheme domain. Data within messages is also self-contained except for references to global objects in the form of global identifiers. Finally, the data within messages is totally encapsulated–no external references to the data exist and hence no changes can be made to the data until it is re-instantiated in some domain. We shall see in a later section that the message format was not completely adequate for the task and extensions were required.

Beyond the selection of the message as the foundation mechanism for object storage and retrieval lay the questions of which *CS* data types could, or should, be made persistent; of how the user interacts with the persistent store; of what naming mechanism should be used to permit retrieval of persistent data by name; and finally of what is an appropriate design for a PISA storage manager. All aspects of the design have been kept lean in terms of functionality, in the hope of allowing for an efficient implementation.

3.1 Persistent Data Types

In the spirit of providing a baseline level of functionality, persistence is not fully extended to all *CS* datatypes. Though the traditional sequential Scheme[25] data types [3] are well supported, only a small amount of context is preserved for the types introduced by *CS* (i.e., *placeholders, domains, threads, ports,* and *delay queues*). Preservation of their full context would entail such a great amount of state that, in the general case, checkpointing the entire computation would be a more suitable approach. The state of a undetermined placeholder, empty/full port, or closed delay queue might include threads blocked accessing it; the thread state would include a current call stack and the domains it currently occupies. The domain state would include a heap, a current thread, and other threads waiting to enter the domain.

3.2 Object Naming

Explicit interaction with the persistent store requires some kind of naming scheme. The prototype allowed items stored in a PISA database to be explicitly retrieved by their external **string** name (e.g., "Toto"). External names are coordinated through a "well known" central coordinator node[4]. This scheme is sufficient for a simple store, but with more users and more objects saved in the store, a more elaborate hierarchical naming scheme may be required.

3.3 Persistent Store Management

Each PISA database is implemented as a distributed store, utilizing the file system at every *CS* node to maximize concurrency and I/O bandwidth. Each thread

---

[3] *Continuations* are not currently supported in either the *Utah Scheme* or the *Concurrent Utah Scheme* implementations[4].

[4] A more elaborate scheme, with perhaps better scalability, might employ conditional local naming and asynchronous abort messages, in case of clashes.

that attempts to access the PISA store on a particular node does so through an internal (i.e., not user visible) domain that contains PISA bookkeeping data structures associated with that portion of the store. Standard domain entry semantics forces serialization of PISA access and guarantees data store integrity. Conventional Unix file locking is performed at the physical store level, to retain store integrity when multiple *CS* systems attempt access to the same data base on a node.

3.4 User Interface

Having determined an appropriate level of persistence for the data types, a procedural interface style of explicit store was chosen. The unit of explicit storage is the individual object. Both explicit and lazy retrieval are supported. Explicit retrieval by name allows specific objects, such as the "root" of an object graph, to be initially retrieved. Lazy retrieval then allows retrieval of only needed portions of an object graph, enabling the incremental access of data sets which may exceed the capacity of the available virtual address space.

Explicit registration is accomplished with the procedure `distill-to-pisa`, which returns a PISA corresponding to the Lisp data. This function abstracts the item into a relocatable format, and writes it to the backing store. A subsequent strict Scheme operation on the PISA, or an explicit application of `condense-from-pisa` to it, retrieves a copy of that entry from the database to the referencing node. These two operations mirror the export and import phases of the standard *CS* message-based copying between domains.

Items registered with a visible name (i.e., via `save-pisa`), will cause the entry of that name into a global table at the "well known" coordinator (node zero). This is then followed by the propagation of that update to the local replicas at the other nodes. Warnings can be issued when names are rebound, by setting a non-`nil` value for the global variable `lisp::*verbose-pisa*`. Similarly, the prevention of name rebinding can be enforced by setting the global variable `lisp::*immutable-name-pisa*`. Name lookup, via `find-pisa`, is first from the (possibly temporally-inconsistent) local replica[5] of this name table, then from the primary copy at node zero. A more decentralized scheme would require use of a more expensive multiple copy update protocol, such as *majority* voting. The higher communications cost of these protocols, while perhaps justified for a mutable persistent store, is overly elaborate for the spartan immutable store of the PISA system.

A default backing store is opened, if non exists, when items are registered or retrieved. Alternatively, the store may be explicitly named by giving an optional argument to the procedure `init-pisa-registry`. This initializes some bookkeeping information and opens the files at each node comprising the PISA store.

---

[5] The alternative would be to funnel all name lookup through the central node as well.

4 Current Implementation

The implementation of *CS* used for this work is Concurrent Utah Scheme (*CUS*). The current network *CUS* system is composed of identical Unix executables running on workstations connected by ethernet. The use of identical code images means that references to compiled procedures can simply be their virtual addresses, which will be identical on all nodes. In addition, symbols may also be referenced by their virtual addresses and identical copies of the symbol table are cached on each node at the same locations. We have taken the standard *CUS* executable and customized it with additional C and Lisp code to support the PISA system.

4.1 Extending the Message Format

Most *CS* datatypes have *by-value* copy semantics when crossing domain boundaries. These "boundaries" define the logical, encapsulated heaps that are private to each domain. This encapsulation at the domain level provides a natural mapping to the distributed-memory architecture of the *Mayfly* multicomputer, allowing each to reside physically at a different node. When instances of these data types are transferred between domains, they are first converted into a relocatable form which is copied to the new domain. Then this message is relocated into the address space of the new domain's heap.

As discussed earlier, our original design was intended to use this mechanism for the PISA system, using the relocatable form as the basis of what we would store. A significant problem with strictly using this message format concerns symbols. As previously mentioned, symbols in *CS*, and the addresses used to reference them, are always consistent across the nodes; this permits them to be passed by address. Since a PISA may be loaded into a version of *CS* that does not include the same set of symbols, or in which the symbols were assigned to different addresses, the original message structure has been enhanced to include symbol names.

The message format could also pass procedures by *reference* based on the assumption of identical code images. A PISA containing a procedure must contain its value, since the code image it is retrieved into may not contain the procedure reference or may contain it but at a different address. Extracting the "value" of a compiled procedure was problematic, since much of the information defining such a function is only included in the **fasl** (binary) files the procedure was loaded from. Our current Scheme compiler does not generate position independent object code. The relocation information, used to patch data and code references during the file load, is not retained at runtime. Each loaded Scheme procedure only retains its fixed start address for execution. In *CUS*, these addresses are kept the same at all the nodes by loading **fasl** files in identical order. Each file is initially loaded on node zero, then sent to the other nodes as a message, and loaded there. Our pragmatic solution is to record a reference to each procedure as it is loaded from a **fasl** file. When a procedure is to be saved into the store, we can extract the corresponding **fasl** fragment from the original object file.

Each function is later retrieved by reloading the fragment, editted to look like an normal **fasl** file, on all nodes.

The final, and quite difficult, issue in extending the message format involved saving closures. Saving the code of a closure is addressed by the method used for other procedures, but properly saving the environment is much more involved. *CS* addressed the issues presented by closure environments with respect to messages by specifying that closures be passed by reference rather than by value. Saving a closure into a PISA does not present this option. The problem arises with potential sharing of the environment with other closures and the fact that an environment may consist of multiple layers, represented as independent entry points or references into the environment. Such sharing must be saved to preserve the semantics of closures. The PISA system peels the contours of the (potentially shared) closure environment into separate items for the store. Each environment contour is *registered* with the store, so that repeated references will be detected and properly preserved.

Reflecting the reference semantics of *CS* closures which have been exported to other *domains*, retrieving such a closure restores a saved *domain* enclosing it also. The exported reference is then returned as the value for the retrieved PISA, maintaining the closure's uniqueness. As with instances of other *CS* global data types, the closure reference is cached in a global table at the node corresponding to that part of the store. On the other hand, local closures (i.e., non-exported) will be restored in the target domain, allowing the possibility of multiple copies when the PISA's value is required at different domains.

4.2 The PISA Type and Lazy Retrieval

The implementation of lazy retrieval was modeled on the placeholder type[16], and a new PISA data type was specified. The type has been designed such that strict operations encountering a PISA cause an *import* of the referenced item into the current *domain* heap. Thus, the PISA is similar to a placeholder, in that it represents a demand for a value, and may be used in place of the value until a strict operation is applied to it.

31 27 26		6 5 3 2	0
node	index	im-pisa. tag	escape immediate tag

Fig. 1. Internal structure of im-pisa datatype.

The type system employed by *CUS* uses the low three bits for the most commonly occuring Lisp items. This limit of eight possible types is expanded in two ways. An *escape pointer* tag indicates that the address in the rest of that

Lisp word points to a heap item preceded by another tag, differentiating the actual types. Alternatively, an *escape immediate* tag indicates that the adjacent three bits in the word designate the actual type. These additional *immediate* tags trade off the possible disadvantage of providing fewer bits for representing a value for the ability to determine the object's type directly from the Lisp item. This is implementationally very convenient when trying to represent items such as placeholders or PISAs, whose values are not necessarily available, and whose identity alone is sufficient for many uses. The new `im-pisa` datatype, adopting an unused *escape immediate* tag value, was introduced to provide a convenient handle to the PISA system for accessing entries present within the backing store. Implementationally, this `im-pisa` (Fig. 1) consists of a single Lisp word, containing the Lisp tag, the *CS* node number, and a node index field. The node number is a positive integer reflecting the portion of the backing store at which the PISA value is contained. This is the physical node for the domain from which the value was originally registered. The index is encoded as offset binary, and converted back to two's complement notation when manipulated as a `fixnum`. Positive index values denote distinct items retrievable from the store, while negative values denote local *annotations* within a single stored item. Local annotations encode the additional out-of-band information for properly restoring items such as closures or placeholders. This PISA type is analogous to the *Object Identifier* (OID) found in many persistent object systems.

4.3 A Detailed Look at the Operational Aspects

Each database entry heap (Fig. 2) consists of a standard (*CS*) message header and an expanded message body. Besides the normal message value, the body contains an additional local annotation count, and a vector of local annotations. The fixed length header contains a number of standard fields used to relocate the message contents into the heap of the target domain. These header fields are: (a pointer to) the message value, the size of header plus body, the original base address of the heap, etc. If present, local annotations are encoded as Lisp lists within the message body.

During the message creation, copied Lisp subitems are compacted into the message body, much like the copying phase of a local garbage collection. As noted earlier, certain data types require special treatment to capture their semantic content. Lisp symbols are translated, or *swizzled*, into symbols within the database's table of print and package names for that node.[6] The occurrence of structures cause the creation of an entry in this table under their type, describing slot names, print method, etc. This translation table is synchronized with the current Lisp image, as part of the initial PISA setup, on the first database access. New symbols, if present in the translation table, are entered into the *CS* symbol table via the standard `intern` mechanism. Registration of items using

---

[6] Utah Scheme is implemented on a base that also supports a Common Lisp implementation; hence, symbols have packages.

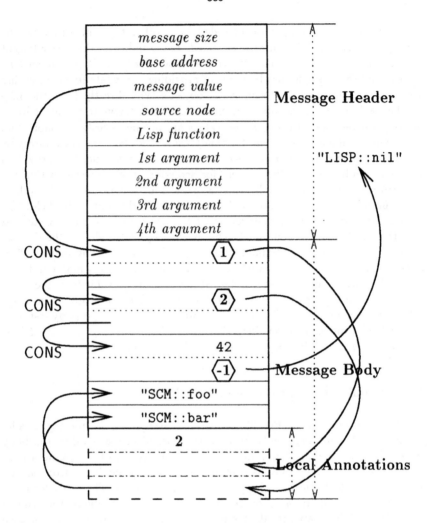

Fig. 2. Database entry heap for the list '(foo bar 42).

additional symbols or structures incrementally update the backing store version of the table. Due to its prevalence, the symbol nil is defined at table creation.

When a strict Lisp operation requires the value of a PISA, a number of caches are checked before retrieval from the store. First, the FIFO (first in, first out) cache at the *domain* is checked. Then the local node's global cache is checked, and finally the store's global cache. Both of these node caches are updated when global items are retrieved. The instances of local items are only cached at the requesting *domain*, and possibly flushed during a garbage collection at that *domain*. The size of retrieved PISA heaps in the FIFO guide the number retained after each GC. An attempt is made to achieve a certain minimal heap free space after the GC, set by a Scheme global variable.

Retrievals are made from the node *suggested* by the node field within the PISA, modulo the current number of nodes. Upon heap retrieval, symbols are translated back to the corresponding global Lisp symbols at the store's node. This message is then sent back to the requesting node. At the target *domain*, addresses within the message are adjusted to their new heap locations. After this, any local annotations are converted back to Lisp items, which are then used to replace local PISA references of that entry.

When encountered during the copying, global *CS* items, such as *CS* placeholders, are registered as separate entries. Each abstracts to a heap with a local annotation of its current state. At present, these *annotations* capture an incomplete description of the item's current state, ignoring *domains* occupied by a *thread*, the current *threads* blocked on a *placeholder*, etc.

CS compiled functions, and their associated constant data, are loaded into a separate BPS (binary program space) heap which is not garbage collected. To support storage of functions, each function is prefaced by a 64 bit header. This header is comprised of information used to retrieve the corresponding fasl code from the object file. The fasl file loader in the Lisp kernel assigns an index number to each file as it is loaded. Each top-level Lisp form results in a characteristic fasl code pattern of BPS heap allocations, followed by fasl commands dealing with data and code, and ended by execution of initialization code. The file offsets for the start of this pattern, and of each function within the form, are packed into the header bits, along with the file index number.

When functions are stored as PISAs, the section of fasl for the top-level form is copied into a heap. Within the heap, this section is preceded by any additional fasl commands for symbols, strings, or constants defined earlier in the original object file used within the section. The offset of the function start within the heap is stored as the last 32 bits of the heap. This offset is used to return the proper function start address back to *Lisp*, as the fasl is reloaded.

4.4 PISA Object System

As a special case, instances of a rudimentary structure-based object system[34] include explicit *CS* and PISA support. These highly stylized structures inherit from a "special" structure type, and are treated differently when registered with the PISA store. They are abstracted into a local *annotation* within the message, which contains the class name and slot values, but not the class methods. Upon retrieval, the slot values are bound to a new instance of the current class with that name, relying on an assumption of compatible methods. Occurrences of other object instances within the slots are separately registered as additional PISAs, unlike instances of conventional *CS* data types.

Ephemeral object classes, specified by a keyword in the class definition, provide support for clustering with the store. Instances of these are registered as local PISAs within the same message as the enclosing Lisp item, possibly violating any object level sharing of these instances with another entry in the store. This convention is similar to the deep versus shallow copying scheme, present in some other systems[10]. This technique allows simple object trees of closely associated items to be registered, and retrieved, as a single entry. Use of more specific hints (such as *Mneme*[18, 19] *segments*, or *Wisconsin Storage System*[5] *pages*) to cluster certain named items near each other is not planned.

Shallow copying (i.e., pass by reference) of instances across *domains* is supported via the specification of **unique** object classes. These are implemented via *proxy* instances which forward each slot or method request to the actual object. The actual object, when created at the original *domain*, is captured in a closure. Support for clustering of **unique** objects [as with other closures] is not presently envisioned.

4.5 PISA Storage Management

At the file system interface, *tdbm*[2] routines are currently used to manipulate the persistent heaps. Each is stored as a value keyed on its global PISA index, in the database for items registered at that node. These routines are also used with a subsidiary database, for symbols and structure descriptions associated with registered items at each node. As part of the PISA initialization on the first store or retrieval from the database, all the stored symbols are **intern**ed into the current *CS* symbol table. Structure descriptions are also re-introduced, if not already present, due to their anticipated frequency of use by the regular items in the PISA store.

The storage layout in tdbm, like *ndbm* in Unix, is based on fixed-size pages. Small items are packed into single *direct* pages, and are found via a binary search of the directory vector at the beginning of the page. The actual items are stored from the end of page. Large items are stored within a number of contiguous *indirect* pages, and referenced from the direct page for that key's hash value. Each top-level commit creates an intention file with actions that will update the database, using *after-image physical logging*[11]. This file contains the shadow pages which will replace pages in the database.

Though transaction semantics are employed within the PISA system, the additional support at the *CS* layer for explicit user level transactions is not planned. The [distributed] garbage collection of unreachable items within the store is not currently performed. At some future date, tdbm may replaced by a more elaborate backend, such as the *EXODUS* storage system[3].

5 Current Status

The PISA prototype currently works well enough to support the Rayshade application, allowing the rendering of some simple images such as the Utah teapot[7, 1] (about 4 K polygons versus a maximum around 1.5 K polygons in CUS).

Table 1. Timings of Basic Scheme Operations (μsecs).

Operation	PISA/CUS
(identity 1)	1.8
(cons 1 '())	2.5
(make-vector 100 0)	112.8
(+ 1.0 1.0)	15.6

Table 2. Timings of Basic Concurrent Scheme Operations (μsecs).

Operation	PISA/CUS local	PISA/CUS remote
(make-domain)	651.1	12635.0
(make-thread)	1761.4	1700.2
(make-placeholder)	45.0	—
(touch 1)	32	—
(touch $\langle ph \rangle$), value 1	892	24444
(determine $\langle ph \rangle$ 1)	844	12748
(determine $\langle ph \rangle$ vec-100)	2624	18364
(apply-within-domain list '() $\langle domain \rangle$)	1856.8	10450.1
(apply-within-domain $\langle closure \rangle$ '())	2761.5	11343.5

Table 3. Timings of Conventional CUS Fasl Loads (msecs).

Operation	Time
1st (load ''840-lines.b'')	1441
other (load ''840-lines.b'')	477
1st (load ''1-line.b'')	53
other (load ''1-lines.b'')	19

Table 4. Timings of Basic PISA Operations (msecs).

Operation	PISA/CUS
1st (load ''840-lines.b'')	1851
other (load ''840-lines.b'')	715
1st (load ''1-line.b'')	145
other (load ''1-lines.b'')	106
(init-pisa-registry ''bar.db'')	5942
(distill-to-pisa 0)	13
(distill-to-pisa vec-100)	465
(save-pisa vec-40 ''foo0'')	981
(save-pisa vec-40 ''foo1'')	439
(touch ⟨pisa⟩) *local*	2.8
(touch ⟨pisa⟩) *cache*	0.6
(touch ⟨pisa⟩) *remote*	1.6
(find-pisa ''foo1'') *local*	1.4
(find-pisa ''foo1'') *remote*	1.2

The addition of PISAs to *CS* has resulted in no significant performance hit on the system. The only noticeable change has been in the speed of loading files. In conventional CUS, the main factors which affect file load time are file system buffering and virtual memory paging. Measurements are shown for a medium size file of 840 lines (55K), and a worst case of a single line file (0.5K), in CUS (Table 3) on a HP9000 model 370 running BSD 4.3 with 64M of swap and 16M of physical memory. The initial load warms up the file system buffers, while subsequent loads just touch new BPS pages. This gives a speedup of 3 for the artificial case of reloading the same file into CUS. The PISA system (Table 4) involve the additional factors of performing a database transaction to update a file name to file index mapping, and recording the file offsets at header of each compiled Scheme procedure in BPS. The additional bookkeeping necessary to support remembering the code fragment locations adds about 30% to the initial medium size file load, and triples the single line file load time.

To illustrate relative speeds, Table 1 has times for some basic sequential Scheme operations, and Table 2 gives the timings of some basic concurrent operations. The latencies of the PISA interface functions are then presented in Table 4.

6 Summary, Contributions, and Future Work

A store for immutable, persistent data has been implemented and integrated into an existing distributed implementation of Scheme. Its use has been demonstrated by incorporation into a distributed ray tracing program. In particular, its ability to persist code fragments is of wide interest, and is being used in the Mach Shared Objects[15] project, a distributed client/server style object manager on top of the Mach operating system supporting bilingual programming in Lisp and C++.

PISAs provide the mechanism to persist objects and their associated methods. We plan to further explore the *use* of these mechanisms from both linguistic and algorithmic points of view. For example, exploiting the space-conserving nature of lazily-loaded objects requires conscious design of data structures and usage. It has proven insufficient to simply move existing code to a persistent, lazily loaded environment in the expectation of achieving the goal of utilizing large datasets in a constrained virtual address space.

A   PISA Interface

This appendix specifies the syntax for the additional built-in procedures introduced by the PISA version of Concurrent Scheme. These supplement the standard procedures of sequential Scheme and Concurrent Scheme.

(init-registry &optional *db-name*)   essential procedure
   Init-registry sets up the backing store, and name tables, on all the nodes using the base filename string *db-name*. The node numbers are appended to *db-name* for the actual tdbm files comprising the store. If the store contains any symbols, or structure definitions, they are interned into the current *CS*. The string *db-name* initially defaults to "t-abstracts."

(distill-to-pisa *item* &optional *no-caching*)   essential procedure
No-caching must be a boolean, indicating whether this *item* should be forgotten after it is written to the backing store. **Distill-to-pisa** explicits registers *item*, and it's transitive closure, with the store. An instance of the PISA datatype which maps to *item* to is returned.

(save-pisa *item* *name* &optional *no-caching*)   essential procedure
No-caching must be a boolean, indicating whether this *item* should be forgotten after it is written to the backing store. **Save-pisa** explicits registers *item*, and it's transitive closure, with the store under the string *name*. An instance of the PISA datatype which maps to *item* to is returned.

(find-pisa *name*)   essential procedure
The value associated with the string *name* within the backing store, if any, is returned; otherwise **nil** is returned.

(touch *item* &optional *wait-outside* *no-stack-splice*)   essential procedure
Wait-outside and *no-stack-splice* must be a boolean. If *item* is neither a placeholder nor pisa, the original *item* is returned. If *item* is a determined placeholder, the value of the placeholder is returned (following standard domain copy semantics). If *item* is an undetermined placeholder, the thread blocks until the placeholder is determined and then returns a copy of the placeholder's value. If

wait-outside is specified as #t, then the thread vacates the domain before doing the touch and re-enters when it can deliver the value. If *item* is a pisa, the associated value is returned from the backing store. This value remains unique if the original was a Concurrent Scheme global datatype, otherwise another copy is returned when the value is no longer cached.

lisp::*verbose-pisa*   essential variable

If #t, a warning is issued when a *name* is rebound.

lisp::*immutable-name-pisa*   essential variable

If #t, rebinding any *name* is treated as an error.

References

1. Jim Blinn. What, teapots again ? *IEEE Computer Graphics and Applications*, 7(9):61–63, September 1987.
2. Barry Brachman and Gerald Neufeld. TDBM: a DBM library with atomic transactions. In *Proceedings of the Summer 1992 USENIX Conference*, pages 63–80, San Antonio, TX, June 8-12, 1992. Usenix Association.
3. Michael J. Carey, David J. DeWitt, Joel E. Richardson, and Eugene J. Shekita. Storage management for objects in EXODUS. In Won Kim and Frederick H. Lochovsky, editors, *Object-Oriented Concepts, Databases, and Applications*, pages 341–369. Addison-Wesley, 1989.
4. Harold Carr. Utah Scheme version 1.0 users guide. Technical Report CSS Opnote 89-02, Center for Software Sciences, Department of Computer Science, University of Utah, Salt Lake City, Utah 84112, 1989.
5. H-T. Chou, David J. DeWitt, Randy H. Katz, and Anthony C. Klug. Design and implementation of the Wisconsin storage system. *Software–Practice and Experience*, 15(10):943–962, October 1983.
6. W.P. Cockshot. Persistent programming and secure data storage. *Information and Storage Technology*, 29(5):249–256, June 1987.
7. Frank Crow. The origins of the teapot. *IEEE Computer Graphics and Applications*, 7(1):8–19, January 1987.
8. Partha Dasgupta, R. Ananthanarayanan, Sathis Menon, Ajay Mohindra, and Raymond Chen. Distributed programming with objects and threads in the Clouds system. *Computing Systems*, 4(3):243–275, Summer 1991.
9. Partha Dasgupta, R. Ananthanarayanan, Sathis Menon, Ajay Mohindra, Mark Pearson, Raymond Chen, and Christoper Wilkenloh. Language and operating system support for distributed programming in Clouds. In *Proceedings of the Symposium on Experiences with Distributed and Multiprocesor Systems (SEDMS II)*, pages 321–340, Atlanta, GA, March 21-22, 1990. Usenix Association.
10. Keith E. Gorlen, Sanford M. Orlow, and Perry S. Plexico. *Data Abstraction and Object-Oriented Programming in C++*. John Wiley & Sons, 1990.
11. Theo Haerder and Andreas Reuter. Principles of transaction-oriented database recovery. *ACM Computing Surveys*, 15(4):287–317, December 1983.
12. R.H. Halstead Jr. Multilisp: A language for concurrent symbolic computation. *ACM Transactions on Programming Languages and Systems*, 7(4):501–538, October 1985.

13. R. R. Kessler and M. R. Swanson. Concurrent Scheme. In T. Ito and R. H. Halstead, editors, *Parallel Lisp: Languages and Systems*, pages 200–234. Springer-Verlag, 1990.

14. Gregor Kiczales, Jim des Rivières, and Daniel G. Bobrow. *The Art of the Metaobject Protocol.* MIT Press, 1991.

15. Gary Lindstrom and Robert Kessler. Mach shared objects. In *Proceedings of the DARPA Software Technology Conference 1992*, pages 279–280, Los Angeles, CA, April 1992, 1992. DARPA.

16. J. S. Miller. *MultiScheme, A Parallel Processing System Based on MIT Scheme.* PhD thesis, Department of Electrical Engineering and Computer Science, MIT, August 1987.

17. David A. Moon. The Common Lisp object-oriented programmin language standard. In Won Kim and Frederick H. Lochovsky, editors, *Object-Oriented Concepts, Databases, and Applications*, pages 49–78. Addison-Wesley, 1989.

18. J. Eliot B. Moss. Design of the Mneme persistent object store. *ACM Transactions on Information Systems*, 8(2):103–139, April 1990.

19. J. Eliot B. Moss and Tony Hosking. Managing persistent data with Mneme: User's guide to the client interface. Technical report, Object Oriented Systems Laboratory, Department of Computer and Information Science, University of Massachusetts, Amherst, MA 01003, March 1989.

20. Andreas Paepcke. PCLOS: a critical review. *ACM SIGPLAN Notices*, 24(10):221–237, October 1989.

21. Andreas Paepcke. PCLOS: stress testing CLOS. *ACM SIGPLAN Notices*, 25(10):221–237, October 1990.

22. Girish Pathak, John Joseph, and Steve Ford. Object eXchange service for an object-oriented database system. In *IEEE 5th International Conference on Data Engineering*, pages 27–34, 1989.

23. Mark P. Pearson and Partha Dasgupta. CLiDE: a distributed, symbolic programming system based on large-grained persistent objects. Technical report, Distributed Systems Laboratory, College of Computing, Georgia Institute of Technology, Atlanta, GA, 1991.

24. Umakishore Ramachandran and M. Yousef A. Khalidi. An implementation of distributed shared memory. In *Proceedings of the First USENIX/SERC Workshop on Experiences with Distributed and Multiprocesor Systems*, pages 21–38, Fort Lauderdale, FL, October 5-6, 1989. Usenix Association.

25. J. Rees and W. Clinger. Revised[3] Report on the Algorithmic Language Scheme. *SIGPLAN Notices*, 21(12):37–79, December 1986.

26. Lawrence A. Rowe. A shared object hierarchy. In Michael Stonebraker and Lawrence A. Rowe, editors, *The Postgres Papers*, number UCB/ERL M86/85, pages 91–117. Electronics Research Laboratory, University of California, Berkeley, June 1987.

27. Guy L. Steele Jr. *Common Lisp: The Language.* Digital Press, second edition, 1990.

28. Michael Stonebraker. The design of the Postgres storage system. In Michael Stonebraker and Lawrence A. Rowe, editors, *The Postgres Papers*, number UCB/ERL M86/85, pages 69–90. Electronics Research Laboratory, University of California, Berkeley, June 1987.

29. Michael Stonebraker and Greg Kemnitz. The POSTGRES next-generation database management system. *Communications of the ACM*, 34(10):78–92, October 1991.

30. M. R. Swanson. *DOMAINS–A Mechanism for Specifying Mutual Exclusion and Disciplined Data Sharing in Concurrent Symbolic Programs.* PhD thesis, Department of Computer Science, University of Utah, June 1991.

31. D.C. Tsichritzis and O.M. Nierstrasz. Fitting round objects into square databases. In S. Gjessing and K. Nygaard, editors, *ECOOP '88: European Conference on Object-Oriented Programming*, volume 322 of *Lecture Notes in Computer Science*, pages 283–299, Oslo, Norway, August 15-17, 1988. Springer-Verlag.

32. Douglas Wiebe. A distributed repository for immutable persistent objects. *ACM SIGPLAN Notices*, 21(11):453–465, November 1986.

33. C. J. Wilkenloh, U. Ramachandran, S. Menon, R. J. LeBlanc, M. Y. A. Khalidi, P. W. Hutto, P. Dasgupta, R. C. Chen, J. M. Bernabéu, W. F. Appelbe, and M. Ahamad. The Clouds experience: Building an object-based distributed operating system. In *Proceedings of the First USENIX/SERC Workshop on Experiences with Distributed and Multiprocesor Systems*, pages 333–347, Fort Lauderdale, FL, October 5-6, 1989. Usenix Association.

34. Benny Yih. Ray tracing in Concurrent Scheme. Technical Report CSS Opnote 91-02, Center for Software Sciences, Department of Computer Science, University of Utah, Salt Lake City, Utah 84112, 1991.

Asynchrony and Real-Time
in Distributed Systems

Mario Tokoro* and Ichiro Satoh **

Department of Computer Science, Keio University
3-14-1, Hiyoshi, Kohoku-ku, Yokohama, 223, Japan
Tel: +81-45-560-1150   Fax: +81-45-560-1151

Abstract. In this paper we attempt to reveal the most essential properties of distributed computations. We classify distributed computation into four forms according to asynchrony and real-time properties. We try to develop formalisms for the four categories based on a process calculus. The formalisms allow us to describe and analyze both globally and locally temporal properties as well as behavioral properties of distributed objects and interactions among them. We also outline a programming language for asynchronous real-time computing. We here discuss issues remaining to be solved and show some prospects.

1   Introduction

In the next decade computing environments will become more widely distributed, open-ended, and ever-changing. In this paper we attempt to extract the most essential problems to be solved in distributed computing and then propose some approaches to solve these problems by both theoretical and practical means.

We first characterize distributed computing in contrast with concurrent computing. Concurrent computing is characterized by its having more than one activity (or object) in computation and no transmission delay in communication among them. Communication without delay means that there is no notion of distance in concurrent computing. Thus, communication is synchronous, in the sense that one gives information to another and the other receives it at the same time. It is impossible that one gives information to another but the other does not receive it. Consequently, a concurrent system has a *unique global view* of the system.

In contrast to this, distributed computing can be characterized by communication delay among activities (or objects). Hence, communication is *asynchronous*, in the sense that one gives information to another and the other will receive it at a later time. It is even possible that one gives information to another and the other will not receive it. The delay prevents distributed objects from

* Email: *mario@mt.cs.keio.ac.jp*, Also with Sony Computer Science Laboratory Inc.
3-14-13 Higashi-Gotanda, Shinagawa-ku, Tokyo, 141, Japan.
** Email: *satoh@mt.cs.keio.ac.jp*

knowing the current status of other objects. Consequently, a distributed system has no *unique global view* of the system.

The lack of the unique global view is one of the most important characteristics of distributed computing, and is the major source of difficulty to design and develop efficient distributed systems. In distributed systems, objects may not be able to escape from dead-lock situations. This is because they must wait for messages which will never arrive each other. Objects and networks can be inactive and faulty. Since it is difficult to detect such situations by means of logical methods, objects often use timeout handling. That is to say, *time* is the last resort that an object can depend on in a distributed environment. Also, many distributed systems must often cooperate with the real-world where the time is *real*. Thus, the necessity of the real-time properties in distributed computing is inevitably derived.

In this paper, we reveal real-time and asynchrony properties in distributed computation. The organization of the paper is as follows. Section 2 proposes a new formalism for reasoning about distributed real-time computing. We classify distributed real-time computing by two criteria, communication and time, and then try to develop formalisms for distributed systems according to the criteria. Section 3 proposes an object-oriented programming language for describing distributed real-time systems. The language provides temporal facilities to manage asynchronously interacting objects by using time constraints. Section 4 relates the notion of asynchrony and real-time with a high level abstract model for future distributed computing called *Computational Field Model* and discusses possibilities of formalizing the model.

2 Formal Systems for Asynchronous Real-Time Computing

In this section we present possibilities of formalizing distributed computation. As we noted above, asynchrony and real-time are characteristic properties in distributed computation. We first classify the computation systems according to two criteria: whether communication is *synchronous* or *asynchronous*, and whether the objects measure time by the *same clock* or *different clocks*. The former means whether the instants of time that the sender object sends and the receiver object receives are the same or not. The latter means whether the time basis of each object is valid for the whole system or only within each object. We show four combinations classified according to the criteria as follows:

- The first combination is a system with synchronous communication using the same clock. This corresponds to a *concurrent* real-time system. In this system, objects can interact with one another following the same global time.

- The second combination is a system with synchronous communication using different clocks. This corresponds to a system where objects following different local clocks interact with one another by using synchronous communications.

- The third combination is a system with asynchronous communication using the same clock. This is a system where objects are distributed and have the same clock. This models a system where distributed objects can share the global clock, such as a world wide system with using a satellite-synchronized clock.

- The fourth one is a system with asynchronous communication using different clocks. This corresponds to a system where objects are distributed and have different clocks. This is the general model for widely distributed systems with high-speed computers.

The correctness of programs for distributed computation depends not only on the logical results of the computation, but also on the time at which the results are produced. Therefore, the construction of its programs is more complex and difficult, especially when we must treat asynchrony in interactions. Consequently, we need the support of formal models for reasoning about asynchrony and real-time properties in computation. Hereafter, we investigate formalisms for the above combinations. The formalisms presented in this paper are based on Milner's CCS [2] for its high expressive power of interactions among concurrent objects.

2.1 RtCCS: Formalizing Real-Time Concurrent Objects

In [3], we investigated a formal model for the first combination, i.e., concurrent real-time systems, by extending CCS to represent temporal properties in real-time computing. In the extension, we represent temporal property by two aspects: the passage of time and timed behavior. We introduced two temporal primitives.

- *The passage of time* is modeled as a special action. The tick action is a synchronous broadcast message over all objects and corresponds to the passage of one unit of the global time. It is described as $\sqrt{}$. The advance of time can be represented as a sequence of tick actions and is viewed as discrete time.

- *Timed behavior* is modeled as a special binary operator which has the semantics of timeout handling, written as $\langle\ ,\ \rangle_t$, and called the *timeout* operator. $\langle P, Q \rangle_t$ denotes an object that after t time units becomes Q, unless P performs any actions prior to that. Intuitively $\langle P, Q \rangle_t$ behaves as object P if P can execute an initial transition within t units of time, whereas $\langle P, Q \rangle_t$ behaves as object Q if P does not perform any action within t units of time.

The definition of RtCCS is given as follows. For details about syntax and semantics, please refer to [3].

Let $a, b, \ldots$ be communication action names and $\overline{a}, \overline{b}, \ldots$ the complementary action of $a, b, \ldots$ respectively. Let τ denote an internal action, $\sqrt{}$ a tick action, and $\mathcal{L}$ be the set of action names and the complementary action names, ranged over by $\ell, \ell', \ldots$. Let $Act \equiv \mathcal{L} \cup \{\tau\}$ be the set of behavior actions, ranged over by $\alpha, \beta, \ldots$. The set $\mathcal{E}$ of RtCCS expressions ranged over by $E, E_1, E_2, \ldots$ is defined recursively by the following abstract syntax.

$$
\begin{aligned}
E ::= \ &0 && \text{(Terminated Object)} \\
\mid \ &X && \text{(Process Variable)} \\
\mid \ &\alpha.E && \text{(Action Prefix)} \\
\mid \ &E_1 + E_2 && \text{(Summation)} \\
\mid \ &E_1 \mid E_2 && \text{(Composition)} \\
\mid \ &E[f] && \text{(Relabeling)} \\
\mid \ &E \setminus L && \text{(Restriction)} \\
\mid \ &\text{rec } X : E && \text{(Recursion)} \\
\mid \ &\langle E_1, E_2 \rangle_t && \text{(Timeout)}
\end{aligned}
$$

The syntax of RtCCS is essentially the same as that of CCS, except for the newly introduced tick action $\sqrt{}$ and timeout operator. Intuitively, the meaning of object constructions are as follows: 0 represents a terminated object; $\alpha.E$ performs an action α and then behaves like E; $E_1 + E_2$ is the object which may behave as E_1 or E_2; $E_1 \mid E_2$ represents processes E_1 and E_2 executing concurrently; $E[f]$ behaves like E but with the actions relabeled by function f; $E \setminus L$ behaves like E but with actions in $L \cup \bar{L}$ prohibited $(L \subset \mathcal{L})$; rec $X : E$ binds the free occurrences of X in E but we shall often use the more readable notation $X \stackrel{\text{def}}{=} E$ instead.

The operational semantics of RtCCS is given as a labeled transition system $\langle \mathcal{E}, Act \cup \{\sqrt{}\}\}, \{ \xrightarrow{\mu} \mid \mu \in Act \cup \{\sqrt{}\} \} \rangle$ where $\xrightarrow{\mu}$ is a transition relation $(\xrightarrow{\mu} \subseteq \mathcal{E} \times \mathcal{E})$. The definition of the semantics is structurally given in two steps. The first step defines the relations $\xrightarrow{\alpha}$ for each $\alpha \in Act$. The inference rules determining $\xrightarrow{\alpha}$ are shown in Figure 1. This is based on the standard operational semantics for CCS except for the addition of the timeout operator. The second step defines the relation $\xrightarrow{\sqrt{}}$ by inference shown in Figure 2. The new action $\sqrt{}$ does not effect the rules of CCS.

We now illustrate how to describe real-time object in RtCCS. Suppose an interaction between a client and a sever object: the client object (*Client*) sends a request message ($\overline{req}$) and then waits for a return message (*ret*). If the return message is not received within 6 units of time, then it sends the request message again; upon reception of a request message (*req*), the server object (*Server*) sends a return message ($\overline{ret}$) after an internal execution of 5 units of time. These objects are denoted as follows:

$$
Client \stackrel{\text{def}}{=} \overline{req}.\langle ret.0, \, Client \rangle_6
$$

$$
Server \stackrel{\text{def}}{=} req.\langle 0, \overline{ret}.Server \rangle_5
$$

RtCCS can formally describe the aspects of time dependence in real-time systems and enjoys many pleasant properties of CCS. As proof techniques, we have introduced some timed equivalences which can verify whether two objects are indistinguishable in their time properties as well as in their functional behavior. We leave details of the equivalences to [3].

2.2 DtCCS: Formalizing Real-Time Objects with Clocks

We here present a possibility of formalizing the second combination, i.e., real-time computing with different clocks. It is well-known that clocks on different

$$\alpha.E \xrightarrow{\alpha} E$$
$$E_1 \xrightarrow{\alpha} E_1' \qquad \text{implies } E_1 + E_2 \xrightarrow{\alpha} E_1', \ E_2 + E_1 \xrightarrow{\alpha} E_1'$$
$$E_1 \xrightarrow{\alpha} E_1' \qquad \text{implies } E_1|E_2 \xrightarrow{\alpha} E_1'|E_2, \ E_2|E_1 \xrightarrow{\alpha} E_2|E_1'$$
$$E_1 \xrightarrow{\alpha} E_1', \ E_2 \xrightarrow{\bar{a}} E_2' \quad \text{implies } E_1|E_2 \xrightarrow{\tau} E_1'|E_2'$$
$$P \xrightarrow{\alpha} P' \qquad \text{implies } P[f] \xrightarrow{f(\alpha)} P'[f]$$
$$P \xrightarrow{\alpha} P', \ \alpha \notin L \cup \bar{L} \quad \text{implies } P \setminus L \xrightarrow{\alpha} P' \setminus L$$
$$P\{\text{rec } X : P/X\} \xrightarrow{\alpha} P' \ \text{implies rec } X : P \xrightarrow{\alpha} P'$$
$$E_1 \xrightarrow{\alpha} E_1', \ t > 0 \qquad \text{implies } \langle E_1, E_2 \rangle_t \xrightarrow{\alpha} E_1'$$
$$E_2 \xrightarrow{\alpha} E_2' \qquad \text{implies } \langle E_1, E_2 \rangle_0 \xrightarrow{\alpha} E_2'$$

Fig. 1. Operational Rules on Global Time

$$0 \xrightarrow{\surd} 0$$
$$\ell.E \xrightarrow{\surd} \ell.E$$
$$E_1 \xrightarrow{\surd} E_1', \ E_2 \xrightarrow{\surd} E_2' \qquad \text{implies } E_1 + E_2 \xrightarrow{\surd} E_1' + E_2'$$
$$E_1 \xrightarrow{\surd} E_1', \ E_2 \xrightarrow{\surd} E_2', \ E_1|E_2 \not\xrightarrow{\ } \text{ implies } E_1|E_2 \xrightarrow{\surd} E_1'|E_2'$$
$$P \xrightarrow{\surd} P' \qquad \text{implies } P[f] \xrightarrow{\surd} P'[f]$$
$$P \xrightarrow{\surd} P' \qquad \text{implies } P \setminus L \xrightarrow{\surd} P' \setminus L$$
$$P\{\text{rec } X : P/X\} \xrightarrow{\surd} P' \qquad \text{implies rec } X : P \xrightarrow{\surd} P'$$
$$E_1 \xrightarrow{\surd} E_1', \ t > 0 \qquad \text{implies } \langle E_1, E_2 \rangle_t \xrightarrow{\surd} \langle E_1', E_2 \rangle_{t-1}$$
$$E_2 \xrightarrow{\surd} E_2' \qquad \text{implies } \langle E_1, E_2 \rangle_0 \xrightarrow{\surd} E_2'$$

Fig. 2. Temporal Rules on Global Time

processors can never run at the same rate. Differences among clocks may lead interactions among objects to failure. Therefore, we need a formalism for reasoning about such locally temporal properties in distributed real-time programs. We here propose such a formalism, called DtCCS, by extending RtCCS, but we leave its detail to [4].

Before giving an exposition of DtCCS, we first present assumptions on the modeling of local time. If relative motion of all processors is negligible, from Einstein's Relativity, the passage of physical *time* in every processor elapses at the same rate. On the other hand, each actual local clock reads its own current time by translating the passage of the global time into its own time coordinate according to its own measurement rate. Clock rates are different from each other and these rates may vary within a certain bound. Therefore, local times measured by different clocks may differ from one another, although the clocks share the same global time.

In order to represent local time properties in distributed computation, we introduce a temporal primitive: *local clock*. In the definition of our formalism, local clocks are introduced as mappings which translate all occurrences of any instant times on local times into instant times in the global time according to the time units of the local clocks. Mappings may be non-deterministic in order to represent inaccurate clocks with drifting time units. Giving the lower and upper bound of the interval of one time unit on a clock, δ_{min} and δ_{max}, respectively, the mapping is defined as follows:

$$\theta(t) \stackrel{\text{def}}{=} \begin{cases} 0 & \text{if } t = 0 \\ \theta(t-1) + \delta & \text{if } t > 0 \end{cases} \text{ where } \delta \in \{\, d \in \mathcal{T}_G \mid \delta_{min} \leq d \leq \delta_{max} \}$$

where $\mathcal{T}_G$ is the global time domain which is the finest and absolute reference time basis for all local times. Please note that, the global time does not imply an actual global clock but only provides the time that each local clock may measure. The extensions, except for local clock, are essentially equivalent to ones in RtCCS.

The syntax of DtCCS is shown below. In the below definition, expressions $\mathcal{S}$, ranged over by $S, S_1, S_2, \ldots$, represent objects on a processor (or a node) with a local clock, and expressions $\mathcal{P}$, ranged over by $P, P_1, P_2, \ldots$, represents interactions among distributed objects following different clocks.

$$
\begin{array}{lll}
S ::= & 0 & (\text{Terminated Object}) \\
\mid & X & (\text{Process Variable}) \\
\mid & \alpha.S & (\text{Sequential Execution}) \\
\mid & S_1 + S_2 & (\text{Alternative Choice}) \\
\mid & \text{rec } X : S & (\text{Recursive Definition}) \\
\mid & \langle S_1, S_2 \rangle_t & (\text{Timeout})
\end{array}
$$

$$
\begin{array}{lll}
P ::= & [\![S]\!]_\theta & (\text{Local Object}) \\
\mid & P_1 \mid P_2 & (\text{Parallel Composition}) \\
\mid & P[f] & (\text{Relabeling}) \\
\mid & P \backslash L & (\text{Encapsulation})
\end{array}
$$

$[\![S]\!]_\theta$ means a sequential expression S executed on a processor with a local clock θ.

In the interpretation of DtCCS, expressions describing concurrent objects with respect to local times are translated into ones in the global time by using the translation rules shown below. And then, the expressions are interpreted as expressions based on the global time. The key idea of the rules is to map time values in descriptions with respect to local time into values with respect to the global time by using the clock mapping. The deadline time of each timeout operator corresponds to the time value.

$$
\begin{aligned}
[\![0]\!]_\theta &\longrightarrow 0 \\
[\![X]\!]_\theta &\longrightarrow X \\
[\![\alpha.S]\!]_\theta &\longrightarrow \alpha.[\![S]\!]_{\theta'} \\
[\![S_1 + S_2]\!]_\theta &\longrightarrow [\![S_1]\!]_{\theta'} + [\![S_2]\!]_{\theta'} \\
[\![\text{rec } X : S]\!]_\theta &\longrightarrow \text{rec } X : [\![S]\!]_{\theta'} \\
[\![\langle S_1, S_2 \rangle_t]\!]_\theta &\longrightarrow \langle [\![S_1]\!]_{\theta'}, [\![S_2]\!]_{\theta''} \rangle_{\theta'(t)}
\end{aligned}
$$

where $\theta', \theta'' \stackrel{\text{def}}{=} \theta$ such that for all t_ℓ, $\theta'(t_\ell) = \theta(t_\ell)$, and $\theta''(t_\ell) + \theta(t) = \theta(t_\ell + t)$.

We briefly explain the intuitive meaning of the main rules. The third rule translates an unpredictable synchronization time for waiting for α into an unpredictable time on the global time domain. The fourth rule shows that all alternative subsequences in a processor share the same clock. The last rule means that deadline time t on local clock θ is mapped into deadline time $\theta'(t)$ on the global time. The clock translation rules can completely eliminate $[\![\cdot]\!]_\theta$ from any expressions in $\mathcal{P}$. Therefore, the syntax of the expressions translated into the global time are equivalent to those of RtCCS and are interpreted by using RtCCS's inference rules presented in Figure 1 and 2.

We now illustrate how to describe distributed object in DtCCS. Suppose that the client and server objects presented previously are allocated to different processors. By the mapping rules, we map the client and the server on the global time domain as shown below.

$$[\![Client]\!]_{\theta_c} \longrightarrow \cdots \longrightarrow \overline{req}.\langle ret.0, [\![Client]\!]_{\theta_c}\rangle\theta_c(6)$$
$$[\![Server]\!]_{\theta_s} \longrightarrow \cdots \longrightarrow req.\langle 0, \overline{ret}.[\![Server]\!]_{\theta_s}\rangle\theta_s(5)$$

where we assume θ_c is the clock of the client and θ_s that of the server. The interaction between the objects is described as $([\![Client]\!]_{\theta_c}|[\![Server]\!]_{\theta_s}) \setminus L$, where $L \stackrel{def}{=} \{req, ret\}$. L makes internal communications encapsulated from the environment. The result of the interaction is dependent on the evaluated values of $\theta_c(6)$ and $\theta_s(5)$. Here we show the possible results:

(1) In the case of $\theta_c(6) > \theta_s(5)$:

$$([\![Client]\!]_{\theta_c}|[\![Server]\!]_{\theta_s})\setminus L$$
$$\stackrel{\tau(req)}{\longrightarrow} (\langle ret.0, [\![Client]\!]_{\theta_c}\rangle\theta_c(6)|\langle 0, \overline{ret}.[\![Server]\!]_{\theta_s}\rangle\theta_s(5))\setminus L$$
$$(\stackrel{\checkmark}{\longrightarrow})^{\theta_s(5)}((\langle ret.0, [\![Client]\!]_{\theta_c}\rangle\theta_c(6) - \theta_s(5)|\overline{ret}.[\![Server]\!]_{\theta_s}) \setminus L$$
$$\stackrel{\tau(ret)}{\longrightarrow} (0|[\![Server]\!]_{\theta_s}) \setminus L$$
$$(success)$$

In this case the client can always receive a return message before it goes to timeout.

(2) In the case of $\theta_c(6) \leq \theta_s(5)$:

$$([\![Client]\!]_{\theta_c}|[\![Server]\!]_{\theta_s})\setminus\{req, ret\}$$
$$\stackrel{\tau(req)}{\longrightarrow} (\langle ret.0, [\![Client]\!]_{\theta_c}\rangle\theta_c(6)|\langle 0, \overline{ret}.[\![Server]\!]_{\theta_s}\rangle\theta_s(5))\setminus L$$
$$(\stackrel{\checkmark}{\longrightarrow})^{\theta_c(5)} ([\![Client]\!]_{\theta_c}|\langle 0, \overline{ret}.[\![Server]\!]_{\theta_s}\rangle\theta_c(6) - \theta_s(5)) \setminus L$$
$$(\stackrel{\checkmark}{\longrightarrow})^{\theta_s(6)-\theta_c(5)}([\![Client]\!]_{\theta_c}|\overline{ret}.[\![Server]\!]_{\theta_s}) \setminus L$$
$$(failure)$$

In this case, the client timeouts before receiving a return message ret. Thus the objects goes into timing failure.

DtCCS allows us to analyze explicitly how the differences among local clocks affect the result of interactions in distributed computing.

Based on DtCCS, we have already developed timed equivalences by extending CCS's bisimulation. They can equate two objects whose functional behaviors completely match and whose timings are different within a given bound. They are appropriate and practical to verify distributed objects with temporal uncertainties and real-time objects with non-strict time constraints. For details of the equivalences please consult [4].

2.3 Toward Formalizing Asynchronous Real-Time Systems

We here attempt to formalize the third and fourth combinations. From the temporal viewpoint, asynchronous communication corresponds to a communication where temporal distance between the occurrences of sending and receiving cannot be ignored. Thus, time is essential in the modeling of asynchronous communication. Also, as mentioned previously, asynchronous communication with time constraints, such as timeout handling, provides a practical method to detect failures. Consequently, formalisms for reasoning about asynchronous communications need the ability to model such distance and time constraints. We are currently extending RtCCS and DtCCS to asynchronous real-time systems. The key idea of the extensions is to express asynchronous communication in terms of synchronous communication and a messenger creation, i.e. asynchronous message sending is represented by creating a process which can engage only in an input action with the same name of the message. We are also investigating the possibility of extending the ν-calculus [1]. The account of research on these should be left to our future papers.

3 DROL: A Programming Language for Distributed Real-Time Systems

We have been thinking about what kind of programming languages for distributed systems should be provided. In order to provide modularity of software, we decided to use the notion of objects. In order to describe concurrent activities, we decided to use *concurrent objects* [9]. However, these notions are not enough to describe safe and efficient distributed systems, since object cannot escape from dead-lock situations such as waiting for a message which will never arrive. Such languages need to provide real-time facilities to manage time-critical responses and to detect failures.

DROL [5] was proposed by Takashio and one of the authors as such a language for describing distributed systems. In contrast to previously proposed real-time programming languages, every object has a clock and real-time properties. DROL proposed the slogan of *best effort and least suffering*. In distributed computing, objects receive request messages and also send request messages. That is, an object is a server as well as client at the same time. As a client, an object should return from a situation where unexpected delay (including deadlock) occurs. This is the notion of *least suffering*. It is achieved by the time-out function at the client (caller) side. As a server, an object should try its best to achieve the requested operation within the limited time. This is the notion of *best effort*. In order to realize the notion, DROL provides a special mechanism, called *time-polymorphic invocation*, which allows the server object dynamically to select one execution body (a method) which can be executed within the timing constraint at that time. It is achieved by the scheduling facility at the server (called) side.

DROL is implemented as an extension of C++ with the capability of describing temporal constraints, and running on a distributed real-time operating system, called the ARTS kernel [8]. The DROL compiler translates a program written in DROL into C++ codes including interfaces for the ARTS kernel. DROL has the following features:

- In addition to C++ objects, DROL is able to define distributed real-time objects which are single threaded active objects and are defined with some timing informations such as timing constraints for each method.

- It supports *time polymorphic invocation* as an invocation expression in order to realize the property of *best effort* and the property of *least suffering*.

In order to illustrate the expressive power of DROL we adopt an example of a distributed real-time system: air traffic control system. Two distributed real-time objects appear in this example: the *airplane object* and the *controlTower object*. The airplane object moves in the sky at a high speed and thus the time allowed for controlling itself is strictly limited. For the airplane object that provides various services with strict timing constraints, a timing constraint for the communication with controlTower takes an important position in order to meet a whole timing constraint.

We suppose a situation shown in Figure 3. The airplane has some trouble in its body in flight. Then, immediately, the airplane object calls a method `emergencyCall()` itself. In `emergencyCall()`, the airplane tries to access the controlTower object, and sends a request to get some information about the airport. The airport has two runways A and B. And the controlTower supports two methods for emergency. One is `emergency_runway()` that returns a minimum information, that is, the name of runway available for landing safely. The worst case execution time of this method is 200 milliseconds. The other is `emergency_all_info()` that returns some useful informations for the airplane in addition to minimum information. The worst case execution time of this method is 500 milliseconds. Of course, the airplane wants to request the latter. However, the timing constraint up to the turning point is 600 milliseconds. If it misses the turning point, the airplane cannot land this airport. So, the airplane has to decide which runway it should land before this timing.

Figure 4 depicts part of the definitions of the controlTower objects in the example of the air traffic control system. Distributed real-time objects are defined by adding the keyword `DRObject` before the C++ `class` keyword. DROL defines methods [3] with timing constraints, where the user can specify the worst case execution time and exceptions. In this class, all methods are declared with tim-

---

[3] A member function in C++ terminology.

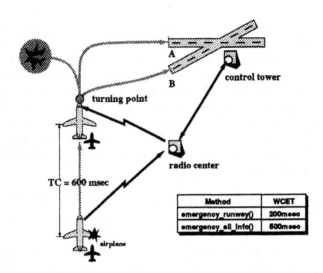

Method	WCET
emergency_runway()	200msec
emergency_all_info()	500msec

Fig. 3. The Air Traffic Control System

ing constraints. For example, the execution of the **emergency_runway()** method needs 200 milliseconds.

The **emergencyCall()** method of the airplane object is defined as shown in Figure 4. In this method, the invocation expression is used to start a time polymorphic invocation. This expression means that if the remaining time up to the deadline on the controlTower object is greater than 500 milliseconds then the **emergency_all_info()** method is executed, and if it is less than 500 milliseconds and greater than 200 milliseconds then the controlTower starts the **emergency_runway()** method. If the airplane object cannot get the reply within 600 milliseconds, it gives up and starts to try to access another control tower object.

In traditional techniques, the airplane can request only one method at a time. Therefore, it can get either "full information" or "no information". This is a serious problem. However, by using the time polymorphic invocation of DROL, we can realize the *best effort* easily. So, the airplane object can get some information that the controlTower object could return at that time. In addition, if the airplane cannot get a reply from the controlTower within 600 milliseconds, it can start to search for the second best that the airplane can do.

For detail, please refer to [5]. We plan to implement it on the Apertos Operating System [10] in the near future. We are also developing a static verification framework for DROL based on RtCCS and DtCCS. Particularly, since DtCCS can analyze locally temporal properties, it provides a very powerful method to verify DROL's applications for distributed systems where objects cannot share the same global clock and thus they follow different clocks.

```
DRObject class ControlTower{
  private:
    ...
    int    recover();
  public:
    EMData emergency_runway(Airplane apid)
              within(0t200ms) timeout();
    EmData emergency_all_info(
                        Airplane apid)
              within(0t500ms) timeout();
    APData airTrafficCondition(
                      Airplane apid)
              within(0t800ms) timeout();
    int    renewData(APData apdata,
                    Airplane apid)
              within(0t02s)
              timeout(recover);
}


Airplane::emergencyCall(ControlTower contT)
{
    ...
    em_data = contT ->>{
        time 0t500ms:
        emergency_all_info(apid);
      time 0t200ms:
          emergency_runway(apid);
      giveup 0t600ms:
          return getAnotherControlTower();
      rejected: print(''Bye Bye...\n'');
      aborted: print(''Bye Bye...\n'');
      ...
}
```

Fig. 4. Definitions of Class ControlTower and Method `emergencyCall()`

4 Towards Formalisms and Languages for the Computational Field Model

In this section we envisage a higher level abstraction of distributed systems. We took note of communication delay as the most essential characteristic of distributed systems. The delay manifests in the function of geographical distance, communication bandwidth, other communication overhead and so on. Whether the delay (distance) can be transparent or not depends on the level of abstraction: For some applications, it is easy to hide the delay (distance) because they employ very fast communication systems. For some other applications, it is difficult and inefficient to hide the delay (distance) because they employ slow communication systems and very widely distributed systems, and because they can utilize their computational resources concurrently with communication. As easily understood, whether the delay can be transparent or not is a matter of the level of abstraction. In order to realize problems to be solved in a wide, complex, and dynamically changing computing environment, we feel the necessity of a higher level abstraction than that modeled by a collection of networked computers.

To do this, one of the authors has proposed a model of distributed computing called *Computational Field Model* [6] [7] as high-level abstraction of distributed computation in coming days. In this model, objects are floating in the continuous field of computation. Some forces, borrowing the idea from the theory of dynamics, such as *gravitational force, repulsive force, friction,* and *inertia* based on the *mass* and *distance* of objects are introduced, so that objects migrate as users move, objects form groups, objects balance the load, and objects avoid faults. This model provides a method of computing in maximally utilizing objects and determining the optimal locations of objects at the next timing taking the cost and effect of migration into consideration.

The metaphor of this model is based on physical phenomenon which essentially contains timed factors, such as acceleration and speed. A formal model and a programming language for the Computational Field Model need to manage temporal properties in this model. The formalisms and language presented in this paper can explicitly deal with properties and thus can provide a theoretical and practical contribution for the model.

5 Conclusions

In this paper, we attempted to extract the most essential properties of distributed computing. Our conclusion at present is its asynchrony and real-time properties. We classified distributed computation into four forms by two criteria; whether communication is synchronous or asynchronous and whether objects refer to the same clock or different clocks. We then presented possibilities of formalizing distributed computations in the four forms. As the first step, we proposed two formal models for concurrent real-time computations and real-time computations with different clocks. These models are extensions of CCS with the notion of the global and local time and thus can provide powerful methods to reason about globally and locally temporal properties and behavioral properties in the computations. We presented some approaches to describe asynchronous real-time computing.

Also, we outlined the programming language for describing asynchronous distributed system called DROL, in which objects provide the properties of *best effort and least suffering* with respect to time and functionality. Fundamental language constructs were shown to give a feeling of how we describe such properties in programs. It is important to note that the synchronous real-time property of DROL program can be validated by using RtCCS and DtCCS. A short remark was also given which relates the notion of asynchrony and real-time with a higher level abstraction of distributed computing called the Computational Field

Model. We feel that we have just come to the starting point of the investigation for distributed objects.

References

1. Honda, K., and Tokoro, M., *An Object Calculus for Asynchronous Communication*, Proceedings of ECOOP'91, LNCS 512, p133-147, June, 1991.
2. Milner, R., *Communication and Concurrency*, Prentice Hall, 1989.
3. Satoh, I., and Tokoro, M., *A Formalism for Real-Time Concurrent Object-Oriented Computing*, Proceedings of ACM OOPSLA'92, p315-326, October, 1992.
4. Satoh, I., and Tokoro, M., *A Timed Calculus for Distributed Objects with Clocks*, to appear in Proceedings of ECOOP'93, July, 1993.
5. Takashio, K., and Tokoro, M., *DROL: An Object-Oriented Programming Language for Distributed Real-time Systems*, Proceedings of ACM OOPSLA'92, p276-294, October, 1992.
6. Tokoro, M., *Computational Field Model: Toward a New Computing Model/Methodology for Open Distributed Environment*, Proceedings of IEEE Workshop on Future Trends of Distributed Computing Systems, September, 1990.
7. Tokoro, M., *Toward Computing Systems for the 2000's*, Proceedings of Operating Systems in 1990's and Beyond, LNCS 563, December, 1991.
8. Tokuda, H., and Mercer, C. W., *ARTS: A Distributed Real-Time Kernel*, ACM Operating System Review, Vol.23, No.3, 1989.
9. Yonezawa, A., and Tokoro, M., editors, *Object-Oriented Concurrent Programming*, MIT Press, 1987.
10. Yokote, Y., *The Apertos Reflective Operating System: The Concept and its Implementation*, Proceedings of ACM OOPSLA'92, p397-413, October, 1992.

Asynchronous Communication Model Based on Linear Logic (Extended Abstract)*

Naoki Kobayashi** and Akinori Yonezawa

Department of Information Science
University of Tokyo
7-3-1 Hongo, Bunkyo-ku, Tokyo, 113 Japan
{koba, yonezawa}@is.s.u-tokyo.ac.jp

1 Introduction

Recently, several applications of Girard's linear logic[4] to logic programming were proposed and shown that they correspond to reactive paradigms[2][3][8]. We propose a new framework called ACL[5] for concurrent computation along this line.

Computation in ACL is described in terms of *proof construction* in linear logic. We restrict inference rules and formulas in linear sequent calculus so that restricted rules have a proof power equivalent to the original rules for the restricted formulas(given in the definition 1). The resulting computational framework contains rich mechanisms for concurrent computation, such as message-passing style asynchronous communication, identifier creation, and hiding operator. They are all described in a *pure logical* form. We also give a model-theoretic semantics as a natural extension of *phase semantics*, a model of linear logic. ACL inference rules can be proven to be sound and complete w.r.t. this model-theoretic semantics. Our framework well captures concurrent computation based on asynchronous communication. It will, therefore, provide us a new insight into other models of concurrent computation from a *logical* point of view. In fact, the actor model[1] and asynchronous CCS[9] can be directly translated into our ACL framework. We also expect ACL to become a formal framework for verification, reasoning, and transformation of concurrent programs with techniques used in traditional logic programming. ACL also exhibits attractive features as a concurrent programming language.

2 ACL Framework

In this section, we introduce the basic (propositional) fragment of ACL. We give transition rules in a form of restricted inference rules of linear sequent calculus.

---

* This is an extended abstract of our technical report[5].
** Naoki Kobayashi is supported by JSPS Fellowships for Japanese Junior Scientists.

2.1 Program Syntax

First, we define the *ACL program clause*.

Definition 1 *A program is a set of clauses, which are defined as follows:*

Clause	::=	Head $\circ\!-$ Goal
Head	::=	A_P
Goal	::=	Terminator|Suicide|A_P	A_m|$?A_m$ |ParaComp |Choice
Terminator	::=	$\top$
Suicide	::=	$\bot$
ParComp	::=	Goal$\otimes$ Goal (parallel composition)
Choice	::=	Receiver |Choice$\oplus$ Receiver
Receiver	::=	Receptor $\otimes$ Goal
Receptor	::=	$A_m^{\perp}$	Receptor $\otimes A_m^{\perp}$
A_P	::=	$P, Q, R, \ldots$ (process predicates)
A_m	::=	$m, n, \ldots$ (message predicates)

We call Goal-formulas above *goal formulas*.

Example. One-place buffer can be defined in ACL as follows:

$$EmptyBuffer \circ\!-put^{\perp} \otimes FullBuffer$$

$$FullBuffer \circ\!-get^{\perp} \otimes (reply \,\otimes\, EmptyBuffer)$$

This definition is quite similar to the following description in CCS[10],

$$EmptyBuffer = put.FullBuffer$$

$$FullBuffer = get.\overline{reply}.EmptyBuffer)$$

though there is a significant difference that communication in ACL is *asynchronous* as is described below, whereas it is synchronous in CCS.

2.2 Operational Semantics

Transition rules are given as a restricted form of inference rules in linear sequent calculus. Please note that the rules should be read that the *conclusion* of an inference rule transits to its *premise formula*. For instance, rule (C2) should be read as $\oplus_j(m_j^{\perp} \otimes A_j), m_i, \Gamma \longrightarrow A_i, \Gamma$.

ACL Inference rules are given as follows:

- Structural Rules
  - (S1) $\dfrac{\vdash \Delta}{\vdash \Gamma}(\Delta$ is a permutation of $\Gamma) \cdots$ (Exchange)
- Parallel
  - (P1) $\dfrac{\vdash A, B, \Gamma}{\vdash A \otimes B, \Gamma} \cdots$ (parallel)
- Communication Rules
  - (C1) $\dfrac{\vdash m, B, \Gamma}{\vdash m \otimes B, \Gamma} \cdots$ (message send)

(C2) $\dfrac{\vdash m_i, m_i^{\perp} \quad \vdash A_i, \Gamma}{\vdash \oplus_j (m_j^{\perp} \otimes A_j), m_i, \Gamma}$(normal message reception)

(C3) $\dfrac{\vdash m_i, m_i^{\perp} \quad \vdash A_i, ?m_i, \Gamma}{\vdash \oplus_j (m_j^{\perp} \otimes A_j), ?m_i, \Gamma}$(modal message reception)

– Termination Rules

    (T1) $\dfrac{}{\vdash \top, A} \cdots$ (program termination)

    (T2) $\dfrac{\vdash A}{\vdash \bot, A} \cdots$ (suicide)

– Clause Rule

    (Cl1) $\dfrac{\vdash B, \Gamma}{\vdash A, \Gamma}$(if $A \circ\!\!- B \in P$)

– Context Rule

    (Co1) $\dfrac{\vdash C[B], \Gamma}{\vdash C[A], \Gamma}$(if $\dfrac{\vdash B}{\vdash A}$ is derived from the other rules)

C[ ], called *positive context*, is defined as follows:

$$C[\,] ::= [\,] \mid C[\,] \,\otimes\, F \mid F \,\otimes\, C[\,] \mid C[\,] \,\&\, F \mid F \,\&\, C[\,] \mid C[\,] \otimes F \mid$$
$$F \otimes C[\,] \mid C[\,] \oplus F \mid F \oplus C[\,]$$

where F is any formula of linear logic.

Rules (C1)-(C3) are rules for communication. $m \,\otimes\, A$ in rule (C1) represents a *sender process* which sends message m. This operation is asynchronous, because $\vdash m, A$ and $\vdash m \,\otimes\, A$ are logically equivalent in linear logic. $\oplus_j (m_j^{\perp} \otimes A_j)$ in rule (C2) represents a *receiver process* which waits for any one of messages $m_1, \ldots, m_k$ and becomes A_i when receiving m_i. $?m$, which we call a *modal message*, is a message which can be copied unboundedly, hence may be used several times by several processes.

The following proposition states that the above inference rules have an equivalent proof power to the original inference rules in linear sequent calculus for the restricted formula.

Proposition 1 *Let P be a program and A be a goal formula. $\vdash A$ is provable by the above inference rules if and only if $\vdash ?P^{\perp}, A$ is provable in linear sequent calculus.*

3 Model based on Phase Semantics

In this section, we give a model for the goal formulas defined in the previous section by extending the *phase semantics*[4] of linear logic.

3.1 Model for ACL

A set of program clauses is written in the form of

$$< P, Q, R, \ldots > \circ\!\!- \mathbf{F}(< P, Q, R, \ldots >),$$

where F is a monotonic function on phase space, which is composed of projection, product, and connectives of linear logic ($\otimes, \&, \oplus, \otimes, ?$).

Given a phase model $(M, \top, m^*)$ where m^* is an assignment of facts to message predicates, we define the model $P^*, Q^*, R^*, \ldots$ of process predicates $P, Q, R, \ldots$ by the following equation:

$$< P^*, Q^*, R^*, \ldots > = \bigoplus_{n \in \omega} (\mathbf{F}^*)^n(0^*)$$

We can prove that the ACL inference rules are sound and complete w.r.t. this model. Proofs are given in [5].

Proposition 2 (Soundness) *The ACL inference rules are sound w.r.t. extended phase model in the following sense: Let G be a goal formula. If G is provable, then G is valid (i.e., $1 \in G^*$) in all the extended phase models.*

Proposition 3 (Completeness) *ACL inference rules are complete w.r.t. the extended phase model in the following sense: Let G be a goal formula. If G is valid (i.e., $1 \in G^*$) in all the extended phase models, G is provable by ACL inference rules.*

4 Extensions of ACL

4.1 First Order Extension

First order existential quantification and universal quantification provide mechanisms for value passing and identifier creation respectively.

First-Order Existential Quantification for Value Passing We introduce first-order existential quantification to the receiver part of a message. Then, communication rules (C2)-(C3) are modified as follows:

$$(\mathbf{C2'}) \quad \frac{(\vdash m_i(a), m_i(a)^\perp) \qquad \vdash A_i(a), \Gamma}{\vdash \oplus_j \exists X(m_j(X)^\perp \otimes A_j(X)), m_i(a), \Gamma}$$

$$(\mathbf{C3'}) \quad \frac{(\vdash m_i(a), m_i(a)^\perp) \qquad \vdash A_i(a), ?m_i(a), \Gamma}{\vdash \oplus_j \exists X(m_j(X)^\perp \otimes A_j(X)), ?m_i(a), \Gamma}$$

The formula $\exists X(m(X)^\perp \otimes P(X))$ represents a process which waits for the values of X via m, and becomes $P(a)$ after receiving message $m(a)$. This extension allows processes to send values in messages.

First-Order Universal Quantification for Identifier Creation First-order universal quantification works as a mechanism for *identifier creation*. Identifier creation is often very important in concurrent computing environment[1][11]. Identifiers work as pointers to access resources including processes such that resources can be accessed only by processes which know their pointers. By passing identifiers in messages, acquaintances can be dynamically changed.

Let us look at $\forall$-rule in linear sequent calculus:

$$\frac{\vdash A(X), \Gamma}{\vdash \forall X.A(X), \Gamma} \quad \text{X not free in } \Gamma$$

We modify this rule as

(ID1) $\dfrac{\vdash A(id), \Gamma}{\vdash \forall X.A(X), \Gamma}$

where *id* is a globally unique identifier which does not appear in $A(X)$, Γ, or any context $C[\ ]$.

4.2 Second-Order Universal Quantification as Hiding Operator

In this section, we introduce second-order universal quantification for message formulas. It works as a *hiding operator* as in CCS. Here is an original rule in linear sequent calculus:

$$\frac{\vdash A, \Gamma}{\vdash \wedge X.A, \Gamma} \quad \text{X not free in } \Gamma$$

We use the symbol $\wedge$, instead of $\forall$ to distinguish from the first-order universal quantification. Notice the side condition. Quantified variable cannot be free outside the scope of $\wedge$. It is, therefore, invisible from outside. We introduce the following ACL rules instead of the above original rules in linear sequent calculus.

- Hiding Rules
  - **(H1)** $\dfrac{\vdash \wedge m.(A, n), \Gamma}{\vdash \wedge m.(A), n, \Gamma}$ where n contains neither m nor process predicates.
  - **(H2)** $\dfrac{\vdash \wedge m.(A), n, \Gamma}{\vdash \wedge m.(A, n), \Gamma}$
  - **(H3)** $\dfrac{\vdash \Gamma}{\vdash \wedge m.(), \Gamma}$

$C[\ ]$ in context rules are also extended to include the form $\wedge m.(C[\ ])$. Then, again this extension can be proven to be equivalent to linear sequent calculus.

5 ACL as a Programming Paradigm

ACL has the following attractive features as a programming paradigm.

1. Variety of communication mechanisms, including:
   - point-to-point communication
   - one-to-many communication
   - one-to-one-of-many communication
2. Multiple messages reception
3. Partial reception of messages
4. Modal messages for sharing information

Details are given in [6].

6 Conclusion

We have proposed a logical framework ACL for concurrent programming languages based on linear logic. We gave the operational semantics of ACL by restricting inference rules in linear sequent calculus and model theoretic semantics based on phase semantics. In ACL, message passing style communication, identifier creation, and hiding operator are formulated pure logically, hence these mechanisms are uniformly treated by the logical semantics. We are currently investigating several process equivalence relations for ACL[7]. Future work includes the application of techniques for traditional logic programming to transformation, reasoning and verification of concurrent programs written in ACL. The full version of this paper is available as [5]. Features of ACL as a concurrent programming paradigm are discussed in detail in [6].

References

1. Agha, G., *Actors: A Model of Concurrent Computation in Distributed Systems*. MIT Press, 1986
2. Andreoli, J.-M. and R. Pareschi, "Linear Objects: Logical processes with built-in inheritance," *New Generation Computing*, 1991.
3. Andreoli, J.-M. and R. Pareschi, "Communication as Fair Distribution of Knowledge," in *Proceedings of OOPSLA '91*, pp. 212–229, 1991.
4. Girard, J.-Y., "Linear Logic," *Theoretical Computer Science*, vol. 50, pp. 1–102, 1987.
5. Kobayashi, N. and A. Yonezawa, "Asynchronous Communication Model Based on Linear Logic," Tech. Rep. 92-5, Department of Information Science, University of Tokyo, 1992.
6. Kobayashi, N. and A. Yonezawa, "ACL – A Concurrent Linear Logic Programming," to appear in Proceedings of International Logic Programming Symposium, MIT Press, 1993.
7. Kobayashi, N. and A. Yonezawa, "Logical, Testing and Observation Equivalences for Processes in a Linear Logic Programming," presented at Linear Logic Workshop, Cornell University, 1993.
8. Miller, D., "The π-calculus as a theory in linear logic: Preliminary results," Tech. Rep. MS-CIS-92-48, Computer Science Department, University of Pennsylvania, 1992. To appear in the 1992 Workshop on Extensions to Logic Programming, LNAI Series.
9. Milner, R., "Calculi for Synchrony and Asynchrony," *Theoretical Computer Science*, vol. 25, pp. 267–310, 1983.
10. Milner, R., *Communication and Concurrency*. Prentice Hall, 1989.
11. Milner, R., J. Parrow, and D. Walker, "A Calculus of Mobile Processes, Part I," Tech. Rep. ECS-LFCS-89-85, University of Edinburgh, 1989.

PART V

Systems

Parallel Inference System Research in the Japanese FGCS Project

Takashi Chikayama and Ryozo Kiyohara*

Institute for New Generation Computer Technology,
1-4-28 Mita, Minato-ku, Tokyo 108, Japan

Abstract. The Fifth Generation Computer Systems (FGCS) project is a national project of Japan aiming at establishing the basic technology required for high performance knowledge information processing systems. One of its most important subprojects has been the research and development of the parallel inference system, aiming at establishing both hardware and software technologies for obtaining massive symbolic computation power through highly parallel processing.
This paper reports an overview of recent research and development on the parallel inference system, including hardware, basic software and experimental application software.

1 Introduction

The FGCS project is a national project of Japan, aiming at establishing the basic technology required for high performance knowledge information processing systems. The research and development principle throughout the project has been to adopt *logic* as the theoretical backbone of knowledge information processing and *parallel processing* as the key technology for obtaining high performance. Thus, one of its most important subproject has been the research and development of the parallel inference system, aiming at establishing both hardware and software technologies for massive symbolic computation power through highly parallel processing.

A concurrent logic language, KL1[UK1], was designed as the kernel language of the system to give the basis of both hardware and software technologies. As the hardware system, the parallel inference machine PIM[TK1] has been developed as a prototype to offer gigantic computation power to knowledge information processing systems. The language processor for KL1 has been developed to run efficiently on PIM. As the basic software system, an operating system PIMOS[CT1] has been developed to provide a comfortable development environment for parallel application software in KL1. PIMOS was also written in KL1. Various experimental application software systems have been developed upon PIMOS.

---

* The second author is currently at: Computer & Information Systems Labratry, Mitsubishi Electric Corp., 5-1-1 Ofuna, Kamakura, Kanagawa 247, Japan.

This paper reports an overview of recent research and development on the parallel inference system, including hardware, basic software and experimental application software.

The following sections are organized as follows. Section 2 describes the design principles of the parallel inference system. Section 3 gives an overview of the system. In Sect. 4, remarks on our experiences with the system are given. Finally, future research plans is described in Sect. 5.

2 Design Principles

There are two most important sets of technologies for high performance knowledge processing systems: One is technologies providing problem solving methods for knowledge information processing; the other is technologies for actually applying such methods, providing massive computational power and ease in programming. The parallel inference system subproject is aiming at establishing the latter, both in hardware and software, through logic-based parallel processing.

Several problems that did not exist with sequential processing arise with parallel processing. The most typical ones and our remedy for them are the following.

Programming language Traditionally, parallel processing software has been written in sequential programming languages augmented with features for parallel processing. This often complicates software further. One of the most typical problems is synchronization between parallel computation activities. Synchronization failures are frequent source of bugs hard to fix.

To solve the problem, we adopted a concurrent logic programming language KL1[UK1], which was based on GHC[UK2]. KL1 is a born concurrent language, where concurrent computation is the default. Its automatic data-flow synchronization mechanism eliminates most of the synchronization problems.

Hardware architecture It was not clear which parallel processing architecture was most suited to knowledge information processing. It was quite difficult to evaluate many architectural ideas only through desk-top analysis. Software simulation is too time-consuming for evaluating with application software with practical complexity and size.

We thus decided to develop several (five, to be precise) models of PIM [TK1] with different processor and interprocessor connection architectures and evaluate them through experimentations with practical application systems.

Software development environment Tools originally designed for sequential programming do not always provide functionality required for debugging highly parallel software, even with extensions made afterwards. The same can be said about the operating system features, such as interfaces to the resource management mechanism and virtualized I/O devices. The original design relies so much on sequential processing that most of the extensions for parallel processing are only suited for small-scale parallelism.

An original operating system PIMOS (Parallel Inference Machine Operating System) [CT1] was thus developed to provide a comfortable software development environment for parallel application software.

The parallel inference system has an overall structure as shown in Fig. 1. A notable difference with conventional computer systems is that the operating system is built upon the level of the programming language processor. For efficient execution, highly parallel application software has to control parallel processing activities in the system, which usually was not needed in sequential or small scale parallel systems. The application layer and the operating system layer thus require the same primitives. We decided to provide their common basis, as the programming language KL1.

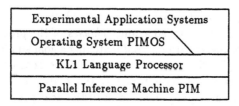

Fig. 1. Parallel Inference System

3   Overview of the System

3.1   The Kernel Language: KL1

This section describes the key features of KL1.

Basic Mechanism KL1 is a concurrent logic programming language based on GHC[UK2]. Its basic execution mechanism is common with other languages of the family, such as Concurrent Prolog[SE2], Parlog[CK1] or Janus[SA1].

KL1 programs consist of *clauses*, each of which corresponds to a logical axiom. Clauses that define a program has the following syntax.

PredName(ArgList, ...) :- Guard | Body.

Each part has the following operational meanings.

PredName gives the name of the predicate (or subroutine, if you like) for which this clause gives (a part of) the definition.

ArgList determines the correspondence of actual arguments given to the predicate and the variables written in the clause definition.

Guard specifies the condition needed to be satisfied to apply the clause. Any number of *goals*, i.e., invocation of predicates, can be written separated by commas and the condition is considered to be satisfied when all of them are satisfied. In the guard, only unifications and invocations of certain predicates defined in the language can be written.

Body specifies the action to be taken when the clause is selected. Like the guard, any number of goals can be given here and all the goals will be executed when the clause is selected. Unlike in guard, user-defined predicates can be invoked from the body, in addition to unifications and language-defined predicates.

Execution of KL1 programs proceeds roughly as follows.

1. First, the initial goal is the only member of a multi-set of goals called the *goal pool*.
2. Some of the goals in the goal pool are picked up.
3. Goals picked up are matched against *clauses* of the program.
4. If there is some clause with its *head* matching a goal and its *guard* is satisfied, the original goal will be reduced to goals in the *body* of the clause and the resultant new goals will be put back to the goal pool.
5. The steps 2 through 4 are repeated until the goal pool becomes empty.

The steps 2 through 4 can be done in parallel for many goals at a time. This is the source of concurrency in this language.

The most notable features of the concurrent logic programming languages are their side-effect free semantics and implicit data-flow synchronization mechanism. As no notion of *assignment* is in the language, value of a variable, once defined, will never change as the computation progresses. The data-flow synchronization mechanism assures that, whenever a decision is to be made for conditional execution, it is suspended automatically until the all the data required for the decision, such as operands to a comparison, get ready.

The combination of these features assures that there would never be synchronization problems such as follows.

— Overwriting a variable before its value is read.
— Reading a variable's value before it is set.

Programs in KL1 are usually organized using the object-oriented programming style [SE1]. Almost the whole PIMOS operating system and many of the application systems running on PIM are written in this way.

Computation Mapping KL1 provides only low level process distribution and priority-based scheduling features for controlling computation mapping. It seems that, at least with the status quo technology, no automatic load distribution schemes are universally effective to all kinds of algorithms. Our decision thus was to provide lower level primitives in the programming language level and make the software written in it responsible for computation mapping.

The primitives provided in KL1 are as follows. Note that, they are no more than pragmas that only suggest the language processor for better performance; they will not change the meaning of the programs.[2]

Processor specification Each body goal may have a processor specification which designates the processor on which to execute the goal.

Priority specification Each body goal may have a priority specification. Each goal has an integer priority associated with it.

Although process distribution is not, data distribution is made automatic. Data referenced by distributed processes are fetched from remote memory automatically on demand. The side-effect free semantics of KL1 allows copying of any data except for undefined variables without affecting the semantics. Executable codes are also distributed on demand, i.e., when a certain piece of code is needed on some processor and the code is not in the memory of that processor, it will be fetched from some other processor automatically. Memory areas occupied by executable code, as well as data structures, no longer needed are reclaimed with the garbage collection mechanism.

Several automatic mapping strategies have been developed for diverse problems using the above straightforward mechanism. Relatively universal ones are provided as libraries and used in many application software systems [FM2].

Metalevel Control With the basic semantics of the concurrent logic programming languages, all the goals in the system form one logical conjunction. This means, a failure or an exception in one of the goals makes the whole system fail. Also, there is no way to control execution of such goals. With this semantics, it is almost impossible to build a system that requires efficient metalevel control on computation activities, such as an operating system.

KL1 thus provides a metalevel execution control feature called "shoen".[3] A shoen is a group of goals. This group is used as the unit of metalevel control, namely initiation, interruption, resumption and abortion of execution. The shoen construct also provides exception handling and resource consumption control mechanisms.

A shoen has two communication streams as its interface: one, called the "control stream", directs inwards from outside of shoen for sending messages to control the execution; the other, called the "report stream", directs the reverse way for reporting events internal to the shoen, such as exceptions (Fig. 2).

PIMOS uses this shoen structure to construct a higher level notion of "task", which is the operating system level unit of resource management. Note that tasks are *not* a unit for parallel execution. There are usually many parallel activities within one task.

---

[2] To be precise, pragmas won't change the partial correctness of programs but certain diverging programs may be assured to stop through pragma specifications.

[3] The Japanese word "shoen" roughly corresponds to the English word "manor".

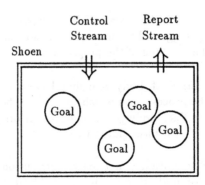

Fig. 2. Shoen and Related Streams

3.2 Parallel Inference Machine PIM

Five models of PIM have been built as listed in the Table 1. They differ in both their processor architecture and their interprocessor connection architecture. Evaluation of their architectures is one of the most important research topics currently going on.

Table 1. Five Models of PIM

model name	PIM/p	PIM/c	PIM/m	PIM/i	PIM/k
processor	RISC+α	horiz. micro.	horiz. micro.	RISC	RISC
device	std. cell	gate array	cell base	std. cell	custom
# PE/cluster	8	8	1	8	4
inter-cluster	hypercube	crossbar	mesh	SCSI	bus
total # PE	512	256	256	16	16

The PIM model M, which was completed first, performs 610 KLIPS[4] with one processor, providing the total peak performance of 150 MLIPS. Its average performance when application software is run upon PIMOS is usually somewhere between one third to one fifth of the peak performance. The PIM model P, which has 512 processors, marks similar total performance.

Some of the KL1 programs on PIM/m with 256 processors or PIM/p with 512 processors run about ten times faster than programs with basically the same (but sequential) algorithm on high-end workstations.

---

[4] LIPS is an execution speed measure unit for logic programming languages, meaning Logical Inferences Per Second. Logical inference corresponds to a subroutine or a function call in procedural languages. It is customary to measure it with a list reversal program.

3.3 PIMOS

PIMOS is an operating and programming system for all models of parallel inference machines. Its overall structure is as shown in Fig. 3. Some of the characteristic submodules of PIMOS are as follows.

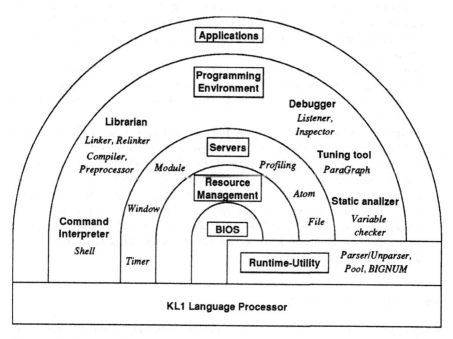

Fig. 3. The Structure of PIMOS

BIOS provides the most basic I/O through SCSI interface. KL1 provides a process model of the SCSI interface through built-in predicates.

Resource management provides a layer for communication management. As all the I/O devices and tasks have message stream interface, management of such streams is resource management means on PIMOS[YH1].

Tasks, implemented using the shoen mechanism, can be nested with arbitrarily many levels. Thus, processes to control tasks form a tree structure, called the "resource tree". Processes to control communication with "servers" (described below) are also in this tree. By distributing such processes to the processor where user programs made request, the overhead of the operating system can be distributed without increasing the amount of communication.

Servers are processes to implement virtual devices upon physical devices[YH1]. Services provided by software systems, such as the database management system[KM1] or the librarian of the PIMOS described below, also have this server interface.

Debugging Tools provide features tailored for debugging parallel programs. It includes the "listener" with tracing and spying functions and the "inspector" to inspect data structures either statically or during their dynamic generation.

ParaGraph is a program tuning tool providing graphic display of execution profile information[AS1]. Such a visualization tool is quite powerful in tuning the performance of programs through changing mapping pragmas stated above.

Note that, as stated above, changing pragmas will not change the meaning of the programs. It only affects the performance. Data and executable code required are automatically distributed. This makes tuning of load distribution much easier.

Librarian is responsible for maintaining the correspondence with executable code modules and their names. It is implemented as a server.

Note that, the side-effect free nature of the KL1 doesn't allow even executable code to be overwritten. Updating some program module means generating a new one and changing the name correspondence. The older version may still be running somewhere in the system (possibly on the same processor). This scheme may seem inefficient but actually not, as updating executable code is not so frequent. The clean semantics, on the other hand, made users' understanding much easier.

3.4 Application Systems

Many experimental application systems have been developed and are running on PIMOS and PIM (currently, PIM/m and PIM/p systems are used mainly). In parallel with the development of independent application systems, performance analysis study from more general standpoint is also going on (see [KK1], for example).

The following is a list of some of such application systems. They all available as free software from ICOT.[5]

Symbolic Processing

PIMOS is the operating system for PIM and Multi-PSI. The entire source code is available as free software.

Strategy management shell which is an experimental multi-task operating system that automatically balances the load of multiple tasks dynamically.

---

[5] For details, please contact ifs@icot.or.jp.

Constraint Programming

GDCC is a parallel constraint logic programming system. It provides highly declarative, flexible and efficient constraint logic programming languages, dealing with various kinds of constraints including non-linear polynomial equations [TS1] .

Consort is a constraint solver for nonlinear inequalities.

Dynamical programming (DP) system is a logic programming system that controls symbolic inferences according to general heuristics based on dynamics.

Knowledge Base

Quixote is a language system providing fundamental facilities for knowledge information processing, such as very high level knowledge representation and inferences [YH2].

Kappa-P is a parallel database management system based on a nested relational model [KM1].

Theorem Proving

MGTP is a massively parallel, high performance bottom-up theorem prover on first order problems [FM1].

The prover tries to generate models satisfying a given axiom set. The system can be used in two ways. As a theorem prover, it will show that no models can satisfy a given axiom set augmented with the negation of the given theorem. As a constraint satisfaction system, models found by the system satisfying a given axiom set are answers to a constraint satisfaction problem. The system showed almost linear speed-up up to 512 processors.

Problem Solving

Andor-II is a language system that allows simple description in a high level language which provides high reasoning power by parallel processing [TA1].

Group problem solving system is a multi-agent system to help task allocation to a group of people cooperatively solving a problem.

Meta Reasoning

Argus/V is a system to analyze properties of Horn logic programs using first-order inference and induction.

SME is a system that extracts the correspondences and similarities of two systems described in tree forms, based on the structure-mapping theory.

Natural Language Processing

PAX is a parallel bottom up parsing system for natural languages.

Dulcinea is an experimental system that generates natural language argument text to justify the given assertion [IT1].

Laputa is a natural language processing system based on concurrent cooperation of morphological, syntactic and semantic analysis [YS1].

Genetic Information Processing

Protein sequence alignment systems have several variations, based on parallel dynamic programming [IM1], parallel simulated annealing [HM1] and through knowledge-based approach using Quixote mentioned above [HM2].

Motif extraction system extracts common motif patterns from amino acid sequences in the same protein category.

Protein conformation prediction system is for predicting 3-D structure of proteins from amino acid sequences based on geometrical stochastic reasoning [OK].

Game Players

GOG is a "go" game (an oriental board game) player system [NK2].

VLSI-CAD

Parallel logic simulator is a system to simulate VLSI circuits to verify their logical and timing specifications.[MY1]

This system adopts a virtual time algorithm, in which simulation done proceeds in a speculative way assuming input signal to be notified from other processors won't change. If such a change is notified later, the simulation will be rolled back. This strategy could extract much higher parallelism than non-speculative algorithm, obtaining 166-fold speed-up on 256 processors of PIM/m (534k events/sec). Although the parallel algorithm used is rather complex, it took only several man-month to build its first version.

Cell placement system automatically designs an optimal placement on standard cell LSI [DH1].

LSI router is a system to route paths between terminals of circuit modules on an LSI [DH1] [DH2].

Case-based circuit design support system helps designing new circuits using knowledge on similar precedential circuits.

Co-Hlex generates a circuit layout given a circuit, chip space and a set of module proximity conditions [WT1].

Rodin is a system for synthesizing LSI circuits given behavior specifications.

Cooperative logic design expert system generates netlists for CMOS standard cell LSI satisfying given area and speed constraints [MY2].

Legal Reasoning

Helic-II is a parallel legal reasoning system referencing to both laws and precedents [NK1].

Reasoning from legal viewpoints is not simple inference process based only laws and regulations, as many of the words and phrases appearing in them are left undefined. Their intepretation is based on precedents. The system keeps two kinds of databases, one on laws and regulations and another on precedents. Given new cases are matched against precedent cases using higher level interpretaion (such as matching a taxi driver and a flight pilot as a traffic operator). The laws and regulations are applied after that, using abovementioned MGTP as the inference engine.

Others

Mendels zone is a software synthesis system for concurrent programs that allow very high level specification.

Desq is a tool to determine ranges of design parameters using qualitative reasoning.

Plant diagnosis and control expert system generates if-then type rules for plant control from high level model description of the plant.

Adaptive model-based diagnostic system generates a probability ordered fault suspect list for given electric circuit with given symptom, estimating fault probability of each component from case records.

4 Through Our Experiences

This section summarize our experiences with building software systems in KL1 on the parallel inference machines.

4.1 Programming Ease

The automatic synchronization mechanism and fine grain concurrency of KL1 made programming much easier. The software productivity became far better than in sequential programming languages with baroque parallel processing extensions.

When we started developing the first version of PIMOS in 1987, there was no parallel KL1 language implementations available. Thus, the operating system was debugged on a sequential (pseudoparallel) implementation, which had only fixed scheduling strategy. When the system was ported to a prototype parallel machine, Multi-PSI, in 1988, we were ready for annoying synchronization bugs that will not reproduce themselves, although the automatic synchronization mechanism of the language should avoid such problems in theory. The theory turned out to be the reality. We found almost no synchronization problems except for a small number of design problems in very high level, although the scheduling on the real parallel machine is quite different from the emulator. We knew this in theory, but actually experiencing this made us much more confident of the great merits of writing a system in a language with automatic data-flow synchronization. When PIMOS was ported to several other models of PIM systems later, each with its own scheduling strategy, we almost never encountered synchronization problems.

Most of the experimental application systems written for PIM were coded by programmers with no experience in parallel programming. Nevertheless, they did not seem to have much problem on synchronization.[6]

4.2 Development Environment

Software development tools, including debugging tools and performance tuning tools, tailored for parallel processing, have been found indispensable for high software productivity.

Not all the PIM systems got ready with the final scale described above. Most of the application software systems were first developed on Multi-PSI system with up to 64 processors, then ported to PIM/m with 128 processors when it got ready, then to its 256 processor version when its production completed, and then to PIM/p with 512 processors. Many programs that showed almost linear speed-up with 16 processors would not with 512 processors. Using the tuning tool ParaGraph was very effective in finding the bottlenecks and it usually took only a few weeks before a new version with improved load distribution algorithm showed good parallelism on larger scale systems.

4.3 High Performance Hardware

Hardware systems with high performance have been very useful. It was helpful to be able to run application systems in their earlier development phases and tune them gradually, rather than having to develop an optimized version from scratch. It is especially true with considerably complicated knowledge processing systems.

5 Future Work

A serious problem with the current parallel inference system is that it runs only on specially devised hardware. Although the system is efficient and self-contained, requiring special hardware is a great obstacle in sharing the environment with researchers world-wide.

Research in subsetting the language to allow more concise and efficient implementation has been conducted with promising preliminary results [UK3]. A separate effort of implementing KL1 by translating into C [CT2] shows reasonable performance with very high portability. These results indicate the future

---

[6] Although those who had been too much accustomed to Prolog found difficulty in realizing large semantic difference of the two languages with similar syntax.

direction of implementing the language and the system on stock hardware to be shared among wider range of researchers in parallel software area.

The Fifth Generaion Computer Systems project ended in March 1993. The Japanese Ministry of International Trade and Industry, considering abovementioned recent research on implementation, launched a new project of two years beginning from April 1993, aiming at disseminating the technologies established in the FGCS project by amalgamating it with conventional computer technologies, such as UNIX and RISC processors. In this project, the following results are expected.

- KL1 implementation with reasonable software development environment on commercially available hardware. An implementation with excellent portability by compilation into C (nicknamed KLIC, for KL1 in C) for UNIX workstations, parallel UNIX systems and network-connected computer systems is planned.
- Knowledge processing software and experimental application software further refined and ported to KLIC. It is also planned to include software already available on UNIX systems as components such software, by utilizing the foreign language interface provided by KLIC.

All the resultant software is planned to be freely available worldwide to be utilized as the basis of further research in the area of knowledge information processing systems.

References

[AS1] Aikawa, S. *et al.*: ParaGraph: A Graphical Tuning Tool for Multiprocessor Systems. Proc. *FGCS '92* (1992) 286–293

[CK1] Clark, K. *et al.*: PARLOG: Parallel Programming in Logic. ACM Trans. Prog. Lang. Syst. 8-1 (1986).

[CT1] Chikayama, T.: Operating System PIMOS and Kernel Language KL1. Proc. *FGCS '92* (1992) 73–88

[CT2] Chikayama, T.: A Portable and Reasonably Efficient Implementation of KL1. Technical Report 747 ICOT (1992)

[DH1] Date, H. *et al.*: LSI-CAD Programs on Parallel Inference Machine. Proc. *FGCS '92* (1992) 237–247

[DH2] Date, H. and Taki, K.: A Parallel Lookahead line Search Router with Automatic Ripup-and-reroute. Proc. *EDAC-EUROASIC 93* (1993)

[FM1] Fujita, M. *et al.*: Model Generation Theorem Provers on a Parallel Inference Machine. Proc. *FGCS '92* (1992) 357–375

[FM2] Furuichi, M. *et al.*: A Multi-Level Load Balancing Scheme for OR-Parallel Exhaustive Search Programs on the Multi-PSI. Proc. *Second ACM SIGPLAN Symp. on Principles and Practice of Parallel Programming* (1990) 50–59

[HM1] Hirosawa, M. *et al.*: Folding Simulation using Temperature Parallel Simulated Annealing. Proc. *FGCS '92* (1992) 300–306

[HM2] Hirosawa, M. *et al.*: Protein Multiple Sequence Alignment using Knowledge. Proc. *26th Annual Hawaii Int. Conf. on System Sci.* 1 (1993) 803–812

[IM1]   Ishikawa, M. *et al.*: Protein Sequence Analysis by Parallel Inference Machine. Proc. *FGCS '92* (1992) 294–299

[IT1]   Ikeda, T. *et al.*: Argument Text Generation System (Dulcinea). Proc. *FGCS '92* (1992) 385–394

[KK1]   Kimura, K. and Ichiyoshi, N.: Probabilistic Analysis of the Optimal Efficiency of the Multi-Level Dynamic Load Balancing Scheme. Proc. Sixth Distributed Memory Computing Conf. (1991)

[KM1]   Kawamura, M. *et al.*: Parallel Database Management System: Kappa-P. Proc. *FGCS '92* (1992) 248–256

[MY1]   Matsumoto, Y. and Taki, K.: Adaptive Time-Ceiling for Efficient Parallel Discrete Event Simulation. *Western Multiconf. on Computer Simulation* (1993) 101–106

[MY2]   Minoda, Y. *et al.*: A Cooperative Logic Design Expert System on a Multiprocessor. Proc. *FGCS '92* (1992) 1181–1189

[NK1]   Nitta, K. *et al.*: HELIC-II: A Legal Reasoning System on the Parallel Inference Machine. Proc. *FGCS '92* (1992) 1115–1124

[NK2]   Nitta, K. *et al.*: Experimental Parallel Inference Software. Proc. *FGCS '92* (1992) 166–190

[OK]   Onizuka, K. *et al.*: A Scheme for Protein Tertiary Structure Prediction Based on Stochastic Reasoning. *submitted to Workshop "Artificial Intelligence and Genome" at IJCAI 93* (1993)

[SA1]   Saraswat, V. A. *et al.*: Janus: A Step Towards Distributed Constraint Programming. Proc. *North American Conf. on Logic Programming* (1990)

[SE1]   Shapiro, E. *et al.*: Object-oriented Programming in Concurrent Prolog. New Generation Computing 1-1 (1983)

[SE2]   Shapiro, E.: Systems Programming in Concurrent Prolog. In Logic Programming and its Applications, M. van Canegham and D. H. D. Warren(eds.), Albex Publishing Co. (1986) 50–74

[TA1]   Takeuchi, A. *et al.*: An Operational Semantics of ANDOR-II, A Parallel Logic Programming Language with AND- and OR-Parallelism, LNCS-491, Concurrency: Theory, Language, and Architecture. Springer-Verlag (1989) 173–209

[TK1]   Taki, K.: Parallel Inference Machine PIM. Proc. *FGCS '92* (1992) 50–72

[TS1]   Terasaki, S. *et al.*: Parallel Constraint Logic Programming Language GDCC and its Parallel Constraint Solvers. Proc. *FGCS '92* (1992) 330–346

[UK1]   Ueda, K. *et al.*: Design of the Kernel Language for the Parallel Inference Machine. The Computer Journal **33-6** (1990) 494–500

[UK2]   Ueda, K.: Guarded Horn Clauses: A Parallel Logic Programming Language with the Concept of a Guard. Technical Report **208** ICOT (1986)

[UK3]   Ueda, K. *et al.*: A New Implementation Technique for flat GHC. In Proc. *Seventh Int. Conf. on Logic Programming*, MIT Press (1990) 3–17

[WT1]   Watanabe, T. *et al.*: Co-HLEX: Co-operative Recursive LSI Layout Problem Solver on Japan's Fifth Generation Parallel Inference Machine. Proc. *FGCS '92* (1992) 1173–1180

[YH1]   Yashiro, H. *et al.*: Resource Management of PIMOS. Proc. *FGCS '92* (1992) 269–277

[YH2]   Yasukawa, H. *et al.*: Object, Properties, and Modules in QUIXOTE. Proc. *FGCS '92* (1992) 257–268

[YS1]   Yamasaki, S. *et al.*: A Parallel Cooperation Model for Natural Language Processing. Proc. *FGCS '92* (1992) 405–413

Massively Parallel Symbolic Computing (Abstract)

David L. Waltz

Thinking Machines Corporation
Cambridge, MA.

and

Department of Computer Science and
Center for Complex Systems
Brandeis University
Waltham, MA

Advances in hardware and computer architecture continue to change the economics of various AI (as well as all other) computing paradigms. The new generation of massively parallel machines extends the potential for applications at the high end of the computing spectrum, offering higher computing and I/O performance, much larger memories, and MIMD as well as SIMD capabilities. Computing costs for the same level of performance are substantially less, and will continue to drop steeply for the foreseeable future.

All this has clear consequences for AI: for example, larger knowledge bases can be stored; hand coding will continue to become less cost-effective relative to learning and simple-to-program brute-force methods as time goes on; and just about any parallel AI paradigm should be capable of executing efficiently.

A brief overview will be provided of recent successful Connection Machine projects: automatic keyword assignment for news articles using MBR nearest-neighbor methods (MBR = Memory-Based Reasoning); automatic classification of Census Bureau returns; protein structure prediction using MBR together with backpropagation nets, and statistics; work on "database mining"; and Karl Sims' generation of graphics using genetically-inspired operations on s-expressions.

1   Introduction

Massively parallel applications must address problems that will be too large for workstations for the next several years, or else it will not make sense to expend development costs on them. Suitable applications include one or more of the following properties: 1) large amounts of data; 2) intensive computations; 3) requirement for very fast response times; 4) ways to trade computations for human effort, as in developing applications using learning methods. Most of the suitable applications that we have found come from the general area of very large databases. Massively parallel machines have proved to be important not only in being able to run large applications, but in accelerating development (allowing the use of simpler algorithms, cutting the time to test performance on realistic databases) and allowing many different algorithms and parameter settings to be tried and compared for a particular task. Nearly all these tasks involve symbolic computing, and make relatively little use of floating point capabilities.

The following sections provide capsule descriptions and references to longer articles on several projects relevant to functional programming. All were done in *Lisp. Several of the projects used methods chosen from the family of methods termed "Memory-Based Reasoning" or MBR.

Methods broadly analogous to the text-search algorithms can be used to build "memory-based reasoning" systems to aid in decision-making. These systems utilize training sets like those used to train artificial neural nets [11, 16] or k-d trees [10]. In memory-based reasoning (MBR) a parallel machine is loaded with the training database; training instances consist of situations together with desired outputs for each situation. When a new problem is encountered, the MBR system compares it to all the known prior cases, and uses the most similar case (or majority vote of several similar cases) to classify the new case. The key to successful MBR operation is the selection of a good similarity metric for matching new problems with known cases. If several near neighbors are used (as opposed to a single nearest neighbor) then combining the cases is also an important MBR issue [13, 15]. MBR is related to nearest-neighbor methods and to Case-Based Reasoning (CBR), but differs from both in that it retains all its training items in a relatively flat database.

2 Automatic Keyword Assignment

This project was done in conjunction with Dow Jones. The goal was to assign keywords, chosen from a set of about 400 possibilities, to each news article. This process is now done by entry level (non-expert) human editors. It is very time-consuming and tedious, and editors tend to quit after a fairly short time at this task unless they are promoted. Dow Jones provided a training sample of 80,000 articles, each with a few keywords (typically five to ten) assigned by these editors. The method used here [8] was a variant of MBR—a nearest neighbor algorithm. A vector similarity text retrieval system (CMDRS—Connection Machine Data Retrieval System—described briefly in [15]) was used to find the 16 articles nearest to an article to be keyworded. Each of these near neighbors was assigned a document score. Roughly, the document score was the sum of the scores for words that occurred both in the article to be keyworded and the best paragraph of the best matching article. Scores are high for rare words, and low or zero for common ones. Finally, each keyword was assigned a score equal to the sum of the scores of all the near neighbors that contained it. The system then used some simple rules to select the highest scored keywords (e.g. the best eight, provided that the eighth had a score at least 1/3 that of the best keyword, otherwise...), and assigned them to the new article.

We were able to test this method against the human editors. We mixed keywords assigned automatically by our system with keywords assigned by human editors to the same articles, and gave the collection (one keyword per article, presented in randomized order) to expert human editors to evaluate. These expert editors graded each keyword as relevant, irrelevant, or borderline. Counting borderline as irrelevant, the automatic system achieved a recall of 80% and a precision of 72%, which compares quite well to human performance of 82% recall and 88% precision. More recent work has used a variant of Koza's genetic algorithm methods [5] to evolve an expression that is used to decide whether to accept or reject each keyword assignment. Using this method, [6, 7] has shown that if some fraction of the articles are rejected and referred to humans for keywording, the system can perform much better than our hand-built rules. For example, one solution generated by the system achieved 79% recall and 77% precision provided that 8% of articles were referred to human editors; another demonstrated 75% recall and 87% precision if 16% were referred; and if 20% were referred, figures of 84% recall and 84% precision were achieved by yet another system. (Generally precision and recall can be traded off; the recall-precision product is a good measure of quality. Recall-precision products were 72% ($= .82 \times .88$) for human editors, 58% for our original system, and 61%, 65%, and 71% for the cases where 8%, 16%, and 20% of articles are referred, respectively).

The original system required two months of effort by a two person team. The genetic algorithm enhancement required roughly an additional person-month.

3   Classifying Census Data: the PACE system

We demonstrated in a joint project with the U.S. Bureau of Census that an MBR system called PACE (for Parallel Automatic Coding Expert [2]) performed impressively on a task to generate one of 241 industry codes and one of 509 occupation codes for individual respondents, by comparing their answers (expressed as free text and multiple choice selections) with 132,000 cases that have already been classified by hand. By limiting decisions to categories where the system has been proven to be correct at least 90% of the time for industry codes and at least 86% of the time for occupation codes, PACE correctly processed 63% of the database for industry codes and 57% of the database for occupation codes. For comparison, AIOCS, an expert system that required 196 person months to develop, achieved only 57% and 37% of the database respectively on these two tasks [1]; the MBR system took less than four person months to build. For this application, the similarity metric for selecting good precedents from the training set was generated on the fly, using statistical operations.

4   Protein Secondary Structure Prediction

In his Ph.D. thesis work at Brandeis University, much of it done while a part-time employee of Thinking Machines, Xiru Zhang implemented a system that for two years held the world's record for accuracy in protein secondary structure prediction [18]. Some background on the protein secondary structure prediction problem is in order: it is now relatively easy to analyze amino acid sequences; the sequences for over 20,000 proteins are now known. However, it is very difficult to find the three-dimensional structures of proteins; fewer than 1000 are known, and a large fraction of these are hemoglobins. The reason is that to find three-dimensional ("tertiary") structure, researchers must crystallize the protein, and then perform X-ray diffraction analysis. This process typically requires 2-3 years time for two or three researchers; moreover, some proteins apparently cannot be crystallized, and so resist tertiary structure analysis. Computer methods for finding tertiary structures for unknown proteins has also proved intractable to date, and most researchers have worked on the simpler problem of finding the portions of an amino acid sequence that correspond to helices, to sheets (two-dimensional structures that consist of parallel bonded strand sections of the amino acid sequence), or to "coil" (anything that isn't a helix or sheet).

Until recently the best secondary structure results had used a backpropagation neural net [9]. Zhang redid this work, but with a larger training set (about 110 non-homologous proteins with helix-sheet-coil labelings) drawn from the Brookhaven database [4], and achieved similar results. He also tried other methods, including a statistical method he devised, which was about as accurate as the neural net, and MBR, which was a little better than the other two. However, Zhang noticed that these three methods only agreed with each other about 80% of the time. He thus devised a hybrid architecture that used all three methods (neural nets, statistics and MBR) separately, and then combined the results of these three using another neural net. The resulting system performed with about 3% greater accuracy than any other system built to date, an increase that is highly significant statistically. Again, the ability to do a number of experiments, each of a large size, led to significantly increased peformance.

5 Database Mining

In a cooperative project with Citicorp, Craig Stanfill of Thinking Machines led an effort that tested the performance of a number of different AI learning and statistical methods for predicting behavior of credit card holders. In each of the experiments, a system was trained on a portion of the database, and then tested on another portion. Training samples for defaulters used fifteen variables (total charges, total paid, number of charges, balance, months overdue, bankruptcy indicator, etc.) for a cardholder as input, and the binary data on pay/default three months ahead as the target output. About ten different methods were tested in all. The best methods tested, in order of effectiveness on this problem, were CART (Classification and Regression Trees), 2-dimensional additive regression, 100 nearest neighbor MBR, and 1-dimensional additive regression. The major advantage of massive parallelism for these tasks is the ability to run a large number of large-scale experiments in a short time. Without fast response times, one might well be tempted to use a small subset of a database, and to stop once a method provided what seemed like reasonable results.

A current project called Darwin, involving Thinking Machines and Epsilon Data Management, Inc. of Burlington, MA, is comparing two forms of genetic algorithms and backpropagation neural nets with CART and statistical methods in a larger and more carefully designed experiment. One of the GA methods is using a Koza-style system [5] which generates candidate Lisp s-expressions whose variables are the attributes in each record along with constants, and whose operators are $+$, $-$, $*$, $/$, square root, log, etc. Each candidate expression can be applied to a record in the database to produce a binary decision (e.g. default or not default). All examples in the database along with correct classifications are stored by distributing them among all the processors of a CM-5. Candidate expressions are initially generated randomly, and broadcast one at a time to all processors, which apply each to the data in each processor, in parallel. Each candidate expression is then scored for accuracy. After a number of these have been tried, the worst ones are discarded, the best ones saved, and numbers of copies generated in proportion to their scores. All candidates are then randomly paired and "mated" by removing subexpressions from each expression and exchanging them between mates. The process continues, using the offspring of this process as candidates.

The other GA system is more in the Holland style [3], and distributes a subset of the database along with a large population of "classifiers" (bitstrings that can each represent a classification method), among the processors. Classifiers are evaluated on subsets of the data local to their processors, and then mated in manners analogous to those above, except that crossover is substituted for exchange of subexpressions.

At this point, early in the experiment, neural nets seem to be exhibiting the best performance—better than fielded statistical methods—but the verdict is still out.

6 Generation of Graphics Using Interactive Evolutionary Methods

Work by Karl Sims has shown how artificial evolution can be used to generate novel graphics images. There are two key parts to this work [12]: 1) a method for taking an s-expression that is a function of (x, y) and using it to generate images; 2) methods for creating (graphically) "interesting" variations of s-expressions; and 3) an interface that allows a user to view a set of images corresponding to variations on a single s-expression and to select one of the variations to serve as the "mother" for the next generation of variations. Several different types of task have been demonstrated: for example, by restricting s-expressions to use particular functions, one can generate 3D plant structures. Recently this program was the basis for an art show at the Pompidou Center in Paris, where visitors were able to use foot treadles to select an image corresponding to a new mother s-expression from among a set of images displayed on large screens. This system in general makes it possible to generate large numbers of images, from which users can select with very few keystrokes, yielding a vast range of images with little user effort beyond the use of esthetic judgement.

7 Summary

Massively parallel machines have proved useful for a number of large database-related tasks. It has generally been important to be able to perform many experiments, and to do so on large amounts of data. Learning and memory-based methods have required modest amounts of time to program, and have yielded excellent performance when compared to other programs as well to to humans.

References

1. Appel, M. & E. Hellerman. "Census Bureau Experiments with Automated Industry and Occupation Coding." *Proc. Amer. Statistical Assoc.*, 1983, 32–40.
2. Creecy, R., B. Masand, S. Smith, & D. L. Waltz. "Trading MIPS and Memory for Knowledge Engineering." *CACM 35, 8*, August 1992, 48–64.
3. Goldberg, D. E. *Genetic Algorithms in Search, Optimization & Machine Learning.* Reading, MA: Addison-Wesley, 1989.
4. Kabsch, W. & C. Sander. "Dictionary of protein secondary structures: pattern recognition off hydrogen-bonded and geomerical features." *Biopolymers 22*, 1983, 2577–2637.
5. Koza, J. *Genetic Programmming: On the Programming of Computers by Means on Natural Selection.* Cambridge: MIT Press, 1992.
6. Masand, B. "Effects of query and database sizes on classification of news stories using memory based reasoning." *AAAI Spring Symposium on CBR*, Stanford, March 1993.
7. Masand, B. "Optimizing Confidence of Text Classification by Evolution of Symbolic Expressions." Unpublished paper, Thinking Machines Corp., Cambridge, MA, 1993.
8. Masand, B., G. Linoff, & D. L. Waltz. "Classifying news stories using memory-based reasoning." *Proc. SIGIR Conf.*, Copenhagen, July 1992.
9. Qian, N. & T. J. Sejnowski. "Predicting the secondary structure of globular proteins using neural network models." *J. Molecular Biology 202*, 1988, 865–884.
10. Quinlan, R. "Learning efficient classification procedures and their application to chess end games." In R.S. Michalski, J. Carbonell, & T. Mitchell (eds.) *Machine Learning: An Artificial Intelligence Approach*, Los Angeles: Tioga Publishing, 1988, 463–482.
11. Rumelhart, D, J. McClelland, et al. *Parallel Distributed Processing*, Cambridge: MIT Press, 1986.
12. Sims, K. "Artificial Evolution for Computer Graphics." *Computer Graphics 25, 4*, July 1991, 319–28.
13. Stanfill, C. & D. L. Waltz. "Toward Memory-Based Reasoning." *CACM 29*, December 1986, 1213–1228.
14. Waltz, D. L. "Memory-Based Reasoning." In M. Arbib & A. Robinson (eds.) *Natural and Artificial Parallel Computation*, Cambridge: MIT Press, 1989, 251–276.
15. Waltz, D. L. "Massively Parallel AI." *Proc. AAAI-90*, Boston, 1117–1122.
16. Waltz, D. & J. Feldman, *Connectionist Models and Their Implications*, Hillsdale, NJ: Ablex Publishing, 1988.
17. Zhang, X. & J. Hutchinson. "Practical Issues in Nonlinear Time Series Prediction." In A. Weigend & N. Gershenfeld (eds.), *Predicting the Future and Understanding*

the Past: Proceedings of the 1992 Santa Fe Institute Time Series Competition, Addison-Wesley, 1993, to appear.

18. Zhang, X., J. Mesirov, & D. L. Waltz. "A Hybrid System for Protein Secondary Structure Predicition." *J. Molecular Biology 225,* 1992, 1049–1063.

Sparcle: A Multithreaded VLSI Processor for Parallel Computing*

Anant Agarwal, Jonathan Babb, David Chaiken,
Godfrey D'Souza (LSI Logic), Kirk Johnson, David Kranz,
John Kubiatowicz, Beng-Hong Lim, Gino Maa, Ken Mackenzie,
Dan Nussbaum, Mike Parkin (Sun Microsystems), and Donald Yeung

Laboratory for Computer Science
Massachusetts Institute of Technology
Cambridge, MA 02139

The Sparcle chip will clock at no more than 50 MHz. It has no more than 200K transistors. It does not use the latest technologies and dissipates a paltry 2 watts. It has no on-chip cache, no fancy pads, and only 207 pins. It does not even support multiple-instructions issue. Then, why do we think this chip is interesting?

Sparcle is a processor chip designed for large-scale multiprocessing. Processors suitable for multiprocessing environments must meet several requirements:

- They must support fine-grain synchronization. Modern day micros pay scant attention to this aspect of multiprocessing, usually providing just a test-and-set instruction, and in some cases, not even that.
- They must be able to initiate communication actions and respond rapidly to asynchronous events such as synchronization faults and message arrival. Traps and other asynchronous event-handling is inefficient on many current microprocessors, often requiring tens of cycles to reach the appropriate trap service routine.
- They must be able to tolerate memory and communication latencies, as well as synchronization latencies. Long latencies are inevitable in large-scale multiprocessors, but current microprocessor designs are ill-suited to handle such latencies.

The goal of the Sparcle chip project was to demonstrate that an architecture that addresses these needs could be evolved without deviating significantly from existing single-processor designs. Indeed the Sparcle processor has been implemented with the help of LSI Logic and SUN Microsystems by modifying an existing SPARC design. The ability to use the existing core of a current RISC design coupled with an efficient communications interface can significantly improve the price-performance ratio of multiprocessors.

Sparcle tolerates long communication and synchronization latencies by rapidly switching to other threads of computation. Sparcle switches to another thread when a cache miss that requires service over the communication network is signalled, or when a synchronization fault is detected. Clearly, such a processor requires a pipelined memory and communications system. In our system, a separate

---

* An extended version of this paper appears in IEEE Micro, June 1993.

communications chip will interface to Sparcle to provide the desired pipelined memory system interface.

The current implementation of Sparcle can switch to another thread of computation in 14 cycles. With slightly more aggressive modifications this number can be reduced to 4 cycles. Unlike previous rapid-context-switching designs like the HEP [1], Sparcle has high single thread performance. In fact, Sparcle's single-thread performance is no worse than that of a SPARC.

Sparcle provides support for rapid response to asynchronous events by streamlining SPARC's trap interface and providing support for dispatching rapidly to the appropriate trap handler. Sparcle achieves this by providing two special trap lines for the most common types of events, namely, cache misses to remote nodes and synchronization faults. A third signal is used for all other types of events. Sparcle also allows servicing traps in dedicated registers to avoid saving and restoring registers. Finally, the trap vectors are spread out in memory so that vital trap codes can be inlined at the dispatch points.

Sparcle supports fine-grain data-level synchronization through the use of full-empty bits, as in the HEP. With full empty bits the probe of a lock and access of the data word protected by the lock can be accomplished in one cycle. If the synchronization attempt fails, then the synchronization trap is invoked to handle the fault. In our system, the external communications chip is responsible for detecting synchronization faults and alerting Sparcle; failure cases are handled in software.

Software handling of failed synchronizations has several advantages. First, the waiting algorithm can be tailored to synchronization type in software. Second, because queuing on the synchronization condition is done in software, hardware complexity is avoided. Because failures are expected to be rarer with fine-grain synchronization that with coarse-grain synchronization, the software handling cost of failed synchronization attempts is not expected to be burdensome. Sparcle also supports control-level parallelism and synchronization based on futures.

Finally, Sparcle supports a highly streamlined interface to the network with the ability to launch and receive interconnection network messages. While the communications interface with the interconnection network is currently being implemented in a separate chip, future implementations will integrate this functionality on the same chip as the processor.

Sparcle was implemented by modifying an existing SPARC design. The register windows in SPARC are used to "cache" multiple threads of computations so that switching between threads requires updating the window pointer and saving and restoring the PSW and PCs. The access to the network is provided through extended address space bits (ASI) and coprocessor instructions available on the SPARC. The context switching and trap handling mechanisms in the SPARC were streamlined to meet our objectives. Unaligned load-store traps are used to detect future-based synchronization. The SPARC was modified for rapid dispatch to an appropriate handler.

The implementation strategy of Sparcle was itself unique and involved multiple participants from industry and university. Sparcle was implemented with help from LSI Logic and SUN Microsystems by modifying an existing SPARC design. First the Sparcle architecture was defined, a Sparcle compiler was written, and a detailed cycle-by-cycle simulator implemented at MIT. Currently, compilers for a parallel version of C and a parallel version of lisp exist. Then, high-level changes to SPARC functional blocks were made at SUN and lower gate-level changes level were made at LSI. These changes were tested against Sparcle binaries produced at MIT. Then net lists were synthesized at LSI and tested against several hundred thousands of test vectors at MIT. The test vectors included both SPARC vectors provided by LSI and Sparcle vectors obtained from the MIT Sparcle simulator. The test set up included a net list module for the floating-point coprocessor, and a behavioral model for the rest of the memory and communication systems. Layout and fabrication was undertaken by LSI.

At MIT, we received working Sparcle chips from LSI on March 11, 1992. A test bed for Sparcle to exercise its multiprocessor functionality has been operational for several months. This test bed allows booting up a multiprocessor system and running multiprocessor code with synchronization operations, context switching, and futures, on a Sparcle processor. The test bed currently allows running Sparcle chips to speeds of up to about 20 MHz. We have currently booted up our runtime system and run several small multiprocessor programs on Sparcle at the maximum speed allowed by the test bed.

We are currently implementing a multiprocessor called Alewife [2] that will allow a more thorough evaluation of our ideas by running the Sparcle chips at their maximum speed in a real system.

The Sparcle project is funded in part by DARPA contract # N00014-87-K-0825 and in part by NSF grant # MIP-9012773. LSI Logic and SUN Microsystems helped implement Sparcle, and LSI Logic supported the fabrication of Sparcle.

References

1. B.J. Smith. Architecture and Applications of the HEP Multiprocessor Computer System. *Society of Photocoptical Instrumentation Engineers*, 298:241–248, 1981.
2. Anant Agarwal, David Chaiken, Godfrey D'Souza, Kirk Johnson, David Kranz, John Kubiatowicz, Kiyoshi Kurihara, Beng-Hong Lim, Gino Maa, Dan Nussbaum, Mike Parkin, and Donald Yeung. The MIT Alewife Machine: A Large-Scale Distributed-Memory Multiprocessor. In *Proceedings of Workshop on Scalable Shared Memory Multiprocessors*. Kluwer Academic Publishers, 1991. An extended version of this paper has been submitted for publication, and appears as MIT/LCS Memo TM-454, 1991.

A New Architecture Design Paradigm for Parallel Computing in Scheme

Carl Bruggeman and R. Kent Dybvig

Indiana University, Bloomington IN 47405, USA

Abstract. This paper describes a new architecture design paradigm
that radically reassigns various system responsibilities among the compiler, operating system, and architecture in order to simplify the design
and increase the performance of parallel computing systems. Implementation techniques for latently typed languages like Scheme are enhanced
and used to support compiler-enforced memory protection and compiler-
controlled exception handling. Hardware design complexity is greatly reduced and hardware modularity is increased by not only eliminating the
need to implement exception handling in the processor state machine,
but also by eliminating global control altogether. In the absence of global
control, techniques such as pipelining and multiple contexts that exploit
instruction-level and thread-level parallelism can be used together without the usual processor complexity problems, to increase the efficiency
of parallel systems. Complexity is reduced and efficiency is increased at
the software level as well. The use of compiler-enforced memory protection and a single shared system-wide virtual address space increases
inter-thread communication efficiency as well as inter-thread protection
resulting in threads that not only are light-weight but also enjoy the
protection guarantees of heavy-weight threads.

1 Introduction

All general-purpose computing systems are implemented partly in hardware and
partly in software. The assignment of responsibilities among the hardware and
software components is critical to both the overall efficiency and design simplicity of a system. The design choices implicit in this assignment should be sensitive
to the most recent advances in hardware and software technology. Many design
choices, however, have been made one way for so long that it is often over-
looked that they are indeed choices. In many cases, conventional architecture is
not taking advantage of modern language features or compiler capabilities; in
other cases, languages and compilers are not sensitive to current hardware characteristics. We are exploring a new system-level architecture design paradigm
with a set of hardware and software responsibilities that is radically different
from traditional architectures. This work demonstrates that a reassignment of
responsibilities among the compiler, operating system and architecture can not
only increase the performance of parallel systems but can also simplify their
design and implementation. Our primary goal is to support symbolic programming languages such as Scheme [7], but the paradigm supports any high-level
type-safe language.

System performance and design simplicity is addressed at both the software and hardware level in the new design paradigm. At the hardware level, performance is most often increased by exploiting parallelism. There are two forms of parallelism that are commonly supported by processor architectures: thread-level parallelism and instruction-level parallelism. Thread-level parallelism is derived from an application by decomposing it into a set of processes or threads that may be run concurrently. Thread-level parallelism is exploited both in multiprocessor systems, where threads run concurrently on different processors, and in multiple-context processors, where several threads are resident within a processor and the processor interleaves their execution in some way. Instruction-level parallelism is parallelism within a thread that is either derived statically by a compiler or dynamically by the hardware. Instruction-level parallelism can be exploited by an architecture to allow the concurrent execution of two or more instructions from a thread.

The exploitation of instruction-level parallelism through pipelining and multiple-instruction issue (superscalar) is one of the primary characteristics of RISC processors [36]. The run-time for a thread is shortened by overlapping the execution of as many instructions from the thread as is possible given the hardware resources of the processor and the data-dependencies of the program [17]. Such processors execute multiple threads sequentially by context switching between threads at synchronization points. Context-switch times for commercial RISC processors, however, are at best on the order of tens of instructions and are often hundreds or even thousands.

The exploitation of thread-level parallelism in shared-memory multiple processor systems is often severely limited by memory and synchronization latencies [4]. Multiple contexts within a processor can be used to hide such latencies by having the processor switch to another context when a memory reference is not local and may take many cycles to complete, or a synchronization attempt fails. Barrel processors, such as the peripheral processor unit from the CDC6600 [45], were among the first architectures to use rapid context switching to tolerate long latencies due to slow memory or other functional units. The HEP [23], Horizon [24], and Tera [2] architectures pursued by Burton Smith have many similar characteristics as does the MASA [15] architecture proposed by Halstead. Dataflow architectures, such as the Monsoon [35], PRISC [31], Epsilon [12], and the ETL EM-4 [37], also exploit multithreading to hide memory and synchronization latencies while at the same time minimizing the amount of processor-resident state for each thread.

In order to improve processor utilization, however, fast context-switch times for multiple context processors are crucial [47]. Fast context switch times on the order of a single cycle are particularly important if these techniques are to be used to cover latencies for second level caches hits that are typically on the order of 4-10 cycles [17]. In multiprocessor systems the performance loss due to memory and synchronization latencies is compounded if traditional pipelined RISC processors are used since the additional resources to exploit instruction-level parallelism are not only idled while the processor waits but the implementation techniques used to exploit instruction-level parallelism increase context-switch time as well.

Techniques such as pipelining and multiple-instruction issue greatly increase the complexity of processor control. Multiple-contexts within a processor also increase processor control. Together these two techniques compound the complexities of the other. Only recently have both techniques been used together in an architecture (*i.e.*, the architecture supports pipelining *within* a thread[1]), the MIT Alewife [1]. In this system, however, the two mechanisms are effectively decoupled, at the expense of concurrency and context switch time, since only a single thread is permitted in the pipeline at one time and the pipeline is required to drain before control can be transferred to another thread.

Indeed, conventional wisdom has it that processor control complexity is overwhelming if pipelining and/or superscalar techniques that exploit instruction-level parallelism are combined with multiple contexts that exploit thread-level parallelism. It is generally assumed that an architecture that permits a thread to run at the full speed of the pipeline must incur a significant delay, such as draining the pipeline, when control switches to another thread. Preliminary work by Laudon [26] suggests such a design might be feasible for sufficiently simple pipelines. This, however, presents the processor architect with a dilemma: either use a much less aggressive (simpler) pipeline design, sacrificing single-thread speed for latency tolerance or use an aggressive pipeline to achieve good single-thread performance, sacrificing latency tolerance (system efficiency) in multiprocessor systems.

The architecture design paradigm proposed in this paper, however, makes the design of aggressively pipelined multiple context processors which allow interleaved (on a cycle-by-cycle basis) or even concurrent execution of multiple resident contexts straightforward to design and implement. In addition, the paradigm enhances hardware design modularity and reuse and encourages the use of asynchronous design methodologies.

At the software level, a number of system performance and design complexity problems arise. First, a multiple-context processor must either replicate the memory protection state for each thread, swap it on a context switch, or require all running threads to share the same address space. Since replication is too expensive and swapping is far too slow, all running contexts must share a single address space. This, however, prohibits separate applications from running concurrently and, even worse, makes all operating system interactions single-threaded. This is unfortunate since operating systems interactions already pose a serious performance concern for high-performance processors, and operating system performance has scaled poorly compared to application performance on

---

[1] All other multiple context architectures to date have employed instruction pipelining where the instructions that may be overlapped come from different threads. As a result, however, single-threaded applications run at only a fraction, 1/N, the speed of the machine, where N is the length of the pipeline. The commercial dominance of pipelined RISC processors, however, present a compelling argument for the importance of pipelining and other techniques that exploit instruction-level parallelism, even for multiple-context processors.

RISC processors [3].

Efficient sharing of information between concurrent threads that require protection guarantees is also crucial for good performance, especially for persistent object-oriented systems as well as application/operating system interactions in more traditional systems. A promising solution is to support a single system-wide address space that all processes share and to support some sort of per-process protection domains [2, 22] within the single address space. In other words, separate the address protection mechanism from the address translation mechanism and allow all threads to share the same address translation resources. This solution has a number of benefits [22]. Shared objects need not be copied between protection domains, since only the per-thread protection tables need to be updated. More importantly, the virtual address of an object can be treated as the identity or "name" of the object since the virtual address is unchanged between protection domains. A single virtual address space also permits the use of simple and fast virtually addressed caches without the complexity and performance loss due to address aliases. Separate protection domains for multiple context processors, however, impose almost as much overhead and are almost as complex as separate address spaces.

From a software engineering point of view this solution is inappropriate. Threads within a protection domain have *no* protection from one another and communication between domains requires (at least) an expensive kernel trap, since the memory protection tables must be updated. Ideally, system-enforced abstraction barriers should be fine-grain and extremely inexpensive so that every part of an application that is logically separate from another part of the application is expressed using an abstraction that enforces the separation.

Separate hardware-enforced protection domains are also inappropriate from the point of view of overall system performance. Hardware-level memory protection precludes the use of most important compiler optimizations, such as procedure integration and constant propagation, between procedures that must run in separate protection domains.

The architecture design paradigm proposed in this paper employs a single system-wide virtual address space and, thus, enjoys all the benefits of single address space systems enumerated above. In addition, system-enforced abstraction barriers are fine-grain and extremely light-weight; the cost of accessing data from another protection domain or the cost of a cross-domain procedure call is, at worst, that of a normal full procedure call. Since all types of compiler optimizations can be performed by the system, however, without compromising protection, the cost of cross-domain accesses can be reduced even further.

The gains in system efficiency and design simplicity are made possible by reexamining traditional system abstractions and reassigning responsibility for various features among the architecture, compiler, and operating system. New system-level abstraction barriers are chosen because the appropriate selection of abstraction barriers is crucial for making implementations simpler to design and reuse (faster to market) and at the same time more amenable to parallelism (faster implementations).

Many of the hardware–software tradeoffs employed by this design paradigm are derived from implementation techniques used for latently-typed languages like Scheme. One reason for doing so is that much research has already been done concerning the explicit [11, 14, 21] and implicit [16] generation of parallel threads from Scheme applications. We have also developed a number of efficient implementation techniques for first-class continuations [19] (threads) and their generalization to concurrent implementations [18], as well as a flexible and efficient storage management system that is amenable to parallel systems [10].

There are two hardware-software design tradeoffs in this new architecture design paradigm that are crucial: software-enforced memory protection and software-controlled exception handling. The issues and benefits related to software-enforced memory protection are discussed in Section 2 followed by a similar discussion for exception handling in Section 3. In Section 4 these issues are generalized into two design principles that together define a very nontraditional set of system abstractions. Section 5 presents a summary, a discussion of potential drawbacks of this design paradigm, and areas for further research.

2   Memory Protection

Primary responsibility for implementing memory protection, when it was implemented at all, has been assigned to the hardware. This was probably the only reasonable choice when most software was written in low-level and assembly languages. Modern versions of such diverse high level languages as Scheme, Fortran, and C++, however, are *type-safe*, *i.e.*, they permit or even encourage compilers to disallow invalid memory references that could lead to security violations in systems without hardware-enforced memory protection. Requiring all languages for a system to be type-safe would, in practice, prohibit only traditional untyped assembly languages since a nontype-safe language, in effect, must *require* that no error be signaled when an unsafe language construction is used or must *require* some aspect of the underlying architecture to be exposed. Even loosely typed languages like C generally leave unsafe language constructions unspecified and strive to hide details of the underlying architecture in the interests of portability. Thus, with recent advances in compiler technology, especially in the realm of latently-typed languages such as Scheme, *compiler-enforced* memory protection is now feasible.

Hardware memory protection can be eliminated by requiring programs to be written in one of these languages or in a higher level "typed" assembly language which similarly disallows invalid memory references. This is useful not only because hardware memory protection comes at a certain (usually small but significant) implementation cost, but also because hardware memory protection is too inflexible. Hardware memory protection is inflexible because it occurs at the memory reference rather than language construct level. As a result, some invalid references (those that do not actually represent security violations) are detected either not at all or in an untimely fashion arbitrarily long after the actual error occurs.

More importantly, hardware-enforced memory protection requires operating system intervention in the case where protection is required and some form of sharing is desired. This intervention, however, is becoming increasingly expensive for high-performance implementations primarily due to increased trap handling latencies [3] while at the same time it is becoming more widely used, both by operating system methodologies such as microkernels that change protection domains frequently and by applications with multiple heavy-weight processes, e.g., X Windows [38]. By placing memory protection under compiler control and utilizing a single large system-wide virtual address space, memory protection can be enforced at a more appropriate level and the difficulty and inefficiency of interprocess communication can be reduced or eliminated.

Even if trap handling latencies were eliminated, hardware-enforced memory protection would still exact a significant efficiency penalty for interaction between any two parts of a system that require protection guarantees. Even in the best case where both partners employ the same representations, where the compilers guarantee that abstraction barriers for data that is exchanged are enforced, and where the system prohibits contact unless such guarantees are made, the existence of a hardware barrier still precludes many important optimizations performed by modern compilers. For example, when compiling user code it would be useless to open-code (inline) system calls that access system data or resources (virtually all system calls) because the system data is in a separate hardware-enforced protection domain. In the worst case without such guarantees, repreated conversions may be required, on both sides of the hardware barrier, between a common "raw" representation and the respective internal representations, even if the internal representations used by both partners are identical.

Because this type of strict enforcement of abstraction barriers is so expensive on systems with hardware-enforced memory protection, software engineering principles are often sacrificed. For example, many systems support a light-weight process abstraction called *threads*. Threads are light-weight because they share a single virtual address space, sacrificing the protection that is implied by a process abstraction for increased interprocess communication efficiency on systems with hardware enforced-memory protection. In a system with compiler-enforced memory protection and a single system-wide virtual address space, threads are not only light-weight and but also have the same protection guarantees that heavy-weight processes enjoy.

Ideally, system-enforced abstraction barriers should be both fine-grain and extremely inexpensive so that every part of a system that is logically separate from another part of the system is expressed using abstraction barriers that guarantee the separation. One approach to fine-grain abstraction barriers, called *capabilities* [9], has been implemented in hardware on a number of systems [5, 33, 48] as well as in kernel software [34, 50]. Hardware-enforced capabilities have often proven to be complex or slow since each instruction and data memory reference must be checked for the appropriate execute or access permissions. Kernel-enforced capabilities are not light-weight since a kernel trap must be taken for each capability access. Compiler-enforced capabilities, however, are both easy to use and inexpensive since protection from improper access to a capability is subsumed by the compiler-enforced type-safety of the various languages. In addition, a number of difficult issues that face hardware-enforced capability systems [27] can be mitigated or avoided using such capabilities (see [6]).

Since protection from improper access is already guaranteed, the implementation of compiler-enforced capabilities is reduced to establishing a convention or interface consisting of two parts: some form of opaque data type encapsulating the resource that can be passed around but not dereferenced and some method of granting controlled access to the resource. Scheme provides a single abstraction that encapsulates both parts, *first-class procedures*. First class procedures are opaque objects that encapsulate both the lexical environment in which they are defined and the code to manipulate it. Since the only way to access the environment (the encapsulated resource) in a type-safe language is to call the procedure, a process creating a capability (procedure) has complete control over how the shared data or resource is viewed or manipulated. Capability access costs very little since a "protected procedure" or "cross-domain" call is simply an ordinary procedure call. As such, they can even be subjected to optimizations such as procedure integration, customized calling conventions, and partial evaluation without loss of protection. The implementation of capabilities in terms of first-class procedures is a good example of how the use of a modern language feature can simplify the design and implementation of an architecture.

3 Exception Handling

Like memory protection, exception handling has traditionally been supported primarily by hardware. Exceptions for the purposes of this paper are divided into two groups: exceptions that occur synchronously with respect to the instruction stream and exceptions that occur asynchronously with respect to the instruction stream. Synchronous exception are changes in control flow that always occur at the same point when executing the same program on the same data set. They are, in effect, conditional branches implicit in the instructions stream. Examples of this type of exception include integer overflow, floating point underflow and overflow, division by zero, and privileged instruction traps. Asynchronous exceptions are changes in control flow that *may* not occur at the same point when executing the same instruction stream on the same data set. Examples include device interrupts and page faults.

Exception handling for both synchronous and asynchronous exceptions is straightforward to design and efficient to implement for architectures that employ microcode, since taking an exception involves just calling another micro-subroutine. The motivation for RISC processors, however, was the observation that the overhead of microcode interpretation penalized the efficiency of simple operations and made pipelined implementations complex [36]. This lead to the adoption within RISC circles of a hardwired global state machine to replace microcode interpretation, all the while retaining the exception handling model that originated with the microcode model. Embedding exception handling in the global state machine, however, is neither natural nor easy to implement in modern pipelined architectures. In fact, it is often the most difficult and time consuming part of the design process [17] and usually the most error prone part as well.

An alternative is to assign primary responsibility for exception handling to the compiler and operating system. Synchronous exceptions can be handled by requiring all functional units to indicate exceptional conditions somewhere accessible to the compiler and by requiring the compiler to generate code that explicitly checks for such conditions. In other words, replace the conditional branch *implicit* in any instruction that might signal an exception with a more general *explicit* conditional branch. Asynchronous exceptions can be handled by requiring that an implementation support multiple hardware contexts and that at least one context be reserved by the operating system to execute a service routine that waits for such events.

For higher-performance implementations, a VLIW [8] (Very Long Instruction Word) type architecture can be used that permits a conditional transfer of control as well as several operations to be specified in a single instruction. An example of an architecture that lies somewhere in between is described in [6]. This architecture could be classified as LIW (Long Instruction Word) since it permits the compiler to specify a general type test for one or both operands as well as an operation on the operands. In addition, it requires exceptions to be signaled in the type or value field of the result generated by the operation. Since the compiler, in many cases, can generate code to perform the check when the result is first used, exceptions can be handled as efficiently as in traditional architectures. In fact, this architecture may run faster since enabling precise exceptions on a number of current architectures effectively disables pipelining.

Eliminating exceptions enormously simplifies processor control because an implicit conditional branch in an instruction that might generate an exception creates a control dependency between that instruction and subsequent instructions. In other words, the effects of subsequent instructions are contingent upon the successful *completion* of the first and the processor state machine must check for and deal with each and every one of these dependencies. Using compiler-controlled exceptions, these control dependencies are transformed into normal data dependencies in branch instructions that check for exceptional conditions. Thus, from the point of view of a context, once an instruction issues, it is guaranteed to complete[2]. Taken one step further, global processor-wide control can be eliminated *entirely* by moving any remaining functionality that may be implemented by the global state machine, such as the register scoreboard, into a related functional unit, such as the register file.

Eliminating the entire global state machine and abandoning the traditional architecture–control paradigm (at least for processor-wide control) is highly desirable for a number of reasons. First, it greatly simplifies the exploitation of parallelism in pipelined, superscalar, and multiple context implementations be-

---

[2] Although page faults, especially on loads, make this invariant appear difficult to maintain, it is actually quite straightforward and useful [6]).

cause parallelism in practice is fundamentally limited by the control interactions necessary to coordinate the efforts of the various functional units. Implementations using a global processor state machine require that all of a processor's functional units proceed in lock-step, presenting status to and receiving control from the global state machine. The addition of even a single functional unit may require that changes be made in the control for all other functional units. In the worst case, this results in a global state machine whose complexity is quadratic in the number of parallel functional units. Often, however, a great deal of design effort is expended refining restrictions that are placed on an architecture which ensure that such complexity problems are avoided, but these restrictions limit the effective parallelism as well.

Second, a global state machine interferes with any modular approach to architecture design and inhibits a systematic exploitation of replication (a primary characteristic and strength of VLSI technology), since the control for each functional unit must be integrated with the control of all the others. For this reason, global control is avoided at the system level in virtually every computer, *i.e.*, no computer has a system-wide controller that orchestrates the step-by-step progress of all processors, caches, memory units, and peripherals in a system. The lack of global control is exploited in the design of highly-parallel and replicatable special purpose processor architectures, such as systolic arrays [25] and other *ensemble* architectures [39], where global control can be severely restricted or eliminated due to restrictions on the problem domain. The elimination of global control, however, has never before been applicable to the design of *general purpose processors*, primarily because there has not existed an acceptable alternative to replace the functionality provided by exceptions.

A number of design methodologies, both synchronous [49] (clocked) and asynchronous [30, 28, 43] (unclocked), have been proposed that enable the design of simple, flexible, and re-usable modules and that allow such modules to be duplicated and composed to form larger modules, where the composition of two or more such modules is often as simple as wiring them together. Asynchronous methodologies, in particular, have made strong claims of modularity because they eliminate an important global design dependence found in synchronous systems: each pipeline stage must require the same amount of time to compute its result since all stages are controlled by the same clock, and that clock must be lengthened to accommodate the slowest stage. In the design of processors, even asynchronous ones, many of the benefits derived from using a hierarchy of modules are lost because global control, by its nature, requires access to all levels of an abstraction, in effect forcing the hierarchy to be flattened. For example, even recent asynchronous processor designs have both an asynchronous architecture (pipeline) and asynchronous global controller, one using microcode [20] and one using hardwired control [29]. The elimination of global control will allow the advantages of hierarchical design methodologies, especially asynchronous ones, to be exploited to full effect.

Third, the use of a global state machine disregards the most important and limiting characteristic of VLSI, the high cost of communication relative to logic and storage [44]. Although the implementation costs for VLSI in terms of area as well as performance favor architectures in which communication is localized [40], the global control paradigm requires many active signals (clock, control, and status) to run to every functional unit and back during each basic clock cycle. Although it has been possible in the past to treat communication delays across a die as negligible compared to cycle time, the decrease in minimum feature size and increase in clock speeds require current designs to devote a significant amount of effort to the treatment of global signals, especially clocks. Future designs will require an ever increasing amount of design effort to minimize the impact of these communication latencies, latencies which will only get worse with larger die sizes (longer signal runs) and faster clock speeds (less time to get there).

Fourth, global control makes fault tolerant processor designs difficult at all levels since a global controller represents a large complex single point of failure whose functionality must in some way be replicated. Dynamic fault tolerance as well as techniques used to increase yields, such as spare cache lines to replace defective ones in on-chip processor caches, will likely be simpler or more widely applicable to other aspects of an architecture in the absence of global control.

4 A New Architecture Design Paradigm

At the heart of the new architecture design paradigm proposed in this paper are two system design principles which expand on the two examples presented above: compiler enforced memory protection and the elimination of global control. The first concerns the use of a new software abstraction barrier while the second concerns the use a new hardware abstraction barrier. These two principles have been chosen because the appropriate selection of abstraction barriers is crucial to making implementations simpler to design and reuse and at the same time more amenable to parallelism. Indeed, the abstraction barriers of traditional systems are often the source of many design difficulties and runtime inefficiencies precisely because they are no longer appropriate in light of the limitations and advances in compiler, operating system, and semiconductor technologies.

4.1 High-level Instruction Set Architectures

The first principle is that user-visible instruction set architectures (ISAs) must be high-level, type-safe, and extensible, and they must use a single shared system-wide virtual address space. An ISA must be high-level in the sense that it provides a simple core set of syntactic forms, such as procedure definition, procedure call, variable assignment, *etc.*, and a core set of primitive functions for system-defined data types and facilities, rather than a set of machine-level representation and location-oriented operations. An ISA must be extensible in the sense that there must be some user-accessible facility to augment, in a type-safe manner, the core set of primitive functions and types in the system.

Traditional ISAs are a language specification for programs that are interpreted by a specific type of processor and, as such, provide a low-level abstraction barrier for compilers to target. Intermediate-level ISAs [41, 42, 46], such as OSF's ANDF [32], provide an additional level of software translation between the output generated by compilers and the code interpreted by the hardware. They specify, in effect, a common assembly language for all compilers in the system, providing an abstraction barrier that hides many of the lowest level implementation details such as instruction scheduling constraints, branch delay slots, and even the number of registers [46]. Intermediate-level ISAs, however, do not enforce type safety because they present a representation-level abstraction barrier, not a semantic-level abstraction barrier. High-level type-safe ISAs and support for a single system-wide virtual address space are both crucial features, for a number of reasons, in systems that employ compiler-enforced memory protection and that enjoy the system integration and optimization benefits outlined earlier in the paper.

First, the efficient exchange of information between programs written in different languages requires standardization of data-type representations across compilers; inter-language linking requires standardization of calling conventions; inter-language optimization, e.g., integration of a procedure compiled by one compiler into code produced by another compiler, requires standardization of back-end formats across all compilers as well. A high-level ISA not only sets these standards but enforces them and defines a framework in which all abstraction barriers, those defined by the system, by a compiler, or by a user program, are rigidly enforced with respect to their semantics but may be folded or collapsed with respect to their implementation by the compiler back-end.

Second, like intermediate-level ISAs, a high-level ISA encapsulates a large number of hardware-specific implementation details, such as instruction latencies, into the common compiler back-end rather than requiring such volatile hardware characteristics to be incorporated into each compiler. Another advantage, shared with intermediate-level ISAs, is that the abstraction barrier simplifies backwards compatibility problems for later implementations since obsolete features need only be supported by the back-end compiler, not the hardware. In addition, new features or the reimplementation of old features are not constrained by design choices that were once optimal for a previous hardware implementation.

Third, since a high-level ISA specification requires each datum to contain a certain amount of semantic content in its type, high-level memory management and storage management facilities, such as cache control and garbage collection, can be optimized in ways that are difficult or impossible on traditional systems. For example, cache or page prefetching may be initiated by the system on a cache miss or page fault if the type of the address indicates that it is a large object that is often accessed sequentially. Or the garbage collector may segregate immutable objects into page-aligned areas creating, in effect, read-only pages that need not be written to backing store when their frame is reclaimed. Even objects that are *usually* immutable can be profitably segregated since it is unlikely the page will need to be written to backing store.

Lastly, and perhaps more pragmatically, by providing a single compiler back-end, the additional complexity and responsibility required of the compiler in a system using compiler-enforced memory protection is centralized in a single compiler back-end. Indeed, for systems without a common compiler back-end, it can well be argued that it is unwise to move a security-enforcement feature, such as memory protection, from hardware where its functionality needs to be validated only once, to every compiler where it must be validated for every release of each compiler.

It may even be argued that it is unwise to base system security on the correctness of a single compiler back-end rather than on the correctness of the hardware. This argument, however, can be countered on at least three fronts. First, hardware implementations are not without their bugs and existing compilers are already trusted to at least compile operating system code correctly and without compromising security. Secondly, compiler writers for latently-typed languages, such as Scheme, already have extensive experience producing compilers that generate efficient code that nonetheless enforces type safety correctly. Lastly, active research is being done on verified compiler implementations that provide proofs of correctness for large parts of a Scheme compiler and runtime system [13] and may well be applicable to systems with compiler-enforced memory protection sometime in the near future.

The requirement that high-level ISAs be extensible addresses the legitimate need on the part of both compilers and applications to define and implement new low-level representations or to provide low-level access to hardware facilities, such as IO. Although the compiler back-end must define and control the representations of data types to a certain degree in order to enforce type safety, the basic framework must be extensible in order to provide some way to dynamically add new types to the system. The compiler back-end must also provide a type-safe abstraction framework for defining assembly code fragments that implement new primitive functions so that such fragments can be safely and seamlessly integrated into the compiler back-end, including all aspects of optimization (see [6] for details).

The requirement for a single virtual address space is important for a number of reasons. First, it makes interprocessor communication simple and efficient since every piece of information (object) in the system has a unique identity (its virtual address) and that information can be shared simply by sharing that address. Second, a single virtual address space permits the use of virtually addressed caches without any of the usual hardware or operating system complexities due to address synonyms (the virtual address alias problem) or homonyms (and the resultant need for PIDs or ASIDs) [22]. Using virtually addressed caches in conjunction with integrated memory and storage management also simplifies cache design. For example, instruction cache flushing can be eliminated, even in the presence of on-the-fly code generation, except for the rare case when the storage management subsystem decides to reuse an area of virtual addresses that has already been used to store code since the last instruction flush. Additionally, data cache flushing for code generated on-the-fly can be performed as it is written to the code object in memory on a per cache-line basis. Virtually addressed caches also make multi-bank data caches feasible since the the virtual address space can be partitioned and each partition assigned to a functionally independent cache bank where the appropriate bank to which an address must be sent can be determined by simply examining the address.

4.2 Data-Distributed Control

The second principle is that global processor control must be replaced by a decentralized form of processor control called *data-distributed control*. In the data-distributed control (DDC) paradigm each functional unit is a simple state machine whose control is entirely local and independent of any other functional unit in the system. For example, an integer ALU may be designed to wait for two source operands, an operation code (add, sub, xor, *etc.*), and a destination register number for the result. After the sources are available, they are acknowledged and the operation is performed. The result is then sent to the register file along with the destination register number. After the register file accepts the result to be written back, the ALU begins the loop again. The name "data-distributed control" is derived from the fact that many control signals which would traditionally be considered global, such as the operation code and the destination register number in the example given above, are encapsulated and distributed with the data (the two source operands) with which they are associated.

A functional unit may wait for only a subset of its sources to become present. For example, a shared bus that can be driven by any one of several functional units is itself a functional unit in the DDC paradigm. A shared bus waits until a set of inputs from one of the functional units is complete, then it acknowledges the receipt of that set and holds it until receipt is acknowledged by the destination. Another example is a register file that may wait for either a read request for registers that are available (no outstanding writes pending) or a register write request for a result from a functional unit to be written back.

In addition to traditional functional units such as integer ALU's, multipliers, and various floating point units, all processor functionality can and must be implemented as functional units in the DDC paradigm. Pipeline hazards are avoided by requiring that each context keep track of pending writes for each register and to postpone the issue of an instruction if the source or destination registers have outstanding writes pending. Page faults on load and store instructions cause the data cache controller (also a functional unit) to signal the *event control unit* rather than to return the data item (on a load) or to signal completion (on a store). The receipt of such a signal in the event control unit will then cause an outstanding load by a system process running in another context to finally complete, effectively waking up the system process so that it can service the fault. After servicing the fault, the system process may then restart the original context by sending the result of the load to the appropriate register in the faulting context or sending a completion signal for the store to the context.

Other types of asynchronous exceptions, such as interrupts, are handled in a similar manner using the event control unit.

The DDC design paradigm is very flexible and there are no paradigm-imposed limits on what can or cannot be done within a functional unit or how one functional unit can exchange information with another. In fact, the exchange of information between functional units can be globally clocked (just as it is in traditional microprogrammed or state machine controlled architectures), completely unclocked (asynchronous), or any number of variations in between.

5 Conclusion

Both design principles interact strongly and depend on each other. For example, data-distributed control requires the type-safety of high-level instruction sets to eliminate the need to support the exception handling implicit in both hardware protection modes, *e.g.*, privileged instruction traps, and hardware enforced memory protection. High-level instruction sets, on the other hand, which employ compiler-enforced memory protection, make far greater use of dynamic type checking than is usual on traditional architectures and will require increased hardware support for high-end implementations. The basic strategy is to support features that are primarily dynamic, *i.e.*, cannot be confidently predicted by the compiler (such as cache misses), in hardware and features that are primarily static in the compiler. For some features there may be no simple way to decide whether a feature is primarily dynamic or static. For example, operand data types in a strongly typed languages are static (known to the compiler) but in some latently typed object oriented languages are inherently dynamic. Other languages, such as Scheme, fall somewhere in between.

There are a number of apparent drawbacks to this new design paradigm for which there exist reasonable alternatives. Compiler-enforced memory protection and especially compiler-controlled exception handling necessarily increase the object code size and the instruction fetch bandwidth over that of traditional systems. Instruction cache size and bandwidth, however, are two of the easiest processor characteristics to increase. There are also many more conditional branches generated by the compiler to implement memory protection and deal with exceptions. The additional branches due to these features, however, are all highly predictable and pipeline breaks can be avoided easily using simple static branch prediction. The cycles lost to the branches themselves can be eliminated if the architecture permits branches to be issued along with other useful instructions using either superscalar or VLIW techniques. The high-level backend language that is, in effect, the only "executable" format for such a system causes problems for commercial concerns that wish to ship binaries rather than sources. But this low-level source code can be "obfuscated" or encrypted to protect commercial interests.

There are also a number of serious drawbacks and unanswered questions for this new design paradigm at the hardware level. First, there is a real potential for increased instruction latency due to the necessary handshaking between functional units. These latencies could be significant for small simple designs where the architect is able to exploit knowledge of the global state to use shortcuts. For large complex designs, where such knowledge is difficult exploit, however, the overhead may be negligible and asynchronous designs may even prove to be faster. Another commercially important feature that has not yet been completely resolved for this design paradigm is testing. Current hardware test procedures rely almost exclusively on the existence of global control and the ability to load a global state vector, step the processor one cycle, and unload the state vector and compare it. Since there is no global control in the new paradigm, a new approach to testing is necessary. (Some possibilities are discussed in [6].)

There are also a number of unknowns at the software level. Although it appears to be quite simple to compile most high-level languages to a common backend language, only time and experience will determine how effectively compilers can handle language features that differ significantly from those in the backend language. Perhaps the most significant unknown and weakest link for this new design paradigm is garbage collection technology. Although garbage collection technology is quite sophisticated and effective for single applications, it has not been exercised extensively at the system level. Many of the assumptions made by current collector technology may be invalid or inappropriate at the system level.

Acknowledgements: We wish to thank David Eby for providing comments on an earlier draft of this paper.

References

1. AGARWAL, A., LIM, B.-H., KRANZ, D., AND KUBIATOWICZ, J. APRIL: A processor architecture for multiprocessing. In *The 17th Annual International Symposium on Computer Architecture* (Seattle, June 1990), pp. 104–114.

2. ALVERSON, R., CALLAHAN, D., CUMMINGS, D., KOBLENZ, B., PORTERFIELD, A., AND SMITH, B. The Tera computer system. In *1990 International Conference on Supercomputing* (June 1990), pp. 1–6.

3. ANDERSON, T. E., LEVY, H. M., BERSHAD, B. N., AND LAZOWSKA, E. D. The interaction of architecture and operating system design. In *Fourth International Conference on Architectural Support for Programming Languages and Operating Systems* (Apr. 1991), pp. 108–120.

4. ARVIND, AND IANNUCCI, R. A critique of multiprocessing von Neumann style. In *The 10th Annual International Symposium on Computer Architecture* (Stockholm, 1983).

5. BERSTIS, V. Security and protection of data in the IBM system/38. In *The 7th Annual Symposium on Computer Architecture* (1980), pp. 245–252.

6. BRUGGEMAN, C. *An Architecture Design Paradigm for Type-Safe Languages*. PhD thesis, Indiana University, 1993. *in preparation*.

7. CLINGER, W., REES, J. A., ET AL. The revised[4] report on the algorithmic language Scheme. *LISP Pointers 4*, 3 (1991).

8. COLWELL, R. P., NIX, R. P., O'DONNELL, J. J., PAPWORTH, D. B., AND ROD-MAN, P. K. A VLIW architecture for a trace scheduling compiler. In *Second International Conference on Architectural Support for Programming Languages and Operating Systems* (1987), pp. 180–192.

9. DENNIS, J. B., AND HORN, E. C. V. Programming semantics for multiprogrammed computations. *Communications of the ACM 9*, 3 (Mar. 1966).

10. DYBVIG, R. K., EBY, D., AND BRUGGEMAN, C. Flexible and efficient storage management using a segmented heap. *in preparation.*

11. GABRIEL, R., AND McCARTHY, J. Queue-based multi-processing Lisp. In *Proceedings of the 1984 ACM Conference on Lisp and Functional Programming* (Aug. 1984), pp. 25–44.

12. GRAFE, V., DAVIDSON, G., HOCH, J., AND HOLMES, V. The Epsilon dataflow processor. In *The 16th Annual International Symposium on Computer Architecture* (Jerusalem, May 1989), pp. 36–45.

13. GUTTMAN, J. D., MONK, L. G., RAMSDELL, J. D., FARMER, W. M., AND SWARUP, V. A guide to vlisp, a verified programming language implementation. Tech. Rep. M92B091, Sept. 1992.

14. HALSTEAD, JR., R. H. Multilisp: A language for concurrent symbolic computation. *ACM Transactions on Programming Languages and Systems 7*, 4 (Oct. 1985), 501–538.

15. HALSTEAD, JR., R. H., AND FUJITA, T. MASA: A multithreaded processor architecture for parallel symbolic computing. In *The 15th Annual International Symposium on Computer Architecture* (Honolulu, 1988), pp. 443–451.

16. HARRISON, W. L. The interprocedural analysis and automatic parallelization of Scheme programs. *Lisp and Symbolic Computation 2*, 3/4 (1989).

17. HENNESSY, J. L., AND PATTERSON, D. A. *Computer Architecture: A Quantitative Approach.* Morgan Kaufmann, San Mateo, California, 1990.

18. HIEB, R., AND DYBVIG, R. K. Continuations and concurrency. In *Proceedings of the Second ACM SIGPLAN Symposium on Principles and Practice of Parallel Programming* (Mar. 1990), pp. 128–137.

19. HIEB, R., DYBVIG, R. K., AND BRUGGEMAN, C. Representing control in the presence of first-class continuations. In *Proceedings of the SIGPLAN '90 Conference on Programming Language Design and Implementation* (June 1990), pp. 66–77.

20. JACOBS, G. M., AND BRODERSEN, R. W. A fully asynchronous digital signal processor using self-timed circuits. *IEEE Journal of Solid-State Circuits 25*, 6 (Dec. 1990).

21. JAGANNATHAN, S., AND PHILBIN, J. A foundation for an efficient multi-threaded Scheme system. In *Proceedings of the 1992 ACM Conference on Lisp and Functional Programming* (June 1992), pp. 345–357.

22. KOLDINGER, E. J., CHASE, J. S., AND EGGERS, S. J. Architectural support for single address space operating systems. In *Fifth International Conference on Architectural Support for Programming Languages and Operating Systems* (Boston, Sept. 1992), pp. 175–186.

23. KOWALIK, J., Ed. *Parallel MIMD Computation: HEP Supercomputer and Its Applications.* M.I.T Press, Cambridge, Mass., 1985.

24. KUEHN, J., AND SMITH, B. The Horizon supercomputer system: Architecture and software. In *1988 International Conference on Supercomputing* (Orlando, Nov. 1988).

25. KUNG, H. T. Why systolic architectures? *IEEE Computer 15*, 1 (Jan. 1982), 65–90.

26. LAUDON, J., GUPTA, A., AND HOROWITZ, M. Architectural and implementation tradeoffs in the design of multiple-context processors. Tech. Rep. CSL-TR-92-523, Stanford University, 1992.

27. LEVY, H. M. *Capability-Based Computer Systems*. Digital Press, 1984.

28. MARTIN, A. J. Compiling communicating processes into delay-insensitive VLSI circuits. *Distributed Computing 1* (1986), 226–234.

29. MARTIN, A. J., BURNS, S. M., LEE, T. K., BORKOVIC, D., AND HAZEWINDUS, P. J. The design of an asynchronous microprocessor. In *Proceedings of the Decennial Caltech Conference on VLSI* (Mar. 1989).

30. MOLNAR, C. E., FANG, T.-P., AND ROSENBERGER, F. U. Synthesis of delay-insensitive modules. *Journal of Distributed Computing* (1986), 218–262.

31. NIKHIL, R., AND ARVIND. Can dataflow subsume von Neumann computing. In *The 16th Annual International Symposium on Computer Architecture* (Jerusalem, May 1989), pp. 262–272.

32. OSF architecture-neutral distribution format rationale. Tech. rep., June 1991.

33. ORGANICK, E. I. *A Programmer's View of the Intel 432 System*. McGraw-Hill, 1983.

34. OUSTERHOUT, J. K., SCELZA, D. A., AND SINDHU, P. S. Medusa: An experiment in distributed operating system structure. *Communications of the ACM 23*, 2 (Feb. 1980).

35. PAPADOPOULOS, G. M., AND CULLER, D. E. Monsoon: an explicit token-store architecture. In *The 17th Annual International Symposium on Computer Architecture* (Seattle, June 1990), pp. 82–91.

36. PATTERSON, D. A. Reduced instruction set computers. *Communications of the ACM 28*, 1 (Jan. 1985).

37. SAKAI, S., YAMAGUCHI, Y., HIRAKI, K., AND YUBA, T. An architecture of a dataflow single chip processor. In *The 16th Annual International Symposium on Computer Architecture* (Jerusalem, May 1989), pp. 46–53.

38. SCHEIFLER, R. W., AND GETTYS, J. The X windows system. *ACM Transactions on Graphics 5*, 2 (Apr. 1986).

39. SEITZ, C. L. Ensemble architectures for VLSI – a survey and taxonomy. In *1982 Conference on Advanced Research in VLSI* (M.I.T., Jan. 1982), pp. 130–135.

40. SEITZ, C. L. Concurrent VLSI architectures. *IEEE Transactions on Computers c-33*, 12 (Dec. 1984).

41. STRONG, J., WEGSTEIN, J., TRITTER, A., OLSZTYN, J., MOCK, O., AND STEEL, T. The problem of programming communication with changing machines: A proposed solution. *Communications of the ACM 1*, 8 (Aug. 1958), 12–13. part 1.

42. STRONG, J., WEGSTEIN, J., TRITTER, A., OLSZTYN, J., MOCK, O., AND STEEL, T. The problem of programming communication with changing machines: A proposed solution. *Communications of the ACM 1*, 9 (Sept. 1958), 9–15. part 2.

43. SUTHERLAND, I. E. Micropipelines. *Communications of the ACM 32*, 6 (June 1989).

44. SUTHERLAND, I. E., AND MEAD, C. A. Microelectronics and computer science. *Scientific American 237* (Sept. 1977), 210–228.

45. THORNTON, J. E. *Design of a computer: the Control Data 6600*. 1970.

46. WALL, D. W. Experience with a software-defined machine architecture. *ACM Transactions on Programming Languages and Systems 14*, 3 (July 1992), 299–338.

47. WEBER, W.-D., AND GUPTA, A. Exploring the benefits of multiple hardware contexts in a multiprocessor architecture: Preliminary results. In *The 16th An-

nual International Symposium on Computer Architecture (Jerusalem, May 1989), pp. 273–280.

48. WILKES, M. V., AND NEEDHAM, R. M. *The Cambridge CAP Computer and its Operating System.* North Holland, New York, 1979.

49. WINKLE, D., AND PROSSER, F. *The Art of Digital Design.* 1900.

50. WULF, W. A., LEVIN, S. P., AND PIERSON, C. *HYDRA/C.mmp: An Experimental Computer System.* McGraw-Hill, New York, 1981.

Customizable Policy Management in the *Sting* Operating System

James Philbin

NEC Research Institute
Princeton, NJ 08540
philbin@research.nj.nec.com

Abstract. Sting is an operating system designed to serve as a highly efficient substrate for modern programming languages. It is designed to run on both parallel and distributed systems. This paper describes one of the important contributions of Sting - customizable policy management at both the kernel and user level of the operating system. Two well defined interfaces separate control issues from policy issues. These interfaces allow different, customized policy management modules to be implemented without changing the rest of the system. Customizable policy management makes Sting suitable for many different operating environments including real time, interactive, and computationally intensive. It also allows the user to choose or implement a policy management strategy that is best suited to a particular program.

1 Introduction

Sting is an operating system designed to serve as a highly efficient substrate for modern programming languages. It is designed to run on MIMD parallel computers, with either shared or disjoint memory, as well as distributed machines composed of networks of workstations.

Sting was designed as an experimental platform for exploring and comparing different models of parallel programming. We have used Sting to implement many different algorithms corresponding to different paradigms of parallelism including: result parallelism, master/slave parallelism, and speculative parallelism.

We have also implemented several different parallel programming models on top of Sting including: futures [Hal85], first class tuple spaces [Jag91], and engines [HF84] and compared them using various parallel algorithms that use these paradigms.

One of the fundamental design goals of Sting was to separate control issues from policy issues to the extent possible. This separation occurs at two different abstraction levels in the system: in the Abstract Physical Processor and in the Virtual Processor. Each of these abstractions is separated into two components, the "controller" which implements the control part of the abstraction and the "policy manager" which makes policy decisions for the controller. Separating control from policy allows us to define different behaviors for what is functionally the same system by modifying only the policy manager part of the abstraction.

Traditionally there have been several classes of operating system including: real time, interactive, and batch. These three classes have provided different interfaces to the user and thus porting a program from one class of OS to another has been difficult. Additionally, since the scheduling decisions made by each class are different it is difficult to debug a program for one, say a real time application, on another, say an interactive development system, and have confidence that the application will run correctly and efficiently on the target system.

The situation is complicated further by the number of different scheduling regimes used in each of these classes of systems. For example, some real time systems use a fixed scheduling order for processes, some use a priority discipline, some use a running quantum discipline, and still others use a combination of these. Interactive operating systems or batch operating systems have at least as many scheduling alternatives if not more.

Separating control from policy allows us to build one operating system that can be easily customized for various classes of operating system. In Sting the modules implementing policy managers are very small relative to the size of the system - consisting in general of less than one hundred lines of code. Thus, we only have to write a small piece of code to build a new system with different policy behavior. Additionally, since the policy manager presents a well defined interface we need only test the new policy manager and not the entire system when we change policy behavior.

Hydra [WLH81] was the first operating system designed with the separation of control and policy in mind, but Hydra only allowed policy customization at the kernel level. Sting goes further than this by allowing the programmer to customize policy decisions as they relate to a particular program. Thus an interactive program such as an editor or window manager can have very different policies from a compute intensive program such as a fluid dynamics simulation or finite elements computation. Separation of control from policy in Hydra was also expensive since it required several context switches between the kernel and the policy manager. Since the Sting policy managers are linked directly into the appropriate address space and require no context switching, they are as efficient as traditional (non-customizable) operating system policy management.

In Sting, virtual processors are multiplexed on abstract physical processors and threads are multiplexed on virtual processors. All policy decisions relating to this multiplexing are decided by policy managers. Decisions relating to the multiplexing of virtual processors on physical processors are made by the Virtual Processor Policy Manager (VPPM) while decisions relating to the multiplexing of threads on virtual processors are made by the Thread Policy Manager (TPM).

Policy managers make three types of decisions: which multiplexor to map a new object (VP or thread) to when it is created or resumed, what order to run the objects mapped on a particular processor, and when to remap or move an object from one processor to another. The large decision spaces that relate to these two levels of policy managers are discussed in detail below.

2 Overview of Sting

Sting is an operating system designed to support modern programming languages such as Scheme, SmallTalk, ML, Modula3, or Haskell. It provides a foundation of low level, orthogonal constructs, that allows the language designer or implementor to build the various constructs required by these languages easily and efficiently.

Modern programming languages have more extensive requirements than traditional programming languages such as Cobol, Fortran, C, or Pascal[1]. The list below identifies some of the requirements that distinguish modern from traditional languages.

Parallelism - The growing availability of general purpose multi-processors has lead to increased interest in building efficient and expressive platforms for concurrent programming. Most efforts to incorporate concurrency into high-level programming languages involve the addition of special purpose primitives to the language.

Multiple Synchronization Models - There are many synchronization protocols used in parallel or asynchronous programming. A modern operating environment should as far as possible provide the primitives to support the various protocols.

Lazy and Eager Evaluation - Many modern languages support either lazy or eager evaluation or both. It is important for the operating system to provide the full range of evaluation strategies from lazy to eager.

Automatic Storage Management - This has become a fundamental feature of many modern languages, because automatic storage management allows more expressive programs, while at the same time reducing both the number of errors in and the complexity of programs.

Topology Mapping - While not yet supported in many programming languages, the ability to control the mapping of processes to processors so as to reduce the communication overhead of a program will become more important as the size of multi-processor computer systems continues to grow and the topologies become more complex.

Sting supports these various requirements efficiently. It does so in an architectural framework that is more general and more efficient than those currently available. It also provides the programmer with an increased level of expressiveness and control, and an unparalleled level of customizability.

The Sting operating system architecture is composed of several layers of abstraction, as shown in Figure 2-a. The first layer is the *abstract physical machine*, which is composed of *abstract physical processors* (PP) connected in some *physical topology* (PT). This layer corresponds to the micro-kernel in newer operating systems. The sec-

---

1. Even though Sting is designed to support modern programming languages it accommodates traditional programming languages just as efficiently.

ond layer consists of *virtual machines* and *virtual processors* (VPs). A virtual machine is composed of a virtual address space into which a set of virtual processors are mapped and connected in a *virtual topology* (VT). Virtual machines are mapped onto abstract physical machines, with each virtual processor mapped onto a physical processor. The third layer of abstraction defines *threads* (T). Threads are lightweight processes that are run on virtual processors.

The threads in a virtual machine are multiplexed on the virtual processors of that machine. At the same time, the virtual processors are multiplexed on the various physical processors. A virtual machine can have a unlimited number of threads and virtual processors, while a physical machine can have only as many abstract physical processors as there are actual hardware processors in the machine.

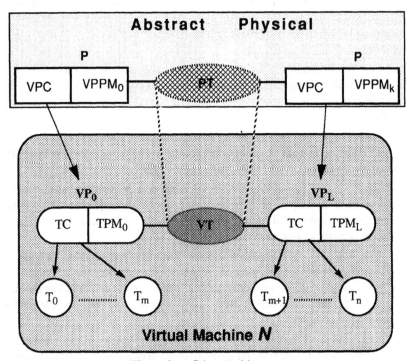

Figure 2-a: Sting Architecture

The virtual processors of a virtual machine are connected together in a virtual topology. The virtual topology maps each virtual processor to a physical processor. For example, a virtual topology might represent a tree of virtual processors that is mapped onto physical processors that are physically connected in a mesh topology. Virtual topologies allow the programmer to express a program in a (virtual) topology that is suitable to the algorithm being implemented, while at the same time obtaining an efficient mapping onto the actual physical topology of the target machine. Virtual topologies also allow parallel programs to be portable across different physical topologies.

Physical processors and virtual processors each have two components a *controller* and a *policy manager*. The controller is a state transition machine for the objects being multiplexed on that processor, i.e. physical processors multiplex virtual processors and virtual processors multiplex threads. The policy manager for a processor makes policy decisions when they are requested by the controller.

Since abstract physical processors multiplex virtual processors, they are composed of a *virtual processor controller* (VPC) and a *virtual processor policy manager* (VPPM). Virtual processors, which multiplex threads, are composed of a *thread controller* (TC) and a *thread policy manager* (TPM). Together the virtual processor policy managers and the thread policy managers make all policy decisions for a Sting system.

Sting is implemented in T [RA82] a dialect of Scheme using a modified version of the Orbit compiler. Readers interested in a more details about Sting should see [JP92a], [JP92b], and [Phi93].

Since the thread policy manager and the virtual processor policy manager are structurally similar in many ways and since users will in general be more interested in customizing the thread policy manager we will discuss it in detail below. After that we will discuss aspects of the virtual processor policy manager that are different from the thread policy manager.

3 Virtual Processors

A Virtual Processor (VP) is an abstraction of a hardware processor. As such, it is responsible for the creation, destruction, scheduling, and migration of lightweight threads. It also handles interrupts (hardware and software) and virtual processor controller up calls, i.e. software interrupts generated by the abstract physical machine, for example, when a thread blocks in the abstract physical machine.

Each VP is associated with both a virtual machine and an abstract physical processor. A physical processor may run VPs associated with many different virtual machines. More than one VP from the same virtual machine can also run on the same physical processor.

Sting's VP's are first class objects. This means they can be passed to and returned from procedure calls, and can be stored in data structures. Being first class, VP's provides Sting with several capabilities that other operating systems lack:

- the user can explicitly map a thread to a particular virtual processor;
- the user can build abstract topologies using VP self-relative addressing; and,
- the policies of any VP can be easily customized.

As explained above, control and policy are separated in the virtual processor. Each virtual processor is composed of two software components: the *thread controller* and the *thread policy manager*. Figure 3-a shows the relationship between the virtual processor, the virtual machine, and user code. The thread policy manager is completely contained within the virtual processor. User code and threads interact with the thread

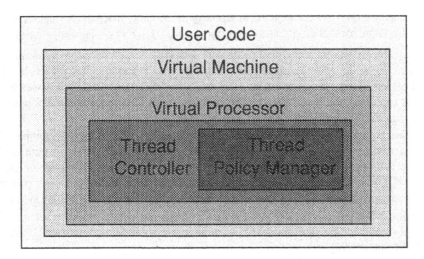

Figure 3-a: Separation of Control and Policy in the Virtual Processor

controller and the thread controller calls the thread policy manager to make policy decisions for it.

The *thread controller* handles the virtual processor's interaction with other system components such as physical processors and threads. The most important function of the thread controller is to handle the state transitions of threads. Whenever a thread makes a state transition that results in it yielding the virtual processor on which it is currently running, the thread controller calls the thread policy manager to determine which thread to run next. The thread controller is discussed in more detail in [JP92a], and [Phi93].

4 Thread Policy Manager

Each virtual processor contains a *thread policy manager*. The thread policy manager makes all policy decisions relating to the scheduling and migration of threads on virtual processors. The thread controller is a client of the thread policy manager and it is inaccessible to user code. The thread controller calls the thread policy manager whenever it needs to make a decision concerning:

- the initial mapping of a thread to a virtual processor;
- which thread a virtual processor should run next when the current thread releases the virtual processor for some reason; or
- when and which threads to migrate to/from a virtual processor.

While all virtual processors have the same thread controller, each virtual processor may have a different policy manager. This ability is particularly important for real time applications where each processor may be controlling a different subsystem with different scheduling requirements.

The thread policy manager presents a well-defined interface to the thread controller. The data structures that the thread policy managers use to make their decisions are completely private to them. They may be local to a particular thread policy manager or shared among the various instances of the thread policy manager, or some combination thereof, but they are never available to any other part of the system. The thread policy manager can thus be customized to provide different behaviors for different virtual machines. This allows the user to customize policy decisions depending on the type of program being run. For example, a computationally intensive program such as a fluid dynamics simulator, might use a non-preemptible lifo scheduling policy, because each thread should run as long as possible and because the lifo scheduling order is optimal for the particular structure of the algorithm being used, while a window manager or user shell might use a priority based fifo policy for the obvious reasons.

It is also worth noting that each thread has an associated priority and quantum. These values are supplied by the user/programmer when a thread is created or scheduled. The only part of the Sting system that uses these values is the thread policy manager. Associating priority and quantum with each thread allows the implementation of the full gamut of scheduling strategies from quantum based real time scheduling to priority based interactive scheduling.

4.1 Thread Policy Manager Interface

The thread policy manager communicates with the thread controller through a simple and easily implemented interface. Whenever the thread controller needs to make a policy decision it calls on the thread policy manager to make that decision. A thread policy manager can be implemented by any module that conforms to the interface.

VP Initialization
   (tpm-initialize-vp *vp*)   -> *no-value*

Initial Placement Policy
   (tpm-allocate-vp *vp thread*)   -> *vp*

Thread Scheduling Policy
   (tpm-dequeue-ready-thread *vp*)   -> *thread | #F*
   (tpm-enqueue-ready-thread *vp thread*)   -> *no-value*
   (tpm-wakeup-suspended-threads *vp*)   -> *no-value*

Scheduling Data Integrity
   (tpm-ensure-priority *priority*)   -> *no-value*
   (tpm-ensure-quantum *quantum*)   -> *no-value*

Migration Policy
   (tpm-vp-idle *vp*)   -> *no-value*

Figure 4-a: Thread Policy Manager Interface

Figure 4-a shows the interface to the thread policy manager. The interface can be divided into five components: policy manager initialization, initial placement policy, scheduling policy, guards used by the thread controller to ensure that priority and quantum data are of the correct type, and migration policy. We emphasize that these policy interface procedures are called only by the thread controller and never by user code. Below we briefly describe the functionality of each of the interface procedures.

tpm-initialize-vp - This procedure is called when a VP is created. It is responsible for initializing any data structures associated with the thread policy manager on the VP that is its argument.

tpm-allocate-vp - This procedure is called whenever a thread is to be scheduled on a VP. While the user may request that a thread be scheduled on a particular VP, the thread policy manager has the final say regarding the VP on which a thread is scheduled.

tpm-dequeue-ready-thread - This procedure returns the next thread that is ready to run or *false* if there is no ready thread. This procedure is called from the thread controller when a thread has yielded the processor for whatever reason.

tpm-enqueue-ready-thread - This procedure is called when a thread becomes ready to run. It is responsible for enqueuing the thread according to the priority and quantum associated with the thread.

tpm-wakeup-suspended-threads - This procedure is responsible for moving any suspended threads into the appropriate ready queue if the real clock time has passed the requested wakeup time.

tpm-ensure-priority - This procedure ensures that it argument conforms to the thread policy manager's notion of a valid priority.

tpm-ensure-quantum - This procedure ensures that it argument conforms to the thread policy manager's notion of a valid quantum.

tpm-vp-idle - This procedure is called if there is no thread runnable. It can do several things:

- It can call the abstract physical processor to inform it that the VP is idle.
- It can migrate threads from either a local or global queue associated with some VP.
- It can decide to do housekeeping chores for the thread policy manager.

We should point out that the categories in the above classification of the thread policy manager's interface procedures (Figure 4-a) are not orthogonal. For example, both **tpm-enqueue-ready-thread** and **tpm-dequeue-ready-thread** could be used to handle load balancing and thread migration on the virtual processor. **tpm-enqueue-ready-thread** could also be used to handle initial mapping of a new thread to a virtual processor. Thus **tpm-allocate-vp** and **tpm-vp-idle** are redundant procedures, but they are useful because they simplify the implementation of both the thread controller and the thread policy manager.

A discussion of memory management and communication in Sting is beyond the scope of this paper, but it should be pointed out that thread policy managers can communicate with each other using any Sting mechanism, in particular shared memory or polymorphic ports.

5 Policy Dimensions

As mentioned above, thread policy managers make three types of policy decisions: (1) which processor to schedule a thread on; (2) which thread to run next on a given processor; and (3) when to migrate a thread to/from another processor and onto which processor to migrate it. There are many different strategies for making these decisions, depending on both the application environment and the implementation of a particular application, but we believe that Sting's thread policy manager interface can support all of them. Below we discuss various strategies for handling these three policy dimensions.

5.1 Initial Thread Placement Decisions

There are many possible criteria for deciding on which virtual processor to run a thread. The two principle criteria that can be used to make this decision are load balancing and "nearness" in the communications topology, to other threads with which data is shared. The reasons for load balancing are obvious, although load balancing strategies are not necessarily so. The reason nearness matters is that it can significantly reduce the cost of communication overhead. A third, though less important reason for mapping a thread to a particular processor is that the processor has a hardware device connected to it that the thread needs to access efficiently.

Below we describe several different load balancing strategies that we have implemented and several that we have not implemented but that may be appropriate under certain circumstances.

Parent's VP - This strategy involves mapping a new thread to the same VP that its parent was running on when it was created. This strategy does not attempt to balance the load on the machine as threads are created, rather it relies on some migration strategy, discussed below, to balance the load on the processor. It does take advantage of the locality normally associated with a parent thread and its children.

Local with Threshold Overflow to Global - This strategy is similar to the Parent's VP strategy. The difference is that when the number of ready threads on a VP reaches a threshold, some number (typically half) of the threads are moved to a global queue. When the local ready queue is empty the VP requests threads out of the global queue. This strategy exploits locality just as the Parent's VP strategy does. It has the further advantage that the load on an individual processor never goes above a particular threshold. The disadvantage of this strategy is possible contention on the global queue.

Topology Mapping - This strategy relies on the programmer to specify the VP onto which a thread is mapped. It has the significant advantage that the programmer can take advantage of the data sharing and data distribution attributes of a particular program to improve its efficiency. It has the disadvantage that it requires more work on the part of the programmer. Any of the other placement strategies can be implemented in such a way so that they honor programmer specified mappings, but make appropriate decisions when the programmer doesn't specify the mapping.[2]

Random Placement - This strategy involves randomly mapping a new thread to a VP. It relies on the randomness to create an even distribution of threads on the processors. This strategy, however, does not take any advantage of the memory or communications architecture of the machine.

Round Robin - This strategy involves relying on a global counter to distribute the threads evenly across all VPs. It has the advantage of being simple and guaranteeing a good distribution. It has the disadvantage that the global counter must have a lock and thus may become a bottleneck, and like random placement, it does not take any advantage of the memory or communications architecture of the machine.

Idle VP - While there are many possible load based strategies the idle processor strategy is perhaps the simplest. Whenever a VP is idle it places itself on the idle VP queue and whenever a new thread is created it is mapped onto the VP at the head of the queue. If no VP is idle some other strategy is used map the thread to a VP. The advantage of this strategy is that idle processors quickly receive new work that is created. The disadvantage is that the number of threads per VP may be very unbalanced, and it does not take any advantage of the memory or communications architecture of the machine.

Load Based - This strategy relies on each VP maintaining some notion of its load and inserting itself in global queue ordered from the least loaded to the most loaded VP. When a thread is mapped to a VP it is always mapped to the least loaded VP. This strategy has obvious advantages, but its disadvantages are that the global queue may be a significant bottleneck if the threads are very lightweight and it does not take any advantage of the memory or communications architecture of the machine.

There are many other possible initial placement strategies. Some can be devised by combining elements of those mentioned above. The performance of a program or algorithm can depend crucially on the initial thread placement strategy used. It is also clear that for programs where computation costs completely dominate communications costs, i.e. embarrassingly parallel programs, initial placement decisions are less important, because they do not need to take advantage of the communications topology; however, initial placement decisions will still effect load balancing. For fine grained parallel programs, especially if run on a machine with a complex topology or distributed hierarchical memory, initial placement decisions can be fundamental to good performance.

5.2 Scheduling

While there are many different strategies for initially mapping a thread to a virtual processor, there are also many other possible strategies for scheduling those threads

---

2 .We discuss topology mapping in more detail in [Phi93].

once they are mapped. Rather than discuss these strategies in detail we will discuss various dimensions along which decisions about the scheduler design must be made.

Local or Global Queues - The first decision the scheduler designer must make is whether the queue(s) will be global, i.e. associated with the virtual machine, or local, i.e. associated with each virtual processor, or some combination of the two. Global queues have the advantage of being more fair, but the disadvantage of being a potential source of contention, and therefore a bottleneck.

Number and Class of Queues - Ready threads can be divided into three classes for the purposes of scheduling:

- Those that have been scheduled but never been run and thus have no execution context.

- Those that have been run before and were in the *running* state immediately prior to going into the *ready* state.

- And those that have been run before and were in the *blocked* state immediately prior to going into the *ready* state.

Ready threads of all classes can be scheduled in one queue, but it may be advantageous to separate threads in different classes into different queues. For example, consider an implementation in which the scheduler maintains one queue for threads that have been scheduled but never run and another queue for threads which have been run.[3] The policy manager can quickly migrate threads that have never been run to other VPs without having to migrate the thread's execution context (because it doesn't have one). The scheduler designer may also wish to discriminate between threads that were *running* and threads that were *blocked*, since the former, having been run more recently, are likely to have more cache/memory locality than the latter.

Ordering Within a Queue - There are various strategies for ordering threads within a particular queue. The two simplest are lifo and fifo, but since threads can have both a priority and a quantum associated with them much more complicated orderings can be created.

Locking Discipline - Another decision the scheduler designer needs to make is locking discipline required for the queues. If the queues are global and have multiple readers and writers, they must be locked on every access. If the queues are local, and have only one reader, i.e. the local VP, and many writers, they only need to be locked for writing. Finally, it is possible that a queue could be completely private to a processor and not need a lock. This is possible if the queue contains only threads that were previously running on that processor and those threads can never be migrated to another processor.

Quantum Discipline - The final decision the scheduler designer must make concerns the amount of time each thread will run before yielding the processor,

---

3. This sort of distinction is interesting in Sting because threads when created are very small data structures (approximately 10 words) and do not acquire an execution context (stack, heap,...) until they begin evaluating. For more information see [Phi93].

i.e. its quantum. There are several possibilities. The quantum for each thread may be determined statically by the programmer. This is generally done when the schedule for the threads is predetermined prior to the execution of a program. Other possibilities are that the quantum is the same for all threads; it is the same for all threads at a given priority, but different for threads at different priorities; or the quantum can vary dynamically under programmer control or under policy manager control.

These various scheduler dimensions allow the thread policy manager to be designed for various real time, computationally intensive, and interactive environments. Another interesting aspect of the thread policy manager is that it is possible to implement a completely static scheduler for a particular program if an optimal or near optimal schedule can be determined for the threads.

5.3 Example Thread Policy Managers

To date, several different thread scheduling strategies have been implemented and tested.

- **Global LIFO** - This scheduler has one global queue in a lifo order.
- **Global FIFO** - This scheduler has one global queue in a fifo order.
- **Local LIFO 1 Queue** - This scheduler has one local queue per VP that is ordered in a lifo manner.
- **Local FIFO 1 Queue** - This scheduler has one local queue per VP that is ordered in a fifo manner.
- **Local LIFO 2 Queue** - This scheduler has two local queues per VP. One contains threads that have never been run and the other contains threads that have been. Both queues are ordered in a lifo manner.
- **Local FIFO 2 Queue** - This scheduler has three local queues per VP. One contains threads that have never been run, one contains threads that have been and were running, and the third contains threads that were blocked. All three queues are ordered in a fifo manner.
- **Local LIFO 3 Queue** - This scheduler has three local queues per VP. One contains threads that have never been run, one contains threads that have been and were running, and the third contains threads that were blocked. All three queues are ordered in a lifo manner.

Each of these thread policy managers were implemented with less than 230 lines of code. 160 of those lines were in a library shared by all of them. Given this library each schedular was implemented with less than 70 lines of code. We think this demonstrates how easily a thread policy manager can be customized. Benchmarks of these policy managers are discussed in the next section.

Each of these thread policy managers that use a local queue can have either of two initial thread placement strategies: round robin or random. Round robin placement uses a global counter that is used to determine the VP onto which the thread should be mapped. Round robin placement does a reasonably good job of load balancing, but the global counter is a potential bottleneck. Random placement is done using a random number generator. It gives a reasonably balanced load without the contention of a global resource. One potential weakness with each of these strategies is that they completely ignore the topology of the physical machine.

These thread policy managers are provided as part of a library of standard thread policy managers that are delivered with the system. Thus, most Sting users will not find it necessary to implement a policy manager, rather they will simply load the appropriate policy manager for their application from the library. The standard policy mangers implement not only scheduling decisions, but also initial placement and migrations decisions.

5.4 Migration Decisions

The final issue in thread policy manager design concerns strategies for thread migration. Thread can be migrated for various reasons. The most common is to balance the load on a virtual machine across the different processors. But there are two other important reasons for migrating a thread from one VP to another. The first is performance. It may be much more efficient to move a thread closer to the resources it is using, whenever possible. The second reason is reliability. If a processor fails, then a checkpointed thread can be migrated to another processor and resumed there.

As with the other policy decisions there are many possible strategies for migrating threads. We discuss a few that relate to load balancing below.

Migration for load balancing usually occurs when a VP is idle. This is because there is little or no overhead[4] in having an idle VP search for work to do, since it would not be doing work otherwise. The strategy does have to be careful to ensure that a VP does not continue to search for work if new work has arrived in the VP's ready queue(s).

Random Search - This strategy entails picking a VP at random and grabbing some number of threads, usually half, from it's queue(s). This strategy can be tuned in several way. The thread policy manager may try to migrate threads that have not yet started evaluation first. In order to reduce the cost of migration. If there are no threads that have not started evaluation then the policy manager may choose to migrate threads that are evaluating, or to look for another processor with threads that have not yet started evaluating. The advantage of this strategy is that the amortized cost of finding work is good. The disadvantage is that it may decrease the locality of the threads in the virtual machine.

Ordered Search - Another strategy is for the thread policy manager to conduct an ordered search starting with VP's that are close to it and gradually moving to those that are further away. This approach has the advantage that it has a better chance of maintaining the locality of threads.

Load Based - If a queue of processors ordered by their load is being kept to improve the initial mapping of threads to VPs, then it can be used by an idle processor to find the most heavily loaded processor and take some, again usually

---

4 . There is the potential to create more contention for shared resources however.

half, of its threads. Because there are many possible ways of measuring the "load" on a virtual processor, the thread policy manager is responsible for calculating it in a manner suitable to the policy being implemented.

There are many other possible strategies for using migration to balance the work on a machine and improve performance. The appropriate strategy will depend not only on a particular program, but also on the memory hierarchy and the communications topology of the physical machine.

6 Benchmark Results

We have benchmarked six different thread policy managers running a program called Abisort.[5] Abisort performs an "adaptive" bitonic sort [BN89] of $n = 16,384$ numbers. The adaptive algorithm achieves optimal complexity ($O(n \log n)$ rather than the $O(n \log^2 n)$ of the standard bitonic sort algorithm) by storing bitonic sequences in a special tree data structure. Adaptive bitonic sort performs about twice as many comparisons as a merge sort, and has somewhat greater bookkeeping costs. However, its parallel divide-and-conquer merge operation allows virtually linear speedup when $n >> p$. Such speedup is not possible with straightforward implementations (on MIMD machines) of other divide-and-conquer sorts such as merge sort and quicksort which contain significant sequential phases. Abisort creates a tree containing 106497 threads.

The program run is exactly the same for each policy manager, i.e. the source is not changed and it is not recompiled. The following thread policy managers were tested:

GLIFO - A policy manager that uses one global queue for scheduling all the threads on virtual processors. The queue is organized in a last in first out manner.

GFIFO - A policy manager that uses one global queue for scheduling all the threads on virtual processors. The queue is organized in a first in first out manner.

L1 LIFO Random - A policy manager that uses one local ready queue on each virtual processor. The queue is organized in a last in first out manner. The initial mapping of thread to virtual processor is done by picking a processor at random.

L1 LIFO Round Robin- A policy manager that uses one local ready queue on each virtual processor. The queue is organized in a last in first out manner. The initial mapping of thread to virtual processor in a round robin manner using a global counter access to which is synchronized.

L1 FIFO Random - A policy manager that uses one local ready queue on each virtual processor. The queue is organized in a first in first out manner. The initial mapping of thread to virtual processor is done by picking a processor at random.

L1 LIFO Round Robin - A policy manager that uses one local ready queue on each virtual processor. The queue is organized in a last in first out manner. The

---

5 .The abisort we used is one of Mohr's benchmarks and the description of the algorithm is largely taken from [Moh91].

initial mapping of thread to virtual processor in a round robin manner using a global counter access to which is synchronized.

The benchmarks were run on an eight processor Silicon Graphics PowerSeries 480 with 256 Mb of main memory. Each processor is a MIPS R3000 running at 40Mhz with a 64kb data cache and a 64kb instruction cache. Table 6-a through Table 6-f show the results of running abisort on a Sting virtual machine composed of eight virtual processors using the various policy managers. These tables give a processor by processor breakdown of various statistics.

The following statistics about *threads* are recorded by each VP:

Created - The number of thread created by the program.

Scheduled - The number of threads scheduled to evaluate.

Absorbed - The number of threads absorbed by other threads.

Blocked - The number of times a thread blocked for any reason.

Resumed - The number of times a blocked thread resumed execution.

Determined - The number of threads that determined (i.e. completed) a value.

Idle - The number of times the virtual processor had no work to do. When a virtual processor has no work it runs its root thread which increments this counter and then spins until there is more work to do.

The following statistics about *thread execution contexts* are recorded by each VP:

Created - The number of thread control blocked created. This occurs when the virtual processors pool of thread control blocks is empty and it must create a new thread control block.

Allocated - The number of thread control blocks allocated from the virtual processor's pool of thread control blocks.

Re-used - The number of thread control blocks that were reused because an unevaluating thread was proceeded by a thread which had just terminated.

The following statistics about *mutexes* are maintained by the system:

Created - The total number of mutexes created by the system.

Acquired - The number of times a mutex was acquired.

Released - The number of times a mutex was released.

An examination of the tables shows that each of the policy managers does a good job of scheduling threads evenly across the processors with the variance in load under 5% for all of them. The round robin schedulers distribute the threads with essentially no variance. However, this even distribution comes at the cost of acquiring an extra lock for each thread scheduled. All of the policy managers show good balance in other respects. The the number of threads absorbed by each processor is well balanced as is the amount of blocking and the number of times a processor goes idle.

Threads	VP$_1$	VP$_2$	VP$_3$	VP$_4$	VP$_5$	VP$_6$	VP$_7$	VP$_8$	Total
Created	13274	13449	12997	13268	13385	13525	13251	13347	106497
Scheduled	13274	13449	12997	13268	13385	13525	13251	13347	106497
Absorbed	10889	11102	10600	10837	10895	11076	10938	10959	87296
Blocked	1472	1526	1547	1506	1514	1576	1491	1546	12178
Resumed	1500	1570	1568	1533	1491	1495	1520	1501	12178
Determined	13191	13527	13123	13209	13372	13443	13357	13275	106497
Idle	30	33	33	22	35	27	21	28	229
Execution Contexts									
Created									50
Allocated	1164	1206	1226	1207	1177	1286	1187	1201	9654
Reused	1181	1191	1180	1214	1148	1191	1204	1238	9547
Mutexes									
Created	13274	13449	12997	13268	13385	13525	13251	13347	106497
Acquired	33351	34073	33363	33524	33540	34156	33611	33729	269347
Released	33351	34073	33363	33524	33540	34156	33611	33729	269347

Table 6-a: Abisort with Global LIFO Policy

Threads	VP$_1$	VP$_2$	VP$_3$	VP$_4$	VP$_5$	VP$_6$	VP$_7$	VP$_8$	Total
Created	13541	13370	13167	13510	13220	13155	13198	13335	106497
Scheduled	13541	13370	13167	13510	13220	13155	13198	13335	106497
Absorbed	13512	13335	13128	13468	13189	13127	13171	13288	106218
Blocked	29	30	27	40	34	30	25	36	251
Resumed	50	26	21	25	39	35	27	28	251
Determined	13572	13364	13148	13493	13244	13161	13200	13315	106497
Idle	21	25	25	22	19	18	27	25	182
Execution Contexts									
Created									38
Allocated	18	21	21	22	20	17	19	21	159
Reused	20	12	13	14	13	18	15	15	120
Mutexes									
Created	13541	13370	13167	13510	13220	13155	13198	13335	106497
Acquired	27259	26849	26412	27143	26607	26448	26507	26775	214000
Released	27259	26849	26412	27143	26607	26448	26507	26775	214000

Table 6-b: Abisort with Global FIFO Policy

Threads	VP$_1$	VP$_2$	VP$_3$	VP$_4$	VP$_5$	VP$_6$	VP$_7$	VP$_8$	Total
Created	13227	13259	13396	13240	13499	13332	13347	13196	106497
Scheduled	13313	13312	13312	13312	13312	13312	13312	13312	106497
Absorbed	10889	11102	10600	10837	10895	11076	10938	10959	87296
Blocked	251	254	258	237	256	243	237	235	1971
Resumed	244	247	267	226	272	244	238	233	1971
Determined	13163	13339	13410	13184	13546	13413	13326	13116	106497
Idle	80	69	75	42	59	85	57	51	518
Execution Contexts									
Created									36
Allocated	257	254	264	237	265	250	246	237	2010
Reused	55	51	52	44	46	68	45	37	398
Mutexes									
Created	13227	13259	13396	13240	13499	13332	13347	13196	106497
Acquired	27386	27696	27906	27350	28088	27810	27647	27228	221111
Released	27386	27696	27906	27350	28088	27810	27647	27228	221111

Table 6-c: Abisort with Local LIFO and Round Robin

Threads	VP$_1$	VP$_2$	VP$_3$	VP$_4$	VP$_5$	VP$_6$	VP$_7$	VP$_8$	Total
Created	13340	13444	13244	13238	13269	13304	13375	13282	106497
Scheduled	13313	13312	13312	13312	13312	13312	13312	13312	106497
Absorbed	13264	13391	13164	13140	13193	13262	13298	13236	105948
Blocked	48	61	56	48	42	57	52	56	420
Resumed	28	59	47	49	64	64	50	59	420
Determined	13296	13458	13211	13198	13260	13366	13381	13327	106497
Idle	22	11	16	23	21	13	22	21	149
Execution Contexts									
Created									38
Allocated	40	42	39	35	29	43	43	41	306
Reused	22	31	28	26	30	30	30	34	243
Mutexes									
Created	13340	13444	13244	13238	13269	13304	13375	13282	106497
Acquired	26798	27166	26659	26594	26707	26942	26962	26867	214695
Released	26798	27166	26659	26594	26707	26942	26962	26867	214695

Table 6-d: Abisort with Local FIFO and Round Robin

Threads	VP_1	VP_2	VP_3	VP_4	VP_5	VP_6	VP_7	VP_8	Total
Created	13332	13322	13258	13191	13309	13332	13440	13312	106497
Scheduled	13318	13400	13233	13096	13297	13504	13023	13254	106497
Absorbed	12835	12800	12709	12727	12867	12845	13023	12745	102551
Blocked	397	405	401	384	411	433	365	415	3211
Resumed	371	359	420	417	385	432	402	425	3211
Determined	13277	13234	13287	13264	13351	13381	13479	13224	106497
Idle	170	115	164	191	175	120	144	122	1201

Execution Contexts

	VP_1	VP_2	VP_3	VP_4	VP_5	VP_6	VP_7	VP_8	Total
Created									52
Allocated	419	400	411	408	432	445	378	410	3303
Reused	80	95	89	82	82	76	64	75	643

Mutexes

	VP_1	VP_2	VP_3	VP_4	VP_5	VP_6	VP_7	VP_8	Total
Created	13332	13322	13258	13191	13309	13332	13440	13312	106497
Acquired	28265	28233	28238	28167	28450	28563	28538	28204	226658
Released	28265	28233	28238	28167	28450	28563	28538	28204	226658

Table 6-e: Abisort with Local LIFO and Random

Threads	VP_1	VP_2	VP_3	VP_4	VP_5	VP_6	VP_7	VP_8	Total
Created	13326	13398	13370	13342	13233	13344	13371	13311	106497
Scheduled	13302	13388	13229	13106	13305	13512	13413	13112	106497
Absorbed	13260	13272	13275	13257	13117	13253	13292	13017	105743
Blocked	81	80	78	72	82	77	75	63	608
Resumed	78	91	97	66	78	56	91	51	608
Determined	13366	13385	13392	13314	13217	13322	13425	13077	106497
Idle	43	27	16	35	19	24	27	15	206

Execution Contexts

	VP_1	VP_2	VP_3	VP_4	VP_5	VP_6	VP_7	VP_8	Total
Created									40
Allocated	61	57	54	51	54	58	44	43	422
Reused	45	40	40	41	48	32	54	33	333

Mutexes

	VP_1	VP_2	VP_3	VP_4	VP_5	VP_6	VP_7	VP_8	Total
Created	13326	13398	13370	13342	13233	13344	13371	13311	106497
Acquired	27059	27094	27092	26953	26764	26959	27133	26412	215466
Released	27059	27094	27092	26953	26764	26959	27133	26412	215466

Table 6-f: Abisort with Local FIFO and Random

Table 6-g show a comparison of the results for the six systems tested. This table shows that for abisort a fifo strategy works better than the lifo strategy and that the global queue works much better than the local queues. The thread policy manager that works best, **GFIFO**, as we might expect, has less idle time, less blocking, and creates fewer execution contexts than any of the others. The one that performs worst, **L1 LIFO Random**, not surprisingly has much more blocking, more idle time, and creates more execution contexts than the others.

Threads	G LIFO	G FIFO	L LIFO Random	L LIFO RR	L FIFO Random	L FIFO RR
Created	106497	106497	106497	106497	106497	106497
Scheduled	106497	106497	106497	106497	106497	106497
Absorbed	87296	106218	102551	87296	105743	105948
Blocked	12178	251	3211	1971	608	420
Resumed	12178	251	3211	1971	608	420
Determined	106497	106497	106497	106497	106497	106497
Idle	229	182	1201	518	206	149
Execution Contexts						
Created	50	38	52	36	40	38
Allocated	9654	159	3303	2010	422	306
Reused	9547	120	643	398	333	243
Mutexes						
Created	106497	106497	106497	106497	106497	106497
Acquired	269347	214000	226658	221111	· 215466	214695
Released	269347	214000	226658	221111	215466	214695
Timing (secs)						
	14.77	11.40	16.94	14.76	14.14	14.68

Table 6-g: Abisort with Various TPMs

The machine we ran these benchmarks on is a physically shared memory machine and the results of these policy managers show less variance than they might on a physically disjoint memory machine. Abisort is only one benchmark; to understand the behavior of various thread policy managers many more benchmarks need to be studied. Finally, there are many other thread policy managers that we would like to test in the future.

7   Virtual Processor Management

As mentioned above there is a second level of policy management in the Sting operating system, i.e. kernel or virtual processor policy management. Each *physical processor abstraction* is composed of a *virtual processor controller* (VPC) and a *virtual processor policy manager* (VPPM). The relationship between the VP controller and the VP policy manager is similar to that between the thread controller and the thread policy manager, i.e. the VP controller is a client of the VP policy manager. Whenever the VP controller needs to make a policy decision it calls the VP policy manager to make that decision.

While all physical processor runs the same VP controller, they can run different VP policy managers. This allows a multiprocessor system to customize the system's use of each physical processor. It is also possible for the system to run the same VP policy manager on each of the physical processors.

When a virtual machine wishes to schedule a virtual processor on an abstract physical processor it calls the virtual processor controller on that physical processor. Likewise, when a virtual machine wishes to remove a virtual processor from an abstract physical processor it calls the virtual processor controller on that physical processor. Each VP controller manages the virtual processors which are mapped onto its physical processor, including all virtual processor state changes.

The VP policy manager makes all policy decisions relating to the scheduling and migration of virtual processors on physical processors. There are three types of decision: First it determines the VP to PP map. This mapping takes place at two distinct times, when the VP is run for the first time and when a VP which has been blocked is rerun. Second, the policy manager also determines the order in and duration for which VPs on a PP are run. Finally, the VP policy manager decides when a VP should be moved (migrated) from one processor to another.

These three decisions allow the VP policy manager to balance the work load on a machine and determine the fairness properties of the physical machine with respect to virtual machines. They also allow VP policy managers to decide where to move the VPs of a fault tolerant VM when a physical processor fails.

Like the thread policy manager the VP policy manager presents a well-defined interface to the VP controller. The data structures which the VP policy manager uses to make its decisions are completely private to it. These data structures may be local to a particular VP policy manager or shared among the various instances of the VP policy manager, or some combination thereof, but no other component of the system has access to them. The VP policy manager can be customized to provide different behaviors to different instances of Sting. This functionality allows it to be customized for different operating system environments as diverse as real time, interactive, or computationally intensive systems.

The principle difference between the thread policy manager and the VP policy manager is that the VP policy manger must be built into the physical machine, i.e. kernel. This means that it must be linked into the operating system when it is built.

Finally, while the thread policy manger is concerned with load balancing and fairness among threads, the virtual processor policy manager is concerned with load balancing and fairness among virtual machines and virtual processors.

8 Conclusion

The fundamental contribution of this work is the development of simple and efficient abstractions that allow the separation of policy management from control in an operation system. Although our system is implemented in Scheme the abstractions developed could be implemented in a more traditional language such as C. It would be relatively easy to add these abstractions to a more traditional operating system such as Unix.

A second important contribution of this work lies in providing the user with the ability to customize the policy management of threads. The ability to customize policy management at the virtual machine level allows the user/programmer to exploit memory and communications properties of a particular algorithm. It also allows the user/ programmer to exploit memory and communications properties when porting a program from one hardware architecture to another without modifying the program itself.

The approach to policy management described in this paper has proven to be extremely flexible. The interfaces to the policy managers are simple and implementing the various policy managers described was easy, requiring less than a day each to code and debug them.

It is unfortunate that we only had a shared memory multiprocessor at our disposal for testing these policy managers. We believe that policy management issues are much more interesting and important on disjoint memory machines. We are currently building a distributed shared memory machine using high performance workstations connected with a fast interconnect, on which to test this hypothesis.

9 References

[BN89]   G. Bilardi and A. Nicolau. Adaptive Bitonic Sorting: An Optimal Parallel Algorithm for Shared Memory Machines. SIAM J. Computing, 18:2, April 1989, pages 216-228.

[CDD+91]   Mark Crovella, Prakash Das, Czarek Dubnicki, Thomas LeBlanc, Evangelos Markatos. Multiprogramming on Multiprocessors. Technical Report 385, Computer Science Department, University of Rochester, May 1991.

[Hal85]   Robert Halstead. Multilisp: A Language for Concurrent Symbolic Computation. *Transactions on Programming Languages and Systems*, 7(4):501-538, October 1985.

[HF84]   Christopher T. Haynes and Danial P. Friedman. Engines Build Process Abstractions. *Proceedings of the 1984 ACM Lisp and Functional Programming Conference*, pages 18-24, 1984.

[Jag91]   Suresh Jagannathan. Customization of First Class Tuple Spaces in a Higher Order Language. *Conference on Parallel Languages and Architectures Europe*, pages 254-276, June 1991.

[JP92a]   Suresh Jagannathan and James Philbin. A Foundation for an Efficient Multi-Threaded Scheme System. *Proceedings of the 1992 Conference on Programming Language Design and Implementation*, June 1992.

[JP92b]   Suresh Jagannathan and James Philbin. STING: A Customizable Sub-
            strate for Concurrent Symbolic Computing. Technical Report 91-003-3-
            0050-1, NEC Research Institute, 1992.

[MP90]   Henry Massalin and Calton Pu. Fine-Grain Adaptive Scheduling using
            Feedback. *Computing Systems*, 3:1, Winter 1990.

[Moh91]   Eric Mohr. Dynamic Partitioning of Parallel Lisp Programs. Technical
            Report YaleU/DCS/RR-869, Yale University, October 1991.

[MVZ90]   Cathy McCann, Raj Vaswani, and John Zahorjan. A Dynamic Processor
            Allocation Policy for Multiprogrammed, Shared Memory Multiproces-
            sors. Technical Report 90-03-02, Department of Computer Science, Uni-
            versity of Washington, March 1990 (revised February 1991).

[Phi93]   James Philbin. The Design of an Operating System for Modern Pro-
            gramming Languages. PhD thesis, Department of Computer Science,
            Yale University, 1993.

{RA82]   Jonathan A. Rees and Norman I. Adams. T : A Dialect of Lisp or,
            LAMBDA: The Ultimate Software Tool. *Proceedings of the ACM Sym-
            posium on Lisp and Functional Programming*, pages 114-122, 1982.

[TG89]   Andrew Tucker and Anoop Gupta. Process Control and Scheduling
            Issures for Multiprogrammed Shard-Memory Multiprocessors. *Proceed-
            ings of the Twelfth ACM Symposium on Operating System Principles*,
            December, 1989.

[WLH81]   William Wulf, Roy Levin, and Samuel Harbison. *HYDRA/C.mmp: An
            Experimental Computer System*. McGraw-Hill, 1991.

10 Acknowledgments

Sting was designed jointly by the author and Suresh Jagannathan. Alvaro Campos
implemented several of the early policy managers.

An Efficient Implementation Scheme of Concurrent Object-Oriented Languages on Stock Multicomputers (Extended Abstract)

Kenjiro Taura, Satoshi Matsuoka and Akinori Yonezawa

Department of Information Science, The University of Tokyo, 7-3-1 Hongo, Bunkyo-ku, Tokyo 113, Japan

1 Introduction

Concurrent object-oriented programming languages (concurrent OOPLs) are promising approach for building large and complex applications on multicomputers, but their dynamic/asynchronous nature makes efficient implementation difficult—support of dynamic concurrent object creation involves scheduling of multiple objects on each node, and sending of asynchronous messages between objects cause buffering of messages, both of which could result in significant overhead. One possible direction to achieve efficiency is to combine dedicated hardware[3, 1] and software tailored for it[2, 7]. The hardware has crucial support for concurrent OOPLs—low overhead remote communication and efficient multithreading. While they are attractive, the majority of current commercial multicomputers such as AP1000[4] and CM5 have no such support. This note summarizes our implementation scheme[5, 8] on these conventional multicomputers, and shows that concurrent OOPLs can greatly benefit from their superior node-local performance while communication performance can be made comparable to dedicated architectures.

Basic operations such as message passing or object creation were implemented very efficiently. Intra-node message passing takes about 15 instructions in addition to the cost of procedure call, unless the receiver object is already executing some other method. Inter-node message passing latency is within $10\mu s$ for small messages. An application benchmark showed good speedup (440 times speedup on 512 nodes system) for a large program.

2 Key Features of Our Implementation

Issues for efficient implementation are roughly classified into two parts:

- How to efficiently schedule concurrent objects within a node (processor).
- How to reduce inter-node communication overhead.

Here we give a rough overview of our approach; the details are found in [5].

2.1 Intra-node Scheduling

To schedule multiple objects within a node, activation frames of methods are typically allocated from heap, because objects might be *blocked* during method execution. Schedulable frames are linked together and serves as a scheduling queue. Such queue-based scheduling causes significant loss of performance, however, especially in OOPLs where small methods are preferably used.

Our scheduling scheme combines two scheduling mechanisms—(1) queue-based scheduling and (2) *stack-based* scheduling which is similar to management of procedure call stack in sequential programming languages. Upon sending an asynchronous message from object S to another object R, method invocation is done in mostly the same way as a standard procedure call when the following conditions are satisfied:

- S and R reside on the same node, and
- R is *dormant* (i.e., not executing another method).

In this case, the activation frame is allocated on the stack and the message is 'sent' via registers, eliminating most of the overhead of the queue-based approach. When R later becomes blocked, a frame is allocated lazily from the heap and frees the stack frame, saving the context into the allocated heap frame. On the other hand, if R happens to be already running another method, the message is buffered to maintain correct semantics.

In our implementation, the second runtime check is eliminated by incorporating it into method lookup. Each class has two kinds of method lookup tables, each of which corresponds to dormant/active case. Each instance of the class switches the pointer to the method lookup table when it becomes dormant/active. Each entry for dormant case has a pointer to a method code, while the corresponding entry for the active case has a pointer to a procedure which buffers incoming messages. To send a message to R, sender merely performs standard method lookup call via the current method lookup table of R. R runs the method immediately in the dormant case, while the message is buffered when R is active.

2.2 Inter-node Communication

In conventional multicomputers, inter-node messages are polled and dispatched on receiver nodes. For correct dispatching, messages carry extra information such as the size of the message, tags to identify the type of each message field, etc. In standard implementation, such information is necessary even for small messages to maintain uniform message format, increasing inter-node communication overhead.

This overhead can be eliminated by removing all such information and instead attaching the address of a message handler which is *specialized* according to the type of the message. For instance, for a message which carries a pointer to the target object and an integer, we precompile a message handler which *knows* that the message contains exactly two words, its first field a pointer to an object, and the second field an integer. The receiver node merely jumps to the message handler as soon as it obtains its address from the network, and the handler performs the remaining extraction and other tasks. This provides large performance gain especially for small messages. Eicken et.al earlier proposed the same mechanism, 'Active Messages'[6].

3 Preliminary Benchmark Results

All benchmarks are run on AP1000 whose node PE is a 25MHz SPARC.

Basic Operation Efficiency: Table 1 lists the cost of several basic operations. The cost of an intra-node message send is different depending on whether or not the receiver object is *dormant*. For the dormant case, method invocation costs about 15 instructions in addition to the cost of standard procedure call, while for the active case, it requires heap allocation of method invocation frame, message buffering etc.

Table 1. Costs of basic operations

	Time (μs)
Intra-node Message (to Dormant)	2.3
Intra-node Message (to Active)	9.6

	Time (μs)
Inter-node Message	8.9
Intra-node Creation	2.1

Inter-node latency, 8.9μs, is obtained by repeatedly transmitting one word asynchronous messages between two objects. This is comparable to implementations on special multithreaded hardware, about a factor of two of [2], or factor of four of [7] even when normalized to the same clock speed.

Application Benchmark: Figure 1 shows the speedup of N-queen exhaustive search algorithm where each branch of the search tree corresponds to a concurrent object, using $N = 8$ and 13 as the test case.[1] As a baseline for speedup measurement, we ran a sequential depth-first search algorithm written in C++ on the same CPU. The program runs less than 100 milliseconds on the single CPU for $N = 8$, while it involves over 4,500,000 object creations and 9,000,000 message passings when $N = 13$. 440 times speedup for $N = 13$ on 512 processors were observed despite that the sequential program needs no termination detection or heap memory allocation.

4 Conclusion

We have proposed a software architecture for concurrent OOPLs on conventional multicomputers. The preliminary measurements have shown that our perfor-

---

[1] We do not claim this is the best way of writing N-queen with concurrent OOPLs. Better performance will be achieved by controlling the number of concurrent objects created, and performing depth-first search near the leaves of the search tree.

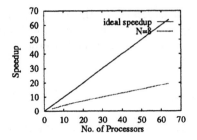 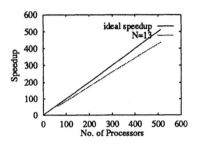

Fig. 1. Speedup for N-queen problem ($N = 8, 13$).

mance compares favorably with the implementations on special multithreaded machines. Restrictions of these mechanisms/techniques are small and they are widely applicable implementations on various multicomputers.

References

1. William J. Dally, Linda Chao, Andrew Chien, Soha Hassoun, Waldemar Horwat, Jon Kaplan, Paul Song, Brian Totty, and Scotto Wills. Architecture of a message-driven processor. In *Proceedings of International Symposium on Computer Architecture*, pages 189–196, 1987.
2. Waldemar Horwat. Concurrent Smalltalk on the message-driven processor. Master's thesis, MIT, May 1989.
3. Shuichi Sakai, Yoshinori Yamaguchi, and Kei Hiraki. An architecture of a dataflow single chip processor. In *Proceedings of International Symposium on Computer Architecture*, pages 46–53, 1989.
4. Toshiyuki Shimizu, Takeshi Horie, and Hiroaki Ishihata. Low-latency message communication support for the AP1000. In *Proceedings of International Symposium on Computer Architecture*, pages 288–297, 1992.
5. Kenjiro Taura, Satoshi Matsuoka, and Akinori Yonezawa. An efficient implementation scheme of concurrent object-oriented languages on stock multicomputers. In *Proceedings of ACM SIGPLAN Symposium on Principles & Practice of Parallel Programming*, pages 218–228, 1993.
6. Thorsten von Eicken, David E. Culler, Seth Copen Goldstein, and Klaus Erik Schauser. Active messages: a mechanism for integrated communication and computation. In *Proceedings of International Symposium on Computer Architecture*, pages 256–266, 1992.
7. Masahiro Yasugi, Satoshi Matsuoka, and Akinori Yonezawa. ABCL/onEM4: A new software/hardware architecture for object-oriented concurrent computing on an extended dataflow supercomputer. In *Proceedings of International Conference on Supercomputing*, pages 93–103, 1992.
8. Akinori Yonezawa, Satoshi Matsuoka, Masahiro Yasugi, and Kenjiro Taura. Implementing concurrent object-oriented languages on multicomputers. *IEEE Parallel & Distributed Technology*, pages 49–61, May 1993.

PART VI

Panel Discussions

PART VI

Panel Discussions

Panel Discussion I:
Massively Parallel Architectures
and Symbolic Computation

Takayasu Ito (chair)
Rishiyur Nikhil
Julian Padget
Norihisa Suzuki
Taiichi Yuasa

Massively parallel computers with thousands of processing elements have been expected to open a new world of computing in the 21st century. However, in this attractive yet challenging area there are various issues to be clarified and many problems to be solved.

Massively parallel architectures have been successful in many applications of numerical computation with vector and array data. What and how about in case of symbolic computation? Small-scale shared architectures have succeeded in parallel processing of Lisp and Prolog. Many Lisp programs written for serial computers have been successfuly transformed into parallel programs for this kind of architecture. Putting Lisp programs on massively parallel architectures has been problematic, since they have dynamically-changing linked data structures. Similar problems also arise in massively parallel symbolic computing for functional programs and logic programs.

The panel discussion will consider the needs of massively parallel symbolic computation in these four areas:

1. Massively parallel architectures.
2. Parallel programming languages and programming environments for massively parallel computer systems.
3. Parallel algorithms and automatic extraction of parallelism.
4. Models of massively parallel machines.

The panel is opened to discuss the optimistic and/or pessimistic futures of massively parallel architectures and symbolic computation.

Position Statement
for panel on
"Massively Parallel Architectures and Symbolic Computation"

Rishiyur S. Nikhil

Digital Equipment Corporation

Cambridge Research Laboratory

Massively Parallel Symbolic Programs (MPSPs) are characterized by very dynamic, heterogeneous processes and data, whose structures are difficult or impossible to analyze and predict at compile time. This is in contrast to traditional parallel programs– mostly scientific– whose structures are regular enough to be easily translated into simple, "marching band" parallel code (manually or by compiler). This has strong implications on languages and architectures for MPSPs.

I believe that MPSPs are best programmed in languages with a shared memory model, *i.e.*, where there is a single, shared object space or heap. Requiring explicit partitioning of process and data, and explicit management of communication, is too complex to be viable for MPSPs. Thus, I do not see SIMD or even SPMD models playing much of a role for symbolic programs, either in languages or in architectures. Even if the underlying machine does not directly support a shared memory model, I believe this should be invisible to the MPSP programmer (to first order). Data parallelism will continue be important, not in its current popular interpretation of homogeneous, lockstep execution, but rather in the more general (and compositional) sense of fine-grain, simultaneous access to heterogeneous data by heterogeneous processes.

Even though MPSPs will be programmed in languages with shared memory models, completely automatic placement of processes and data is perhaps infeasible. I expect that the programmer may still have to provide executable hints to improve the proximity of processes to their data. Such hints may be of the form: "execute this function or allocate this data structure on processor J", where J is itself a computed value, perhaps using the address of some other dynamically allocated data structure. Note that the computation model remains a shared memory model; the hints are just that— they do not affect correctness, and the way we express computations and data structure-access remains unchanged. It is interesting to note that even in the field of scientific computation, High Performance Fortran (HPF) demonstrates a similar evolution back to a shared memory model with explicit help from the programmer for data placement.

I believe the problem of automatic extraction of massive parallelism from sequential MPSPs is intractable. However, this does not mean that programmers must resort to explicit and tedious specification of parallelism. Instead, I have great hope in *implicitly parallel* languages (my favorite is Id, a mostly functional language) where parallelism is obvious and abundant in the language semantics.

These languages not only have implicit parallel processes (*e.g.*, via parallel argument evaluation), but also have implicit data synchronization (*e.g.*, via logic variables, I- and M-structures). In fact, the programmer is explicit only about occasional sequentialization, which is the opposite of traditional approaches.

A fundamental problem in efficient implementation of MPSPs is tolerance of asynchrony. Asynchrony is unavoidable, both for architectural reasons and because of the dynamic nature of MPSPs themselves. Since we cannot precisely schedule process and data placement, non-local data accesses (which involve communication) will be frequent, fine-grained and unpredictable. Thus, the latency of a particular memory access can vary by orders of magnitude. Further, some of these accesses may be synchonizing (*e.g.*, reading a logic variable or I-structure), introducing further unpredictable delays. To tolerate such asynchrony, I believe it is essential for MPSP implementations to be based on multithreading, *i.e.*, each processor has a collection of threads amongst which it multiplexes rapidly so that it does not waste time waiting for the response to a long-latency access. To be effective, this thread multiplexing must be very efficient— the overhead must be smaller than typical remote-access latencies. Thus, it must be done entirely at the user-level (not in the operating system) and perhaps with architectural support.

I believe that, for economic reasons, architectural support for MPSPs can be added only where such features are widely applicable, *i.e.*, where they are beneficial to a wide range of parallel applications. Promising possibilities include:

- Support for a shared memory abstraction on machines with physically distributed memories: There is at least one commercial machine (the KSR-1) already providing this support in hardware. In addition, there is an increasing number of exciting research efforts on directory-based global cacheing, distributed shared memory, *etc.*, using various combinations of hardware, operating system and runtime system support.
- Tight integration of communication and computation: Today, inter-processor communication overheads are extremely high for reasons of protection (requiring kernel intervention) and protocol processing (based on worst-case assumptions about the interconnection network). In the near future, I expect user-level access to the communication network (with hardware protection); very high performance (low latency, high bandwidth), reliable, switched interconnection networks; and, lightweight, user-level mechanisms for message-handling (such as lightweight interrupts, multithreading, or programmable message co-processors).
- Support for producer-consumer synchronization, such as FULL/EMPTY bits on every location, and fast dispatching based on this state: A major source of parallelism in symbolic programs comes from concurrent execution of a computation C1 that produces a data structure with a computation C2 that consumes it. For example, C1 may grow a tree structure (in parallel at all the leaves) while C2 may traverse the tree (also in parallel). Since the rate at which the frontier of the tree is growing may be unpredictable and irregular, if C2 is to proceed concurrently with C1, it needs to be able to block at each

point in the frontier which is currently still under construction by C1. The brute-force method of placing a barrier between C1 and C2 throws away too much potential parallelism. On the other hand, support for efficient, fine-grain synchronization on individual data locations permits exploitation of this kind of parallelism.

Languages and MP systems with these features are currently under construction in several research projects. I am optimistic that MPSPs can become a reality in the next three or four years.

Massively Parallel Architectures and Symbolic Computation
Position Statement

Julian Padget
School of Mathematical Sciences
University of Bath
BATH, BA2 7AY, United Kingdom

"Massively Parallel" used to mean array processing and hence SIMD programming. Although pure array processors such as the Maspar and CM-2 are still available, it seems that simple processing elements operating on a bit at a time are being replaced by complex 32-bit processors, either custom, as in the Maspar or KSR-1, or off-the-shelf, as in the CM-5 and Meiko CS-2. That list of hardware covers a range of low-level programming models from pure SIMD, through shared memory MIMD to distributed memory MIMD. However, whatever the architecture, we can be sure that the FORTRAN community will be served well through FORTRAN-90 and High Performance FORTRAN. The computational model still remains that of manipulation and operation on vast regular datasets. What about non-numeric irregular computation on these systems?

To use Valiant's term, we have yet to find our "bridging model" between non-numeric irregular software and the diversity of parallel architectures. The lack of a widely-accepted solution is not for a want of effort, but perhaps that effort suffers from too many languages and too many slightly incompatible models none of which ever reaches a sufficiently large audience to gain significant acceptance or can be compared practically with another in a common environment. How is one concurrency abstraction or one data-parallel abstraction better than another?

While one problem is that we do not have the means to compare these abstractions effectively, this may also be a red herring, because concurrency versus data-parallelism preserves the MIMD/SIMD divide. Although massively-parallel processing contains the dichotomy (now) of both MIMD and SIMD systems, FORTRAN is succeeding by having chosen a simple unifying model, which works well on SIMD systems and can be mapped without great difficulty on to MIMD. Can the same be done for languages oriented to non-numeric processing?

Lisp (here I reveal my true colours!), has been implemented on array processors, but offers little more than the FORTRAN model. It seems clear that we need to move up a level of abstraction if we are to make progress. Dataflow is a move in that direction, but I do not know why it has not succeeded and neither do I know enough to speculate. The so-called "architecture independent" languages, Unity and Gamma are similar attempts, but seemingly less radical. These both have a strong SIMD feel about them and while they are presently simple and elegant, having little or no support for data structures, adding to them may be like augmenting the APL diamond. Should the programming model for massively-parallel non-numeric processing attempt to encompass data-parallelism?

Here are three possible scenarios:

1. Assume SIMD architectures will disappear.
2. Recognize them as useful adjuncts.
3. Accord them equal status with MIMD architectures.

The last leads to the FORTRAN situation; the weaker architecture dominates the model. Data-parallelism is intrinsically concerned with regular datasets and is, as such, orthogonal to the problem posed to the panel. Therefore, we should not start from data-parallelism, as has FORTRAN, because it is a dead-end. The first and second can be accommodated by the same approach: support for data-parallel operations, which can be run on array processors, if available, or chunked and run on MIMD systems. Thus, our fundamental model assumes the existence of many processors, but has no notion of the cost of transfer between those processors. However, it does not seem practical to expect anything other than non-uniform access cost. The next question is where is the hardware for program development?

Those resources are all around us: they are our existing networks of machines. In practice, it seems that a network of workstations could serve well for development purposes and even for production runs, although the same program should be able to run on whatever massively-parallel architecture is available.

The challenge now is to build languages capable of orchestrating control *and* data-parallelism on networks of workstations, array processors, shared-memory multi-processors and distributed memory multi-processors, or, in one word multicomputers.

Is there a role for a massively parallel computer?

Norihisa Suzuki

IBM Tokyo Research Laboratory

It is not straightforward to predict that the massively parallel computer (MPC) will be widely accepted.

There are several factors against MPC.

- One is the rapid increase of the speed of a single-chip (or sometimes multi-chip) microprocessors, and the other is the advance of hardware and software for small scale shared memory multiprocessors. These progresses enable a tremendous computation at a relatively inexpensive price; most of the computation requirements previously accomplished only by supercomputers and MPCs can be done by powerful workstations and small scale multiprocessors.
- The second progress is the high speed switch and the associated software to connect a large number of workstations to form a cluster. This will further enhance the reach of the computation power of inexpensive systems.
- The third factor is the ecological consciousness that discourages the consumption of huge electric power required by MPCs.
- The fourth factor is the dwindling supply of government funding for scientific and military research, which paid for most of the MPCs.

In conclusion MPC will be very popular only if its performance is an order of magnitude faster than a cluster of powerful workstations or small scale multiprocessors, and even then only if it is cost-effective, even from an ecological point of view.

Is the world ready for massively parallel symbolic computation?

Taiichi Yuasa

Toyohashi University of Technology

As reported in our paper presented at the workshop, we have been working for the design and implementation of a Lisp language and system, called TUPLE, for massively parallel (MP) SIMD architectures. Having finished the implementation, we are now interested in testing (or, hopefully, proving) the effectiveness of symbolic computation on MP SIMD architectures.

For this purpose, we chose two applications in symbolic computation, and are porting them onto TUPLE.

1. Computer algebra, which frequently handles matrices whose elements are general mathematical formulas, such as polynomials. Since many efficient algorithms have been exploited for MP computation on matrices with numeric elements, we hope we can obtain efficient MP implementation of computer algebra systems.
2. Natural language translation, which requires dictionary lookups. By executing the lookup operation in MP, we have the chance to drastically improve the performance of the translator.

Although we have just started the porting, our experience so far shows that the porting will not be so hard as was imagined. This result encourages us to try more applications in symbolic computation that are potentially suitable for MP computation.

Through the implementation of TUPLE and the porting of applications, we found that three features of the underlying architecture are the keys to the future success of MP symbolic computation.

- Smooth communication between the processing elements (PEs) and the processor (FE: Front-end) with which the user interacts. Even for MP applications, FE executes some part of the program, by operating on the results of PE computation. In addition, systems for symbolic computation are characterized by their high interaction with the user.
- Efficient local indexing, which allows PEs to access different addresses independently. This will be obvious since symbolic computation inevitably requires pointer operations.
- Large memory space for each PE. Until recently, systems for symbolic computation had been suffering from the small memory size. We, working on MP symbolic computation, have the same problem.

Unfortunately, as far as we know, none of the currently available SIMD machines provide all these features. This is mainly because these machines are intended for non-symbolic applications, such as fluid dynamics and digital signal processing.

Some brand-new MP MIMD machines may provide solutions to these problems. Although our experiences are limited to MP SIMD computation, our technology may possibly be applied to MIMD computation. In addition, it is expected that SIMD programs run much more efficiently on MIMD (or SPMD) machines. Unfortunately, so far, we have no data to verify this possibility.

Panel Discussion II:
Applications for Parallel Symbolic Computation

Robert H. Halstead, Jr. (chair)
Takashi Chikayama
Richard Gabriel
David Waltz
Aki Yonezawa

Research projects have developed a whole range of interesting technology for supporting parallel symbolic computation, but this technology has not seen much "production" use. In contrast, parallel processing for numerical applications is receiving a lot of attention and is beginning to be taken very seriously as a computing technology. What are the reasons for this difference and what (if anything) should be done about it?

This panel discussion will grapple with questions such as:

1. What are the symbolic applications that need parallel computation?
2. Are there symbolic "grand challenge" applications analogous to the numerical "grand challenges" that currently get so much publicity?
3. What software and hardware developments, if any, must occur before parallel symbolic computing can become commonplace?
4. What properties make an application "symbolic," anyway?

List of Workshop Participants

Kamal Abdali	NSF
Anant Agarwal	MIT
Mario O. Bourgoin	Thinking Machines
Carl Bruggeman	Indiana University
Robert Cassels	Apple Cambridge Research Center
Takashi Chikayama	ICOT
David C. De Roure	U. of Southampton
Kent Dybvig	Indiana University
Marc Feeley	University of Montreal
Richard P. Gabriel	Lucid
Masami Hagiya	University of Tokyo
Robert H. Halstead Jr.	DEC Cambridge Research Lab
W. Ludwell Harrison III	Connected Components Corporation
Carl Hewitt	MIT
Kinson Ho	University of California at Berkeley
Takayasu Ito	Tohoku University
Suresh Jagannathan	NEC Research Institute
Laxmikant Kale	University of Illinois
Yukio Kaneda	Kobe University
Shin-ichi Kawamoto	Tohoku University
Robert Kessler	University of Utah
Naoki Kobayashi	University of Tokyo
David A. Kranz	MIT
J.P. Massar	Thinking Machines
Satoshi Matsuoka	University of Tokyo
Eric Mohr	Archetype
Rishiyur S. Nikhil	DEC Cambridge Research Lab
Randy Osborne	Mitsubishi Electric Research Lab
Julian Padget	University of Bath
James Philbin	NEC Research Institute
Christian Queinnec	Ecole Polytechnique & INRIA-Rocquencourt
Ichiro Satoh	Keio University
Tomohiro Seino	Tohoku University
Norihisa Suzuki	IBM Tokyo Research Lab
Hidehiko Tanaka	University of Tokyo
Kenjiro Taura	University of Tokyo
Mario Tokoro	Keio University
David Waltz	Thinking Machines & Brandeis University
Akinori Yonezawa	University of Tokyo
Taiichi Yuasa	Toyohashi University of Technology
John Zuckerman	Motorola

Lecture Notes in Computer Science

For information about Vols. 1–670
please contact your bookseller or Springer-Verlag

Lecture Notes in Computer Science

This series reports new developments in computer science research and teaching, quickly, informally, and at a high level. The timeliness of a manuscript is more important than its form, which may be unfinished or tentative. The type of material considered for publication includes

– drafts of original papers or monographs,

– technical reports of high quality and broad interest,

– advanced-level lectures,

– reports of meetings, provided they are of exceptional interest and focused on a single topic.

Publication of Lecture Notes is intended as a service to the computer science community in that the publisher Springer-Verlag offers global distribution of documents which would otherwise have a restricted readership. Once published and copyrighted they can be cited in the scientific literature.

Manuscripts

Lecture Notes are printed by photo-offset from the master copy delivered in camera-ready form. Manuscripts should be no less than 100 and preferably no more than 500 pages of text. Authors of monographs and editors of proceedings volumes receive 50 free copies of their book. Manuscripts should be printed with a laser or other high-resolution printer onto white paper of reasonable quality. To ensure that the final photo-reduced pages are easily readable, please use one of the following formats:

Font size	Printing area		Final size
(points)	(cm)	(inches)	(%)
10	12.2 x 19.3	4.8 x 7.6	100
12	15.3 x 24.2	6.0 x 9.5	80

On request the publisher will supply a leaflet with more detailed technical instructions or a T_EX macro package for the preparation of manuscripts.

Manuscripts should be sent to one of the series editors or directly to:

Springer-Verlag, Computer Science Editorial I, Tiergartenstr. 17,
D-69121 Heidelberg, Germany

ISBN 3-540-57396-8
ISBN 0-387-57396-8